Valery Perry (ed.)

EXTREMISM AND VIOLENT EXTREMISM IN SERBIA

21st-Century Manifestations of an Historical Challenge

BALKAN POLITICS AND SOCIETY

Edited by Jelena Dzankic and Soeren Keil

1	*Valery Perry (ed.)*
	Extremism and Violent Extremism in Serbia
	21st Century Manifestations of an Historical Challenge
	ISBN 978-3-8382-1260-9

Valery Perry (ed.)

EXTREMISM AND VIOLENT EXTREMISM IN SERBIA

21st-Century Manifestations of an Historical Challenge

Bibliografische Information der Deutschen Nationalbibliothek
Die Deutsche Nationalbibliothek verzeichnet diese Publikation in der Deutschen Nationalbibliografie; detaillierte bibliografische Daten sind im Internet über http://dnb.d-nb.de abrufbar.

Bibliographic information published by the Deutsche Nationalbibliothek
Die Deutsche Nationalbibliothek lists this publication in the Deutsche Nationalbibliografie; detailed bibliographic data are available in the Internet at http://dnb.d-nb.de.

Original cover art designed by Aleksandar Dadić and Ivana Zuber, Novi Sad, Serbia.

While the research presented in this publication was undertaken as part of an OSCE Mission to Serbia project, the views herein expressed are solely those of the editor and contributors and do not necessarily reflect the official position of the OSCE Mission to Serbia.

British Embassy
Belgrade

The research in this book has been supported by the British Embassy in Belgrade. The content of this book does not reflect the official position of the British Embassy in Belgrade. Responsibility for the information and views expressed in the book lies entirely with the authors.

∞

Gedruckt auf alterungsbeständigem, säurefreien Papier
Printed on acid-free paper

ISBN-13: 978-3-8382-1260-9
© *ibidem*-Verlag, Stuttgart 2019
Alle Rechte vorbehalten

Das Werk einschließlich aller seiner Teile ist urheberrechtlich geschützt. Jede Verwertung außerhalb der engen Grenzen des Urheberrechtsgesetzes ist ohne Zustimmung des Verlages unzulässig und strafbar. Dies gilt insbesondere für Vervielfältigungen, Übersetzungen, Mikroverfilmungen und elektronische Speicherformen sowie die Einspeicherung und Verarbeitung in elektronischen Systemen.

All rights reserved. No part of this publication may be reproduced, stored in or introduced into a retrieval system, or transmitted, in any form, or by any means (electronical, mechanical, photocopying, recording or otherwise) without the prior written permission of the publisher. Any person who does any unauthorized act in relation to this publication may be liable to criminal prosecution and civil claims for damages.

Printed in the EU

Table of Contents

Acknowledgements 7

Defining, Framing and Contextualizing Extremism and
Violent Extremism in Serbia: An Introduction to the Volume
by Valery Perry 9

Using the Past to Extremes in Serbia: Narratives of Historical
Violence in Right-Wing Extremism and Islamism
by Niké Wentholt 69

The Eurasian Wings of Serbia: Serbian Affinities
of the Russian Radical Right by Ana Dević 109

(Non)violent Extremism Online: How Opinion Leaders Use
Online Channels to Disseminate Radical Messages and
Intolerance by Davor Marko 139

The Nexus between Online Violent Extremism and Serbian
Youth: How Do Young People in Novi Sad, Bor, Zaječar,
and Tutin Perceive Online Extremist Narratives?
by Kristina Ivanović 183

Mapping Extremist Discourse
among Serbian 4Chan /pol/ Users by Boris Milanović 223

Violent Extremism and Radicalization in the Context of the
Migrant Crisis: Evidence from Serbia by Tijana Rečević 281

Inclusive Intangible Cultural Heritage Protection as an
Instrument for the Prevention of Identity-Based Conflicts:
The Case of Serbia by Miloš Milenković 319

Concluding Remarks by Valery Perry 353

About the Contributors 367

Acknowledgements

This research project began in autumn 2017 with one key objective: to find out from a wide range of experts what research questions they think deserve consideration and attention when thinking about extremism and violent extremism in Serbia. The open call for proposals yielded nearly two dozen proposals, and it was consistently impressive to see the sophisticated understanding each of the selected researchers brought to the effort. Each author pursued their own research, and participated in peer review on other papers relevant to their own topic. This facilitated a collegial learning and working environment, and hopefully planted seeds for future collaboration. One contribution, by Boris Milanović, was integrated into the collection later in the collaborative process, as the topic was both innovative in its subject matter and approach and complementary to the other research topics. Together the contributions combine historical and contemporary analysis and approaches that nicely reinforce themes, observations, and policy recommendations.

Many of the authors used various online sites, portals and tools in their review and analysis. These links were confirmed as of late October/early November 2018. The fluidity of online content can make it difficult to stay current, but they have provided sufficient references to ensure interested readers can find more information as needed.

I would like to thank each of the authors for their professionalism throughout the process, and their patience with seemingly endless peer reviews, conversations on methodology and substance, style suggestions, and copy-editing. It was a pleasure to work with Aleksandar Dadić and Ivana Zuber on the cover art — a process that helped us to appreciate the visual branding of some of the "-isms" that surround and shape these issues. Thanks to Predrag Nikolić for his patience as I've pondered themes and topics and engaged in comparative pontificating on the emergence of new and more troubling extremisms in the region and globally. Boris

Milanović, in addition to being an astute analyst, has been an excellent formatting guru. Jovana Vujanović brought a set of fresh eyes to the manuscript in the final stages, just when we needed it. And thanks are due to the OSCE Mission to Serbia and the British Embassy in Serbia, as they supported independent scholarship on this issue, allowing for fruitful exploration and collaboration.

It has been a true pleasure to work with the contributors in this volume, as they have each brought with them unique yet complementary perspectives and skill sets that have made the process a learning experience for everyone. It is our hope that similar research will be supported in other parts of the region, based on the issues and needs defined by experts on the ground, who understand the issues that deserve attention and scrutiny.

The collection is dedicated to the researchers and activists who are fighting against the violence of extremism described in this volume, and who instead imagine a society where inclusion overcomes exclusion, engagement trumps marginalization, and hope eclipses fear.

Valery Perry
Belgrade, Serbia
November 2018

Defining, Framing and Contextualizing Extremism and Violent Extremism in Serbia: An Introduction to the Volume

Valery Perry

Introduction[1]

The topics of extremism, violent extremism, and in particular violent extremism grounded in militant jihadi ideologies have been at the forefront of the foreign policy architecture of the United States and its allies since September 11, particularly since the long and devastating war in Syria led to the emergence of the Islamic State of Iraq and Syria (commonly and variably referred to as ISIS, ISIL, or *Daesh*[2]). The increase in violence, prolonged and intensified through shifting yet steady proxy war dynamics, has contributed to a notable rise in the number of individuals and families fleeing towards the west, adding to a human migration already occurring from Afghanistan, Pakistan, and sub-Saharan Africa. Spectacular acts of violence in Syria and Iraq, coupled with attacks in its name elsewhere (including in Europe), have been seared onto the consciousness of a global population who have been exposed to the news and imagery through pervasive social media as never before. It is not a coincidence that in this same period of time the world has seen a sharp trend towards rising and increasingly visible and emboldened populism and nationalism undergirded by small, but growing, vocal and empowered far-right factions, some of whom

---

1   I would like to thank Georgia Holmer, Predrag Nikolić, Niké Wentholt and two anonymous reviewers for their comments, critiques, and suggestions. All of the usual disclaimers apply.

2   In this introduction ISIS will be used to refer to the various activities conducted by Islamic State/*Daesh* and its formal and informal affiliates. This does not confer any presumed dominance or legitimacy on their claims, nor does it exonerate other violent jihadist groups such as Al-Qaeda. It is simply for ease of writing. The authors in the volume that refer to this phenomenon use and define various terms as well, as informed by their study as well as the terminology confronted and heard throughout their own research.

have successfully shifted political centers to the right through a process of social normalization of their own increasingly extreme messages, sometime buttressed by violence as well. As increasingly noted by experts—but often ignored by voters and policymakers fearful of confronting their own domestic extremist demons—reciprocal radicalization in Western Europe and the United States has created a vicious cycle of growing extremism and entrenched social discontent, political polarization grounded in identity politics, and a heightened fear of the "other."

Politicians, policymakers, and law enforcement agencies are struggling with these challenges in established and wealthy democratic states. Summoning the political will to not only introduce counter-terror measures but to also address the *drivers* of extremism through more effective policies and budgetary allocations is difficult in France, Germany, the United Kingdom, the U.S.; in fact *everywhere*, as defensive domestic postures and the politics of economic austerity have shrunk the public pie. It should therefore be no surprise that countries with much weaker institutional and economic foundations are facing even greater challenges. The Western Balkans[3] provide an interesting case, as these countries occupy complex middle ground, geographically, politically, economically, and metaphorically. They enjoy a European perspective, but have not yet been assessed to have progressed enough to become European Union (EU) members in spite of years of post-war enlargement engagement in support of reform.

Being "in between" leads to a regional flavor of extremism that is distinct. The region continues to suffer from the pain of post-Cold War economic transition (and from the additional damage of the aftermath of the 2008 financial crisis). Yet at the same time, for that very reason, the Western Balkan region is not itself an attractive destination for refugees or migrants—a dynamic in the west that has fuelled far-right, anti-migration elements. The "us vs. them" narratives common in mainstream and extremist discourse on the

---

3   In this volume the Western Balkans will refer to Albania, Bosnia and Herzegovina (BiH), Croatia, Kosovo, Macedonia, Montenegro, and Serbia. While Croatia is already in the EU and NATO, its recent wartime history and continuing impact mean that it too contributes to regional dynamics of reciprocal extremisms.

position of Islam in society is also different. While countries in western Europe frequently struggle with poorly assimilated second- or third-generation populations of often Muslim migrants, in the Balkans the centuries-long presence of an indigenous Muslim tradition sets it apart from its neighbors to the north and west. However, the region's recent experience of war and ethnic cleansing grounded in the politics of violent ethno-national, clerical and sectarian distinctions skillfully manipulated by ethnic entrepreneurs (Gagnon 1994/95) has left a legacy of weakened social fabric, majority-minority tensions, and weak civic and bridging social capital. The development of liberal democracy and open markets hasn't emerged as smoothly as some in the west might have hoped, and countries in the region have been described less as examples of democracy and more as models of partitocracy (Kleibrink 2011; Kleibrink 2015; Stiks and Horvat 2014), or elastic authoritarianism (Mujanović 2017). And just as the region is in greater need of a unified and incontrovertible values-based future perspective, the geopolitics of "spheres of influence" is returning amidst a trans-Atlantic alliance unmoored by the interrelated and cumulative impact of the politics of the Trump Administration (Bassuener and Perry 2017), Brexit, and the rising influence of Turkey and Russia (Bajrović et al 2018; Dević, this volume). At the same time globalization has brought actors such as China and the Gulf states to the region, each pursuing their own interests (Bartlett et al 2017) and often different values.

Against this fluid and complex backdrop, the engagement of outside actors through the "international community" — primarily through efforts in support of future membership in the EU and/or NATO — continues.[4] Reforms remain heavily focused on EU-required technical support related to judicial independence, public administration reform, market access, and others, as broadly outlined in annual status reports (EC 2018). However, over the past several years a new external donor interest in preventing and coun-

---

[4] Croatia joined the EU in 2013. Albania, Croatia, and Montenegro are NATO members. Serbia does not aspire to NATO membership, and BiH is divided internally, with its Serb leaders mirroring Serbia's position.

tering violent extremism (P/CVE) has become increasingly prominent, with outside actors having their own interests, contexts, and narratives. This leads to questions about the extent to which extremism and violent extremism are and need to be domestic, regional, and broader international priorities, what this means for long-standing regional reform strategies, and what the impact of securitization of reform could be in both the short- and the long-terms.

This volume contributes to the exploration of these phenomena with a focus on Serbia, though with references to the wider Western Balkan region, and in particular the post-Yugoslav space. Serbia, as an EU candidate with a long accession perspective and mixed results in terms of its economic and democratic transitions since the violent break up of Yugoslavia, is increasingly being linked to these trends, both as a target case study in its own right, and as a critical piece in the larger Balkan geostrategic puzzle due to its size and both its past and more recent historical engagement with its neighbors. This book explores these dynamics in Serbia through original research that examines a range of aspects of extremism and violent extremism in the country today, from a variety of multi- and interdisciplinary perspectives.[5] This broad and holistic research approach is important for Serbia and its neighbors, as the security lens through which most research has been focused to date has done little to explain the deep and structural dynamics of manifestations of radicalization and extremism in the region. This book aims to add to the growing literature on the topic, and to spur foreign actors — in particular, the US, the United Kingdom (UK) and the EU countries funding various relevant efforts — to better understand the nature of the threats and dynamics of extremism in Serbia, and to recalibrate their strategies accordingly.

---

5   The majority of research ideas were solicited through an initial call for proposals in October 2017 for experts from Serbia, as well as non-Serbian researchers engaged in the Serbian context. The fact that the vast majority of the proposals selected were from Serbian experts demonstrates that people on the ground have an advanced and nuanced understanding of the issue of extremism and violent extremism in their own communities.

This chapter therefore serves as an introduction to the issue of extremism and violent extremism in Serbia, and as a review of the response to these challenges, providing an overarching background and conceptual framework for the volume. This introductory chapter is organized as follows. First, there is a fairly lengthy discussion of some often tricky and always controversial terms and definitions—a sensitive issue with which many of the authors struggled as they sought to use terms that would ensure clarity among readers of all backgrounds while not unintentionally reinforcing misconceptions. This definitional context at the same time introduces some of the phenomena being explored. This is followed by a brief historical review of Serbia's recent past, and an introduction to the emergence of the P/CVE focus in the Western Balkans over the past several years. Short overviews of the contributions in the volume illustrate common themes and issues; the concluding chapter further extrapolates critical observations and policy implications. Taken together it becomes increasingly clear that there is less a problem of *violent extremism* in Serbia than there is a prevalent and unresolved *culture of extremism*, grounded in the reciprocal dynamics of the socio-political ecosystem that has emerged since the wars in the 1990s, and that efforts to transform the country (and the region) through support for open and democratic systems have been woefully inadequate in addressing the drivers of all kinds of extremisms.

Terminological challenges and conceptual fluidity

As a first step it is important to provide a review of a number of terms and definitions; an exercise that will draw criticism from many but which reveals the ambiguity and unsettled nature of this topic. Broadly speaking, from the beginning the authors were encouraged to use terminology that reflected their own evolving understanding of the associated concepts in their selected contexts, their engagement with the literature, and their interaction with interlocutors. The language used by respondents themselves can shed light on the understanding of these trends in any given local context.[6] The review below is aimed at being indicative of the nuances, and the authors in this volume make no claim to offer or agree on any single, discrete definition.

The issue: terrorism, radicalization, (violent) extremism

As the notion of terrorism has an extensive pedigree and history, it may be useful to begin with this concept, though this approach can admittedly color the terms that follow. There is no universally accepted definition of terrorism — to use the over-worn adage, whether someone is viewed as a terrorist or a freedom fighter is almost always subjective. Whether or not the term is used very often depends on the extent to which a government (state actors) wants to be seen as conferring legitimacy upon or condemning certain actions (Schmid 2004). The United Nations (UN) has struggled with this for years, with some members seeking to ensure that the right to self-determination is not painted as terrorism through an overly broad definition (UNGA 2012). The universal agreement that ISIS be labeled and treated as a terrorist group is in that sense an exception, a rare case in which all Security Council members could agree on this designation (UNSC 2015a; UNSC 2015b; UNSC 2017). Schmid and Jongman (1988) provide a comprehensive overview of the concept in the pre-9/11 world, which provides useful historical background. Gill et al (2014) define terrorism as, "the use or threat of action where the use or threat is designed to influence the government or to intimidate the public or a section of the public, and/or the use or threat is made for the purpose of advancing a political, religious, or ideological cause" (no page number), careful

---

6   As an example of the tricky linguistic terrain, in 2016 the author conducted interviews as part of research for the Regional Cooperation Council (Perry 2016). Throughout the research many respondents used the term "Salafism" or "Wahhabism" (or variants) as they sought to describe from their perspective observed changes or trends in their country. When presenting the report findings at an event in Belgrade in spring 2017, using the same terminology as had been used by the respondents, the author was criticized by participants from domestic or foreign Islamic communities for using the term Salafism in this context. However, the author noted that this was the language used by respondents, reflecting their own stated framing.

to reflect both the intimidation and ideological characteristics. While contemporary reports on P/CVE issues often painfully wrestle with definitions, Crenshaw's classic piece examining the causes of terrorism has almost no detailed discussion on the definition, noting simply, "terrorist violence communicates a political message; its ends go beyond damaging an enemy's material resources" (Crenshaw 1981, 379).

While terrorism has been in the lexicon of security specialists for decades, the realization that it is important to understand how someone *becomes* a terrorist, and the way by which they begin to go down such a path, opened the door for additional concepts that might identify and describe the process of coming to adopt and perhaps even act on extreme views. The term radicalization is often used for this pathway explanation, to understand a journey that includes both real-world and cognitive, psychological characteristics.

A 2018 report comprised of contributions by a number of authors defines radicalization as the process of individual or group leanings to extremist thoughts and beliefs (Austin and Giessmann 2018). (As noted below, the definition of extremist or radical beliefs is itself not simple.) The radicalization process describes a move from an initial "default" state which likely conforms to the broader social norms of one's society, towards something quite substantially different and outside the norm of one's environment. The process can be cognitive, thereby affecting one's thoughts, opinions and beliefs, and can also be behavioral, affecting one's actions and behavior (McCauley and Moskalenko 2017; Horgan 2008). While either type of radicalization may be viewed as deviant by others living in line with one's expected social norms, it does not have to be inherently viewed as violent. A 2014 Organization for Security and Cooperation in Europe (OSCE) definition notes, "Radicalization is not a threat to society if it is not connected to violence or other unlawful acts, such as incitement to hatred, as legally defined in compliance with international human rights law. Radicalization can actually be a force for beneficial change. For instance, people advocating the abolition of slavery or who championed universal suffrage were at one time considered to be radical as they stood in opposition to the prevailing views in their societies" (OSCE 2014, 35). It goes on to note, "Terrorist radicalization is a dynamic process whereby an individual comes to accept terrorist violence as a possible, perhaps even legitimate, course of action" (ibid). Another definition used by the OSCE specifies the phrase "radicalization that leads to terrorism," which is defined as, "the dynamic process whereby an individual comes to accept terrorist violence as a possible, perhaps even legitimate, course of action. This may eventually, but not necessarily, lead this person to advocate, act in support of, or to engage in terrorism" (OSCE 2018, 7).

Coolsaet provides a good overview of the struggle to agree on terms and definitions; for instance, the terms radicalization vs. violent radicalization. However, he also warns against the ultimate potential policy implications of focusing on the process of any given individual rather than on the environment or ecosystem in which that person lives. "Focusing on the process an individual undergoes from his or her original 'normal' status to becoming a terrorist seemed a lot easier than addressing the environment that made him or her vulnerable to the siren song of extremism" (Coolsaet 2016, 14). Considering the process within the context of any specific environment forces one to begin to conceptualize radicalization as a complex, whole of society phenomenon. In that vein, Neumann's conceptualization of radicalization looks at a number of dynamics, including grievance, needs, ideas, people, and violence (Neumann 2017). Further, while this cognitive/behavioral process has clearly existed for some time, Coolsaet cites Silke and Brown, noting that one would not have encountered the term radicalization in relation to the Irish Republican Army (IRA) or the Red Brigades in trying to understand *their* motivations and individual pathways,[7] leading one to wonder whether that was a weakness of past analysis of those movements, or whether contemporary radicalization is in fact somehow different.

---

[7] Andrew Silke and Katherine Brown, "'Radicalisation': The Transformation of Modern Understanding of Terrorist Origins, Psychology and Motivation." In: Shashi Jayakumar (ed.), *State, Society, and National Security: Challenges and Opportunities in the 21st Century*. Singapore, World Scientific Publishing, 2016, pp. 129–150.

So what does a process of radicalization *lead to* if one is shifting *away* from an accepted social norm? This question requires introduction of the terms radicalism and extremism, and their variants. Radicalism tends to be associated with a belief system, while extremism tends to convey belief *plus* action. Writers on this topic again take pains to note that not all forms of radicalism are necessarily regressive (in terms of rights), bad or violent. The early 20th century women's suffrage movement will again be noted as an example that was at the time considered to be "radical," but ultimately resulted in an expansion of rights. This example is meant to convey the subjectivity of the cultural and socio-political context; once an idea is mainstreamed in a society (like women's voting rights) it is no longer radical. Radicalism does not have to be equated with violent action or intent to perpetrate violent actions.

However even this is subjective, and the emergence of definitions squarely drafted based on the presumption of Western liberal values may be cited in this context. A 2004 report by Dutch intelligence sought to define "radicalism" as something different from extremism. They defined radicalism as, "The (active) pursuit of and/or support to far-reaching changes in society which may constitute a danger to (the continued existence of) the democratic legal order (aim), which may involve the use of undemocratic methods (means) that may harm the function of the democratic legal order (effect). In line with this, radicalization can be interpreted as a person's (growing) willingness to pursue and/or support such changes himself (in an undemocratic way or otherwise), or his encouraging others to do so" (as cited in Coolsaet 2016, 12).[8] This is interesting as it suggests a deviation from some presumed accepted set of social and political norms (similar to the British definition of extremism noted below). However, in a contextual vacuum one might fairly apply this definition, presumably aimed at non-state, unofficial actors, to some of the illiberal political experiments unfolding in states such as Hungary (Magyar 2016).

---

8   Coolsaet cites, *From dawa to jihad*. The Hague, AIVD, December 2004, p. 40; Annual Report 2004. The Hague, AIVD, 2005, p. 16.

Further complicating the lexicon, there is no single agreed definition of either extremism or violent extremism, and perhaps not coincidentally little agreement on where one ends and the other begins. (Is it possible to be a peaceful neo-Nazi? Can one pursue extremist ends through dull and procedural means?) Echoing the discussion above, Ebner cites the British government definition of extremism as, "vocal or active opposition to fundamental British values, including democracy, the rule of law, individual liberty and mutual respect and tolerance of different faiths and beliefs" (Ebner 2017, 13; UK DOE 2015, 5). Austin and Giessmann (2018) and Meleagrou-Hitchens and Kaderbhai (2017) also provide good overviews of these concepts.

In an effort to avoid confusion regarding the means, USAID offers this definition of *violent extremism*: "advocating, engaging in, preparing, or otherwise supporting ideologically motivated or justified violence to further social, economic or political objectives" (2011, 2–3). When one parses this definition, it leads to some challenging terrain. What if a speaker (or a "key influencer") makes spoken or online comments advocating for the use of violence, in general, but without specificity or themselves pulling a trigger? (*"All xxx should be eliminated."*) Should they always be held to account? Or must calls for violence be actionable and specific? (*"Go tomorrow to kill xxx in such and such a place."*) Criminal codes vary by jurisdiction, but the waters are very often murky and up for interpretation. When one begins to wrestle with balancing freedom of speech and belief with social interests to minimize hate speech and (resultant) hate crimes, these are not simple academic discussions.[9] Where is the line in terms of provoking hate and implying the need for violent action, and specifically calling for acts of violence? (Davor Marko and Boris Milanović each explore some of these quandaries in their chapters.)

---

9   In the Serbian context, a long-time leader of the country's far-right, Vojislav Šešelj, during the wars openly and regularly called for violence. Following a years-long war crimes case he was (partially) acquitted, as he was found to have held no formal command responsibility, and that his speech did not amount to incitement (RFERL 2018; Escritt 2016).

Neumann has engaged closely with these issues and the terminological struggles. He explains that the increase in use of the term *violent extremism* was intended to, "shed the political baggage that was associated with the word terrorism" (2017, 15). He also notes that there is no good answer to the relationship between violent and non-violent forms of extremism (15), and that many meanings are subjective and based on definitions of what is considered to be mainstream in a given society.

Coolsaet offers a forensic dissection of the EU's own evolutionary struggles with terminology and policy, in particular as these phenomena play out on EU soil. A 2008 EU expert group decided to focus on extremism rather than radicalization, arguing that, "while radicalism can pose a threat, it is extremism, and particularly terrorism, that ought to be our main concern since it involves the active subversion of democratic values and the rule of law. In this sense violent radicalization is to be understood as socialization to extremism which manifests itself in terrorism" (Coolsaet 2016, 23). The use of the word "active" emphasizes the line between thought and action, marking a move from cognitive processes to real-life and active behavior; such movement implies flux along a spectrum of belief—and then possibly behavior—viewed as deviant from the norm. The OSCE provides yet another interesting example of the delicate policy tango that shapes adoption and use of terms, as both the political interests of the 57 participating States must be taken into account, as well as the role the Organization plays as a security body that engages on human rights. Therefore, the OSCE doesn't refer to just extremism (which could convey judgment on thought) but instead *violent* extremism (qualified) and radicalization *leading to terrorism* (action)—cumbersomely shortened to VERLT (OSCE 2018; OSCE 2014).

These concepts reflect policy objectives and imperatives that employ terminology that seeks to accommodate non-violent dissent, while at the same time discounting any possible justification underlying acts of violence. Extreme violence and attacks on civilians are hardly new. The notion of a distinction between violence committed by state and non-state actors is also not a novel debate. And the family of a victim of a random shooting incident in the US may not care whether the attack was or was not preceded by release of a manifesto of potential political relevance; discussions on which violent attacks in the US deserve the label terror are increasingly common (ACLU, n.d.). Yet in the current political climate one must at minimum be aware of the potential for selective abuse of the "terror" label in an increasingly securitized environment. A recent terrorist conviction upheld by the courts in Hungary against a Syrian asylum seeker found guilty of perpetrating violence in a melee at the Hungarian border demonstrates the potential for misuse of this concept (Amnesty 2018). Later in this chapter, the different legal/prosecutorial approaches used in Serbia depending on whether its nationals have gone to fight in Syria or in Ukraine provide another example of the at times flexible or selective application of the "terror" label.

The lack of clarity this review provides likely brings little closure or satisfaction to the reader. However, these distinctions, nuances and debates are complicated for (relatively) long-established democracies. The discussions are even more complicated in a region such as the former Yugoslavia, which is merely a generation removed from wars that included organized state/government backed violence as well as "freelance" crimes against humanity. How does one define or delimit definitions of violent extremism in countries in which many (if not most) citizens have a direct connection with some act of violence underpinned by political/religious/ideological overtones? This is the question that blurs the P/CVE field in this region.

The dynamic: reciprocal radicalization

Next, the term reciprocal radicalization deserves mention, as this concept provides a relevant and useful theoretical framework for understanding the dynamics of extremism in Serbia, as well as the Western Balkans as a whole.

Eatwell described the phenomenon of cumulative extremism in a study of community cohesion—and threats to cohesion—in Great Britain (2006). Others have looked at the way extremisms can interact and spiral into violence, and can mobilize over real or simply perceived threats (Goodwin 2013). Julia Ebner's 2017 *The Rage: The Vicious Circle of Islamist and Far-Right Extremism* provides a readable and thoughtful book-length study of this issue, with particular relevance for the destructive social-political dynamics playing out in Europe, with special attention to developments in Germany and the UK. Ebner's exploration of the symbiosis between the far-right and Islamist extremism does a solid job of describing this phenomenon. She notes Eatwell's 2006 concept of cumulative extremism, describes "tit for tat" extremism, and considers the interplay of hate crimes and reciprocal radicalization studied at a 2014 Royal United Services Institute conference (Cole and Pantucci 2014). She asks, "Do we need to combat far-right extremism to fight Islamist extremism?" (Ebner 2017, 13). In addition, these works have echoes in Barber's 1995 work, which foresaw a clash resulting from and among the interrelated and fast-paced forces of economic changes, media consolidation, social insecurities, and competing and escalating tribalisms (Barber 2001).

While Ebner doesn't touch on the Balkans, her description of opposing groups falling deeper into fear, grievance, and exclusionary world views increasingly incompatible with one another, and often tied less to concrete issues but to one's sense of identity and ambient alarm, paints a picture that forces readers to consider whether the Western Balkans are echoing contemporary trends in Europe, or whether the west has perhaps caught up with the Balkans, which began this descent a generation ago.

Application of these terms has come to the region surprisingly late. While some of the early relevant work in Serbia touches on the interplay of extremisms, the focus of the raft of studies in the region from 2014–2018 on foreign terrorist fighters and militant jihadism largely neglects this dynamic. In a 2018 British Council series of country reports on extremism (described further below), the Serbia report does the most thorough job of addressing reciprocal dynamics, referring to far-right nationalism as a driver of Islamist extremism, which then remains the main focus of the study (Petrović and Stakić 2018). In another report, Sead Turčalo provides a specific and current example of this dynamic in practice: "Just a small detail how it works: recently, we had a story about a radical Serbian group

Srbska Čast ("Serb Honor"). Everywhere, they posted photos from training camps, etc. A few days afterwards, one of the Salafi groups posted their video about a camp where they actually train children—not in military skills, they are taught about Salafist thinking—with men in long beards in the background and so on. That's how it actually happens. And it happens constantly, all the time" (Austin and Geissmann 2018, 75). Actions and reactions occur; and actors on both sides can in fact even *need* the other to support their own propulsion. (Wentholt explores some of these dynamics in her chapter.)

Scholars of conflict resolution might be surprised to learn that this concept has only so belatedly been acknowledged, as while applying the concept to a post-ISIS world may be novel, the underlying concepts are not. In their discussion of escalation, Rubin and Pruitt wrote, "As conflicts escalate, they go through certain incremental transformations. Although these transformations occur separately on each side, they affect the conflict as a whole because they are usually mirrored by the other side" (Rubin et al 1994, 69). They later link this to the conflict spiral model that "results from a vicious circle of action and reaction" (74). They further studied the structural evolution of conflict dynamics that integrate sources and drivers on all sides, as well as conflict moments that change the structure of a conflict in ways that can make the initial conflict sources almost unrecognizable upon release of some immediate trigger. Mitchell's decades-long study of conflict reveals similar tit for tat dynamics, and also strategies for problem solving in such a polarized environment of deep individual and social positioning (Mitchell 2011).

This volume is very much grounded in the concept of reciprocal radicalization, with several authors (Rečević, Marko, Ivanović, and Wentholt) explicitly exploring the interplay of Serbia's extremisms in their work. Their approaches reveal much about the narratives of supporters of extreme views in both camps, and the surprising similarities in some foundational elements as these extremes meet, through history and today.

The focus: extremisms in Serbia

Two manifestations of extremism are explored in this volume. The first, militant jihadist or ISIS-inspired has been by far the bigger focus by both international actors and also domestic law enforcement authorities in spite of the fairly limited scope of the problem. The second, far-right nationalism, is more pervasive, but to a large extent has been normalized due to years of war and post-war politics. The Serbia-specific dynamics of each are briefly introduced in the background section that follows.

A full discussion on the typology of mainstream and non-mainstream Islam is beyond the scope of this introduction. Throughout this research project, the team continually struggled with terminology, and how to best address clarity and style while also seeking to avoid deep explanations about theological issues. This was particularly the case when referring to ISIS-related extremism. Abu-Nimer urges a delinking of Islam/Muslims from P/CVE by avoiding terms such as Islamic terrorism, Muslim terrorists, and jihadists (Abu-Nimer 2018). However, Abdel-Samad (2016) proposes a more open reckoning with these issues in his book *Islamic Fascism*. In his study of Salafi-Jihadism, Maher (2016) traces the history of the idea that violence can and even must be a part of Salafist practice. Olidort writes that, "[T]he political prominence of Salafists is remarkable given that most Salafists are skeptical of violent *and* nonviolent political participation" [emphasis added] (2015, 4). Some authors, including in the region (Kursani 2015) use terminology related to *takvir*, or the Kharadjites, to avoid these quandaries.

Academic dissections are ongoing in various quarters, and in the Western Balkans, undergoing various post-Communist and post-war transitions, the emerging nature of new approaches to religion makes description even more difficult. As noted below, when speaking about the nature of Islam (often described as changing) in the region since the wars, individuals will often refer to the increase in individuals practicing Islam according to highly conservative Salafist interpretations, often referring to these believers (sometimes pejoratively) as Wahhabis. Much of the difficulty—for both insiders and outsiders — is determining who can legitimately interpret religious texts; this echoes the discussion above on labels to describe beliefs that deviate from some norm. Other terms, such as "fundamentalist" might be more appropriate for such groups, reflecting the spectrum of religious interpretations within *any* given faith, in which more or less conservative or fundamentalist interpretations may occur.

However, this term is also subjective, as defining the "fundamentals" of a faith system can be a matter of some interpretative license and even dispute, and reflects the extent to which a given religion is more or less centralized or decentralized. "Puritanism" can be viewed as a more atomistic and literal reading of a text, devoid of context that could be construed as inappropriate interpretative liberty. For example, Abou El Fadl makes a distinction between moderate and what he calls "puritan" Islam, avoiding the term "fundamentalist," and arguing that all Islamic groups claim that their ideas in fact best represent the true intention of the religion (Abou El Fadl 2005).

As noted above, right-wing extremism is also viewed as existing upon some spectrum and some presumed "normal" from which the extremes deviate. Terminology varies. Rush (1963) considered the term "radical right" as semantically confusing, preferring the term "extreme right." In the US context, terms such as extreme right, far-right and radical right are defined by the Anti-Defamation League as "right-wing political, social and religious movements that exist outside of and are more radical than mainstream conservatism," potentially involving skinheads, neo-Nazis, nationalists and anti-government elements (ADL). The term "Alt-right" has rather recently emerged in the US, coined in 2008 to describe a new form of American conservatism that embraces white identitarianism, white nationalism, or white supremacy (SPLC n.d.). In their discussion of the evolution of the right in Europe, Eremina and Seredenko (2015) note that the various terms (far-right, radical right, ultra right, extreme right, etc.) can be used as synonymous labels to describe sets of shared beliefs that are based on all or some common characteristics (nativism, xenophobia, anti-Semitism, anti-Islam sentiment, etc.). They also consider the extent to which such self-identifying individuals or organized movements can be said to have fascism and Nazism as underlying ideological constructs or simple inspiration, noting some authors will apply varying labels based on the promotion or use of violence as a means. Their ability to normalize by participating as minor but at times key partners in coalition governments suggests the potential for further consolidation and mainstreaming;[10] in the context of Europe and the Western Balkans, this is perhaps a critical distinguishing marker from political Islamism and puritanical interpretations of Islam. In this volume Dević explores the affinity of the Russian right for the Serbian right, illustrating the potential for broader regional nationalist congruence under banners of white nationalism and Eurasianism.

It is clear that this is complex and far from settled. Therefore, each author is using language that they heard in conversations, or encountered in their desk research, and their selected wording should not be read as prejudice but as the language they experienced in various contexts when discussing this topic.

The response:
countering, preventing, and transforming violent extremism

Each of the social phenomena described above are being addressed by various policies, and often programmatic initiatives, aimed at stopping these trends and actions, or at least reducing their likelihood. For the policy descriptions and recommendations that follow, some short definitions are helpful. Just as there is some cloudiness on the spectrum with the problems, so there is not always a clean divide among the efforts to address them.

Counter-terrorism is traditionally understood as law enforcement efforts to interdict, disrupt, investigate, and prosecute individuals or groups alleged of planning or carrying out terrorist acts. Guidance from the US Chairman of the Joint Chiefs of Staff (CJCS)

---

10   However, this cannot be ascribed solely to parliamentary systems, as the acquiescence of the Republican party in the US to many of the themes and actions of the alt-right that has been witnessed since the election of Donald Trump in 2016 cannot be discounted as a similar demonstration of normalization (Beckett 2017).

narrows the definition of counter-terrorism to "actions and activities to neutralize terrorists, their organizations and networks," explicitly avoiding references to actions to address root causes, or desired end-states, in the guidance (CJCS 2014, iii). For the purposes of this volume, counter-terrorism activities are characterized by activities by law enforcement agencies, intelligence services and the military. This reflects a security and criminal approach, which is different than P/CVE efforts which are pre- or non-criminal in nature.

Countering violent extremism was the term first applied to this developing policy imperative, perhaps most publically in a summit organized by the Obama administration. As important as seeking an end to the Syria quagmire (an unsuccessful endeavor, sharpened by the belief by some that the chemical weapons "red line" was allowed to be crossed without real consequence) (Lynch 2015; Fisher 2018), there was an increasing recognition that something was driving people to believe that going to Syria/Iraq to build "the Caliphate" was a rational choice to make. There was a need to understand and counter the drivers of these choices. In February 2015 the Obama administration convened a "Summit on Countering Violent Extremism," bringing together participants from over 60 countries. President Obama's remarks were clearly very heavily focused on ISIS/ISIL, Al-Shabaab and others claiming to be fighting jihad, while he explicitly noted this was not a war against Islam. While the "P" in P/CVE wasn't used, the broad remedies he outlined were even then structural and long-term: addressing the dearth of educational opportunities among the young (and subsequent perceptions among youth of being "trapped"), economic stagnation, injustice, grievance, and "the humiliations of corruption" (Obama 2015); in effect, a structural and whole of society approach.

This was soon augmented by *preventing* violent extremism. As the two are by necessity very often connected, P/CVE has become the common parlance. Reflecting the phenomena being addressed, these definitions are often considered along a scale or a spectrum. Preventing violent extremism is viewed as the earliest entry point, in terms of preventing the emergence of (violent) extremist views and the process of radicalization from beginning or taking deep root in an individual or a community. As described more in the pages that follow, while the theory may suggest a need for special effort in targeting particularly "at risk" individuals or groups, in the post-war Western Balkan context there is a risk that doing this could in fact only further increase the drivers of extremism by reinforcing a sense of marginalization and exclusion. In addition, such an approach would not satisfactorily address the sources of reciprocal radicalization, nor provide a systematic framework for long-term structural policy reforms. (Quite bluntly, while one might have an interest in trying to work in one village that saw several young Muslims go to Syria, solely, directly and heavily targeting that one village could very well be counter-productive, and would be unable to touch the structural economic, social, educational, and political issues that require a systemic approach.) Prevention activities are generally aimed at a whole community, aimed at reaching (and "inoculating") everyone in order to achieve strong community "resilience" or social-political herd immunity. This can happen through education, school, youth, and other activities, often aimed at promoting tolerance, respect for diversity, critical thinking, and other "soft" skills. The development and peacebuilding communities should be involved, for their analysis and their tools (Holmer and Bauman 2018). A collected volume explicitly grappling with the "ecology of violent extremism," including a host of peace and conflict studies researchers, shows that this complex, multilayered, and structural approach is gaining academic attention (Schirch 2018; Holmer 2013).

Efforts to *counter* violent extremism come in the next pre-criminal stage, targeting a narrower range of individuals who have already been identified as having begun a trek down the pathway of radicalization. In the best case scenario, a teacher, cleric, coach, social welfare worker, friend, relative, or other community member would recognize changes in an individual's (often a young person) behavior (dress, activities, social circles, etc.) and seek to find that person help, to determine whether or not the change is standard adolescence or perhaps something deeper, ranging from substantial family problems, drugs, abuse, psychological trauma, or radicalization of some sort. The process by which a community is able to identify and respond to reports of possible problems, and in turn respond with some package of support (ranging from counseling to jobs training, education, etc.) is often referred to as a referral mechanism. The Prevent program's Channel method in the UK is one of the more well known, both for its scope but also for concerns about its approach (HMG 2015; HMG 2012; Economist 2016); others include the Danish model (Hemmingsen 2015), or the Swedish approach (Löfven 2015). As with prevention, this is also pre-criminal; the challenge here is to seek to *reverse* a process that has begun, and to work with both community services and also law enforcement in case there is the chance of the possibility to shift gears from cognitive to behavioral radicalization (Horgan 2008). Further, some CVE efforts may also be needed in a post-criminal environment, either through treatment during incarceration, or post-prison parole or other services for a former inmate or their family, in an effort to reduce recidivism. This is further complicated by different legal, sentencing, and post-prison approaches based on the extent to which an individual was a direct perpetrator to violence, or a witting or unwitting accessory (CoE 2016; UNODC 2016; SAR Consulting 2018).

The overwhelming focus on the foreign terrorist fighter issue (described more below) requires quick note of a few more terms. "Return" tends to refer to the return to their home country of individuals who have fought or been on or near the battlefield, almost exclusively referring to Syria/Iraq (Renard and Coolsaet 2018), rather than, for example, those Serbian citizens who went to Eastern Ukraine. De-radicalization and counter-radicalization measures can imply efforts aimed at explicitly supporting, "a cognitive transformation of behaviors away from extremist ideological positions and from the aspiration to use violence as a means to achieve specific goals" (Ernstorfer 2018, 51). However, some experts and organizations, anxious to not be perceived as policing or criminalizing thought rather than action, prefer the term reintegration, perhaps in tandem with rehabilitation, to identify how to integrate people who have been in these environments, and then possibly in prison, back into their home country and community (Holmer and Shtuni 2017). Horgan provides a good introduction to these issues, and to the knotty distinction between disengagement and deradicalization (2008).

It is important to note that preventing non-violent extremism is not always an explicit element of P/CVE. According to human rights frameworks, individuals have a right to freedom of thought, belief, and conscience. The broader public interest is in preventing the action—the violent action. While not always explicit, in the Western Balkan context there is an assumption or hope that the principles and values of PVE, and of a liberal system grounded in critical thinking, tolerance, respect, and appreciation for diversity, etc.—will deter and prevent people from harboring (let alone acting on) extremist thoughts. However, while the liberal democratic grounding may remain critical to the whole of society approach needed, the liberal peace as a construct, and particularly as a Euro-Atlantic organizing principle, seems to be on shakier ground than at any time since its post World War II establishment, exactly when a firm and shared values framework is most needed.

Serbia: some recent historical context

While the region's history of political assassination, war, and political violence fills volumes, some baseline context focusing on the most recent past in Serbia can be useful. Wentholt's contribution provides an historian's lens into some key and recurring themes.

Yugoslavia's dissolution and the new political context

Serbia, as the seat of Belgrade, the former capital of Yugoslavia, played a pivotal role in late Cold War events precipitating the violent dissolution of the country. Early markers of impending troubles became glaringly evident with the 1986 publication of the SANU (Serbian Academy of Arts and Sciences) memorandum warning of the historical victimization of the Serbian people and the need for renewed centralization that would reverse decentralizing trends since the early 1970s. Efforts at a smooth economic and political transition failed, as populist and nationalist voices drowned out messages of gradual reform and moderation (Glaurdić 2011; Glenny 1996; Silber and Little 1996; Ramet 2002).

Grievances and agendas between the two largest and most prominent Yugoslav republics of Serbia and Croatia, harkening back to World War II, led to an escalatory spiral of divisive rhetoric and politics, as Slobodan Milošević and Franjo Tuđman alternately blamed one another for the deteriorating situation and collaborated on how to potentially dissolve, including how to divide a Bosnia that was geographically, demographically, and politically caught in the middle (Glaurdić 2011; Donia 2014; Burg and Shoup 1999).

Slovenia's declaration of independence in June 1991 was secured following 11 days of violence. Croatia declared independence at the same time, but was then mired in violence from autumn 1991 until August 1995, as fully one third of its territory was claimed and held by Serbian fighters who had declared their own republic. Around 20,000 people were killed (BBC 2014). The war that erupted in Bosnia and Herzegovina in spring 1992 would last until December 1995, claiming just under 100,000 lives, the majority of which were civilians, and Bosniaks (Bosnian Muslims) (Sito-Sučić and Robinson 2013). Creeping political and physical oppression against Albanians in Kosovo (an autonomous part of the Serbian Republic in Yugoslavia) was a consistent feature, peaking through acts of violence reciprocally perpetrated by Serbian police and soldiers and the Kosovo Liberation Army (KLA). Heightened violence in 1997 and 1998, and inconclusive peace talks, culminated in 78 days of NATO air strikes against Serbia and Montenegro in 1999 (at that time both republics were still joined in the *Savezna Republika Jugoslavija*), with around 500 civilian casualties (HRW 2000), and approximately 1000 military/police officers killed (RTS 2013). Following the military action a substantial international presence in Kosovo was established, and Kosovo declared independence in 2008 (a status still contested by Serbia). Macedonia's proclamation of independence in 1991 was peaceful, though the country later experienced violence in early 2001 between insurgent Albanian militants and Macedonian security forces. Following a referendum in 2006, Montenegro peacefully divorced Serbia and declared its independence. While the level of violence accompanying these political processes varied greatly, violence as a tool in over a decade of political developments was prevalent. With the exception of the fighting in the province of Kosovo and the NATO airstrikes, Serbia did not experience war on its territory. However, the long rule of Slobodan Milošević, the 2003 assassination of Prime Minister Zoran Đinđić, and the continuing struggle between forces of liberalism and illiberalism have contributed to years of charged and at times violent politics (Gordy 1999; DiLellio 2009; Edmunds 2009; Guzina 2003).

The role of Belgrade in all of these developments is contested by the various parties involved, with defense and offense being framed differently depending on one's side, and one side's separatist freedom fighters being framed by the other as terrorists. Direct and indirect support of Serbian irregulars in Croatia and Bosnia has been well documented through research and scholarship, as well as the archives associated with cases tried at the ICTY and International Court of Justice (HLC 2018; ICTY n.d.; ICJ n.d.; Donia 2014). While broadly viewed as wars based on nationalist power struggles, there has from the beginning also been framing as a Christian-Muslim "clash of civilizations" (DeLiso 2007). When a notorious paramilitary leader spoke from an ethnically cleansed Bijeljina (in Bosnia) in 1992, he referenced Muslim terrorists, framing Serb actions as defensive.[11] As the SANU Memorandum was seized upon by non-Serbs as a sign of their intentions, so the Islamic Declaration written by Alija Izetbegović (Izetbegović 1969/70) has been used as a sign of the exclusive intentions of some Bosniak leaders. The arrival of foreign jihadists to Bosnia during the war to support Muslims viewed as having been left to fend for themselves is framed by some as having been unsuccessful in terms of transforming the Bosnian battlefield into one grounded in jihad, yet left a lasting trace, and provided continuing fuel for competing exclusive agendas (Kepel 2002; Li 2015).[12]

---

11 One such video is entitled, "Bijeljina posle Borbi 1992 Arkan," available at https://www.youtube.com/watch?v=KieshyeZHXo [Date accessed October 29, 2018] Željko Ražnatović, aka "Arkan," was synonymous with ethnic cleansing in the earliest days of the war, building on a pre-war criminal career around Europe. He never faced justice as he was killed in a Belgrade hotel in 2000 (Vulliamy 2000).

12 Kepel writes that as many of 4000 foreign jihadis came to Bosnia to fight; Li notes around 1000. Azinović notes there were around 3000 (Sadović 2008).

Within the borders of Yugoslavia as in today's Serbia, the country includes territory with substantial Muslim populations, though they comprise fewer than 4% of the overall population today.[13] While a small number are Albanian speakers in the south of Serbia, the majority are Bosniaks—Slavic Muslims who speak what was once known as Serbo-Croatian—in the south west of Serbia known as Sandžak to Muslims (and Raska to Orthodox Serbs).[14] Considered simply an internal region of Serbia (neither a republic nor an autonomous province like Vojvodina or Kosovo), Sandžak was widely viewed as having no basis for autonomy or self-rule. However, as tensions ratcheted up there were political moves to raise the so-called "Sandžak question." Sandžak did not see war as in Bosnia, but experienced acts of violence and general suppression (Morrison and Roberts 2013; Lyon 2008; ICG 2005; ICG 1998). The key political players involved in the early 1990s remain active in political life today.

Serbia in 2018 faces unfinished business in terms of both international and domestic affairs. On the international side the Kosovo status question has not been resolved in spite of years of dialogue, as no Serbian politician wants to be viewed as "giving up" the emotionally charged territory, while few harbor realistic hopes of reasserting control of territory well over 90% Albanian. Talks are focused primarily on ensuring the rights of Serbs in Kosovo—in the north (bordering Serbia) but also in municipalities in the south. Talks of partition gained public prominence in 2018 as the specter of wrangling over maps led to concerns of other regional territorial

---

13   The 2011 census reported 222,828 Muslims in Serbia, or about 3.1% of the population (Statistical Office, 2011, 13). This did not include Albanians in Bujanovac, Presevo, and Medveđa who largely did not participate in the census count. A count in these municipalities in 2015 reported a total of 75, 342 people, overall, of all faiths (BETA 2015). Therefore it is safe to note that the population of Serbia is less than 4% Muslim. Thanks to Boris Milanović for providing this data analysis.

14   In the Ottoman period, Sandžak emerged as a geographical-historical construct. Today there are six municipalities in southwest Serbia that previously fell within the Sandžak of Novi Pazar (Novi Pazar, Nova Varoš, Priboj, Prijepolje, Sijenica, and Tutin) and five from Montenegro (Berana, Bijelo Polje, Plav, Plevlja and Rožaje.) Raska—a current geographical and administrative term with medieval etymology, is the name of the existing administrative district of Serbia which includes Novi Pazar and Tutin, and has its administrative seat in Kraljevo.

agendas being pursued (Filipović 2018). In addition, Serbia's stated domestic and foreign policy goal—membership in the European Union—continues in spite of efforts by Belgrade to maintain a special relationship with Moscow that seems increasingly at odds with the values thought to underlie EU membership. Domestically, power in Serbia has centralized over the past several years through the stewardship of Aleksandar Vučić and his Serbian Progressive Party (*Srpska Napredna Stranka*, SNS). In 2018 virtually every part of the country is controlled by the ruling SNS/coalition; one of the rare towns held by an opposition party, Šabac, has complained about inappropriate pressures (N1 2018b). Some have referred to the situation as less a democracy and more a partitocracy (Kleibrink 2011; Kleibrink 2015). This centralization provides fuel to actors seeking decentralization for often divisive means, through calls for increased autonomy in Vojvodina (which traditionally enjoys autonomy in many areas) and calls for autonomy for Sandžak (RFERL 2009; N1 2018a).

A tale of two extremisms

Two primary strains of radicalism or extremism are of concern in Serbia today. These are far-right nationalism, and extreme or puritanical Islam, potentially including militant-jihadism. Petrović and Stakić estimate around 7000 people could fall under the label "Islamist extremist," which they say is "a slightly higher figure than right wing extremists" (Petrović and Stakić 2018, 13).

The far-right in Serbia today cannot be delinked from the violent disintegration of Yugoslavia; nor, as Wentholt explains, can it be delinked from other narratives of the country's more distant past. One can view the escalation of tensions and violent rhetoric leading up to the wars, and then the wars themselves, through a prism of violent extremism. The use of dehumanizing and divisive speech pervaded "mainstream" media in Serbia, normalizing anti-Muslim, anti-Albanian rhetoric and other external "enemies." The influx of paramilitaries and "weekend warriors" from Serbia into Croatia and BiH, and later Kosovo, driven either by a commitment to a greater Serbia ideology or a personal interest in violence, provided space for a physical and territorial expression of and outlet for the rising ethno-national tensions.[15] During the 1990s the Serbian Radical Party (SRS) of Vojislav Šešelj was the most visible and important force on the right, not only due to the ongoing effectiveness of Šešelj in using the media to send his message but due to the party's role in the government, as its electoral success not only resulted in Parliamentary seats but demonstrated the level of public support for their positions (Delauney 2016). While two of the party's most prominent members—Aleksandar Vučić and Tomislav Nikolić—left the SRS, rebranding their policies within the SNS, Šešelj has remained relevant since returning to Serbia after years in the Hague fighting war crimes charges.[16] (In her chapter, Dević explores the extent to which some on the far right perceive that Vučić, and even Šešelj, have "sold out" their values, viewing instead Milorad Dodik in neighboring BiH as the "true Serb" protecting Serb interests.) Following elections in 2016 Šešelj's party holds 22 seats in Serbia's 250 member National Assembly.

However, the relative decline in SRS's position in Serbia was accompanied by the rise of a variety of other far-right parties and groups, including *Dveri, Obraz, Nacionalni Stroj, Krv i čast, Srbska Akcija* and *Srpski narodni pokret 1389* (Bakić 2013a; Bakić 2013b Stakić 2013; Stakić 2015; Džombić 2014; Đoric 2014). Ivanović provides a useful review of a number of these groups in her chapter, and Marko as well notes that the current diffusion of the right reflects dispersed popular support in a manner that is distinct from the more centralized era of the SRS. The role or influence of the Serbian Orthodox Church cannot be discounted for its symbolic or direct

---

15 There was an interesting case in early 2018 when two explosive devices were thrown at the US embassy in Podgorica. The perpetrator was killed in the process; no one else was injured. As the story unfolded initial speculation about a suicide bombing ended when it was confirmed that the man in question was a resident of Montenegro, born in Serbia, who had fought in Kosovo and received commendation from Milosević for his service (SEEBiz 2018). This incident was not framed as terrorism, but as an individual act of discontent and possibly mental illness. It is reasonable to speculate on the subsequent reaction had the perpetrator been later identified as a Muslim.

16 See footnote 9 above.

support of activities by these groups (Džombić 2014). Further, consideration of the links with hooligan groups and the far-right in terms of providing real or potential shock troops for this ideological base has been discussed, including in terms of their role in violence related to LGBT events (Džombić 2014; Đorić 2012).

The Serbian far-right has been viewed through a fresh lens in the past two years in light of broader geopolitical developments and consequent regional impact. The broader shift to the right in the Euro-Atlantic zone, driven in part by reactions against the mass waves of migration in 2014/2015, has emboldened and empowered the far-right (Ebner 2017) including in Serbia (see Rečević, this volume). This has been visible in terms of the links between Russia and its orthodox brethren in the region, ranging from "pan-Slav" motorcycle gangs such as the Night Wolves (Lakić and Živanović 2018), to allegations of involvement in a coup attempt in Montenegro (Bajrović et al 2018). (Dević explores the intellectual roots of this Russian-Serbian affinity.) It has also been seen in connection with *Srbska Čast* in the Repubika Srpska in BiH, where that extremist group has been hosted by the entity government in Banja Luka (Klix 2018; Lakić and Kovačević 2018).[17] The participation of Vučić and other officials in the opening of an autumn 2018 conference organized by the National Avant Garde[18] (Zorić 2018) surprised some, as the group is characterized as at minimum far-right, and even neo-fascist in orientation.

This is by necessity a cursory review. The literature and the contributors in this volume reveal a few key points worth noting. First is the continuity in narratives and messaging since the late 1980s through the war to today. While some players are the same,

---

17 This meeting was not missed by SAFF, the publication arm of Active Islamic Youth in BiH, often described as Wahhabist, which on March 27, 2018 posted on Facebook mocking the notion that Srbska Čast is humanitarian in nature, and noting the organization's statement that they are ready for mobilization for Kosovo. Available at https://www.facebook.com/magazinsaff/posts/ovo-je-ta-srbska-%C4%8Dast-za-koju-dodik-ka%C5%BEe-da-je-humanitarna-organizacija-vo%C4%91e-srb/683484 511775143/ [Date accessed October 9 2018]

18 Their web site notes their three pillars: an archeofuturistic ideology; the practical goal of the liberation of the Serb nation; and the establishment of a new, freedom-oriented Serbian elite. See http://www.nacionalnaavangarda.rs/o-nama/

and new ones have emerged, narratives and tropes are rather consistent. Second is the normalization of right-wing rhetoric in public discourse, which can be considered as dangerous hate speech by some, but is dismissed by others as simple tabloid fodder and clickbait. Third, and perhaps most important, one can clearly see space for exclusion in a social-political system with such a strong nationalist pedigree, and in which the notion of a civic vs. ethnic democracy seems an illusion (Smooha and Jarve 2005). Miloš Milenković explores issues of culture, citizenship, and identity in his study in this volume.

The second form of extremism in Serbia—and the one which has garnered much more attention by domestic authorities but also the international community, is related to new and more puritanical forms of Islam in the country, particularly in Sandžak and in the Albanian speaking south, and in particular fears of violent militant jihadism or ISIS-inspired extremism. As with the far-right, there are links between politics, politicians, and religion. This summary begins with a description of the divided Islamic Community, a characteristic, one can argue, that both contributes to potential vulnerabilities while also making coordinated and effective activities more difficult, a situation noted by some of the authors as well.

The divide has its roots in the dissolution of Yugoslavia and the subsequent wars, which brought divisive ethno-nationalist politics and varying radical flavors of Bosniak/Muslim religious identification. Yugoslavia's Islamic communities had been organized within the framework of the Islamic Community in the SFRJ, based in Sarajevo, from 1945–1991. This fragmented as Yugoslavia fell apart. The Serbian Islamic Community (*Islamska zajednica*, IZ), administered from Belgrade and led by Mufti Hamdija Jusufspahić, emerged in April 1992, but was viewed as a Milošević tool. Sulejman Ugljanin, reflecting his political aims, established the Islamic Community of Sandžak in October 1993, installing Mufti Muamer Zukorlić as the head. However, far from uniting the Bosniaks under the banner of a shared faith, for years a dual struggle has played out: between the two Islamic communities, but also between Ugljanin and his protégé Zukorlić, who began to play an increasingly prominent and aggressive role, eventually edging out his mentor in political relevance. The rivalry was further complicated by the political turmoil in Belgrade following the assassination of Prime Minister Zoran Đinđić in 2003 and the rise of Vojislav Koštunica, as personal agreements and preferences between Belgrade and Sandžak again shifted.[19]

The Law on Churches and Religious Communities was adopted in 2006, identifying the Belgrade-based Islamic Community as the legitimate community based on the Kingdom of Yugoslavia structure inherited from the early 1900s, and ignoring all of the more recent developments. Following an effort to simultaneously unite the IZs and stem Zukorlić's rise by once again reorganizing the IZ and centering it in Belgrade (without either Novi Pazar or Sarajevo as reference points), in January 2007 Zukorlić formed the Islamic Community in Serbia of the Bosnia and Herzegovina Riyaset (Morrison and Roberts 2013). The split between an IZ in Belgrade and one in Novi Pazar continues to this day, in spite of attempts to reconcile the two communities, including by the Turkish government, when then Turkish Minister of Foreign Affairs Ahmet Davutoglu made multiple visits from 2010 to 2014 to try to mediate the conflict, yet failed. As a result, neither IZ is in fact able to formally influence the religious life of all of the country's Muslims — or over lucrative religious buildings and properties. This split makes engaging with the broad-based Islamic community institutionally difficult as leaders from each dispute the legitimacy of the other.[20]

In 2018 Ugljanin remains a vocal critic and is an again increasingly radical voice in Sandžak's political life, while Zukorlić is a member of the Serbian Parliament, with his party allied with the ruling coalition led by Vučić. However, the Serbian government

---

19 Following Ugljanin's political break with Rasim Ljajić (who was at that time heavily backed by Zukorlić), Ugljanin signed an agreement with Koštunica in 2004 switching allegiance in support of the Belgrade based Islamic Community.
20 It is much more difficult to engage programmatically in Serbia. In BiH, the Islamic Community is united and has a long history, and has engaged in a unified way on a number of efforts to reduce vulnerabilities to extremism. Further, this split, together with the overwhelming strength of the Serbian Orthodox Church, complicate efforts at inter-faith dialogue at the highest levels. This is again in contrast to neighboring BiH, which has an Inter-Faith Council.

maintains closer connections with the Islamic Community *of* Serbia (Belgrade), despite the ruling SNS party being in coalition with Zukorlić's Party for Justice and Reconciliation (SPP). The Islamic Community *in* Serbia has become quite established, particularly in its base in Novi Pazar. While there is no official data, it is commonly understood that the Islamic Community in Serbia enjoys support from the majority of mosques in Sandžak, where most of Serbia's approximately 250 official mosques are located.

In addition to these domestic developments, it is critical to note another and no less important development in Islamic life in Serbia — the introduction of more conservative strains of Islam, often referred to colloquially as Wahhabism or Salafism. Studies of such conservative and self-isolated communities are always challenging, as it is difficult for outsiders to gain access and trust with any private, closed social group. However, there are examples of regional research which look at trends that could have regional implications, as in BiH by Bećirović (2016) and Puhalo (2016) who have explored the rise of Salafism in BiH.

Interviews in the region — including in Sandžak — in 2016 revealed the term, "the democratization of religion" to describe a regional phenomenon, as after years of tight state control on non-state activity, religious plurality suddenly enjoyed more openness and flexibility.[21] These changes led to some examples of social/cultural clashes in places like Novi Pazar, and discomfort with unfamiliar new practices that led to increased concerns of radicalization potential and the subsequent impact on security (Ćorović 2017; Damad 2015a; Damad 2015b). The context of this change was always the introduction of more conservative interpretations of Islam in a region that had traditionally adhered to more moderate, Turkish-style Islam, which, in the diverse religious environment of the region by necessity led to more interaction with other faiths and flexible worldviews (Bringa 1995; Bougarel 2017; Morrison and Roberts

---

21 Some of Karčić's descriptions of similar dynamics in Bosnia are instructed when thinking about developments among Bosniaks and Serbia as well (Karčić n.d.).

2013).[22] While the most striking influx of an outside form of Islam was through the arrival of jihadis to Bosnia to fight during the war (as noted above), this occurred in other ways as well. For example, students from the region were able to study in the Middle East, where they were immersed in a different culture and approach to Islam (Perry 2016). Organizations from the Persian Gulf also became involved in various educational, cultural, and humanitarian engagements in the region, particularly in Bosnia. Following 9/11 a number of these were closed or shut down as links to organizations associated with the attacks (financially or otherwise) were identified or suspected (Racimora 2013; Weinberg 2015). But the influence continued in various ways. Well before the war in Syria, "In 2006/2007, 15 Salafis from Novi Pazar were arrested, and in 2009, 12 of them were convicted of crimes related to terrorism" (Petrović and Stakić 2018 10). Ćorović (2017) explains the emergence of Islamic youth associations (like Al-Furqan), and Kladničanin (2013) examines the online presence of Wahhabis in the region through portals aimed at engaging young people. (In this volume, Marko explores this issue in his study of the online presence of a cleric at the largest mosque in Novi Pazar, which is at times colloquially referred to as "the Salafi mosque.") In their report on Serbia, Petrović and Stakić note that their research "estimates that there are no more than 100 violent Islamic extremists who are grouped into three masjids in Novi Pazar" (4).

Extremists from Serbia on foreign battlefields

Both of these extremisms have included an element of recent real-world battlefield experience, with Serbian citizens going to fight in wars in Syria and Iraq, and also Ukraine.

Citizens from around the world, including the Western Balkans, began to go to Syria, and then also to Iraq, to fight or otherwise provide support. The motivation varied: from support for the people resisting Bashir al-Assad's suppression of the Syrian manifestation of the Arab

---

22 Several of these sources are related more to Bosnia than to Sandžak. However the ties and similarities in dynamics ensure their relevance in the absence a significant body of literature on Sandžak.

Spring; to aiding some of the various other factions that subsequently mushroomed; to foreign fighters viewing this as the latest in a series of battlefields for "global jihad," following the tradition of Afghanistan, Bosnia, and Chechnya (Kepel 2002). While this movement of fighters was notable, even more remarkable was the migration of women and children—whole families—to the region, as the experience shifted from one of simple war to one of apparent *hijra*—a dynamic that was seen among people coming from Bosnia (Azinović and Jusić 2015). While a growing humanitarian crisis and security nightmare, western policy urgency also cannot be de-linked from the mid-2014 ISIS declaration of the so-called Caliphate. This declaration presented a new manifestation of a globalized jihadist movement, for the first time formally linking territory to the group's ideological goals and calling on believers to come to fight, but also to build. Savvy yet gruesome use of media and social media brought this group and their tactics onto screens across the globe.

Available data shows that 37 men and 12 women from Serbia went to Syria and Iraq, as well as around 10 minors (Azinović 2018, 4). In real terms this number is low when compared to countries such as Belgium, France, the UK, and Germany. The numbers are a bit higher when viewed against the total number of Muslims in Serbia, where it ties with the number from Macedonia (see Table 1). The fact that these numbers are proportionally the highest in two countries where the Muslim population is the smallest (compared to the majority Serbian and Macedonian populations) is an issue that deserves consideration.

Table 1: Regional data on WB citizens who went to Syria and Iraq (Azinović 2018, 3–6)

	Number of Adults per 100,000 Muslims	Prevalence of foreign fighters in the Muslim Population
Albania	7	1 in 14,286
BiH	13	1 in 7692
Kosovo	18	1 in 5555
Germany	18	1 in 5555
Montenegro	19	1 in 5263
Macedonia	22	1 in 4545

Serbia	22	1 in 4545
UK	26	1 in 3846
France	30	1in 3333
Belgium	83	1 in 1204

There have been no new cases of individuals from the region going to Syria/Iraq since mid-2016 (Azinović 2018, 4), a development that can broadly be attributed to the increase in violence following Russia's increasingly aggressive involvement, much stronger border enforcement and penalties at home, and ISIS's own losing streak which made recruitment more difficult.

There are estimates that around 300 adults have returned to the region, and that as of 2017 around 460 people from the region remained in Syria/Iraq, including 197 combatants. Ten adults are reported to have returned to Serbia (Azinović 2018, 9–10). There is no certainty regarding how many may still return, refuse to return, or be killed in final actions. Arrests in the region continue. For example, in August 2018, seven Macedonian citizens were arrested for having participated in the war in Syria (Beta 2018).

In terms of Serbian citizens who went to fight in Ukraine, the phenomenon has been more open and public in many ways, perhaps reflecting the comparative "normalization" of this phenomenon. Petrović and Stakić write that around 70 Serbian citizens joined the pro-Russian side in Ukraine (Petrović and Stakić 2018, 6); others suggest the number could be as high as 300 (Živanović 2018b). In late August 2018, a prominent and very public Serbian citizen who had gone to fight in Ukraine, Bratislav Živković, was arrested (Rudić 2018). Pro-Russian Serbian nationalists mourned the death of Aleksandar Zakharchenko, the leader of the self-proclaimed Donetsk republic in Eastern Ukraine (Živanović 2018a). Investigation, prosecution, and conviction has been spotty; most returning cut deals with the prosecution, pleading guilty and receiving suspended sentences. Petrović and Stakić (2018) point out the differing legal treatments applied for different wars, with those going to Ukraine prosecuted as foreign fighters, while those going to Syria and Iraq are indicted on terrorism related charges. The way that individuals returning to Serbia are treated is important, as respondents, particularly Muslims, will point to this issue as an example of their ongoing social stigmatization and selective justice.

This too provides only a brief survey, but again some trends provide a useful framework for the discussions in this book. First, the politics of the split in the Islamic communities in Serbia is fundamental to both reducing the vulnerabilities to extremism (which, globally, often include the sense that "mainstream" society—including Islam—is corrupted (Chayes 2015)) as well as enabling a more effective prevention approach integrating Serbia's religious communities. Second, the evolution of the role of religion in a society with a strong recent history of top-down and imposed secularism opens up new spaces for a battle of ideas. And third, the openness of support for extremist ideas and actions on the side of Serbian nationalists, in the general public sphere but also among prominent political leaders, has normalized one of the country's variants of extremism.

VERLT and P/CVE as a policy priority in the Western Balkans—the research

Long-time terrorism researcher John Horgan started a lunch lecture at a CVE conference in Singapore in 2013 by asking for whom the future of terrorism was important, suggesting four possible answers: the responders, the victims, the recruits, and the researchers (CENS 2013, 14). Since 2014, the number of research initiatives and conferences occurring on the topic of P/CVE has mushroomed. This section summarizes some main developmental points in the emergence of P/CVE studies in the region. It is not a comprehensive literature review, and while it doesn't include unpublished analyses and project inception reports drafted by the many organizations and companies now engaging on P/CVE, those reports have influenced consideration on this issue more broadly. A literature review included as part of the regional British Council funded research project can provide additional references, though it should be noted that this set of country surveys is very heavily focused on aspects of ISIS-inspired extremism and radicalization (Bećirović et al 2017). Further, each of the authors in this volume makes a contribution to the overall literature review through their own unique studies and conceptual frameworks.

It is important to emphasize that Serbian writers have been ahead of the curve in terms of both thinking about the nature of extremism, and focused analysis on right-wing extremism. Đorić wrote on hooliganism in 2012, including on the phenomenon in Serbia (Đorić 2012). The Center for the Development of Civil Society, with support from the Open Society Foundation, published a book-length collected volume on the topic, *Politički Ekstremizam u Cyber Prostoru Srbije (Political Extremism in Serbian Cyberspace)*, based on research conducted in 2012 and 2013, and with chapters on various manifestations of extremism in Serbia, from the far-right to the "Wahhabis" (Jelinčić and Ilić 2013). Bakić (2013b), Stakić (2013; 2015), Biserko (2014) and Đorić (2014) have studied Serbia's far-right for years; Đorić has also written on the extreme left (2016). This variety should perhaps not be surprising, as there has been quality political analysis by independent experts from the Milošević era to today. The prominence of right-wing nationalism has been unavoidable in the broader political context, and the small number of Muslims in the country has been dwarfed by the broader environment and lived experience of far-right extremism. However, one can also consider the role of foreign funding in the *other* countries of the region, most notably those with larger Muslim populations, and the explicit requests for research solely on that phenomenon, particularly since 2014. This is finally beginning to change. As of this writing in autumn 2018, a number of research efforts underway in BiH, for example, are finally beginning to look at other forms of extremism, but have not yet been published.

It is also useful to note that research on relevant issues was underway before P/CVE became a regional policy imperative; just a few are noted in this summary. In *Jihad: The Trail of Political Islam*, Kepel (2002) included a chapter entitled, "The Failure to Graft Jihad on Bosnia's Civil War." (The book was originally published in French in 2000; the English version included an introduction addressing the 9/11 attacks.) In *The Coming Balkan Caliphate* (DeLiso, 2007), the author provides a provocative early look at this issue, but only considered issues related to violent Islamist extremism. (In the opinion of this author, DeLiso offered a subjective analysis of drivers, overlooked the concept of right-wing nationalism or reciprocal radicalization, and at times echoed "clash of civilizations" argumentation by attributing eschatological fundamentalist thinking solely to adherents of Islam.) Morrison's "Wahhabism in the Balkans" (2008) examines the rise of this fundamentalist interpretation through both pre-war ideological discourse but then also the arrival of mujahidin fighters during the war, particularly in BiH, concluding, "The moderate character of Balkan Islam will continue to be challenged by the narrowness of the Wahhabi doctrine" (11).[23]

But the volume increased beginning in 2014. Regionally the wave of P/CVE efforts was security focused, and often related to reports on the approximately 900 citizens of the region who had gone to Syria and Iraq. A policy brief entitled "We Did Criminalize it — Now What? Western Balkans Response to the Foreign Fighters Threat" was published in September 2014 by the Macedonia-based NGO Analytica, focusing less on the specific trends in the region than on short anecdotes based on experiences from Germany, the UK, and Belgium (Bogdanovski 2014). In 2015 the Atlantic Initiative in Bosnia and Herzegovina, with support from the Norwegian Embassy in BiH, published the report "The Lure of the Syrian War: the Foreign Fighters' Bosnian Contingent" on the phenomenon, including data on the number of BiH citizens who had travelled to Syria from December 2012 through December 2014 (then estimated at 156 men, 36 women and 25 children), and early data on the number of returned as of January 2015 (48 men and 3 women). The authors also began to tease out recruitment strategies and motivations (Azinović and Jusić 2015). The Kosovo Center for Security Studies (KCSS) published, "Report Inquiring into the Causes and Consequences of Kosovo Citizens' Involvement as Foreign Fighters in Syria and Iraq," in April 2015, similarly providing a baseline for thinking about the issue of extremism in Kosovo, with a focus on ISIS-inspired ideology. The report, funded by the US Embassy in

---

23   Morrison, together with Elizabeth Roberts, published *The Sandžak: A History in 2013*, the most comprehensive English language history on the region.

Pristina, also began to delve into ideological considerations of Wahhabism and *takvir* (Kursani 2015). The Institute for Democracy and Mediation (IDM) in Albania published a book length report, *Religious Radicalization and Violent Extremism in Albania*, funded through the US Embassy in Tirana and providing a baseline on religious (primarily Islamist) extremism based on polling and other data collection (Vurmo et. al. 2015). In September 2015, "Countering the Cultivation of Extremism in Bosnia and Herzegovina: The Case for Comprehensive Education Reform," applied a post-war/conflict transformation lens to the issue, for BiH but also the region (Perry 2015).

In addition, regional efforts were launched. A September 2015 workshop in Belgrade resulted in a collected volume, *Violent Extremism in the Western Balkans*, notably looking at radical Islam and nationalist violent extremism (Ejdus and Jureković 2015). The Balkan Investigative Reporting Network (BIRN), with funding from the United Kingdom, published a report (*Balkan Jihadists: The Radicalization and Recruitment of Fighters in Syria and Iraq*) and held a related launch conference in Sarajevo in March 2016, bringing together short-form reporting from throughout the region (BIRN 2016). In July 2016 the collected volume, *Jihadist Hotbeds: Understanding Local Radicalization Processes* included a chapter, "Beyond Gornje Maoče and Ošve: Radicalization in the Western Balkans," exploring the trend of the rise of conservative and/or extremist Islam in the region (Qehaja 2016). The Regional Cooperation Council (RCC) published a survey of P/CVE efforts in July 2016, which included Turkey. Research for that report (conducted from February through May) revealed that the definition of the issue, and the vast majority of ongoing research and projects in the region was focused on the issue of militant jihadist violent extremism (Perry 2016).

More recently the research has continued. An edited volume entitled *Between Salvation and Terror: Radicalization and the Foreign Fighter Phenomenon in the Western Balkans,* and funded by the Norwegian Embassy in BiH, again focused on foreign fighters who had gone to Syria/Iraq from Albania, BiH, Croatia, Montenegro, Kosovo, Macedonia, Serbia, and Slovenia (Azinović 2017). (It is interesting to note that there is no mention of the impact of far-right nationalism or reciprocal radicalization as a concept.) UN Women supported two studies: "The Role of Women in Supporting, Joining, Intervening in and Preventing Violent Extremism in Sandjak," based on four days of field research (Speckhard and Shajkovci 2016), and "Drivers of Radicalization and Violent Extremism in Kosovo: Women's Roles in Supporting, Preventing and Fighting Violent Extremism," looking at drivers of radicalization and specifically pertaining to the participation of 44 women from Kosovo believed to have gone to Syria and Iraq (Speckhard and Shajkovci 2017). "The Islamic State Narrative in Kosovo: Deconstructed One Story at a Time" was published by KCSS (funded by the US government) in September 2017, focusing on Islamic State narratives, propaganda and distribution techniques targeting Kosovo's Albanians (Kraja 2017). "Understanding Push and Pull Factors in Kosovo: Primary Interviews with Returned Foreign Fighters and their Families," was commissioned by UNDP and published in November 2017, based on 13 semi-structured interviews with returnees either in prison or under house arrest (Xharra and Gojani 2017).

In mid-2018, a regional research effort on extremism in the Western Balkans funded by the British Council (and first initiated in mid- to late 2016) was published, with country-specific reports and an overarching introductory regional framework and literature review. Initial talks on the project revealed an interest in ensuring a "baseline report" for each country,[24] though as noted above some countries already had such reports. The focus was again very strongly on threats of Islamist extremism, though notably the Serbia report was able to most strongly link to the impact of far-right nationalism as a driver (Petrović and Stakić 2018). Schmid's (2014) framing of "not now violent" extremists was frequently referenced in this collection, to demonstrate the broad sense of threat from peaceful extremism in the region.[25]

---

24 Personal discussion, Sarajevo autumn 2016.
25 The next wave will likely focus on two emerging trends—online radicalization and prison radicalization. For example, KCSS published "New Battlegrounds: Extremist Groups' Activity on Social Networks in Kosovo, Albanian and FYROM in November 2017 (Kelmendi and Balaj 2017), funded by the EU. "Bosnia and Herzegovina

This non-exhaustive review reveals several trends. First, with the exception of Serbia there has been little written on extremism of any variant in the region prior to the deluge. As other countries begin to acknowledge reciprocal radicalization, work by independent experts in Serbia to date could serve as a roadmap. Second, the emergence of the P/CVE framework in 2014 was heavily biased towards counter-terrorism and security lenses, shaped by the foreign terrorist fighter phenomenon and ISIS. The policy, economic, social, and ideological situation in the region did not suddenly change; however, from 2014 already existing issues were securitized through the VE lens. And third, the increase in the number of reports and authors shows increasing nuance on the issue, and the greater relevance of reciprocal radicalization.

VERLT and P/CVE as a policy priority in the Western Balkans—the projects

While P/CVE has been an increasingly prominent focus of donors in the region, it is important to remember that the region had already been on the democratization and development radar screen (Carothers 2009), due both to the post-war reconstruction, reconciliation and democratization efforts, but also in support of the region's broader Euro-Atlantic integration perspective. Many organizations—both international and non-governmental—were already active. The EU has a presence and Special Representatives throughout the region, as does the Council of Europe, the UN Family (in particular UNDP, UNESCO, UNDP and UNICEF) and the International Organization for Migration (IOM). The OSCE is in the field throughout the region, including, for example, a Mission in BiH that was opened in 1994, and a Mission in Serbia established in 2001. There are/have been US/USAID funded efforts ranging from

---

Daesh Tracker," an unpublished study by Moonshot CVE (2017) used big data techniques to measure "appetites" for *Daesh*-related content; a similar study was done for Kosovo. Other are in the pipeline at the time of this writing. A report on the potential for prison radicalization based on a study conducted in Zenica (BiH) was presented in autumn 2018 (SAR 2018); an OSCE conference on the topic of prison (de)radicalization was held in Tirana, Albania in November 2018.

ICITAP (International Criminal Investigative Training Assistance Program) (supporting police/law enforcement reform, from local policing to modernization of Ministries of the Interior); NDI (National Democratic Institute) and IRI (International Republican Institute) supporting election processes with parties and candidates, as well as get out the vote efforts and women's engagement; IREX and Internews (supporting independent media and civic engagement); and more. German efforts include GIZ (German Corporation for International Cooperation) and various political foundations (Konrad Adenauer, Heinrich Boell, Friedrich Ebert, etc.) and others, working on similar democratization initiatives. The United Kingdom has engaged on projects related to parliamentary reform, governance, the rule of law, and other topics, working through NGOs or implemented by the Westminster Foundation or British Council, to name a few. Countless other organizations such as Save the Children, CARE, World Vision, the Open Society Fund, and Nansen Dialogue Centers have been on the ground at varying times, as have local think tanks and NGOs (Puljek Shank and Memišević, n.d.; Belloni 2008). In Serbia, a combination of large organizations in Belgrade and smaller groups around the country implement an array of projects and initiatives based on donor support or local need, often with substantial funds through EU civil society support mechanisms (GI 2017). This is more than simple background context, as it demonstrates that present P/CVE efforts are often in practice plugging into existing institutional structures and frameworks. This should raise questions both of the impact of work to date prior to the P/CVE focus, and the ability of new or rebranded efforts to effectively address long-elusive structural post-war reform challenges (Spasojević 2017; CRTA 2016; Grødeland 2006; Greenberg 2010).

Just as research has increased over the past several years, so have activities on the ground, to the point where work has been conducted to map the activities.[26] A number of different thematic

---

26 There is imperfect agreement on what constitutes a PVE project. If after school youth football projects funded through PVE budget lines and taking a holistic peacebuilding approach to PVE counts, does an after-school youth football project funded through a "youth" budget line that has existed for a decade or more also count?

issues are becoming key focus areas of engagement, research, and practice. All of these issues are being addressed throughout Europe (France, Belgium, the UK, etc), with methods and pilots being exported to the Western Balkan region. And just as wealthier and more consolidated democracies are struggling with addressing these issues and drivers, the challenges in terms of governance, public administration, and community resilience are similarly daunting in the Western Balkans. From a classic security perspective, programs are developing related to the issue of returning foreign terrorist fighters and their families; terrorist financing; addressing issues of prison radicalization and the role of prisons in rehabilitation of incarcerated extremists; and efforts to address possible risks related to migration (an issue explored by Rečević in this volume). In terms of P/CVE, there is a trend in developing programming related to community "referral mechanisms" for early warning and response; efforts aimed at providing specific support to women and girls in terms of preventing radicalization or responding to gender specific threats and vulnerabilities; understanding the role of the Internet in prompting or facilitating radicalization, and as a counter-point developing projects to use the Internet and social media to deter or counter radicalization; work with religious communities in support of promoting moderate faith interpretations, tolerance, and inter-faith dialogue; education reform, in terms of promotion of critical thinking, intercultural education, and media/digital literacy; and a large number of efforts aimed at providing young people with alternatives to extremist lifestyle choices, targeted at particularly "at-risk" youth and young people in general.

The field is becoming crowded—less so in Serbia than in BiH and Kosovo, but still crowded. The 2016 RCC report noted provided an initial survey (Perry 2016), and from 2018 the EU is funding a project entitled, "Communities First—Creation of a Western Balkans Civil Society Hub to Prevent and Counter Violent Extremism," in six countries which includes a P/CVE project mapping

---

Should all efforts aimed at increasing intercultural skills and tolerance, building media and digital literacy, and supporting youth critical thinking abilities be included?

component.²⁷ In Serbia alone, activities have been supported and initiated by the US Embassy, the OSCE,²⁸ the German Marshall Fund, Hedayah, and others, and implemented by the Belgrade Center for Security Policy, the Helsinki Committee for Human Rights, Damad, CeSID (Center for Free Elections and Deomcracy), Forum 10 and many others. Information sharing and coordination among donors and implementers is often weak, ad hoc, and personality-based. As is discussed in the conclusion, one can argue about the extent to which these prevention approaches are new, or a rebranding of peacebuilding, education, and youth engagement projects that have been underway for years (Perry 2017).

An interdisciplinary approach

This volume provides a broad look at the dynamics of extremism and violent extremism in Serbia, to make a contribution to the literature but also potentially to ongoing policy discussions. While conscious of the flurry of activity on this topic, it is hoped that the interdisciplinary approach will add a different perspective. All of the chapters were developed based on the authors' own identification of important issues and themes; the topics were not commissioned.

The collection opens with an historical piece by Niké Wentholt, who brings together classic historical archive work with a contemporary and timely assessment of current messaging and policy implications. Wentholt applies historical analysis to narratives of terror and violence that forge links between long-standing historical narratives and interpretations and contemporary political discourse. She studies the language and messaging of the far-right group *Zavetnici*, and of the web site *Putvjernika*, which promotes interpretations of Islam often viewed as extreme in nature or intention. She reviews a selection of messaging from these resources, and compares them to discourse in selected Parliamentary debates and

---

27 The project is being coordinated by Forum MNE in Montenegro. More information on the project is available at http://www.forum-mne.com/images/Project_facts heet_EN.pdf
28 From September 2017 – March 2019 the author served as project coordinator for a two-year UK-funded P/CVE project implemented by the OSCE Mission to Serbia.

the mainstream print daily *Politika*, to begin to determine the nexus between historical myth and expressed experience and grievance, and contemporary calls to engage and act. She concludes that reciprocal radicalization is evident as messaging from these extremist groups play and build off one another, at times based on the same historical moment, but with different perspectives.

Providing additional deep context, Ana Dević takes a sociological approach to the issue of Serbian right-wing extremism and the influence of contemporary Russian academic/para-academic thought. Following a review of three phases in Russian-Serbian relations, she examines the impact of writings and activities by Yelena Gus'kova and Aleksandar Dugin, and their conceptual and practical support and affinity for Serbian nationalism. She identifies echoes of the Serbian right wing from a Russian and Eurasian perspective, in which an "aggressive" and "immoral" west is viewed as preventing a more "righteous" Slav brotherhood and destiny. The rigor of such Russian extremity leads to an embrace in particular of Vojislav Šešelj and Milorad Dodik in the Republika Srpska in neighboring Bosnia and Herzegovina, as other "mainstream" Serbian politicians are viewed as having sold out to the west as a part of European Union aspirations. She also introduces the real-world links between these Russian intellectuals and Serbian far-right organizations, and is critical of the ability of the EU to offer a salient alternate vision to the population that could compete with the emotional appeals from the Russian-Serbian right.

These scene-setting chapters are followed by contributions by three authors who each focused their research on specific aspects of the role of the Internet in cultivating online extremism. As the role of online networks and social media use is one of the truly unique elements of modern forms of extremism and violent extremism, these perspectives are useful in complementing some of the historical reviews. Davor Marko provides an interesting comparative case study that looks at two prime influencers who each enjoy a prominent social media presence: Goran Davidović, a far-right Serbian nationalist proponent with a significant profile on Twitter, and Sead Islamović, a Muslim cleric with strong conservative/Salafist views who relies heavily on YouTube as a means of ideas propagation. In contrast to some studies on online social network analysis underway that rely on big data and volume, Marko engages in limited yet deeper qualitative analysis of the subject matter, considering the level of interaction between influencers and followers in each case study, the tone and content of rhetoric, and the extent of their online followers. While methods of outreach and network-building are different, each influencer emphasizes the need for self-preservation of "their" group, through sophisticated language that eschews open calls for violent action, but certainly conveys messages that could be interpreted by some as supportive of extreme measures to support one's "own."

Whereas Marko focuses on the role of the influencer (the product), Kristina Ivanović considers the target reader or "consumer" of online extreme content. Her research explores the issue of online radicalization and its impact on Serbian youth through original focus group discussions with several dozen young people in three parts of Serbia: Tutin, a small municipality in the Sandžak region; Zaječar/Bor, small towns in the far east of the country; and Novi Sad, in Vojvodina. Her selection of regions provides an opportunity to understand the views of young people on both militant jihadist extremism, as well as right-wing nationalism and neo-Nazi groups. Her method included discussing examples of online ideological propagation with focus group participants, to seek their comments on whether they had seen such materials, their impressions on the tools and quality of outreach and messaging, and the overall effectiveness of these online tactics. Through these discussions she also seeks to better understand the drivers of extremism in these communities, and to begin to identify remedies, which, in her assessment, require more effective education, youth engagement, and inter-religious dialogue—all noble objectives which have to date proved elusive.

Boris Milanović delves into the online world of 4chan in Serbia, introducing readers to an online discussion platform active for a decade, but gaining prominence with the more recent rise of the alt-right. Following a description of the forum's basic elements, he explains the impact of the anonymous nature of posts, which can be viewed as empowering or enabling, but certainly provides a different snapshot of opinion and dynamics than sites in which users require personal profiles. He then proceeds to give an analysis of the more than half a million posts linked to Serbian IP addresses, focusing on the use of "traditional" extremist nationalist narratives, the ever-present threats to the Serbian people, the sense of connections with other similarly minded far-right groups outside of Serbia, and the explicit or implicit readiness of users to either incite or note their readiness to use violence in pursuit of their aims. His inclusion of illustrative discussion comments and visual memes that often convey a basket of far-right symbolism provides insights into a poorly understood online ecosystem. And while the anonymous nature of the forum could lead some to argue it provides a "safety valve" for hate, it is difficult to surmise that the simmering rage and grievance does not provide fuel for potential real-world violent acts.

The refugee crisis that affected the European continent a few years ago has slowed significantly due to stronger border security, more aggressive preventive measures, and a deal with Turkey to stem the flow of refugees. However, the crisis continues to have an impact on domestic politics in key countries throughout Europe, most notably Germany. As Serbia is not a destination, but a transit country, the vast majority of these people are just passing through the country en route to an increasingly inaccessible European Union. There are around 3000 refugees "stuck" in Serbia as they await an unknown fate; while there is some flux, some have been living in refugee/migrant centers for years now. Tijana Rečević spoke to local officials, aid workers, and citizens in three communities affected by the crisis and hosting centers—Preševo (in the Albanian speaking south), Šid (in central Serbia, by the border with Croatia), and Subotica (in Vojvodina in the north, near the border with Hungary.) She seeks to understand whether the ongoing limbo situation might be increasing tensions and radicalization tendencies not only among individuals stuck in these centers (and stuck in Serbia), but also in the host communities themselves. She finds that while there is potential for reciprocal radicalization, to date the situation has been fairly stable. She notes however that another increase in numbers, or the continuing lack of a long-term perspective for migrants desperate to get on with their lives, could lead to an increase in tensions; continued constructive vigilance by all involved stakeholders is therefore required.

Miloš Milenković brings an anthropologist's eye to the issue, considering the role of social inclusion or exclusion in cultural policy, and the extent to which cultural heritage is or is not supportive of an open and multicultural identity in Serbia. He views identity-based conflicts as a source of potential social instability and division, but also of a manifestation of intolerance, exclusion, and grievance that can create conditions conducive to extremist leanings. He specifically focuses on the issue of the UNESCO declaration of examples of intangible cultural heritage (ICH) in Serbia, considering the number of applications for ICH by the majority (Serbian Orthodox) population when compared to the country's national minorities. He argues that more proactive and inclusive cultural policies can not only support the constructive engagement of minorities, but can prevent the emergence of hegemonic cultural fundamentalism by a dominant majority group.

In comparison to some of the other noted publications, this is a rather eclectic volume. This is by design, grounded in an interest in a more nuanced, inter-disciplinary, and whole society analysis of historical and contemporary experience with extremist thoughts and actions. The various approaches used by the authors are unique, but strong common themes emerge in terms of diagnosis and prescription. In the concluding chapter a number of evident commonalities are further explored, as are some over-arching conclusions that can be drawn from the authors' research and analysis. It is perhaps most notable, at the beginning of this volume, to point out that the themes and challenges explored by each contributor are not new, but have been around for decades, and are rooted in generations; however, today these dynamics are playing out in a very new and uncertain global environment, which could affect future developments in unanticipated ways.

References

Abdel-Samad, Hamed. 2016. *Islamic Fascism*. New York: Prometheus Books.

Abou El Fadil, Khaled. 2005. *The Great Theft: Wrestling Islam from the Extremists*. San Francisco: HarperOne.

Abu-Nimer, Mohammed. 2018. "Alternative Approaches to Transforming Violent Extremism: The case of Islamic Peace and Interreligious Peacebuilding." *Transformative Approaches to Violent Extremism*. Austin, Beatrix and Hans J. Giessmann (eds.) Berlin: Berghof Foundation.

ACLU. nd. "How the USA Patriot Act Redefines 'Domestic Terrorism.'" ACLU Web Site. Accessed October 1, 2018. https://www.aclu.org/other/how-usa-patriot-act-redefines-domestic-terrorism Accessed October 1, 2018.

Amnesty International. 2018. "Hungary: Conviction Upheld for Syrian Accused of Terrorism for 'throwing stones'." Accessed Sept 21. 2018 https://www.amnesty.org.uk/press-releases/hungary-conviction-upheld-syrian-accused-terrorism-throwing-stones.

Anti-Defamation League (ADL). 2018. "Extreme Right/Radical Right/Far Right." https://www.adl.org/resources/glossary-terms/extreme-right-radical-right-far-right

Austin, Beatrix and Hans J. Giessmann. 2018. *Transformative Approached to Violent Extremism*. Berlin: Berghof Foundation.

Azinović, Vlado. 2017. *Between Salvation and Terror: Radicalization and the Foreign Fighter Phenomenon in the Western Balkans*. Sarajevo: The Atlantic Initiative.

Azinović, Vlado. 2018. "Regional Report: Understanding Violent Extremism in the Western Balkans. British Council Extremism Research From June 2018." Accessed October 27, 2018. bit.ly/erfreport_wb

Azinović, Vlado and Muhamed Jusić. 2015. "The Lure of the Syrian War: the Foreign Fighters' Bosnian Contingent." Accessed October 26, 2018. http://atlanticinitiative.org/2016/06/17/the-new-lure-of-the-syrian-war-the-foreign-fighters-bosnian-contingent-atlantic-initiative-sarajevo-2016-2/

BBC. 2014. "Croatia Accuses Serbia of 1990s Genocide." *BBC*, 3 March, 2014. https://www.bbc.com/news/world-europe-26415503.

Bajrović, Reuf, Vesko Garčević and Richard Kraemer. 2018. "Hanging by a Thread: Russia's Strategy of Destabilization in Montenegro." Accessed September 5 2018. https://www.fpri.org/wp-content/uploads/2018/07/kraemer-rfp5.pdf.

Bakić, Jovo. 2013a. "Delanje Organizacija Srpske Krajnje Desnice u Cyber-Prostoru." *Politicki Ekstremizam u Cyber Prostoru Srbije*. Jelinčić, Jadranka and Snezana Ilić (eds.), 111–119. Zrenjanin: Centar za Razvoj Civilnog Drustvo.

Bakić, Jovo. 2013b. *Right Wing Extremism in Serbia*. Belgrade: Friedrich Ebert Stiftung.

Biserko, Sonja (ed.). 2014. *Ekstremizam kako prepoznati društveno zlo*. Belgrade: Helsinški odbor za ljudska prava u Srbiji.

Barber, Benjamin R. 2001. *Jihad vs. McWorld: Terrorism's Challenge to Democracy*. New York: Ballantine Books

Bartlett, Will, James Ker-Lindsey, Kristian Alexander and Tena Prelec. 2017. "The UAE as an Emerging Actor in the Western Balkans: The Case of Strategic Investment in Serbia." *Journal of Arabian Studies*. 7, no., 1: 94–112.

Bassuener, Kurt and Valery Perry. 2017. "Erratic Ambiguity: The Impact of Trump's Unpredictable Foreign Policy in the Western Balkans." Democratization Policy Council Policy Paper. Accessed October 2, 2018. http://www.democratizationpolicy.org/pdf/DPC_Policy_Paper_Erratic_Ambiguity_Trumps_Foreign_Policy_in_W_Balkans.pdf.

Beckett, Lois. 2017. "How Leftwing Media Focus on Far-Right Groups is helping to Normalize Hate." *The Guardian*. March 5, 2017. https://www.theguardian.com/world/2017/mar/05/left-wing-media-far-right-normalize-hate-trump

Bećirović, Edina. 2016. "A Rhetorical Fight for the 'Hearts and Minds' of Bosnian Muslims." Accessed October 29, 2018. http://www.helsinki.org.rs/doc/Edina%20Becirevic%20-%20Salafism%20vs.%20Moderate%20Islam.pdf.

Bećirović, Edina, Majda Halilović and Vlado Azinović. 2017. "Literature Review: Radicalization and Violent Extremism in the Western Balkans." Extremism Research Forum. Accessed October 30, 2018. https://www.britishcouncil.rs/sites/default/files/erf_literature_review_2017_radicalisation_and_violent_extremism.pdf.

Belloni Robert. 2008. "Civil Society in War-to-Democracy Transitions." *From War to Democracy: Dilemmas of Peacebuilding*. Jarstad A and Sisk T (eds), 182–210. Cambridge: Cambridge University Press.

Beta. 2015. "Procenjen brok stanovnika u Bujanovcu, Medvedi i Presevu." *Radio-Televizija Vojvodina*. July 7, 2015. http://www.rtv.rs/sr_lat/drustvo/procenjen-broj-stanovnika-u-bujanovcu-medvedji-i-presevu_617896.html ccessed October 29, 2018]

BETA. 2018. "Uhapseno sedam drzavljana Makedonije zbog ratovanja u Sirii." *N1*, August 7, 2018. Available at http://rs.n1info.com/a409 961/Svet/Region/Uhapseno-sedam-drzavljana-Makedonije-zbog-r atovanja-u-Siriji.html

BIRN. 2016. "Balkan Jihadists: The Radicalization and Recruitment of Fighters in Syria and Iraq." *Balkan Investigative Reporting Network*. March 2016. http://www.balkaninsight.com/en/file/show/Balka n-Jihadists.pdf.

Bogdanovski, Andreja. 2014. "We Did Criminalize it — Now What? Western Balkans response to the Foreign Fighters Threat." Analytica Policy brief, Accessed October 26, 2018. https://www.analyticamk.or g/images/stories/files/2014/Foreign_Fighters.pdf.

Bougarel, Xavier. 2017. *Islam and Nationhood in Bosnia-Herzegovina: Surviving Empires*. London: Bloomsbury Academic.

Bringa, Tone. 1995. *Bring Muslim the Bosnian Way: Identity and COmmunity in a Central Bosnian Village*. Princeton: Princeton University Press.

Burg, Steven L. and Paul S. Shoup. 1999. *The War in Bosnia-Herzegovina: Ethnic Conflict and International Intervention*. New York: M.E. Sharpe.

Carothers, Thomas. 2009. "Democracy Assistance: Political vs. Developmental." *Journal of Democracy* 20, no.1: 5–19,

Center of Excellence for National Security (CENS). 2013. "Cens-Warwick Gr:een Workshop, Countering Violent Extremism: The State of Play." Workshop Proceedings. Accessd September 2 2018 http://w ww.academia.edu/6111322/CENS-WARWICK_GR_EEN_WORKS HOP_COUNTERING_VIOLENT_EXTREMISM_THE_STATE_OF_P LAY.

CJCS (Chairman of the Joint Chiefs of Staff). 2014. "Counterterrorism." Joint Publication. Accessed October 26, 2018. http://www.jcs.mil/ Portals/36/Documents/Doctrine/pubs/jp3_26.pdf.

Chayes, Sarah. 2015. *Thieves of State; Why Corruption Threatens Global Security*. New York: W.W. Norton & Company.

Cole, Jennifer and Raffello Pantucci (eds.). 2014. "Community Tensions: Evidence-Based Approaches to Understanding the Interplay between Hate Crimes and Reciprocal Radicalization." STFC/RUSI Conference Series No. 3. Accessed October 9, 2018. https://www w.connectfutures.org/wp-content/uploads/2018/01/RUSI-Laura-Zahra-McDonald_community_tensions.pdf.

Coolsaet, Rik. 2016. "All Radicalization is Local: The Genesis and Drawbacks of an Elusive Concept." Egmont Paper 84. Royal Institute for International Relations. Accessed October 29, 2018. http://ww w.egmontinstitute.be/content/uploads/2016/05/ep84.pdf?type=p df

Ćorović, Aida. 2017. "Radicalization in Serbia: The Youth of Sandžak between a Hammer and an Anvil." In *Between Salvation and Terror: Radicalization and the Foreign Fighter Phenomenon in the Western Balkans*, Azinović, Vlado (ed.), 125–136. Sarajevo: The Atlantic Initiative

Council of Europe (COE). 2016. *Council of Europe Handbook for Prison and Probation Services Regarding Radicalization and Violent Extremism*. Accessed October 27, 2018. https://rm.coe.int/16806f9aa9.

Crenshaw, Martha. 1981. "The Causes of Terrorism." *Comparative Politics*. 13 (4): 379–399.

CRTA. 2016. "Research on citizens' participation in democratic processes 2016." Accessed October 28, 2018. http://otvoreniparlament.rs/istrazivanje/15.

Delauney, Guy. 2016. "Serbia Elections: Radical Šešelj Back in Parliament." *BBC News*. April 25, 2016. https://www.bbc.com/news/world-europe-36128489.

Di Lellio, Anna. 2009. "The Missing Democratic Revolution and Serbia's Anti-European Choice: 1989–2008." *International Journal of Politics, Culture and Society*. 22, no 3, (September): 373–384.

Damad. 2015a. *Extremism and Radicalism among Youth in Novi Pazar – Perceptions, Risks and Threats*. Novi Pazar: Damad Cultural Center.

Damad. 2015b. *Integrated Response of the Community to Human Security Challenges in Novi Pazar*. Novi Pazar: Damad Cultural Center.

DeLiso, Christopher. 2008. *The Coming Balkan Caliphate: The Threat of Radical Islam to Europe and the West*. Santa Barbara: Praeger Security International.

Đorić, Marija. 2014. *Ekstremna Desnica*. Belgrade: Udruzenje Nauka i Društvo Srbije.

Đorić, Marija. 2016. *Ekstremna Levnica: Ideoloski Aspekti Levicarskog Ekstremizma*. Belgrade: Udruzenje Nauka i Društvo Srbije.

Đorić, Marija. 2012. *Huliganizam: Nasilje i Sport*. Belgrade: Udruzenje Nauka i Društvo Srbije.

Donia, Robert. 2014. *Radovan Karadžic: Architect of the Bosnian Genocide*. Cambridge: Cambridge University Press.

Džombić, Jelena. 2014. "Rightwing Extremism in Serbia." *Race and Class*. 55, no. 4: 106–110.

Eatwell, Roger. 2006. "Community Cohesion and Cumulative Extremism in Contemporary Britain.) *The Political Quarterly*. 77, no. 2: 204–216.

Economist. 2016. "Driving Away the Shadows." *The Economist*. August 20, 2016. https://www.economist.com/britain/2016/08/20/driving-away-the-shadows.

Ebner, Julia. 2017. *The Rage: The Vicious Circle of Islamist and Far-Right Extremism*. London: I.B. Taurus.

Edmunds, Timothy. 2009. "Illiberal Resilience in Serbia." *Journal of Democracy*, 20: 128–142.

Ejdus, Filip and Predrag Jureković (eds.). 2015. *Violent Extremism in the Western Balkans*. Belgrade: Regional Stability in South East Europe Study group.

Eremina, Natalia and Sergei Seremenko. 2015. *Right Radicalism in Party and Political Systems in Present-day European States*. Cambridge: Cambridge Scholars Publishing.

Ernstorfer, Anita. 2018. "Effective Approaches to Preventing Violent Extremism: A Peacebuilding Systems Perspective." *Transformative Approached to Violent Extremism,* Austin, Beatrix and Hans J. Giessmann (eds.), 49–60. Berlin: Berghof Foundation

Escritt, Thomas. 2016. "U.N. Tribunal Acquits Serbian Firebrand Šešelj of War Crimes." *Reuters*. March 31, 2016. https://www.reuters.com/article/us-warcrimes-warcrimes-acquittal-idUSKCN0WX10D.

European Commission (EC). 2018. "Enlargement Package: Commission Published Reports on Western Balkans and Turkey." European Commission Press Release. Accessed September 15 2018. http://europa.eu/rapid/press-release_IP-18-3342_en.htm.

Fisher, Max. 2018. "America's Three Bad Options in Syria." *The New York Times*. April 10, 2018. https://www.nytimes.com/2018/04/10/world/middleeast/syria-us-chemical-weapons.html.

Gagnon VP. 1994/1995. "Ethnic Nationalism and International Conflict: The Case of Serbia." *International Security* 19 (3):132–68.

Gill, Paul, John Horgan and Paige Deckert. 2014. "Bombing Alone: Tracing the Motivations and Antecedent Behaviors of Lone Actors Terrorists." *Journal of Forensic Science*s. 10: 425–435. https://www.ncbi.nlm.nih.gov/pmc/articles/PMC4217375/.

Glaurdić Josip. 2011. *The Hour of Europe: Western Powers and the Breakup of Yugoslavia*. New Haven: Yale University Press.

Glenny, Misha. 1996. *The Fall of Yugoslavia*. London: Penguin Random House.

Goodwin, Matthew. 2013. "Woolwich Attack and the Far Right: Three Points to Consider When the Dust Settles Down." *The Guardian*. May 23, 2013. https://www.theguardian.com/commentisfree/2013/may/23/woolwich-attack-far-right-three-points.

Gordy, Eric. 1999. *The Culture of Power in Serbia: Nationalism and the Destruction of Alternatives*. University Park: Penn State University Press.

Gradjanske Inicijative (GI). 2017. "Serbia: Country Paper." Western Balkans CSOs for Global Development, Austrian Development Cooperation. Accessed October 28, 2018. https://www.gradjanske.org/wp-content/uploads/2017/09/Serbia-Country-Study-_final2017-1.pdf.

Greenberg, Jessica. 2010. 'There's Nothing Anyone Can Do About it': Participation, Apathy and 'Successful' Democratic Transition in Postsocialist Serbia." *Slavic Review* 69, no. 1: pp. 41–64.

Grødeland, B. 2006. "Public Perceptions of non-Governmental Organisations in Serbia, Bosnia & Herzegovina, and Macedonia." *Communist and Post-Communist Studies* 39 (2): 221–246.

Guzina, Dejan. 2003. "Socialist Serbia's Narratives: From Yugoslavia to a Greater Serbia." *International Journal of Politics, Culture and Society* 17, no. 1: 91–111.

Hemmingsen, Ann-Sophie. 2015. "An Introduction to the Danish Approach to Countering and Preventing Violent Extremism and Radicalization." Accessed October 2, 2018. https://www.ft.dk/samling/20151/almdel/reu/bilag/248/1617692.pdf.

Her Majesty's Government (HMG). 2012. "Channel: Protecting Vulnerable People from being Drawn into Terrorism. A Guide for Local Partnerships." Accessed October 28, 2018. https://www.npcc.police.uk/documents/TAM/2012/201210TAMChannelGuidance.pdf.

Her Majesty's Government (HMG). 2015. "The Prevent Duty: Departmental Advice for Schools and Childcare Providers." Accessed July 26 2018. https://assets.publishing.service.gov.uk/government/uploads/system/uploads/attachment_data/file/439598/prevent-duty-departmental-advice-v6.pdf.

Holmer, Georgia. 2013. "Countering Violent Extremism: A Peacebuilding Perspective. United States institute for Peace (USIP) Special report 336). Accessed July 23, 2018. https://www.usip.org/sites/default/files/SR336-Countering%20Violent%20Extremism-A%20Peacebuilding%20Perspective.pdf.

Holmer, Georgia and Bauman, Peter. 2018. "Taking Stock: Analytic Tools for Understanding and Designing P/CVE Programs." United States Institute of Peace. Accessed October 27 2018. https://www.usip.org/publications/2018/09/taking-stock-analytic-tools-understanding-and-designing-pcve-programs.

Holmer, Georgia and Adrian Shtuni. 2017. "Returning Foreign Fighters and the Reintegration Imperative." United States Institute for Peace Special Report 402. Accessed September 7 2018. https://www.usip.org/sites/default/files/2017-03/sr402-returning-foreign-fighters-and-the-reintegration-imperative.pdf.

Horgan, John. 2008. "Deradicalization or Disengagement? A Process in Need of Clarity and a Counterterrorism Initiative in Need of Evaluation." *Perspectives on Terrorism* 2, No. 4: 3–8.

Humanitarian Law Center (HLC). 2018. *Dossier: The JNA in the Wars in Croatia and BiH*. Belgrade: Humanitarian Law Center.

Human Rights Watch (HRW). 2000. "Civilian Deaths in the NATO Air Campaign." Accessed October 29, 2018. https://www.hrw.org/sites/default/files/reports/natbm002.pdf.

Filipović, Gordana. 2018. "Serb Leaders Floats a Kosovo Partition, Triggering Alarm." *Bloomberg*. August 9, 2018. https://www.bloomberg.com/news/articles/2018-08-09/serbian-president-Vučić-says-he-favors-partitioning-kosovo.

International Crisis Group (ICG). 1998. "Sandzak: Calm for Now." *ICG Report No. 48*. November 9, 1998. Available https://www.crisisgroup.org/europe-central-asia/balkans/serbia/sandzak-calm-now.

International Crisis Group (ICG). 2005. "Serbia's Sandzak: Still Forgotten." ICG Report No. 162. Accessed September 15, 2018. https://www.crisisgroup.org/europe-central-asia/balkans/serbia/serbias-sandzak-still-forgotten.

International Court of Justice (ICJ). n.d. "International Court of Justice web site." Accessed October 26, 2018. https://www.icj-cij.org/en.

International Criminal Tribunal for the Former Yugoslavia (ICTY). n.d.. "ICTY Court Records." Accessed October 28, 2018. http://icr.icty.org/.

Izetbegović, Alija. 1969/70. *The Islamic Declaration*. Sarajevo: n/a.

Jelinčić, Jadranka and Snezana Ilić. 2013. *Politicki Ekstremizam u Cyber Prostoru Srbije*. Zrenjanin: Centar za Razvoj Civilnog Drustvo.

Karcic, Harun. n.d. "Islamic Revival in Bosnia and Herzegovina 1990–2010." Sarajevo: Center for Advanced Studies.

Kelmendi, Vesë and Shpat Balaj. 2017. "New Battlegrounds: Extremist Groups' Activity on Social Networks in Kosovo, Albanian and FYROM in November 2017." Accessed October 29, 2018. http://www.qkss.org/repository/docs/New_Batelgrounds_Extremist_Groups_in_Social_Media_738865.pdf.

Kepel, Gilles. 2002. *Jihad: The Trail of Political Islam*. Cambridge: Belknap Press of Harvard University Press.

Kladničanin, Fahrudin. 2013. "Vehabije u sajber prostoru." Jelinčić, Jadranka and Snezana Ilic eds. *Politicki Ekstremizam u Cyber Prostoru Srbije*, 127–134. Zrenjanin: Centar za Razvoj Civilnog Društva,

Kleibrink, Alexander. 2011. "How Partitocracy Puts Limits to the EU's Transformative Power." LSE Ideas. Accessed October 28, 2018. http://blogs.lse.ac.uk/ideas/2011/08/how-partitocracy-puts-limits-to-the-eu%E2%80%99s-transformative-power/.

Kleibrink, Alexander. 2015. *Political Elites and Decentralization Reforms in the Post Socialist Balkans*. New York and Basingstoke: Palgrave MacMillian.

Kraja, Garentina. 2017. "The Islamic State Narrative in Kosovo: Deconstructed One Story at a Time." Accessed October 28, 2018. http://www.qkss.org/en/Reports/The-Islamic-State-narrative-in-Kosovo-deconstructed-one-story-at-a-time-991.

Klix. 2018. "Udruženje 'Srbska Čast' radi na formiranju paravojne formacije u Republici Srpskoj." *Klix*. January 12, 2018. https://www.klix.ba/vijesti/bih/udruzenje-srbska-cast-radi-na-formiranju-paravojne-formacije-u-republici-srpskoj/180112086.

Kursani, Shpend. 2015. "Report Inquiring into the Causes and Consequences of Kosovo Citizens' Involvement as Foreign Fighters in Syria and Iraq." Kosovo Center for Security Studies. Accessed October 28, 2018. http://www.qkss.org/repository/docs/Report_inquiring_into_the_causes_and_consequences_of_Kosovo_citizens'_involvement_as_foreign_fighters_in_Syria_and_Iraq_307708.pdf.

Lakić, Mladen and Danijel Kovačević. 2018. "Russia. Bosnian Serbs Scorn 'Paramilitary Unit' Claims." *Balkan Insight*. January 13, 2018. http://www.balkaninsight.com/en/article/russia-bosnian-serbs-scorn-paramilitary-unit-claims-01-13-2018-4.

Lakić, Mladen and Maja Živanović. 2018. "Russia's 'Night Wolves' to Tour Bosnia Despite Ban." *Balkan Insight*. March 20 2018. http://www.balkaninsight.com/en/article/night-wolves-to-continue-their-tour-in-serbia-and-republika-srpska-03-19-2018.

Li, Darryl. 2015. "Jihad in a World of Sovereigns: Law, Violence and Islam in the Bosnia Crisis." *Law and Social Inquiry* 41, no. 2: 371–401.

Löfven, Stefan. 2015. "Prevent, Preempt and Protect—the Swedish Counter-Terrorism Strategy." Government Communication 2014/15:146. August 27, 2015. Accessed October 28, 2018. https://www.government.se/contentassets/b56cad17b4434118b16cf449dbdc973d/en_strategi-slutlig-eng.pdf.

Lynch, Marc. 2015. "Obama and the Middle East: Rightsizing the US Role." *Foreign Affairs*. September/October 2015. https://www.foreignaffairs.com/articles/middle-east/obama-and-middle-east.

Lyon, James. 2008. "Serbia's Sandžak Under Milosevič: Identity, Nationalism and Survival." *Human Rights Review* 9: 71–92.

Maher, Shiraz. 2016. *Salafi-Jihadism: The History of an Idea*. New York: Oxford University Press.

Magyar, Bálint. 2016. *Post-Communist Mafia State: The Case of Hungary*. Budapest: Central European University Press.

McCauley, Clark and Sophia Moskalenko. 2017. "Understanding Political Radicalization: The Two-Pyramids Model." *American Psychologist* 72, no. 3: 205–216. https://www.apa.org/pubs/journals/releases/amp-amp0000062.pdf.

Meleagrou-Hitchens, Alexander and Nick Kaderbhai. 2017. "Research Perspectives on Online Radicalization: A Literature Review, 2006–2016." Accessed October 28, 2018. https://icsr.info/wp-content/uploads/2017/05/ICSR-Paper_Research-Perspectives-on-Online-Radicalisation-A-Literature-Review-2006-2016.pdf.

Mitchell, Christopher R. 2011. "Conflict, Change and Conflict Resolution." *Advancing Conflict Transformation: The Berghof Handbook II*. Austin, B., Fischer, M. and Geissman, H. J. (eds.). Opladen/Framingham Hills: Barbara Budrich Publishers.

Moonshot CVE. 2017. "Bosnia and Herzegovina Daesh Tracker." Unpublished report.

Morrison, Kenneth. 2008. "Wahhabism in the Balkans. Advanced Research and Assessment Group Balkans Series 08/06." Accessed September 27, 2018. https://www.files.ethz.ch/isn/50179/2008_March_Wahabism.pdf.

Morrison, Kenneth and Elizabeth Roberts. 2013. *The Sandzak: A History*. London: C. Hurst and Co.

Mujanović, Jasmin. 2017. *Hunger and Fury: The Crisis of Democracy in the Balkans*. London: C. Hurst & Co. Publishers.

Neumann, Peter R. "Countering Violent Extremism and Radicalization that Lead to Terrorism: Ideas, Recommendations, and Good Practices from the OSCE Region." Accessed October 26, 2018. https://www.osce.org/chairmanship/346841?download=true.

N1. 2018a. "Bosniak Leader in Serbia: I'll Fight for Autonomous Sandzak." *N1*. July 26, 2018. http://rs.n1info.com/a407249/English/NEWS/Bosniak-leader-in-Serbia-says-he-will-continue-political-fight-for-Sandzak-region-autonomy.html.

N1. 2018b. "Opposition in Serbia to Inform CoE about Regime Pressure." *N1*. October 25, 2018. http://rs.n1info.com/a430834/English/NEWS/Serbia-s-opposition-to-complain-to-CoE-about-ruling-party-pressure-on-local-authorities.html.

Obama, Barack. 2015. "Remarks by the President at the Summit on Countering Violent Extremism." The White House. Accessed September 24, 2018. https://obamawhitehouse.archives.gov/the-press-office/2015/02/19/remarks-president-summit-countering-violent-extremism-february-19-2015.

Olidort, Jacob. 2015. *The Politics of "Quietist" Salafism*. Washington DC: The Brookings Institution.

OSCE. 2014. *Preventing Terrorism and Countering Violent Extremism and Radicalization that Lead to Terrorism: A Community Policing Approach*. Vienna: OSCE.

OSCE. 2018. *The Role of Civil Society in Preventing and Countering Violent Extremism and Radicalization that Lead to Terrorism: A Focus on South-Eastern Europe*. Vienna; OSCE.

Perry, Valery. 2015. "Countering the Cultivation of Extremism in Bosnia and Herzegovina: The Case for Comprehensive Education reform." Accessed September 10 2018. http://www.democratizationpolicy.org/pdf/DPCPolicyNote_10_ExtremismandEducationinBiH.pdf.

Perry, Valery. 2016. *Initiatives to Prevent/Counter Violent Extremism in South East Europe: A Survey of Regional Issues, Initiatives and Opportunities*. Regional Cooperation Council. Accessed October 26, 2018. https://www.rcc.int/pubs/38/initiatives-to-preventcounter-violent-extremism-in-south-east-europe-a-survey-of-regional-issues-initiatives-and-opportunities.

Perry, Valery. 2017. "Reflections on Efforts to Prevent and Counter Violence Extremism and Radicalization in the Balkans." Democratization Policy Council Policy Note #15. Accessed July 23, 2018. http://www.democratizationpolicy.org/summary/valery-perry-reflections-on-p-cve-efforts-in-the-balkans/.

Petrović, Predrag and Isidora Stakić. 2018. "Serbia Report." Accessed September 15, 2018. https://www.britishcouncil.rs/sites/default/files/erf_report_serbia_2018.pdf

Puhalo, Srđan (ed.). 2016. "Selefije u Bosni i Hercegovini: Ko Su Oni, Kako ih Drugi Vide i Kako se izvjestava o Njima." Accessed September 15, 2018. http://www.media-diversity.org/en/additional-files/srdjan-puhalo-selefije.pdf.

Puljek-Shank, Randall and Tija Memišević. n.d. "Donor Support for Civil Society Advocacy in BiH." Accessed September 15 2018. http://www.mirovna-akademija.org/rma/images/2013/donor_support_en.pdf.

Qehaja, Florian. 2016. "Beyond Gornje Maoce and Osve: radicalization in the Western Balkans." *Jihadist Hotbeds: Understanding Local Radicalization Processes*. Arturo Varvelli (ed). Milan: Instituto per gli Studi di Politica Internazionale (ISPI).

Racimora, William. 2013. *Salafist/Wahhabite Financial Support to Educational, Social and Religious Institutions*. Brussels: Directorate-General for External Policies of the Union.

Ramet, Sabrina. 2002. *Balkan Babel: The Disintegration of Yugoslavia from the Death of Tito to the Fall of Milosević*. Boulder: Westview Press.

RFERL. 2009. "Serbia's Vojvodina Regains Autonomy." *Radio Free Europe/Radio Liberty*. December 15, 2009. https://www.rferl.org/a/Serbias_Vojvodina_Regains_Autonomy/1904999.html.

RFERL. 2018. "UN Court Partially Overturns Serbian Nationalist Šešelj's Acquittal." *Radio Free Europe/Radio Liberty*. April 11, 2018. https://www.rferl.org/a/un-court-Šešelj-appeal-war-crimes-crimes-against-humanity/29158554.html.

Renard, Thomas and Rik Coolsaet (eds.). 2018. *Returnees; Who are They, Why are They (not) Coming Back and How Should we Deal With Them?* Egmont Paper 101.

Radio-Televizija Srbije (RTS). 2013. "Stradalo 1,008 Vojnika i policajaca." *RTS*. February 11, 2013. https://web.archive.org/web/20160105214010/http://www.rts.rs/page/stories/sr/story/9/Politika/1264384/Stradalo+1.008+vojnika+i+policajaca.html

Rubin, Jeffrey Z., Dean G. Priutt and Sung Hee Kim. 1994. *Social Conflict: Escalation, Stalemate and Settlement*. New York: McGraw Hill.

Rudić, Filip.. 2018. "Batislav Živković: Serbia's Facebook-Mad Warrior in Ukraine." *Balkan Insight*. 27 August 2018. http://www.balkaninsight.com/en/article/bratislav-zivkovic-serbia-s-facebook-mad-warrior-in-ukraine-08-25-2018-1.

Rush, G.B.. 1963. "Towards a Definition of the Extreme Right." *The Pacific Sociological Review* 6, no. 2: 64–73.

Sadović, Merdijana. 2008. "Bosnia: The Mujahedin Unmasked." Accessed October 26, 2018. https://iwpr.net/global-voices/bosnia-mujahedin-unmasked.

SAR Consulting. 2018. *Understanding the Nature and Extent of Radicalization and Extremism in Prisons and Places of Detention in BiH. Prison radicalization Assessment Report, Zenica Prison*. Kildare: SAR Consulting

Schirch, Lisa (ed.). 2018. Th*e Ecology of Violent Extremism: Perspectives on Peacebuilding and Human Security*. London: Rowman and Littlefield.

Schmid, Alex P.. 2004. "Terrorism—the Definitional Problem." *Case Western Reserve Journal of International Law* 36 (2): 375–419.

Schmid, Alex P. 2014. "Violent and Non-Violent Extremism: Two Sides of the Same Coin?" Accessed September 15, 2018. https://www.icct.nl/download/file/ICCT-Schmid-Violent-Non-Violent-Extremism-May-2014.pdf.

Schmid, Alex P. and Albert J. Jongman. 1988. *Political Terrorism: A New Guide to Actors, Authors, Concepts, Databases, Theories and Literature*. Piscataway: Transaction Publishers.

SEEBiz. 2018. "Vojnik Bivse Vojske SRJ, bacio bombu na ambasadu SAD u Podgorici." *SEEBiz*. February 22, 2018. http://www.seebiz.eu/vojnik-bivse-vojske-srj-roden-u-kraljevu-bacio-bombu-na-ambasadu-sad-u-podgorici/ar-171334/.

Silber, Laura and Alan Little. 1996. *The Death of Yugoslavia*. London: Penguin Books.

Sito-Sucic, Daria and Matt Robinson. 2013. "After Years of Toil, Book Names Bosnian War Dead." *Reuters*. February 15, 2013. https://www.reuters.com/article/us-bosnia-dead/after-years-of-toil-book-names-bosnian-war-dead-idUSBRE91E0J220130215.

Smooha, Sammy and Priit Jarve (Eds.). 2005. "*The Fate of Ethnic Democracy in Post-Communist Europe*. Flensburg: European Centre for Minority Issues and Open Society Institute.

Southern Poverty Law Center (SPLC). nd. "Alt Right." Accessed 25 September 2018. https://www.splcenter.org/fighting-hate/extremist-files/ideology/alt-right.

Spasojević, Srdan. 2017. "Country Report: Serbia." Accessed October 28, 2018. http://www.erstestiftung.org/publication/civil-society-in-cee/.

Speckhard, Anne and Ardian Shajkovci. 2017. "Drivers of Radicalization and Violent Extreimsm in Kosovo: Women's Roles in Supporting, Preventing and Fighting Violent Extremism." Accessed October 28, 2018. http://www.icsve.org/research-reports/drivers-of-radicalization-and-violent-extremism-in-kosovo-womens-roles-in-supporting-preventing-fighting-violent-extremism/.

Speckhard, Anne and Ardian Shajkovci. 2016. "The Role of Women in Supporting, Joining, Intervening in and Preventing Violent Extremism in Sandjak." Accessed September 10, 2018. http://www.icsve.org/research-reports/the-roles-of-women-in-supporting-joining-intervening-in-and-preventing-violent-extremism-in-sandjak/.

Stakić, Isidora. 2013. *Odnos Srbije Prema Ekstremno Desničarskim Organizacijama*. Belgrade: Belgrade Center for Security Studies.

Stakić, Isidora. 2015. "Serbian Nationalism and Right-Wing Extremism." *Violent Extremism in the Western Balkans*. Ejdus, Filip and Predrag Jureković (eds.), 133–148.

Statistical Office of the Republic of Serbia. 2011. Religion, Mother Tongue and Ethnicity: Data by Municipalities and Cities. Accessed October 28, 2018. http://pod2.stat.gov.rs/ObjavljenePublikacije/Popis2011/Knjiga4_Veroispovest.pdf.

Stiks, Igor and Srećko Horvat. 2014. "The New Balkan Revolts: From Protests to Plenums, and Beyond." Accessed September 20 2018. https://www.opendemocracy.net/can-europe-make-it/igor-%C5%A1tiks-sre%C4%87ko-horvat/new-balkan-revolts-from-protests-to-plenums-and-beyond.

UK Department of Education. 2015. "The Prevent Duty: Departmental Advice for Schools and Childcare Providers." Accessed October 26, 2018. https://assets.publishing.service.gov.uk/government/uploads/system/uploads/attachment_data/file/439598/prevent-duty-departmental-advice-v6.pdf.

UNGA (United Nations General Assembly). 2012. "Legal Committee Urges Conclusion of Draft Comprehensive Convention on International terrorism." Sixty-seventh General Assembly, 8 October 2012. Accessed October 4, 2018. https://www.un.org/press/en/2012/gal3433.doc.htm.

USAID. 2011. *The Development Response to Violent Extremism and Insurgency: Putting Principles into Practice*. Washington DC: USAID.

United Nations Office on Drugs and Crime (UNODC). 2016. *Handbook on the Management of Violent Extremist Prisoners and the Prevention of Radicalization to Violence in Prisons*. Vienna: UNODC.

UNSC (United Nations Security Council). 2015a. "Resolution 2199." Accessed September 15, 2018. https://www.un.org/en/ga/search/view_doc.asp?symbol=S/RES/2199%20(2015).

UNSC (United Nations Security Council). 2015b. "Resolution 2253." Accessed September 15, 2018. http://www.un.org/en/ga/search/view_doc.asp?symbol=S/RES/2253(2015),

UNSC (United Nations Security Council). 2017. "Resolution 2368." Accessed September 15, 2018. Available at https://www.un.org/press/en/2017/sc12917.doc.htm.

Vulliamy, Ed. 2000. "Bloody Handiwork of Arkan." *The Guardian*. January 16, 2000. https://www.theguardian.com/world/2000/jan/16/balkans3.

Vurmo, Gjergji, Besfort Lamallari and Aleka Papa. 2015. *Radicalization and Violent Extremism in Albania*. Tirana: Institute for Democracy and Mediation.

Xharra, Behar and Nita Gojani. 2017. "Understanding Push and Pull Factors in Kosovo: Primary Interviews with Returned Foreign Fighters and their Families." Accessed 5 September 2018. http://www.ks.undp.org/content/dam/kosovo/docs/PVE/UNDP_Push%20and%20Pull%20Factors_ENG.pdf.

Weinberg, David Andrew. 2015. "King Salman's Shady History." Foreign Policy. January 27, 2015. https://foreignpolicy.com/2015/01/27/king-salmans-shady-history-saudi-arabia-jihadi-ties/.

Živanović, Maja. 2018a. "Pro Russian Serbs Mourn Ukraine Rebel's Death." Balkan Insight. 3 September 2018. http://www.balkaninsight.com/en/article/serbian-right-wingers-mourn-ukraine-rebel-s-murder-09-03-2018.

Živanović, Maja. 2018b. "Ukraine Probing Serbian pro-Russian Fighters, Report Says." *Balkan Insight*. June 27, 2018. http://www.balkaninsight.com/en/article/fighters-from-serbia-under-investigation-by-ukrainian-authorities-media-06-27-2018.

Zorić, Jelena. 2018. "Ko Je Iza Nacionalne Avangarde Koja Olako Okupi Drzavni Vrh?" N1. October 9, 2018. http://rs.n1info.com/a426623/Vesti/Ko-je-iza-Nacionalne-avangarde-koja-olako-okupi-drzavni-vrh.html

Using the Past to Extremes in Serbia: Narratives of Historical Violence in Right-Wing Extremism and Islamism

Niké Wentholt

Introduction[1]

From graffiti to hooligans' chants, from literature to political speech, violent history[2] is visible and almost tangible in Serbia. Explanations for this salience range from the cultural to the political to the historical, but the state-propagated justification of violence in the wars of the 1990s has undoubtedly contributed. The memory of this conflict still resonates in wider Serbian society.

This and more distant violent history can provide a source for the acceptance and "legitimization" of the use of violence by extremist groups (Pavićević 2014, 81). As much as it is important to acknowledge that radicalization is fueled by structural and political economic injustice,[3] it is also a "dynamic process whereby an individual comes to accept (terrorist) violence as a possible, perhaps even legitimate, course of action" (Milojević, Simonović, Janković, Otašević, & Turanjanin 2013, 20; CeSID & UNDP Serbia Country Office 2016, 8). This chapter can thus contribute to understanding the recruiting success of two types of extremism that currently endanger Serbian society and security: right-wing extremism with its track record of mostly street violence, and Islamist extremism as a

---

1. I gratefully note the excellent and inspiring cooperation with the research team, and coordinators from the OSCE: Valery Perry, Boris Milanović, and Predrag Nikolić. This chapter has highly benefitted from the constructive feedback from internal peer review by other research team members.
2. Here I do not intend to say that the whole history of Serbia is inherently violent. Rather, as the focus of this report is on violent extremist groups, my focus is limited to violent events and actors in history.
3. The topics of violence, extremism, and radicalisation are often approached from the angle of "push" and "pull" factors. In the cited UNDP report from 2016 example, seven out of eight drivers of VERLT are "negative" factors. The only "positive" driver, the "banalization of violence in the media," is also framed in negative terms.

perceived but to date latent threat (Regional Cooperation Council 2016, 48).

The central question in this chapter is thus: how do extremist right-wing and Islamist organizations use narratives of violent events and violent actors from the region's history? First, the study will explore the memory politics of the violent history of the past decades in Serbia. The second part will investigate the use of these narratives by extremist right-wing groups, and the third part will consider some Islamist platforms. Throughout these analyses, the chapter assesses to which extent both sides frame each other as an historical enemy.

Literature review

Interested in "dominant or hegemonic narratives" of historical violence, this study first of all searches for the Serbian "national imaginary" stemming from the 1990s wars and beyond (Roper, Dawson, & Ashplant 2000, 22). This helps to understand the salience of violent history in mainstream and extremist spaces. Additionally, the official political dimension matters because of the close ties[4] between extremist right-wing groups and political parties (Mrševič 2016, 17; Stakić, Interview, 2017; Bakić, Interview, 2017).

Much of the actual street violence comes from hooligan groups rather than extremist right-wing organizations. Football fan groups like *Grobari* and *Delije*, associated with *Partizan* and *Crvena Zvezda* respectively, and their various sub organizations in particular need to be mentioned. These hooligan groups have, however, little ideological basis (Dimitrijević 2018; Bakić interview, 2017; Savez antifašista Srbije 2018). Hooligans rather function as the extremist right-wing's foot soldiers. In this role, they *do* reproduce the latter's conservative and nationalist values (Živanić 2017). So while

---

4   However, the nature of these ties varies from one extremist right-wing group to the other, and moreover often changes through time. In general, it is safe to say that important and tight relationships exist between the political party level and level of extremist right-wing groups in society. Some of these groups even move between both levels. Several, like *Zavetnici* and *Dveri*, started out as societal movements and now take part in political elections.

the extremist right-wing organizations in question are not necessarily big in terms of numbers (Stakić, Interview 2017; Savez antifašista Srbije 2018), for their political and societal reach they have the "potential to be very dangerous" (Bakić, Interview 2017).

While largely leaning on the 1990s as a basis for legitimacy, extremist right-wing groups go beyond recent history to frame their heritage and identity (Bakić, Interview 2017; Dragišić 2017). Religious and political attachment to the Orthodox Church play into this narrative. Ironically, this claim on history is not always in line with historical facts. As stressed by Bakić, groups often falsify the past before using it (Bakić, 2013, 3–4). In this light, it is helpful to connect Isidora Stakić's recent research into the use of securitization discourse by right-wing groups to frame and justify their violence (Stakić, 2015) to the dominant "ante morale-myth" (Antić 2003).[5] This myth holds that the Serbian nation faces perpetual threats from inside and outside. It functions in tandem with the notion of historical Serbian victimhood, also present in school textbooks (Antić 2003, 261). The perception of enemies is essential here (Bakić 2013, 4). An important adversary in Serbian historical memory is fascism, mainly represented by the Croats for their regime's collaboration with the Nazis during the Second World War.

Islam and Muslims constitute another important "other" in Serbian historiography, sometimes dismissed as a "leftover of the Ottoman past" (Elbasani & Roy 2015, 460). This "enemy" has gained all the more relevance with the growth and prominence of Islamist terrorism itself and, most importantly, the (international) attention to it. This is also reflected in attitudes towards the fight against terror. As Ana Antić argues, Serbia framed the 9/11 attacks through its own memory of victimhood at the hands of Islamist violence in the 1990s. Because of this, the country expected to hold a special place in the global anti-terror coalition (Antić 2003, 270).

Despite disagreement on the precise numbers, it seems safe to note that several hundred Muslim Albanians and Bosniaks, an estimation shared by the recent British Council report on the Western

---

5   This myth is not an exclusive feature of Serbia, but is at play in other countries of the Western Balkans as well (and probably, in some form or another, also beyond).

Balkans (Azinović 2018, 4), travelled to Syria and Iraq from the Western Balkans to engage in the war there, including as jihadists. According to some findings, a "significant portion" of these foreign fighters are mujahedeen who travelled to Bosnia in the 1990s and settled down after the war (Dronzina & Muca 2017, 27–28). Together with propagation and the large sums of money invested by Saudi Arabia, this begins to explain the observed growth in Salafist/Wahhabist practices and radicalization (Bećirević 2016, 18, 25, 64). A well-informed report puts the fear of returning foreign fighters in perspective, but highlights some weaknesses in "prevention-centered interventions" (Azinović & Bećirević 2017, 7, 9, 16).

Trying to approach the question from a more holistic perspective, a 2015 study explains the rise of conservative Islam in Bosnia as the "indirect attempt to introduce new norms into a society that is practically without any in the post-conflict and transitional space it still occupies" (Azinović & Jusić 2015, 47). It is important to recognize that Islamist platforms do not tell "as simplistic a story as often suggested" (Winter 2018, 110). We already know from wider research that Islamist ideologists look for legitimacy in the long history of political Islam and its conflicts (Ebner 2017, 55). The Islamic State relied upon a variety of "tropes" in their communication to attract followers, including those of Muslim victimhood and utopic images of the caliphate (Winter 2018, 110–113).

Motivations for jihadist radicalization in the Western Balkans are similarly complex. Recent research has indicated that fighters are not so much radicalized "in relation to injustices (real or imagined) that they may be directly exposed to in their communities of origin, but to their perception of the suffering of a wider, global community which they also perceive as their own" (Azinović & Jusić 2015, 43). At the same time, regional attachment still matters. This chapter focusses on the political and geographical space of Serbia, but acknowledges that Muslims from Serbia may seek spiritual, cultural, and religious identification beyond these borders. Jihadist recruitment from platforms based in Bosnia and Herzegovina (BiH) (or, in some cases, even Vienna) similarly does not keep to borders (Simeunović & Dolnik 2013, 99). A part of the Muslim recruits from Bosnia and Serbia, the latter mostly from Sandžak, see their fight "as continuation of the jihad they felt was ended prematurely in 1995" (Azinović & Jusić 2015, 8, 41). It is for this reason that this report looks at Islamist platforms that, while based in BiH, seek readership from Bosniaks across borders. The term Bosniak connotes ethnicity and has since 1993 generally replaced the term "Bosnian Muslim." It therefore includes, most importantly in the context of this study, the Muslim population in Serbia that has Bosniak ethnicity[6] but Serbian citizenship.

Because of the legacy of the 1990s wars and other constructed (or even invented) historical animosities, this report considers the possibility that the historical narratives of both right-wing extremists and Islamists are "two sides of the same coin" (Ebner 2017, 18, 26). As "'rhetorical allies'", Ebner has recently argued in line with other recent studies (Ebner 2017, 28), their narratives "complement and amplify each other". This results in "a bizarre form of interdependency between the two" (Ebner 2017, 197). In addition to studying extremist right-wing and Islamist narratives in their own right, this chapter will thus also explore whether both groups exploit the historical "threat" of the other.

Methods and case selection

The author is aware of her position as an "outsider" as a Dutch researcher. While such a perspective may have its merit, it seems essential to have Serbian researchers engage with these questions too. This chapter was written on the basis of a fairly small set of evidence due to the limited research timeframe. More research is welcome to validate (or contest) the findings of this study.

The research project consists of four research questions:

---

[6] The author is aware that the term "Bosniak," especially in relation to ethnicity and in research connected to religious fundamentalism, can be very problematic. This study tries to stay away from perpetuating narratives of ethnic and religious essentialism, but will use this term to give due to the most common descriptions of realities in the region. For more in-depth reflection on the realities of ethnic identity, see the chapter by Miloš Milenković in this book.

*How have politics and violent history
been related in Serbia since the 1990s wars?*

This section studies some dominant historical narratives and landmark events in dealing with the past in Serbia. Central is the interpretative policy analysis[7] of three parliamentary debates, each between 100 and 200 pages in length, and selected for their relevance to three different "pasts" in Serbia: the 2003 lustration law (Narodna skupština 2003) dealing with the Yugoslav socialist heritage;[8] the 2005 law that gave četnik fighters from the Second World War equal status as their partisan counterparts (Narodna skupština 2005);[9] and the 2010 declaration to condemn the crimes in Srebrenica in 1995 (Narodna skupština 2011).[10] Research relied upon qualitative research (see the respective footnotes for further explanation of specific methods); no content analysis software was employed. Rather, combining distant and close reading, sources were read "back and forth" between text and context (Yanow 1999, 14, 15, 22).

*Which narratives of historical violence do right-wing extremist
organizations use and how?*

For this and the third sub-question the discourse-historical method is used. More interested in the argumentative than linguistic quality of the narratives studied, this chapter pays specific attention to how different historical arguments are used in relation to each other ("interdiscursivity") and context (Reisigi & Wodak 2009).[11] *Srpski*

---

7   Reading "back and forth" between "policy or agency artefacts" meaning and "context", I use Dvora Yanow's critical method of interpretative policy analysis (Yanow 1999, 14, 15, 22). Although not all the debates on laws and declarations studied directly qualify as policy, this method enables me to track political arguments as well as the actual changes following from these.
8   Full name: Zakon o odgovornosti za kršenje ljudskih prava, but often spoken of as Zakon o lustraciji.
9   Full name: Zakon o pravima boraca, vojnih invalida i članova njihovih porodica, but often spoken of as Zakon o izjednačavanju partizanskih i četničkih boraca.
10 Full name: Deklaracija o osudi zločina u Srebrenici, but often spoken of as Deklaracija o Srebrenici.
11 I am aware of several limitations in the application of this method: first, I am not a native speaker of Serbian. While I can fully read the language I will stay away from claims about specific linguistic meanings and instead focus on the context in which the argument is presented. Secondly, the limited scope of this paper makes the highly extensive application and presentation of the full method difficult. Therefore,

sabor Zavetnici (hereafter called: *Zavetnici*) is the main case study. *Zavetnici* is not the biggest or most well-known, although it was involved in the disruption during the *Miredita-Dobar Dan* festival in 2017. Exactly because it is relatively new to the scene it is keen to build a profile. The study looks at material published on *Zavetnici's* website in the period November 2014 until February 2018. After the analysis of *Zavetnici* was completed, the findings' representativeness was explored through two additional cases of high-profile extremist right-wing groups. A targeted search word analysis[12] was conducted for the websites of *Obraz*, which was banned by the Serbian constitutional court in 2012, and *Srpski Narodni Pokret Naši* (*Naši*) (Bakić 2013; Stakić 2013). The online presence of these organizations is further contextualized in the right-wing extremist scene in Kristina Ivanović's and Davor Marko's chapters in this book. Additionally the study analyses a video, mainly containing recordings of demonstrations, uploaded by the official channel of *Zavetnici* on YouTube in 2014.[13]

Which narratives of historical violence do Islamist platforms use and how?

Put Vjernika is selected here as the main case study. It is known for having recruited Serbian Muslim citizens for armed jihad — most notably from the Sandžak region (Simeunović & Dolnik 2013, 105).[14] To give due to the timeline of global Islamist activity, this research is focused on articles from the longer period 2010–2018.

---

the case studies and genres in question are necessarily very limited and the eight steps are not individually presented but all were executed for the overall analysis.

12 Key words "heroj", "istorija" and "prošlost", in different forms to match grammatical use (i.e. "istoriji", "istorije").

13 Called "For the Fatherland" and a little less than eight minutes in length (Zavetnici 2014).

14 According to research from 2013, the Wahhabist organizations Salaam and Ansari Sharriah, founded and run from London by Abu Hamza al-Mazri, use *Put Vjernika* "for recruiting young followers" (Simeunović & Dolnik 2013, 91). *Put Vjernika's* website is sometimes inactive for longer periods of time. It is unclear at the time of writing whether this is due to technological errors or security measures from the authorities. At the time of this writing in, the website is currently online. Researchers struggling with access to the articles used in this report can contact the author for these data.

Taking into account that case selection was limited as some platforms have been removed by the authorities because they considered their call for jihad a security threat (most notably the Sandžak website *kelimetul-haqq*), the websites IslamBosna.ba[15] and Istina.ba[16] are additionally selected to put the findings of *Put Vjernika* to the test.[17] No suitable video has been found for analysis as was done for *Zavetnici*. The large part of Islamist platforms' video material can be categorized as either pedagogic and religious compilations, religious sermons and lectures, or episodes of the documentary "The real face of the (non-)Islamic Community".

The three websites are all associated with the Wahhabist movement. It needs to be emphasized however that these platforms are not inherently violent or exclusively jihadist. Like the above discussed extremist right-wing organizations, they partially function as an expression of civil society, providing a platform for discussion on Islam, values and even citizenship — in the case of *Islam Bosna* especially for the Bosniak diaspora (Jevtić 2017a, 60–63). The majority of articles has a religious or even pedagogic character, probably underlying the platforms' appeal.

The selected platforms however, with varying levels of visibility, support the armed jihad in Syria and Iraq. *Put Vjernika* is the most outspoken and has been used as recruitment platform before, although it is clear that the platform tries to circumvent increasing control by religious or other authorities. Through interviews with, for example, an "activist of the opposition in Aleppo" (Islam Bosna

---

15 Founded in 1997 as a non-governmental organization in Sarajevo by Senad Ukka (who, according to research available in 2017, is the site's administrator), in 1997 *Islam Bosna* decided to focus on establishing as a website instead. For more information on the origins and readership of *Islam Bosna*, see Jevtić, 2017a, pp. 59–61; Jevtić, 2017b, 71. According to research by Steven Oluic from 2008, the website is run by the Muslim Brotherhood (Muslimansko bratsvo) (Oluic 2008, 44).

16 Istina.ba presents itself as a mainly informative platform and has had a social media presence on Facebook and Twitter since November 2014. It is not known, according to the author's best knowledge, who runs the platform.

17 All articles filed under relevant categories were analysed since the format and structure of these two Islamist cases did not allow a targeted search word analysis, as was employed for the respective cases of right-wing extremism. For IslamBosna.ba, these were the categories "genocid" [genocide], "Srebrenica", and "Ožiljci vremena" [scars of time]. For Istina, this was "Historija BiH" [History BiH].

2016a), and videos of civilian suffering at the hand of Assad's forces, and writing about "the good jihadists of El-Nusra" and Al-Qaeda (Senusija 2014), *Islam Bosna* avoids direct calls for jihad but still presents a favorable image of the armed fight. *Istina* mostly speaks of spiritual jihad (in fact, *Islam Bosna* and *Put Vjernika* also emphasize the various ways of exercising jihad, including financially and spiritually) and is less congratulatory in its writing of jihadist forces in Syria, but still justifies their violence by demonizing Assad and his allies. Illustrating the interlinkages between Islamist networks, they cross-post each other's articles (e.g. Putvjernika 2015b). Cross-posting with *Sandžak Press* also regularly occurs.

How do right-wing extremist organizations frame the threat of Islamist violence in its historical narratives, and vice versa?

The aforementioned thesis of Julia Ebner on "reciprocal radicalization" of right-wing and Islamist narratives guides this question. This thesis is specifically applied to both groups' *historical narratives* (Ebner 2017, 17). It is addressed throughout the broader analyses on both right-wing extremist and jihadist platforms. However, as convincingly argued and illustrated by Tijana Rečević in her respective chapter, "microradicalization" on the societal level is essential to understanding the impact of extremism. This paper is unable to study this in full, but will explore whether the findings for right-wing e-platforms extend to more mainstream reporting on jihadism and Islamism in newspaper articles by *Politika* and *Blic*[18] in 2014–2018, using the built-in search engines on their websites.[19] Such a "reality check" is interesting since, as Boris Milanović mentions in his chapter in this book, the extremist expressions on such Internet platforms is not necessarily directly connected to action in the "real world."

---

18   Both newspapers are read nationwide, but represent different segments of the media landscape: *Politika* is a more traditional newspaper with a long history and historical reputation, while *Blic* is much newer and often categorized as a tabloid. Both are generally considered "right-wing", which is the most common orientation of media in Serbia.

19   Key words džihad, Islam, Islamska Država, in different forms to match grammatical use (e.g. "džihada")

There is indeed a seeming methodological asymmetry, even apart from the differences between these groups' organizational structures. The study does investigate mainstream right-wing platforms in politics and media, but not Islamist ones. Given this study's geographical focus on Serbia, this however reflects the asymmetry of the present day situation where the right-wing, and even the radical right-wing, is very much institutionalized. The aim is not a methodologically perfect comparison, but instead an exploration of both cases in their own right, accounting for existing limitations and differences. The assessment of Ebner's thesis eventually links both cases.

Politicizing the past and historicizing politics: dominant narratives of historical violence throughout the decades

This section aims to show how the historical narratives used today are grounded in radical nationalism and enemy images constructed during the 1990s wars. Four factors will be respectively discussed here: the influence of these enemy narratives on present-day political narratives; the international attention for dealing with the war past, especially the impact of (European Union enforced) cooperation with the International Criminal Tribunal for the former Yugoslavia (ICTY); measures to deal with the socialist past; and the rehabilitation of the četnik movement.

During the early 1990s, military and political leaders constructed and re-activated historical narratives to mobilize people and resources for the war effort. History always offers a rich repository for such "a political unconscious filled with resonant imaginative figures and scenarios from the national past" (Roper, Dawson, & Ashplant 2000, 22). In the case of right-wing Serbia, the frame of civil war was dominant in the 1990s (Campbell 1998, 44). According to the narratives that guided the armed Serbian nationalist movement, četnik fighters defended Serbia from the threat of the Croat fascist ustaša, helped by the Bosniak "traitor." In the case of Islamist framing of the Bosniak authorities supporting secession and then leading the war effort, the dominant frame is a fight for independence and defense against Serbian nationalists' attack. Viewed through this lens, their armed forces, partially because of their own lack of military resources, welcomed the foreign mujahedeen fighter as "dedicated, and in some cases, highly trained and skilled foreign combatants" that could moreover intimidate the Serbian enemy (Mustapha 2013, 747). This way, the mujahedeen fighter became part of this war narrative as well, alongside the frame of domestic defense.

1990s war narratives and enemy narratives in the Serbian political sphere

As much as this historical construction is a fascinating process, this research question focusses on why and how these narratives still survive into the present day. From the parliamentary debates studied, four enemy narratives become apparent. Apart from the presence of some Muslim representatives from Sandžak, Muslims, let alone radical Muslims, are not well represented in the mainstream political sphere in Serbia to which this paper is geographically limited. The following enemy narratives are thus more insightful to understand the basis from which extremist right-wing groups can build (Pavićević 2014, 85). As further elaborated upon in the methodology section, they were identified through use of the discourse-historical method. Selection criteria included frequent recurrence in terms of users (several parliamentarians representing more than one party) and presence (throughout the debate or several debates rather than just at one point).

A first enemy present in parliamentary debates, referred to by both liberal and more conservative parties, is the Yugoslav socialist guilty of "communist evil" (Narodna skupština 2003, 265). Stalin, the Soviet Union, and Russia also feature in this narrative. A second frequent historical enemy is the fascist committing "terror" in Serbia (Narodna skupština 2005, 11). This narrative often narrows down to the fascist Croat ustaša (Narodna skupština 2005, 14; Narodna skupština 2011, 115, 151). A third historical enemy is the international community, often mentioned in tandem with alleged weak leaders in Serbia. Sometimes the international community is blamed for supporting Serbia's opponents, especially Croats and Muslims (Narodna skupština 2011, 155–156), while other times it is directly accused of committing violence against Serbs, especially during the 1999 NATO bombings. (Narodna skupština 2011, 106, 115, 168–169; Narodna skupština 2003, 292; Narodna skupština 2005, 21). A fourth, but remarkably less frequent narrative, used in the selected debates exclusively by parliamentarians of the Radical Party, is that of the historical Muslim[20] enemy (Narodna skupština 2003, 343; Narodna skupština 2011, 112, 115). In the debate on the Srebrenica declaration, specific mention is made of "Muslim leaders from Sandžak" who during the Second World War allegedly sent a dead child as a "present" to the Serbian inhabitants of the region (Narodna skupština 2011, 112).

While many tend to associate the term "terror" these days with Islamist violence, parliamentary parties have long used the word to delegitimize this wide range of historical opponents. The recent attention for Islamist violence has however foregrounded the narrative of the historical Muslim threat. There is indeed reason to share the worry that "the exploration of the Islamic phenomenon is left to the mercy of nationalist and post-conflict paradigms, which necessarily essentialize the revival of Islam according to the ethno-religious divisions of the day" (Elbasani & Roy 2015, 457). Countering this nationalist interpretation, more liberal actors refer to similarly historicized — but not at all fully imagined — narratives of the Bosnian type of "inclusive Islam" (Bećirević 2016, 10; Campbell 1998, 49). However, up until the present day the post-war context seems to offer more fertile soil to exclusive and nationalist narratives.

Changing the narrative of Serbia's anti-fascist historical movement

These narratives also developed through post-war and post-socialist politics of "dealing with the past." Starting with the former, the international community has not only been heavily involved in the

---

20 This includes both Bosniaks and Albanian Muslims.

1990s wars, but also in their aftermath. The ICTY came to symbolize this. Right-wing actors heavily opposed the arrests of "Serbian patriots" as demanded from this court (Subotić 2009). The fact that the European Union and United States enforced cooperation with the court further entrenched notions of the West as anti-Serb (Komšić 2007, 9–10; Pantić 2007, 319).

The debate on the socialist past eventually gave even more impetus to this nationalist discourse. After the October 5, 2000 transition, opposition parties had initially been keen to propose lustration measures and disclosure of the socialist secret service archives. Laws in this direction were adopted during the early 2000s, but never implemented. Instead, "dealing" with the socialist past increasingly came to mean revision of the history of the četnik national movement (Radanović 2011).

In the years from 1945 leading up to the early 2000s, the official historical narrative was clear: the četniks had been fascist collaborators, whereas the partisans had fought fascism, liberated Serbia, and created Yugoslavia. But in the past fifteen years, parties from the right side of the political spectrum have set out to rehabilitate the četniks or the "*ravnogorski pokret*," since "both [the partisan and četnik movements] were antifascist" (Bogoljub Pejčić in Narodna skupština 2005, 3–4). Armed Serbian forces in the 1990s had also directly identified with the četnik nationalist movement. In 2005, a law on soldiers' pensions was adopted that in practice equalized both movements. Two rehabilitation laws in 2006 and 2011 allowed socialist convictions in the early years of Yugoslavia to be revised. Symbolizing this development, 2015 saw the rehabilitation of the četnik General Dragoljub (Draža) Mihailović. He had been tried and executed in Yugoslavia in 1946. Cases of other wartime leaders like Milan Nedić are still pending, despite ongoing accusations that they, including Mihailović, collaborated with the fascists and Nazis (Savez antifašista Srbije 2018).

Parliamentarians were and are eager to connect these various violent pasts. The suffering in the 1990s wars and under the ICTY were brought into the debate on četnik rehabilitation (Narodna skupština 2003, 87, 316, 329, 355; Narodna skupština, 2005, 12, 24, 60; Narodna skupština 2011). Ivica Dačić from the Socialist Party for example accused those proposing četnik rehabilitation of fake patriotism, as they in reality wanted "to send today's fighters for freedom to The Hague" (Narodna skupština 2005, 24). This endorses the narrative of perpetual Serbian victimhood. It furthermore confirms the mainstreaming or "normalization of nationalism" (Stakić 2013, 3).

Extremist right-wing groups directly benefit from this. The asymmetry in this paper's methodology, reflecting the fact that radical Islam functions in the margins while the radical right-wing (although not necessarily the extremist right-wing)[21] is much institutionalized, does not allow for a similar analysis for Islamist platforms. However, the salience of grand narratives of historical continuity benefitted right-wing and Islamist platforms alike. While the former recycle četnik symbols, the latter could profit from the "living memory" of the wars and distant past by referring for example to the *Mladi Muslimani* (Young Muslims), a movement active in the first half of the twentieth century, but still existing, grounded in religious, political and ethnical identities (Jevtić 2017b, 66–69). The last section of this paper will mention some examples of this use by Islamist platforms.

Extremist right-wing and Islamist historical narratives thus do not need to be contrasted to each other: they are in a certain way part of the same problem. In a country and region where "radical is the new norm" (Bećirević 2016, 12, 19)[22] and the past is salient, it is not difficult to exploit historical narratives to extremes—no matter the direction. The chapter by Ivanović further confirms the relation

---

21　While both groups may have similar goals, this (by all means very complex) distinction hints at the difference in strategy: extremists are more inclined to place themselves outside society and the rules that apply there. This indeed explains the different level of institutionalization: radicalism can exist within the boundaries of regular politics and media. An organization like *Zavetnici* even moves between both categories, taking part in political elections while also employing activities that are extremist (i.e., the disruption of public events). *Obraz* is probably the most extremist organisation from this paper's selection: it was banned by the Serbian constitutional court in 2012 after its leader Mladen Obradović had been convicted for prison sentences.

22　In the referenced article, this phrase is used to describe Bosnia and Herzegovina. The characterization seems however apt for Serbia as well, and indeed for the broader region.

between post-war transition and appeal of extremist discourses, especially on youth.

Narratives of violent history by extremist right-wing groups

Since its establishment in 2012, as it explains on its website, *Zavetnici* has operated in Serbia, Montenegro, and the Republika Srpska (in Bosnia), and specific mention is made of the Serbian diaspora as well. *Zavetnici* prides itself for the "concrete measures" it proposes, and also takes part in elections (Zavetnici, O nama 2017a). In line with conclusions from the literature, it is clear that *Zavetnici* uses violent events and actors from Serbian history as a main component of its identity narrative. Established on February 15, 2012, *Zavetnici* explains that this date "symbolically determined our path". February 15 refers to the start of the First Serbian Uprising on that date in 1904, while 2012 denotes the centennial of the liberation of "Old Serbia and Kosovo and Metohija." The organization's logo contains the "medieval Serbian hero and knight Miloš Obilić" (Zavetnici, O nama 2017a). Remembering Bakić's observation that right-wing organizations often falsify history in order to use it, *Zavetnici's* call for "revision of textbooks for primary and secondary schools" is noteworthy.

Figure 1: "Support for the rehabilitation of Draža Mihailović"

Reference: (Zavetnici 2014)

Such revision is "necessary", the group argues, because in these history books Serbian history is "falsified" (Zavetnici 2016a; Zavetnici, O nama 2017a).

Identification with history:
the fascist enemy and their own četnik pride

The previous section described how the revision of Serbia's Second World War history significantly changed the narrative of fascism and anti-fascism. Many of Zavetnici's historical references are enabled by this conflation of Serbia's nationalist and anti-fascist movements. Carrying a banner with Mihailović's image, the main face of this historical revision, Zavetnici demonstrated for his rehabilitation (Zavetnici 2014, 4.44).

Četnik nationalism is praised alongside enemy narratives of the fascist Croat ustaša, but also alongside dismissal of the Yugoslavian idea and socialism. The same article that described Mihailović as a "hero" who fought "against fascism", condemned Tito's "dictatorial" regime (Zavetnici 2015g). *Naši* described Tito's socialism as a "dictatorship" (Opačić 2017), while *Obraz* directly contrasted the heroism of a soldier from both World Wars to the anti-patriotism and weakness of both Yugoslav states (Bokan 2015).

The state-led rehabilitation of the četnik movement both legitimized and foregrounded nationalist symbols which right-wing groups were happy to pick up on. *Zavetnici*'s video shows two moments where several participants hold a hand gesture with thumb, middle, and index finger touching (Zavetnici 2014, 3.48, 4.57). There can be some confusion about what symbols and signs are considered "traditional."

Figure 2: The četnik greeting, as shown two times in the video

Reference: (Zavetnici 2014)

While right-wing sources have recently warned that the sign with three unconnected fingers has in fact no nationalist origin, this version of the gesture is agreed to be a traditional četnik greeting. It is indicative that the gesture is used during a demonstration in 2013 to commemorate the victims of Operation Storm (Zavetnici 2014, 4.57). This Croat military operation from the 1990s is described by *Zavetnici* in terms of a "genocidal" crime against the Serbian nation (Zavetnici 2015e). Images shared by *Obraz* through their online presence also demonstrate this hand gesture, including in references to Srebrenica (Obraz 2015a).

Three minutes into *Zavetnici*'s video, a main figure of the organization and some other adherents are shown wearing St. George ribbons during a church ceremony. These ribbons, originally a Russian military decoration, carry different meanings. Throughout Europe the ribbons are a symbol of the fight against fascism. In Russia they are of late often worn as a patriotic symbol.

Figure 3: Wearing the St. George ribbon

Reference: (Zavetnici 2014)

The appearance of this ribbon on the *Zavetnici*'s jacket most likely reflects both *Zavetnici*'s claim on anti-fascism, after all one of the most powerful historical motifs in Serbia, and its support for the Russian nation and politics. Together these create an interesting nationalist, pro-Russian take on the narrative of Serbia's anti-fascist struggle. *Zavetnici* regularly speaks about Russian "heroes" and emphasizes the historical brotherhood and unity between the two nations in times of war (Zavetnici 2017f; Zavetnici 2016d; Zavetnici 2015a; Zavetnici 2015b). The organization commemorates the Russian soldiers that gave their lives "for the defense of the Serbian state and Serbian nation" (Zavetnici 2016b). *Obraz* connects the Russian friendship with more recent history. It placed a Russian flag at a monument for Serbs killed in Srebrenica "as a sign of gratefulness to Russia" for preventing the United Nations Security Council (UNSC) from adopting a resolution on the "imagined 'genocide'" committed by Serbia (Obraz 2015a). Ana Dević's contribution in this volume further explores this contemporary and historical Russia-Serbia dynamic.

Connecting enemies and heroes from the past: a perpetual struggle

The 1990s wars are, like the literature suggested, indeed central to extremist right-wing groups' historical frames. "Heroes" from the conflicts in Bosnia, Croatia, and Kosovo are regularly mentioned. In line with experts' opinions, the main figure here is General Mladić, convicted by the ICTY for the genocide in Srebrenica in 1995 (Bakić Interview, 2017; Stakić Interview, 2017; Dragišić Interview 2017).

The analyzed material shows however that also the more distant past and less contemporary figures function as important components of identity narrative. *Obraz* held a march in 2015 to honor the 200-year anniversary of the Second Serbian Uprising (Obraz 2015e). With the same urgency as *Zavetnici* praises Mladić for preventing the Serbian nation from suffering "the same fate" as twice before this century at the hands of "terrorists of [Bosnian Muslim general] Orić" (Zavetnici 2017b), it calls for a monument for the "heroes of the First World War" (Zavetnici 2018a) — a cause also supported by the parliamentary party DSS (DSS 2017). Similarly, *Obraz* and *Naši* call Mladić a hero who liberated Srebrenica (Obraz 2015a; SNP Naši 2016), but devote as much attention to national figures from centuries ago like Sveti Sava (Velimirović 2014; Obradović 2016), Knez Lazar (Ivanović 2015) and the aforementioned heroic deeds of a soldier during both World Wars (Bokan 2015).

Most of the time, this distant past is connected to more recent events or even the present day. One *Zavetnici* article speaks in the same paragraph of the "centuries of Ottoman occupation," the current Vučić regime and "communists" who apparently in the "same way" suppressed religion (Zavetnici 2015c). References to heroes are also not limited to the historical episodes in which they lived.

An article by *Naši* describes the honor with which "we fight for the same thing" as a range of Serbian historical figures, including Knez Lazar and Karađorđe, striving for a "final victory" "with our holy ancestors" (Ivanović 2015).

The battle in Kosovo on June 28, 1389 is living memory as testified by the organization's annual activities on so-called *Vidovdan* and the several references to it (Zavetnici 2017e; Zavetnici 2015h; Ivanović 2015). While this important national day originally commemorates the fallen "martyrs" in the fight against the Ottomans more than 600 years ago, recordings in the *Zavetnici* video show a banner with the image of Gavrilo Princip. Also on June 28, but 525 years later, Princip's assassination of the Austrian-Hungarian Empire sparked the beginning of the First World War. The text next to the portrait reads: "Serbian Princip lives forever" (Zavetnici 2014, 0.45).

Figure 4: Using Princip's image at a Vidovdan protest in Sarejevo

Reference: (Zavetnici 2014)

The use of his portrait in a *Vidovdan* protest illustrates the ease with which *Zavetnici* morphs different historical eras together in the same narrative. The alleged perpetual struggle for "freedom," "independence," and sovereignty fought by the "Serbian nation throughout the centuries" is a recurring motif (Zavetnici 2016c;

Zavetnici 2016b). A similar rationale of historical continuity also exists in *Obraz* and *Naši* articles, where Sveti Sava is presented as relevant today as ever (Ivanović 2015; Velimirović 2014; Obradović 2016), and hope is expressed that the days of King Milutin, born in the thirteenth century, will return (Obraz 2015b). "The truth is," *Obraz* writes, "that Sveti Sava lived 700 years ago," but his nationalism had lived and grown "through all seven centuries until today" (Velimirović 2014).

Just as heroes are picked from a wide range of history, depicted enemies are both ever-changing and always looming. They range from fascists (often Croats) and Muslims, to Serbian progressive and pro-West NGOs, Western organizations, the international community, and even Serbian state authorities. *Zavetnici* states that the country's leaders commanded "one of the greatest heroes" of the Kosovo war, Vladimir Lazarević to hand himself over to ICTY solely in a bid to please the West (Zavetnici 2017c), while *Naši* directly blames former President Boris Tadić for handing over "heroes" Mladić and Karadžić to the "anti-Serbian" Hague Tribunal (SNP Naši 2017). *Obraz* similarly expresses the idea of Serbian-West betrayal by writing about the "Merkel-Vučić plan on changing the consciousness of the Serbian nation" (Obradović 2016).

Even more salient in the articles by *Obraz* than those by *Zavetnici* is the emphasis on the internal enemy. *Obraz* is keen to narrate about the alleged U-turn of prominent Serbian politicians Aleksandar Vučić and Tomislav Nikolić: formerly being the "most outspoken adversaries of the US, EU and NATO," in comparison with "Americans, Muslims and Croats" they now come out as the most dangerous (Obraz 2015d). *Naši* calls October 5, 2000 a "day of occupation" (SNP Naši 2015). Frames of spreading lies about the wars, especially Srebrenica, and accusations of outsiders denying Serbian victimhood are assigned to several actors: the EU (Zavetnici 2017c), the ICTY (Zavetnici 2017d), unpatriotic Serbs for whom "all others are more important, innocent, respected, bigger martyrs than whatever which Serb" (Obraz 2015c), and organizations like REKOM (a regional fact-finding initiative targeted at the 1990s wars) and Radio Free Europe (Zavetnici 2017g; SNP Naši 2014).

Islam as historical enemy of the right-wing?

In line with findings from the literature review and dominant political enemy narratives, right-wing organizations furthermore find an historical enemy in Islam. This concerns both Bosniaks and Albanian Muslims. *Zavetnici* recently warned "the world" that, "Albanian terrorism is again activated." Without implying to which history ("again") it refers, the article claims that the Albanian "terrorists" aim for the creation of a "genocidal Great Albania," an "ethnically clean Kosovo" and wish to erase "Serbian historical continuity" (Zavetnici 2018b).

Additionally, according to *Zavetnici* the events in Srebrenica in 1995 should not be remembered as "war crimes," but as "the liberation and defense" of the nation from and against "Islamic fundamentalism." Muslim forces instead committed "genocide" on the Serbian nation (Daniel Igrec & Zavetnici 2017; Zavetnici 2015f; Politika 2016b). One article states that "the first victims of radical Islamism in Europe were Serbs." In this way, *Zavetnici* establishes a clear link with the current fear of Islamist terrorism (Daniel Igrec & Zavetnici 2017).

The evidence however does not suffice to apply Julia Ebner's thesis to *Zavetnici*'s use of history. The above-noted excerpt may in isolation seem to put the Muslim enemy central, but *Zavetnici*'s broader material makes clear that other historical enemies are still equally or even more salient. The same applies to the analyzed material of *Naši* and *Obraz*. The current international attention to Islamist terrorism is however likely to add further legitimacy and significance to this frame. To initially explore where this process is at, a brief exploration of articles by mainstream right-wing media outlets *Politika* and *Blic* follows.

In general, the targeted search on keywords gave more results on *Blic* than *Politika*, but the large part of both newspapers' articles from 2015–2017 mentioning jihadism and Islamism in relation to the Balkans remains mainly factual. They, for example, simply report on the death of Albanian fighters of Islamic State, or the trial against a Bosniak jihadi. Also, the majority of articles that do use a sensationalist tone to report on jihadism and Islamism related to the

Balkans, do not turn to history to further instill a sense of fear. One *Politika* article for example makes claims that (as later appears from the article, remain unconfirmed) about camps of radical Islamists in Bosnia and Herzegovina. While it extensively speculates about life and ideology in the camps outside state control, it does not draw parallels to the past (Stanišić 2015). The opposite is also true: *Blic* for example extensively quoted Mladić's lawyer who described the wartime jihad in Bosnia and wrote about the 1995 crimes by "*El Mudžahid*" [italics by author], but did not connect both stories to a supposed present-day threat of Islam (Blic 2016a; Blic 2017). These findings indicate that the Islamist enemy as a historical narrative is not a given in the right-wing mainstream media.

Analyzed articles that do wish to explain the problem's historical origin, mostly limit themselves to the 1990s wars. Articles describe these wars as the start of jihadism and describe how Muslim countries' so-called humanitarian help created a foundation for the spread of "Wahhabism" (Politika 2016a; Politika 2016c; Blic 2016b). Both newspapers sometimes contrast the current day threat of Islam to the reported "tolerant Muslim community" before the wars (Politika 2016c). Confirming the earlier observation that even the popular newspaper *Blic* does not always seek the most sensationalist reporting, one of its articles ends with a quote that the indigenous form of Islam is tolerant and in harmony with other religions (Blic 2016c).

Some articles from *Politika* and *Blic* do however suggest that the problem has deeper historical roots, extending beyond the 1990s. Think tank analyst Gordon Bardoš[23] in *Politika* deliberately draws an "historical parallel" between the "several hundreds of Islamic extremists" fifty years ago, mainly in the circle of former Muslim fighter and late Bosnian statesman Alija Izetbegović, and the "several hundreds of thousands people" attracted to the Islamic State today (Bardoš 2015). Similarly looking back half a century, an article from *Blic* directly compares current Bosnian politician Bakir

---

23 Bardoš is a controversial author and researcher. His analyses often perpetuate a popular nationalist Serbian perspective, and the example mentioned in this paper testifies to this.

Izetbegović and his aforementioned father Alija (Vukašinović 2017). Whereas the latter in the mid-1980s "got a nine year prison sentence," referring to the Sarajevo process in 1983 that saw the conviction of thirteen Bosnian intellectuals on grounds of hostile activity,[24] *Blic* states that his son "today receives applause" and aims to continue his "father's dreams" of the region's Islamization (Vukašinović 2017).

Revealingly, the narrative of Muslim violence is connected to another, stronger historical adversary: the West, accused of ignoring and even hiding Serbian victimhood at the hand of Islam (Jakšić 2015; Bardoš 2015). Focusing on a French opinion maker who now warns of Islam in Europe, one *Politika* article ridiculed how back in the 1990s he ignored Serbian suffering by the "first Al Qaida regiment in Europe" (Kremenović 2016). These articles thus underscore the extremist right-wing narrative of Serbs as the first European victims of Islamist violence, but mostly confirm the narrative of the anti-Serb West.

Narratives of violent history by Islamist platforms

Like the studied material from *Zavetnici*, history is very present on the website of *Put Vjernika*. Even articles that deal with present topics frequently feature elaborate reflections on history. The websites *Islam Bosna* and *Istina* both contain special historical categories: respectively "traces of the past" and, most specifically, "Srebrenica," and "history," including a sub-category "History BiH." Confirming the position presented in the literature review, the three websites display a sense of identification with the history of the broader global Muslim community. Next to regional history, numerous articles discuss Islam and Arab history, ranging from the fall of Granada to the Palestinian conflict. In line with this, the structure of the websites and context of the articles of these platforms, while often

---

24   The process is often described in terms of a "show trial" and should indeed be seen in the broader light of developments in socialist Yugoslavia at the time. The accused were politicians, activists, and members of the group Mladi Muslimani (Young Muslims), striving for independence and, according to some (but this remains contested), Islamization of Bosnia.

emphasizing the specific history of Bosnia and Herzegovina, suggest that they target all BHS-speaking[25] Muslims. *Islam Bosna* for example has special labels "Sandzak" and "npazar," indicating Novi Pazar, the main city of the Serbian Sandžak region. This indicates that they actively report on events from and topics important to this part of their readership. As mentioned in the methodology section, cross-posting with *Sandžak Press* is common.

Identification with history: the "genocidal" enemy and the loyal ally

Interestingly, the historical frame of "fascism," popular amongst extremist right-wing organizations, is also used by Islamist platforms. *Put Vjernika* calls Serbs dancing on Muslim graves "fascist" (Putvjernika 2010a), but also uses the term for the convicted Croatian war criminal Slobodan Praljak (Putvjernika 2017a). In addition to the enemy, *Islam Bosna* also clearly identifies the ally: an article from late 2011 extensively describes the "enormous support" of Saudi Arabia during the 1990s. Underscoring the importance of remembering this history, the title of the article asks the reader whether "we are indeed that forgetful, or what is still worse unthankful?" (Islam Bosna 2011).

Figure 5: Graves of mujahedeen in Bosnia

Reference: (Beganović 2013b)

In general, *Islam Bosna* seems more focused on narratives of heroism than *Put Vjernika*, which prefers enemy narratives of threat. *Islam Bosna* honors the memory of mujahedeen showing pictures of their

---

25 BHS stands for: Bosnian, Croatian and Serbian, as these languages (formerly referred to as Serbo-Croatian) are highly related and mutually intelligible.

graves (Beganović 2013b), gives elaborate testimony of the lives of two "special heroes" from the 1990s' *El Mudžahidin* (Beganović 2013a) and describes this unit's "brilliant victory" (Islam Bosna 2013a).

The most frequent historical narrative is however that of genocide. The latter word is used to refer to numerous atrocities of the 1990s wars (Putvjernika 2017b; Putvjernika 2012a; Beganović 2013b), as well as one in 1943[26] (Islam Bosna 2012). One article, without specifying the massacre, speaks of the "the newest/most recent genocide" from the 1990s (Putvjernika 2010a). This suggests that Muslims in the region suffered genocide before as well. *Istina* is even more explicit by describing a Serbian document from 1844 the inspiration for "numerous genocides on Bosnian Muslims" since (Istina 2016a).

The massacre in Srebrenica in July 1995 plays an important role in this narrative of perpetual (threat of) Serbian genocide against Muslims. This crime is recognized by the International Court of Justice and ICTY as genocide. Using the frame retrospectively, *Islam Bosna* calls the aforementioned 1943 massacre "Sandžak Srebrenica" (Islam Bosna 2012). As noted, it even features a special label/category for Srebrenica on its website. The frame is also connected to the present situation. One article ridicules a Sufi leader for denying the Srebrenica genocide, connecting this to his apparent stance towards the Syria conflict: such denial is to be expected "from a person who defends the Satanist Assad regime" (Putvjernika 2015a). Aware of the weight of this frame, *Put Vjernika* and *Islam Bosna* use titles like "Aleppo [Haleb] = a new Srebrenica?" (Islam Bosna 2016b) and "Srebrenica in Syria" to describe present-day massacres by "Shi'ite" forces on Sunnis abroad (Putvjernika 2013).[27] *Islam Bosna* published an interview with a soldier of the

---

26 During the Second World War, as a result of foreign invasion and civil war between partisans, četniks and ustaše, numerous atrocities were committed across the region of the former Yugoslavia (this article specifically refers to one in Sandžak).

27 The explicit mentioning of "shi'ite" is interesting here too and reveals one more alleged historical enemy: Iran and shi'itism in general. Various articles and videos on the website of Put Vjernika highlight Iran's alleged negative role in the 1990s wars and its ongoing involvement in Bosnian society and culture. Speeches by Iranian political and religious leaders are translated and commented upon to show their

"liberating forces" who iterated how people in Aleppo admire and find inspiration in "the resistance put up against the aggressor during the war in Bosnia" (Islam Bosna 2016a). Drawing more parallels, the soldier described the conflict as "not a civil war" but a "war against regime and foreign Shi'ite forces," after which he compared these enemies to those during the war in Bosnia and Herzegovina (Islam Bosna 2016a).

While not as strong a frame as in extremist right-wing narratives, the West features as well as an historical enemy. Playing into the wide international attention for the Srebrenica genocide, one article emphasizes how specifically the Dutch "betrayed" Srebrenica. It draws attention to the ongoing trials in The Hague to argue that Europe and the Netherlands should be "ashamed" of the way they express "hatred" about Islam in Bosnia (Putvjernika 2012a).

Recent articles express awareness of, and play with, the international attention to Islam and the changing meaning of the word "terror" in Serbia and the West. In one article, *Put Vjernika* claims that Serbian media tries to blame everything on Muslims. Even when reporting on a violent incident of a Serb against a Muslim, the article sarcastically explains, Serbian media will find a way to flip the roles and then instead describe the violence as a deed of an "'Islamic terrorist'" (Putvjernika 2012b). An article by *Istina* applies the same rationale to the West and ridicules the "war against terrorism." It is used, the article suggests, as a "moral license to execute massacres" in Syria (Nurković 2017). Although these are just some examples, this awareness of the international focus on Islamist terror combined with the expressed adversity towards Serbia and the above-noted anti-Muslim themes common on the right, all indicate fertile soil for Ebner's thesis.

---

malice, and articles emphasize that Iran supports Assad's regime. Wahhabists, of which Put Vjernika is part, generally receive support from Saudi Arabia (Simeunović & Dolnik 2013, 91–92). This country's main enemy is Iran and this rivalry also plays out in Bosnia and Herzegovina.

Connecting enemies and heroes from the past: perpetual threat

The applicability of Ebner's thesis to Islamist historical narratives is further supported by Islamist platforms' claims of historical victimhood at the hand of Serbs. Mirroring the findings of extremist right-wing organizations and even going further, the Islamist platforms frame contemporary danger in a narrative of continuous historical threat. A *Put Vjernika* article speaks about the "genocidal ideology of četniks" and refers to an influential Serbian bishop during the 1990s to underscore the urgent danger of "četnik religious extremists" (Putvjernika 2012a).[28] In an article on a specific incident in Bosnia's Republika Srpska, *Put Vjernika* calls present day actions against Bosniaks "terror" and stresses the risk of "a new genocide" (Putvjernika 2010a). Illustrating the broader focus and target readership of *Put Vjernika*, another article expresses concerns about "Bosniaks" from Sandžak and other regions at the periphery of BiH (Putvjernika 2015b). It is indeed important that *Put Vjernika*, as well as *Istina* and *Islam Bosna*, seem to describe the group they are representing as well as the Serbs as their present-day adversary in terms of ethnicity and religion ("Bosniaks," "Muslims;" "Serbs," "Christians"), sometimes inspired by history ("četniks"), rather than nationality. This is, of course, very much in parallel with the frames used by the extremist right-wing groups analyzed above: for all three, the Serbian ethnicity as well as the orthodox Christian identity are important identity frames, while "Muslims" (from the Balkans) in general are described as an adversary, rarely distinguishing between Albanians and Bosniaks from Serbia or BiH.[29]

Other articles start out with a local, recent scandal and then position the incident in the broader historical context. *PutVjernika's* website for example reported on celebrations by a Serbian antiterrorist division on the location of the Batajnica mass grave of 744 Albanian civilians. After describing the shameful event, the article extensively describes the developments in the 1990s leading up to the massacre (Putvjernika 2017c). The opposite also happens: an article

---

28 Generally, no distinction is made between Bosnian Serb or Serbian forces.
29 For an analysis on the construction of these frames during and after the 1990s' wars in Bosnia, see Campbell 1998, 44, 42–48.

by *Islam Bosna* on the aforementioned 1943 "Sandžak Srebrenica" connects this distant past both with the 1990s war and the present day, by pointing at the alleged current support of the Serbian state for the četnik movement (Islam Bosna 2012).

This narrative of victimhood is also used to delegitimize the current attention for Islamic radicalization. *Put Vjernika* implies that such messages in fact cover up a very old desire to kill and persecute the Muslim population (Putvjernika 2010b). Serbian media, it claims, write about "the dangers of "radical Islamists" to distract attention from Muslim suffering at the 15-year anniversary of the Srebrenica genocide (Putvjernika 2010c). Another article suggests that now Serbian authorities target Muslims not because of Wahhabi radicalism, but simply "because we said that we are Muslims", like in 1992 (Putvjernika 2010b). The dominant frame here is the assertion that "history repeats itself" (Putvjernika 2016), warning Muslims to be vigilant and ready to defend themselves to prevent another genocide or massacre. This also feeds into the frame of internal weakness and the important Islamist recruitment motive of becoming a "better Muslim" (Azinović & Jusić 2015, 44).

Further bolstering the master historical narrative of perpetual victimhood, two *Put Vjernika* articles argue that the current prosecution of Salafism has the same characteristics as the prosecution of the *Mladi Muslimani* during the 1980s in Yugoslavia (Young Muslims) (Putvjernika 2016; Putvjernika 2015b).

The articles specifically single out the Islamic Community, a longstanding and powerful organ in Bosnia, as an enemy that "betrayed" and "persecuted" the Mladi Muslimani and Muslims in general during communist times, and still does so today towards

Salafists.[30] It directly warns Muslims that what happened in "our recent past" can happen again (Putvjernika 2015b).

Figure 6: Comparison between Mladi Muslimani and Salafists ("selefije")

Reference: (Putvjernika 2015b)

A similarly elaborate article on the aforementioned Sarajevo process against the Young Muslims by *Islam Bosna* however lacks such a parallel. The process is connected to ethnic cleansing in the 1990s, the Serbian Memorandum and the creation of an "atmosphere of hate," but does not connect this to the present day (Džunuzović 2013). Possibly, the article assumes that this link is self-evident.

---

30 Translation: please note that the original is itself clumsy. Titles two columns: "Young Muslims (fundamentalists) (1945...)/Salafists ("Wahhabis") (1995...). List (largely similar): 1. Staged court processes, 2. State terror on them, 3. Betrayal from hodža and Islamic Community/from Daija and Islamic Community, 4. Persecutions from the media, 5. Unceasing tracking from the intelligence services, 6. Media persecutions and lynching, 7. Very weak support amongst the nation, 8. Called by any names, 9. Indicted for destruction of the state, 10. Indicted for terror, 11. Murders of followers. Ending: Are there similarities? Take away the lesson. History repeats itself. Do not follow people, follow the Kuran and Sunnet!

However, it is important to note that history also seems to be considered an important story in itself. *Istina* published a series of four elaborate articles to discuss the coming of Islam to Bosnia, starting out in the fifteenth century. Blaming the "myth" of Balkan Islamization, they explicitly warn of the danger of falsification of history (Istina 2016b; Istina 2016a; Istina 2015b; Istina 2015a). This reminds of *Zavetnici*'s similar concern about alleged "lies" spread in history textbooks.

Conclusion

This analysis has indicated that both right-wing extremist and Islamist groups refer to the violent past to increase legitimacy and appeal. It has not only studied how extremist right-wing and Islamist platforms use the violent history, but has also "located" these narratives within the political memory politics and related developments of the past two decades.

The findings, first, suggest that both sides benefit from the radical political atmosphere created by the enemy narratives of the 1990s wars. Extremist right-wing organizations in addition concretely benefit from the state-led rehabilitation of the četnik movement as an alleged anti-fascist force. Interestingly, both groups have several historical enemies in common: the fascist, the Yugoslav state, the internal traitor, and the West. Ideas of conspiracy and international weakness connect the latter two groups. Western organizations operating with or in Serbia should be aware of their role in these narratives.

As a second and related finding, both groups paint an image of history and the present day as a continuous battle against the enemy. In the material studied, violent history is rarely directly used to justify violence in the present day. Instead, history is portrayed as a warning. Right-wing groups connect violent events (e.g. *Vidovdan*, Srebrenica) and heroes (e.g. Sveti Sava, Mladić) from different historical periods to emphasize the ongoing looming threat to Orthodox Christian Serbs. Similarly, Islamist platforms honor heroes from the distant and recent past (e.g. *Mladi Muslimani, El Mudžahidin*) and explicitly and repeatedly speak about the risk of a new "genocide" to underscore that Muslims should always be ready to defend themselves. Such circular reasoning potentially justifies the use of violence to protect their own community. It is therefore worth exploring if extremist interpretations of history could fall under hate speech law, and, if not, what this could mean for long-term social cohesion. On a positive note, there is a potential for reformed history education to stress particularism and multi-perspectivity in interpreting the past, to fight the construction of such master historical narratives from its basis.

Third, extremist right-wing groups and Islamist organizations frame each other as an important historical enemy, albeit not the dominant one. Therefore, Ebner's thesis partially applies to the use of historical narratives by these two groups. Islamist platforms in particular exploit historical narratives to portray Serbia, whether its institutions or people, as perpetual threat. Right-wing extremist narratives focus more on the Western and internal enemy. However, in an international context prone to polarize and exacerbate both perceived threats, right-wing and Islamist extremism in Serbia may further tailor their violent historical narratives towards the other. This merits attention from academia and policy alike. After all: if violence in history is made to look normal and just, the actual use of violence is only one step away.

References

Antić, Ana. 2003. "Evolucija i uloga tri kompleksa istorijskih mitova u srpskom akademskom i javnom mnjenju u poslednjih deset godina." *Historijski mitovi na Balkanu*. 1: 259–290. Beograd.

Azinović, Vlado, & Bećirević, Edina. 2017. *A Waiting Game: Assessing and Responding to the Threat from Returning Foreign Fighters*. Sarajevo: Regional Cooperation Council.

Azinović, Vlado, & Jusić, Muhamed. 2015. "The Lure of the Syrian War. The Foreign Fighters' Bosnian Contingent." https://wb-iisg.com/wp-content/uploads/bp-attachments/4798/Foreign-Terrorist-Fighteres_-BiH.pdf.

Azinović, Vlado. 2018. "Regional Report. Understanding Violent Extremism in the Western Balkans.". British Council Western Balkans Extremism Research Forum. https://docs.google.com/viewer?url=https%3A%2F%2Fwww.rcc.int%2Fp-cve%2Fdownload%2Fdocs%2Ferf_report_western_balkans_2018.pdf%2Fb6227266ac466b5034c7693e8936c87f.pdf&embedded=true&chrome=false&dov=1

Bakić, Jovo. 2013. *Right-wing extremism in Serbia*. Belgrade: Friedrich Ebert Stiftung.

Bakić, Jovo. 2017. Interview with author, December 12.

Bardoš, Gordon N. 2015. "Od Balkana do Islamske države." *Politika Online*, 5 December 2015. http://www.politika.rs/sr/clanak/344826/Tema-nedelje/Od-Balkana-do-Islamske-drzave.

Bećirević, Edina. 2016. *Salafism vs. Moderate Islam. A Rhetorical Fight for the Hearts and Minds of Bosnian Muslims*. Sarajevo: Atlantic Initiative.

Beganović, Ezher. 2013a. "Heroji Bosne: Adil Bosnić i Emir Planja." http://islambosna.ba/heroji-bosne-adil-bosnic-i-emir-planja/

Beganović, Ezher. 2013b. Uspomena na velikane našeg vremena: Mudžahidski mezari u BiH. http://islambosna.ba/uspomena-na-velikane-naseg-vremena-mudzahidski-mezari-u-bih/

Blic. 2016a. "Zavšna reč odbrane u Hagu 'Mladić je nevin, kriv je samo što je Srbin i što je branio srpski narod'." *Blic*, 9 December 2016. https://www.blic.rs/vesti/hronika/zavsna-rec-odbrane-u-hagu-mladic-je-nevin-kriv-je-samo-sto-je-srbin-i-sto-je-branio/lwgr3v9

Blic. 2016b. "Švajcarski list upozorava: BiH kolevka evropskog džihadizma, vehabija Bilal Bosnić vrbovao po Švajcarskoj." *Blic*, 7 November 2016. https://www.blic.rs/vesti/republika-srpska/svajcarski-list-upozorava-bih-kolevka-evropskog-dzihadizma-vehabija-bilal-bosnic/cy58gqb

Blic. 2016c. "Iz bede u džihad Stotine sledbenika ISIS dolazi iz jedne zemlje na Balkanu." *Blic*, 19 October 2016. https://www.blic.rs/vesti/svet/iz-bede-u-dzihad-stotine-sledbenika-isis-dolazi-iz-jedne-zemlje-na-balkanu/hqnv90j

Blic. 2017. "Hrvatski mediji: Mudžahedini su odsecali glave srpskim vojnicima, a Izetvegović ih je svečano postrojio." https://www.blic.rs/vesti/svet/hrvatski-mediji-mudzahedini-su-odsecali-glave-srpskim-vojnicima-a-izetbegovic-ih-je/bj4re08

Bokan, Dragoslav. 2015. "O užasima rata i strahotima mira." www.obraz.rs: http://www.obraz.rs/2015/12/23/o-uzasima-rata-i-strahotama-mira/

Campbell, David. 1998. *National Deconstruction. Violence, Identity, and Justice in Bosnia*. Minneapolis and London: University of Minnesota Press.

CeSID, & UNDP Serbia Country Office. 2016. "Survey of the drivers of youth radicalism and violent extremism in Serbia." http://www.rs.undp.org/content/dam/serbia/Publications%20and%20reports/English/Resilience/UNDP_SRB_drivers%20of%20youth%20radicalism%20and%20violent%20extremism.pdf?download.

Daniel Igrec and Zavetnici. 2017. "Dekonstrukcija srebreničkih laži." http://zavetnici.rs/?p=7151

Dimitrijević, B. 2018. Interview with author, February 9.

Dragišić, Zoran. 2017, Interview with author, December.

Dronzina, Tatyana, & Muça, Sulejman. 2017. "De-radicalising the Western Balkans." *New Eastern Europe* 3, 25–33.

DSS. 2017. "Podići spomenik majoru Dragutinu Gavriloviću." http://www.dss.rs/podici-spomenik-majoru-dragutinu-gavrilovicu/

Džunuzović, Anes. 2013. "'Sarajevski proces' suđenje Muslimanima i muslimanima." http://www.islambosna.ba/sarajevski-proces-suenje-muslimanima-i-muslimanima/

Ebner, Julia. 2017. *The Rage. The Vicious Circle of Extremist and Far-Right Extremism*. London & New York: I.B. Tauris.

Elbasani, Alroda, & Roy, Olivier. 2015. Islam in the post-Communist Balkans: alternative pathways to God. *Southeast European and Black Sea Studies*, 15 (4), 457–471.

IslamBosna. 2016a. "Ekskluzivno: Razgovor sa aktivisticom opozicije u Halebu." *Islam Bosna*, October 9 2016. http://www.islambosna.ba/ekskluzivno-razgovor-sa-aktivisticom-opozicije-u-halebu/

IslamBosna. 2011. "Jesmo li zaista toliko zaboravni ili, što je još gore nezahvalni?" http://islambosna.ba/jesmo-li-zaista-toliko-zaboravni-ili-to-je-jo-gore-nezahvalni/

IslamBosna. 2012. "Sandžačka Srebrenica: 69 godina od genocida nad Bošnjacima Limske doline." http://islambosna.ba/sandaka-srebrenica-69-godina-od-genocida-nad-bonjacima-limske-doline/

IslamBosna. 2013a. "Dan kada je Armija R BiH predvođena Odredom "El Mudžahidin." http://www.islambosna.ba/10-09-1995-dan-kada-je-armija-r-bih-predvodena-odredom-el-mudzahidin-oslobodila-vozucu/

IslamBosna. 2013b. "Poruke prošlosti za bolje razumijevanje sadašnjosti: Pismo ruskom caru iz Istanbula." islambosna.ba/poruke-prolosti-za-bolje-razumijevanje-sadanjosti-pismo-ruskom-caru-iz-istanbula/

IslamBosna. 2016b. "Haleb = nova Srebrenica?" http://islambosna.ba/haleb-nova-srebrenica/

Istina. 2015a. "Proces privatanja Islama u BiH – prelazak na Islam tokom 15-og stoljeća." https://istina.ba/proces-privatanja-islama-u-bih-prelazak-na-islam-tokom-15-og-stoljeca/

Istina. 2015b. "Mit o islamizaciji Bosne." https://istina.ba/mit-o-islamizaciji-bosne/

Istina. 2016a. "Čija je Bosna? 2." https://istina.ba/2-cija-je-bosna/

Istina. 2016b. "Čija je Bosna?" https://istina.ba/cija-je-bosna/

Ivanović, Ivan. 2015. "Ivan Ivanović – Vidovdanska ideologija." https://nasisrbija.org/ivan-ivanovic-vidovdanska-ideologija/

Jakšić, Boško. 2015. "Šejtanski posao." *Politika*, 28 April 2015. http://www.politika.rs/sr/clanak/326062/Sejtanski-posao

Jevtić, Jana. 2017a. "Reforming Islam Online: The Study of IslamBosna and New Sources of Religious Knowledge Among East London's Bosniak Diaspora." In *European Muslims and New Media*, edited by Merve Kayikci & Leen D'Haenens, 53–70. Leuven: Leuven University Press.

Jevtić, Jana. 2017b. "Bosnian Muslims and the Idea of a "European Islam" in Post-War Sarajevo. Generation, Class and Contests over Religious Authority." *Journal of Muslims in Europe*, 6 (1), 52–75.

Komšić, Jovan. 2007. "Političke stranke u Srbiji i evropske vrednosti. Programi i praksa." In *Političke stranke u Srbiji i Evropska unija*, edited by Zoran Lutovac, 9–50. Beograd: Friedrich Ebert Stiftung, Fakultet političkih nauka.

Kremenović, Mladen. 2016. „Kako je zaštitnik bosanskih muslima postao islamofob." *Politika*, 15 March 2016, http://www.politika.rs/sr/clanak/351148/Region/Kako-je-zastitnik-bosanskih-muslimana-postao-islamofob.

Milojević, Saša, Simonović, Branislav, Janković, Bojan, Otašević, Božidar, and Turanjanin, Veljko. 2013. *Youth and Hooliganism at Sports Events*. Belgrade: Organizacija za evropsku bezbednost i saradnju.

Mršević, Zorica. 2016. Navijačko nasilje: incidenti ili rituali. In *Bezbjednost i osnovna prava: Dimenzije i perspektive sigurnosti LGBT* edited by Aleksandar Zeković, 11–26. Podgorica: Vlada Crne Gore.

Mustapha, Jennifer. 2013. "The Mujahideen in Bosnia: the foreign fighter as cosmopolitan citizen and/or terrorist." *Citizenship Studies*, 17 (6–7), 742–755.

Narodna skupština. 2003. "Osma sednica prvog redovnog zasedanja (četvrti dan rada), 30 maja 2003." In *Narodna skupština Republike Srbije, Stenografske beleške. Osma sednica prvog redovnog zasedanja. 27, 28, 29. i 30. Maj 2003. Godina*, 291–403. Beograd: Biblioteka Narodne skupštine.

Narodna skupština. 2005. "Sedma sednica drugog redovnog zasedanja, 15. decembar 2004. godine (drugi dan rada)." In *Republika Srbija narodna skupština, Stenografse beleške. Sedma i osma sednica drugog redovnog zasedanja 14, 15, 16, 17, 21 i 22. decembar 2004. Godine*, 8–70. Beograd: Narodna skupština.

Narodna skupština. 2011. "Treća sednica prvog redovnog zasedanja, 30. mart 2010. godine." In *Republika Srbija narodna skupština, Stenografske beleške. Dan za poslanička pitanja druga i treća sednica prvog redovnog zasedanja 25. i 30. mart 2010. Godine*, 94–266. Beograd: Narodna skupština.

Nurković, Mirza. 2017. "Civilne žrtve i priča o terorizmu." https://istina.ba/civilne-zrtve-i-prica-o-terorizmu/

Obradović, Mladen. 2016. "Evropska Srbija protiv Svetog Save." http://www.obraz.rs/2016/01/29/evropska-srbija-protiv-svetog-save/

Obraz. 2015a. "Obraz položio rusku zastavu na spomenik stradalim Srbima." http://www.obraz.rs/2015/07/12/obraz-polozio-rusku-zastavu-na-spomenik-stradalim-srbima/

Obraz. 2015b. "Sveti Kralj Milutin, Krsna slava Obraza." http://www.obraz.rs/2015/11/12/sveti-kralj-milutin-krsna-slava-obraza/

Obraz. 2015c. "Veći muslimani od Muhameda." http://www.obraz.rs/2015/04/22/veci-muslimani-od-muhameda/

Obraz. 2015d. "Srbi na Srbe ili Srbi za Srbe?" http://www.obraz.rs/2015/12/17/srbi-na-srbe-ili-srbi-za-srbe/

Obraz. 2015e. "Marš povodom dva veka od Boja na Ljubiću." http://zavetnici.rs/?p=5428

Oluic, Steven. 2008. "Radical Islam on Europe's Frontier—Bosnia & Herzegovina." *National Security and the Future*, 9 (1–2), 35–52.

Opačić, Dušan. 2017. "SNP Naši – Treći put je garant vladavine narodne većine." https://nasisrbija.org/snp-nasi-treci-put-je-garant-vladavine-narodne-vecine/

Pantić, D. 2007. Prihvaćenost programskih opredeljenja među pristalicama partija. Na primeru nekih aktuelnih spoljnopolitičkih dilema. In *Političke stranke u Srbiji i Evropska unija*, edited by Zoran Lutovac, 299–321. Beograd: Friedrich Ebert Stiftung, Fakultet političkih nauka.

Pavićević, Olivera. 2014. "Nasilje i kultura." *Zbornik Instituta za kriminološka i sociološka istraživanje*, 33 (1), 75–94.

Politika. 2016a. "Albanija i Kosovo izvor džihadista." *Politika*, 3 January, 2016. http://www.politika.rs/sr/clanak/346523/Svet/Albanija-i-Kosovo-izvor-dzihadista

Politika. 2016b. "Komemorativni skup u znak sećanja na srebreničke žrtve." *Politika*, 11 July, 2016. http://www.politika.rs/sr/clanak/358998/Komemorativni-skup-u-znak-secanja-na-srebrenicke-zrtve

Politika. 2016c. "Njujork tajms: Kako je Kosovo postalo regrutna baza za džihadiste." *Politika*, 22 May, 2016. http://www.politika.rs/sr/clanak/355531/Politika/Njujork-tajms-Kako-je-Kosovo-postalo-regrutna-baza-za-dzihadiste

Putvjernika. 2010a. "Srpski sindrom: Marko pije uz ramazan vino." http://putvjernika.com/srpski-sindrom-marko-pije-uz-ramazan-vino/

Putvjernika. 2010b. "Upozorenje muslimanima!" http://putvjernika.com/upozorenje-muslimanima/

Putvjernika. 2010c. "Užas u Bogojnu je djelo stranih obavještajnih službi?" http://putvjernika.com/uas-u-bugojnu-je-djelo-stranih-obavjetajnih-slubi/

Putvjernika. 2012a. "Sram te bilo, Evropo." http://putvjernika.com/sram-te-bilo-evropo/

Putvjernika. 2012b. "Muslimanska čakija za jabuke opasnija od srpskih bombi!" http://putvjernika.com/muslimanska-cakija-za-jabuke-opasnija-od-srpskih-bombi/

Putvjernika. 2013. "Srebrenica u Siriji: Šiitske snage za nekoliko dana izmasakrirale preko 1500 muslimana." http://putvjernika.com/srebrenica-u-siriji-siitske-snage-za-nekoliko-dana-izmasakrirale-preko-1500-muslimana/

Putvjernika. 2015a. "Šejh Imran Husein presudio: U Srebrenici nije bilo genocida!" https://putvjernika.com/sejh-imran-husein-presudio-u-srebrenici-nije-bilo-genocida/

Putvjernika. 2015b. "Šta znači nekoga proglasiti vođom selefija/'vehabija'?" http://putvjernika.com/sta-znaci-nekoga-proglasiti-vodom-selefijavehabija/

Putvjernika. 2016. "Obavezno pročitati: Nevjerovatna sličnost između Titove i današnje 'Islamske zajednice Bosne i Hercegovine'." https://putvjernika.com/obavezno-procitati-nevjerovatna-slicnost-izmedu-titove-i-danasnje-islamske-zajednice-bosne-i-hercegovine/

Putvjernika. 2017a. "Nakon izricanje presude u Hagu, hrvatski fašista umro u bolnici." http://putvjernika.com/nakon-izricanja-presude-u-hagu-hrvatski-fasista-umro-u-bolnici/

Putvjernika. 2017b. "Crkva kao duhovna sigurna kuća za ratne zločince: Patrijarh Irinej stao u odbranu Ratka Mladića." http://putvjernika.com/crkva-kao-duhovna-sigurna-kuca-za-ratne-zlocince-patrijarh-irinej-stao-u-odbranu-ratka-mladica/

Radanović, Milan. 2011. "Istorijska politika u Srbiji nakon 2000. Primeri manifestovanje sprege između akademskog istorijskog revizionizma i državne revizije prošlosti." In *Izgubljeno u tranziciji. Kritička analiza procesa društvene transformacije* A. Veselinović, P. Atanacković, & Ž. Klarić, 258–303. Beograd: Rosa Luxemburg Stiftung.

Regional Cooperation Council. 2016. "Initiatives to Prevent/Counter Violent Extremism in South East Europe." http://www.rcc.int/download/docs/RCC-CVE-Case-Study%20(3).pdf/88adfd3c5fd8007d87bfc2e7ecba2cc2.pdf.

Reisigi, Martin, & Wodak, Ruth. 2009. The discourse-historical approach (DHA). In *Methods for Critical Discourse Analysis* edited by Ruth Wodak, & M. Meyer, 87–121. London: Sage.

Roper, Michael, Dawson, Graham, & Ashplant, T. G. 2000. *The Politics of War Memory and Commemoration*. London: Routledge.

Savez antifašista Srbije. 2018. Interview with author, February 8.

Senusija, Halil. 2014. "Razgovor s dezerterom iz IDIŠ-a" http://www.islambosna.ba/razgovor-s-dezerterom-iz-idis-a/

Simeunović, Dragan & Dolnik, Adam. 2013. "Security Threats of Violent Islamist Extremism and Terrorism for South East Europe and Beyond." In *Shaping South East Europe's Security Community for the Twenty-First Century*, edited by S. Cross, S. Kentera, R. Nation, & R. Vukadinović, (pp. 87–113). London: Palgrave Macmillan.

SNP Naši. 2014. "Radio Slobodna Evropa širi sramnu propagandu i laži o Srebrenici." https://nasisrbija.org/radio-slobodna-evropa-siri-sramnu-propagandu-i-lazi-o-srebrenici/

SNP Naši. 2015. "5 oktobar – dan okupacije Srbije." https://nasisrbija.org/5-oktobar-dan-okupacije-srbije/

SNP Naši. 2016. "Srećan rođendan Đenerale!" https://nasisrbija.org/srecan-rodjendan-djenerale/

SNP Naši. 2017. "Izdajničku DS treba zabraniti, a Tadić mora da dgovara zbog hapšenja Madića." https://nasisrbija.org/izdajnicku-ds-treba-zabraniti-a-tadic-mora-da-odgovara-zbog-hapsenja-mladica/

Srpski pokret obnove. 2008. *Evropska desnica Srbije Program*. Belgrade: Srpski pokret obnove

Stakić, Isidora. 2013. "Odnos Srbije prema ekstremno desničarskim organizacijama." Beograd: Beogradski centar za bezbednosnu politiku.

Stakić, Isidora. 2015. "Securitization of LGBTIQ Minorities in Serbian Far-right Discourses. A Post-structuralist Perspective." *Intersenctions East European Journal of Society and Politics*, 1 (1), 183–206.

Stakić, Isidora. 2017. Interview with author, December 22.

Stanišić, D. 2015. "Radikalni islamisti kampuju kod Donjeg Vakufa." *Politika*, December 12, 2015. http://www.politika.rs/sr/clanak/344928/Region/Radikalni-islamisti-kampuju-kod-Donjeg-Vakufa

Subotić, Jelena. 2009. *Hijacked Justice. Dealing with the Past in the Balkans*. Ithaca: Cornell University Press.

Velimirović, Nikolaj. 2014. "Nacionalizam Svetog Save." http://www.obraz.rs/2015/05/03/nacionalizam-svetog-save/

Vukašinović, S. 2017. "Ekskluzivno otkrivamo istorijska dokumenta Alija počeo, Bakir nastavio: Izetbegović bi da dosanja očev san o Bosni bez Srba." *Blic*, November 20, 2017. https://www.blic.rs/vesti/politika/ekskluzivno-otkrivamo-istorijska-dokumenta-alija-poceo-bakir-nastavio-izetbegovic-bi/ttgvj51.

Winter, Charlie. 2018. "Apocalypse, later: a logitudinal study of the Islamic State brand." *Critical Studies in Media Communication*, 35 (1), 103–121.

Yanow, Dvora. 1999. *Conducting Interpretive Policy Analysis*. London: Sage Publications.

Zavetnici. 2014. "Srpski sabor Zavetnici – Za otadžbinu!" https://www.youtube.com/watch?v=FGOZaTb_RUY

Zavetnici. 2015a. "Zavetnici Kragujevac: Sprečiti skrnavljenje grobova ruskih heroja!" http://zavetnici.rs/?p=4310

Zavetnici. 2015b. "Međunarodna konferencija: "Srbi i Rusi zajedno kroz vekove!" Retrieved from Zavetnici: http://zavetnici.rs/?p=4199

Zavetnici. 2015c. "Skrnavljenjem Valjevske Gračanice vlast urušava identitet srpskog naroda!" http://zavetnici.rs/?p=4128

Zavetnici. 2015e. "Proslavom 'Oluje' vrši se revizija istorijske istine!" http://zavetnici.rs/?p=4092

Zavetnici. 2015f. "Rezolucijom o Srebrenici ugrožava se samostalnost Republike Srpske!" http://zavetnici.rs/?p=3906

Zavetnici. 2015g. "Rehabilitacijom đenerala zadovoljena istoriska pravda!" http://zavetnici.rs/?p=3784

Zavetnici. 2015h. "Okupimo se na Gazimestanu!" http://zavetnici.rs/?p=3867

Zavetnici. 2016a. "Zavetnici o merama za obnovu srpske kulture." http://zavetnici.rs/?p=5360

Zavetnici. 2016b. "Zavetnici obeležili dan ruskih dobrovoljaca!" http://zavetnici.rs/?p=5428

Zavetnici. 2016c. "Haška presuda Radovanu Karadžiću napad na Republiku Srpsku!" http://zavetnici.rs/?p=5192

Zavetnici. 2016d. "Tradicionalni susret Lavrova i Zavetnika!" http://zavetnici.rs/?p=6268

Zavetnici. 2017b. "Zavetnici o presudi generalu Mladiću!" http://zavetnici.rs/?p=7484

Zavetnici. 2017c. "Danijel Igrec: 'Evropski standardi' – drugo ima za ucenjivanje Srbije." http://zavetnici.rs/?p=7477

Zavetnici. 2017c. "Kad ministar policije Srbije zaigra na masovnoj grobnici." http://putvjernika.com/kad-ministar-policije-srbije-zaigra-na-masovnoj-grobnici/

Zavetnici. 2017d. "Oslobađanje Nasera Orića poruka da zločini nad Srbima nisu kažnjivi!" http://zavetnici.rs/?p=7294

Zavetnici. 2017e. "Zavetnici obeležili Vidovdan na srpskom Kosovu i Metohiji!" http://zavetnici.rs/?p=7114

Zavetnici. 2017f. "Hitno pronaći vandale koji su oskrnavili spomenik Caru Nikolaju!" http://zavetnici.rs/?p=7107

Zavetnici. 2017g. "UPOZORENJE: Ne potpisujte peticiju Kandićkinog REKOM-a!" http://zavetnici.rs/?p=6856

Zavetnici. 2018a. "Zavetnici: Podići ćemo spomen kompleks braniocima Beograda i majoru Gavriloviću!" Retrieved from www.zavetnici.rs: http://zavetnici.rs/?page_id=7540

Zavetnici. 2018b. "Zatražiti hitnu sednicu SB UN! Objaviti svetu da je albanski terorizam ponovo aktiviran!" http://zavetnici.rs/?p=7725

Zavetnici. 2017a. "O nama." http://zavetnici.rs/?page_id=7542

Živanić, Jovana. 2017. "Odnos prema naciji organizovanih navijača F.K. Crvene Zvezde – Delija." *Kultura Polisa*, 14 (33), 405–416.

The Eurasian Wings of Serbia: Serbian Affinities of the Russian Radical Right

Ana Dević

> *"Antifascism is for any nationalist an unpleasant reminder of the fact that fascism is an extreme, but in essence, a normalized form of nationalism"* (Kuljić 2018).

Introduction[1]

This chapter addresses the radicalization of Serbian nationalist discourse in the form of the burgeoning of a new Serbian extreme right in the last fifteen years, in relation to its transnational support — namely, its links to Russian academic, para-academic, and political circles. The study seeks to find common historical and social dynamics and denominators of this alliance in their anti-Western (anti-U.S., anti-European Union, and anti-NATO) discursive positions and actions. Three spheres and periods of the Serbian-Russian "alliances" are addressed: 1) support for Serbian nationalism from the era of Milošević to its far-right forms in the area of Russian political science and international relations; 2) post-2000 para-academic links (Aleksandr Dugin's "geopolitics") in the sphere of social science and humanities; and 3) joint patterns of violent or potentially violent far-right activism. The discourse and activities reviewed address the following main themes (although not exclusively): 1) the threat of the "unipolar" post-Cold War political and economic order, represented as the "menace" of the U.S. and its NATO and EU allies, bringing about the corruption of "genuine" national and cultural identities in Serbia and Russia; and 2) protecting Serbia's territorial integrity, where Russia comes as a "natural" stronger partner, due to its allegedly unchanging primordial-historical affinities with Serbia. The two themes are taken as ideal types, as in reality the protagonists routinely merge them: for example, LGBTI people are perceived as corrupting the "right" ethno-

---

1   I am grateful to Valery Perry, Srđan Barišić and Miloš Milenković for their comments on earlier drafts of this chapter.

national and patriarchal "core" of Serbian and Russian peoples, while their sheer presence is also considered an intrusion of a Western "fifth column." As a major issue that transverses the main topics of Russian-Serbian right-wing activism, the chapter also considers the ways in which these groups relate—critically or approvingly—to the current ruling party in Serbia for its positions on the above issues.

Methodology, state of the art in research and clarification of hypotheses

The study relies on a mix of materials: a review of secondary literature, such as academic studies and reports, which come primarily—and significantly—from researchers affiliated with the non-governmental sectors in Serbia and Russia. Here, the emphasis is on defining the political weight of right-wing extremism in the wider context of Serbian (and to a lesser degree Russian) nationalism, in terms of the positioning of relevant stakeholders, such as the state (political parties), the military, and church authorities.[2] The study is also based on a mix of media materials, including print, television, and Internet/online, which reflect the activities of the far-right groups. There is a focus on the "patriotic" media that popularize (are sympathetic toward) far-right groups, those that are neutral, and the media that aim to warn against the harmful activities of the far-right.

The research on violent extremism and radicalization threats in Serbia is still in its nascent stage and is in need of analysis

---

2   In Serbia, the ruling Serbian Progressive Party (*Srpska napredna stranka*) under President Aleksandar Vučić (between 2012 and 2017, he served, twice, as the Prime Minister, as well as Deputy Prime Minister, and as Minister of Defence), forged a political scheme that "swallowed" state institutions and public enterprises. In the words of Marion Kraske, "Opposition and civilian actors are, in spite of all the pro-European lip service, rigorously combated, criminalized, and, not least, threatened" (Kraske 2017). The Progressive Party, however, did not invent the mechanism. An earlier systematic analysis of this process, which grew out of Milošević's 1990s and the disintegration of socialism is presented in Vesna Pešić's *State Capture and Widespread Corruption in Serbia* (Pešić 2007).

through further studies and observations. However, based on available studies and commentaries by local social scientists, such as, among others, Dušan Janjić, Srđan Milošević, Filip Ejdus and Predrag Jureković, and the 2014 volume edited by the Helsinki Committee for Human Rights in Serbia, it is possible to make initial hypotheses about the origins and state of extremism and radicalization.

There are two types and directions of the *nascent extreme right* active in Serbia, which are the product and accompaniment of Serbian ethnic nationalism. The first began during the violent disintegration of Yugoslavia in the 1990s, and its function was to assist the formation of new states through mobilization of the population for wartime violence. One such typical para-state organization that was a carrier of these actions at the time was the Serbian Radical Party (*Srpska radikalna stranka* — SRS). The processes were echoed in other parts of the dissolving Yugoslavia: in Croatia, the counterpart of the SRS was the Croatian Party of Rights (*Hrvatska stranka prava*) with its military faction, the Croatian Defense Force (*Hrvatske obrambene snage* — HOS). The second type, which emerged in the past eighteen years or so, is linked to the wider political and economic European context: the developments in global politics and what is now perceived as the crisis of liberal democracy. The first and most numerous extremist groups (some now outlawed), characteristic of this second type, that came to prominence in Serbia since around 2002 include the National Front, the Serb People's Movement *Naši*, the Serb People's Movement *1389*, and *Obraz* (Honor) (Huseinović 2011). More far-right groups emerged after 2010, which is also the period of the intensification of ties with Russia.

The principal focus of all of these groups, emerging after the NATO military intervention in Serbia, is Kosovo, i.e., the struggle for liberating the "Serbian Jerusalem" from the "alien" Albanian and Muslim rule — hence its Islamophobia, hate speech against Muslims and Albanians, and the anti-US/NATO/European Union attitudes. Another relevant focus of radicalism and (potential) violence of these groups targets the local Roma population and LGBTI community, accompanied by a discourse of racial purity, defense of the "sanctity" of the heterosexual family, and patriarchal relations. An offspring of this type of radicalization is also the more recent right-wing mobilization in response to the war in Ukraine, where dozens of fighters and mercenaries from the post-Yugoslav region joined either Kiev or pro-Russian forces. It has been argued that these groups are linked to several local soccer fan clubs (the violent members of which are often referred to as hooligans), and that they are, significantly, operationalized by the state (and in particular by/through the police) (Đorić 2012). The stark difference between the violence that occurred during the LGBTI Pride Parade in 2010 and the peaceful atmosphere in which it took place in 2017 (and 2018) led several observers to note that it is ultimately the Serbian state that is responsible for both the anti-Pride street violence of the "hooligan" groups in 2010, and their quiescence several years later (Stojanović 2017).

Introduction: the origins of far-right "friendships"

This paper builds upon previous studies that define the recent burgeoning of the radical right in Serbia as a product and synthesis of several characteristics of Serbian nationalism that it developed since the end of its war phase and the fall of Milošević's regime (Biserko 2014; Stakić 2016; Milosavljević 2007). Among these features, two are relevant for understanding the transnational framework of the Serbian radical right: 1) the closer association of Serbian elites and nationalist opposition parties with the Russian political regime and cultural sphere; and 2) the growing importance of the Serbian Orthodox Church as an agent of Serbian nationalism, manifested in its assertiveness in the social sphere and foreign relations, and the accompanying naturalization of a "timeless" (meta-social) religious "brotherhood" between the Serbs and Russians. While one could agree with Stakić (2016, 142–145) that the greater leniency of the Serbian state and elites toward Serbian right-wing groups is a major factor in their radicalization and increasing presence in the popular media and social networks, I would propose that their "normalization" and popularity are also due to the moral, ideological and material support they receive from a plethora of actors in the Russian

Federation. Furthermore, I would propose that the structural and historical causes of such affinity and alliances have to do with the recent shared pressures for nationalist whitewashing of the communist past in both Russia and Serbia, where Serbia found an additional benefit in legitimizing its role in the Yugoslav wars by the cases of the Russian annexation of Crimea and the creation of the Donetsk and Lugansk Republics.

The analysis will address the three spheres in which the affinity and alliances between the Russian and Serbian right wing are being built: academic-ideological (including para-academic), cultural (which in many cases overlap with the academic-ideological), and activist (where the emphasis is on right-wing radical mobilization, including taking part in military actions), which may also overlap with affinities in the cultural sphere.

The stage of the wars and state violence: the 1990s

Before moving to the first stage and forms of the Russian-Serbian far-right "kinship," it is important to note that since the end of the Cold War and throughout the 1990s the interest of Russian politics in Serbia was rather discontinuous. The Russian government supported the international sanctions against Serbia in 1992, as well as the creation of the International Criminal Tribunal for the former Yugoslavia (ICTY). Then, in 1999, following the NATO bombing, Russian troops arrived to the Priština airport from their positions in Bosnia, ahead of and in spite of the impending NATO deployment. After a tense standoff, Russian forces agreed to withdraw and to not claim an independent peacekeeping zone in Kosovo.

To illuminate the rather disjointed interest of Russia in Serbian affairs, it is useful to start from the period of the mid-to-late 1980s, leading to and during the "perestroika" reforms. This was also the moment when in Serbia, for the first time since 1948, there appeared a resurgence of the theme of "brotherhood" between Serbs and Russians in terms of cultural, ethnic, and religious ("spiritual") affinities, limited at first to some intellectual-literary and clerical circles (Deretić 2013). These "culturalist" attitudes in Serbia notwithstanding, official views of the situation in Yugoslavia held by Soviet foreign policy circles at the time were still very much informed by the polarities of the Cold War. Yugoslavia's post-Tito era, with its deepening economic and political crises, was perceived as heading for a state of grave financial indebtedness and political instability, resulting in the end of Yugoslav socialist self-management, pushing its leadership away from its previous Western associations, and driving them closer to the Soviet Union politically.[3] However, the situation in the Soviet Union was also changing rather rapidly with the coming to power of Mikhail Gorbachev, announcing the end of the Cold War confrontation. When Gorbachev visited Yugoslavia in 1988, the impression that the Soviet delegation conveyed to its hosts was that Yugoslavia was considered several steps ahead of the USSR in terms of pursuing the desired reforms of socialism. Emphasizing the high opinion that the new Soviet leadership held of the Yugoslav path of socialism and the Non-Aligned Movement, Gorbachev addressed both U.S. and NATO leaders while standing in the Yugoslav Federal Assembly, asking for a freeze of the arms race in the Mediterranean (Biserko 2008, 8).

The Belgrade visit by Gorbachev, despite its framework of a joint reformist socialist front, in fact brought about a renewed ethnicization, clericalization, and mystification of Serbian-Russian relations. The Serbian Orthodox Church publicized at the time the fact (or "fact") that Gorbachev belonged to the family of churchgoers, while the painter Milić of Mačva portrayed Gorbachev as Archangel Michael dressed in a Serbian folk costume. Bishop Danilo Krstić wrote in the main church newsletter, "We Serbs respect all peoples, but love Greeks and Russians above all others…" (Biserko 2008, 9).

The cosmopolitan anti-Cold War stances held by Gorbachev and foreign minister Eduard Shevardnadze at the time were by no means shared across all sectors of the Soviet elites. The orientations

---

3   Raif Dizdarević, a former high-ranking politician and diplomat, the foreign minister of Yugoslavia in the late 1980s, states in his memoirs that the Institute of Social Studies of the Russian Academy of Sciences had prepared a policy paper with such predictions (Dizdarević 1999, 12, 167).

and agendas of the Soviet military were quite opaque, which became apparent during the 1991 army coup attempt against Gorbachev, which was internationally supported only by the top Yugoslav Army generals, themselves plotting a military coup in Yugoslavia.[4] Following the breakdown of the USSR, during the first half of the 1990s of the Yeltsin era, positions toward the ex-Yugoslav space and the wars raging there were rather vague. The situation changed decisively in 1996, when Evgenii Primakov became the Minister of Foreign Affairs, chastising the "bowing of Russia before the West", and charting his doctrine of multipolarity, with a plan to build a strategic three-way axis between Russia, China and India. From this moment on, the official stance of Russia was to support Slobodan Milošević and Serbia's positioning in the post-Dayton Accords space (Vignjević 1997).

During this beginning stage of active Russian interest in Serbia, the main point of concern for this paper is the work and activities of Yelena Gus'kova, an historian and international relations specialist, and the head of the Center for Balkan Crisis at the Institute of Slavistics of the Russian Academy of Sciences. Gus'kova's extensive visits to Serbia, starting from the mid-1990s, corresponded with the onset of new foreign orientations of the Kremlin, i.e., the reestablishment of a powerful position vis-a-vis the European Union, NATO, and the U.S. In 1994–1995, Gus'kova worked as a fieldwork expert in the office of the UN Special Envoy Yasushi Akashi in Zagreb, which resulted in a volume she edited, "Our Peacemakers in the Balkans" (Gus'kova 2007), in which she laments the period of the first half of the 1990s, when Russian observers in the region were very few and disinterested in supporting the Serbian cause in the war. She reports on her meetings with Radovan Karadžić and Ratko Mladić, and their shared disappointment in the actions of the Russian foreign minister Andrei Kozyrev. She praises

---

4   In the spring of 1991, the Yugoslav federal secretary of national defense, General Veljko Kadijević, visited in secret his Soviet counterparts Yazov and Kryuchkov, seeking their approval for the planned military coup in Yugoslavia. On the day of the attempted coup in the USSR, in August 1991, Mihajlo Marković, the president of Milošević's (ruling) Socialist Party, sent his greetings to the generals that aimed to oust Mikhail Gorbachev (Vasić 2005).

Mladić's simple "rural philosophy," and quotes him saying that he would "finish" the problems that Russia has with its "Turks" (Chechens) in two weeks (Bulatović/Gus'kova 1996). A decade later, Slobodan Milošević extensively used Gus'kova's book "The Yugoslav Crisis" (Gus'kova 1993) for his defense at the ICTY. At the Tribunal, Gus'kova acted as a defense witness for Bosnian Serb general Stanislav Galić, who was found guilty of acts of violence and terror (indiscriminate shelling and sniping) against civilians in Sarajevo. Starting from the late 1990s, Gus'kova concentrated on academic visits to Serbia, where she became a member of the Serbian Academy of Sciences in 2007. She was also invited to Serbia through diplomatic channels, giving presentations in the *Russian House* in Belgrade (a cultural institute, attached to the Russian diplomatic mission).

The downfall of Milošević's regime: post-2000

Starting from the fall of Milošević's regime in 2000, Gus'kova transferred her allegiances to the extreme nationalist Serbian Radical Party of Vojislav Šešelj, focusing on the Kosovo issue, intensifying her support for anti-NATO and anti-Western attitudes in Serbia, and lamenting over the marginalization of Vojislav Koštunica and domination of Zoran Đinđić in the elite constellation after 2000. In interviews given to the Serbian press, Gus'kova warned against the loss of the Serbian "heroic identity" of the 1990s. She argues that the 1999 NATO bombing could not bring down Milošević's regime and the Serbian Army, due to their heroic struggle and broad support among ordinary Serbs, so Western powers had to resort to different means of overthrowing the Serbian regime (Gus'kova 2004). Gus'kova argues that the EU and the U.S. pumped millions of dollars into building the resistance movement "*Otpor*" in Serbia as a prototype for future "colored revolutions" elsewhere, where, she argued, allegedly no popular resistance against ruling regimes could be found. Further, NATO and the U.S. created a sort of dependence by post-Milošević' elites on Western support, and made the Serbs, as Gus'kova laments, "forget who bombed them." With regard to the secession of Montenegro from Serbia in 2006,

Gus'kova argues that this act was prepared by the U.S. as well, to guarantee the safety of its military bases in the Mediterranean and Kosovo, and prepare for future NATO enlargement.

> "Therefore, by joining NATO, the Balkan states will force Serbia, Montenegro, Macedonia and Republika Srpska to take an anti-Russian stand. We do have something to pause and think about, we — Slav brothers."

Following the voluntary surrendering of Vojislav Šešelj to the ICTY in 2003, and especially after the split in the Serbian Radical Party, with Aleksandar Vučić and Tomislav Nikolić, formerly first aides to Šešelj, forming a new conservative, "moderate-nationalist" party (*Srpska Napredna Stranka*, SNS), Gus'kova started paying greater attention to developments in the Republika Srpska within Bosnia and Herzegovina. The parliament of the Bosnian Serb statelet appointed Gus'kova as an honorary member of its Senate, which gave her a new launching pad for renewed involvement in Serbian foreign affairs. Gus'kova now presents Milorad Dodik, the president of the Republika Srpska, as a model Balkan politician, replacing the "betrayed" Milošević and Šešelj. Dodik, in her view, made the people of Republika Srpska united, and will lead their country (sic) to become a new Serb Piedmont in the Balkans.[5] Moreover, Gus'kova sees Dodik as a politician with courage, who was able to say "no" to Western powers since 2006 (when they attempted to transfer more powers from Republika Srpska to the Federation), and asks: Why it is not the case with Serbia?

> "In contrast to Aleksandar Vučić, Dodik is the one who takes care of Serbs in different states. Vučić only pays attention to what the West tells him... The government in Belgrade cannot balance between the European Union and NATO, on the one hand, and its relations with Russia, on the other... Serbs are a good people, and lucky are those who were able to know them... The truth about Srebrenica and the Balkan war will come to light, and, with

---

5 Serbia's Piedmontese role was once (since the end of the 19th century until the end of WWI) defined by its political activists and elites as an agenda to unite all South Slav people in one state (Yugoslavia). In a dark twist or irony, the current "Piedmont" role of the Republika Srpska is to unite Serbs only, and, thus, dismantle the Dayton Agreement, as Milorad Dodik frequently proclaims during his visits to Serbia.

the help of Russia, the truth will be recorded for the future generations of politicians and historian alike" (Gus'kova 2018a).

Dodik's October 2018 election as the Serb member of Bosnia's triple-headed presidency can be expected to further reflect and exploit these dynamics and affinities.

Echoing the principal tunes of Serbian right-wing, extreme nationalist parties since the 1990s—about the ICTY being an "anti-Serb court," and praising Ratko Mladić as a national hero (for both Serbs and Russians)—Gus'kova frequently switches between her roles as an advocate for Serbian wartime policies and her pragmatic view of the current situation in Serbia from the official perspective of the Kremlin:

> "Russia will not oppose what Serbia decides. If your government decides to recognize Kosovo's independence and calls the Kremlin to say "we are forced to do it," Moscow will support you. But let's take a different scenario: Belgrade tells Moscow: "We will recognize Kosovo, but you should block its membership in the UN Security Council so that we don't look guilty"... I remember the 1990s here when the talk was: We will never give up on Kosovo. We'll die, but not give it away. What Moscow does is right. Russian authorities stick to their rule of maintaining relations with the elected government, and they will never support the opposition. Its current strategy is directed to keeping the peace here, not pushing Serbia toward Russia" (Gus'kova 2018b).

In her expanding support for the "Piedmont role" of Milorad Dodik (thus, advocating the division of Bosnia-Herzegovina) and Vojislav Šešelj (whom she visited, as a victorious hero, in his home immediately upon his return from The Hague), and in treading a fine line between the radical nationalist and official Russian line vis-à-vis Kosovo, Gus'kova may seem to be creating ideological confusion about the policies of Russia in Serbia. The flip side of this may be that she is actually *affirming* strategic choices that Russia maintains vis-à-vis Serbia, regardless of what Belgrade may ultimately do. I would further argue that this mix-up of affirmative stances (being both for, and against the official European Union aspirations of the ruling Serbian Progress Party), facilitates support and legitimacy for the ideas and actions of Serbian far-right groups who extol Russia as their ally.

Eurasian ideological consolidations: Aleksandr Dugin in Serbia

Following the longtime presence of Gus'kova in Serbia as a foreign relations expert and interpreter of Russian policies in the Balkans, the second tier of Russian ideological concentration in Serbia comes in the face of Aleksandr Dugin, a philosopher and sociologist, and creator of the notion of "Eurasian geopolitics." Dugin first came to prominence in Russia when he, together with the (once) dissident writer Eduard Limonov,[6] formed the National-Bolshevik Party in 1994, a direct-action movement that was supposed to unify the radical left and radical right and dismantle the regime of Boris Yeltsin. Following several mostly comic attempts to disrupt the office routine of the Kremlin (Eduard Limonov, in an article he was invited to write for an anarchist portal based in the U.S. and Canada, called it "punk" or subcultural activism),[7] the National Bolshevik Party was banned in 2007, with Dugin then pursuing his academic career. His earliest interests in Serbia can be found on the Russian web site Srpska.ru, which is dedicated to the common Christian Orthodox, monarchist, political (Kosovo, Ukraine, Donetsk Republic), and right-wing views that Russia and Serbia share. Srpska.ru (now defunct) had links to several Serbian right-wing groups' web sites.

In the spring of 2008, writing before the general elections in Serbia and following the declaration of the independence of Kosovo, Dugin introduced what he saw as a "major turning point in Serbian politics." At the same time, a news presenter of the Russian state TV channel, speaking about the fifth anniversary of the assassination of Serbian Prime Minister Zoran Đinđić, called him (Đinđić), "a Western marionette," who deserved the bullet (Blic

---

6   Limonov is known in the post-Yugoslav region mostly for his famous visit to the hills above the besieged Sarajevo, where he came to take part in the "Pale Poetry evening" in 1992. Delivering his greetings to Radovan Karadžić, "on behalf of the Russian people and all free people of the world," he then begged to be allowed to fire a machine gun at Sarajevo, his wish granted (Halimović 2016).

7   One such action was the "occupation" of the Bolshoi Theater on May 7, 2004, the day Putin was inaugurated. Putin was supposed to arrive in the Bolshoi that evening, so National-Bolsheviks first appeared on stage, and then occupied the presidential box (Limonov 2011).

2008). Comparing the agendas of the Serbian Radical Party, the former Prime Minister Vojislav Koštunica, and the Democratic Party leader Boris Tadić, Dugin foresaw that if the latter remained in power, Serbia would join the European Union and would have to pay the price—Kosovo will then be "betrayed." Further, he proposed that:

> "(T)he factor of Russia, it seems, will be the decisive one. If the Serbs would feel that Russia truly supports them, then the overwhelming majority will vote for Tomislav Nikolić or Koštunica, and for other groups from the patriotically-motivated political block" (Dugin 2008).

In March 2008, Dugin visited the University of Belgrade, taking part in the conference "Russia and the Balkans: Current Issues on Security and Cooperation," organized by the Faculty of Law. There, he introduced Serbian audiences to his theory of "Eurasian geopolitical realities," where a small state like Serbia can assume the role of the biblical David, waking, first, the sleeping giant "brother" (Russia), as well as China, and saving itself and others from "the continuous sadism and humiliations of the U.S. and its satellites, and also provoking a powerful wave of reactions and inciting a new historical process" (Dugin 2008).

According to Dugin, geopolitical turns can occur quite unexpectedly, as seen in the case of Russia, which has been seeking to regain its position as a world power since Vladimir Putin assumed leadership. Speaking to the Serbs, Dugin argued that the case of Kosovo, similar to that of separatist Chechnya in Russia, can trigger a new balance of powers, where Serbia will start a global process and Russia will assist it. The participation of Serbia in the "multipolar world order" (Dugin 1997), appears to be, according to Dugin, the only chance that Serbia has to build its political future. According to this scheme of recognizing the "correct geopolitical course," the "hasty" movement of Serbia toward joining the European Union can bring about not only the loss of Kosovo, but can trigger further dismantling of Serbia—the secession of Vojvodina and Sandžak—and the disappearance of Republika Srpska in Bosnia.

Apart from the strategic-political affinities, Dugin's scheme recognizes the second foundation of the special Serbian geopolitical place—its primordial complementarities with Russia.

> "Russians love their leaders, whom they deem "sacred," whereas Serbs consider sacred their people. This is the reason why Russians respect and value Serbs, along with their freedom-loving and patriotic traditions" (Dugin 1997).

Dugin's visits to Serbian academic arenas became more frequent since 2008, and have been regularly accompanied with interviews with conservative, right-wing, tabloid, clerical orthodox, but also mainstream media, tabloids, and portals in Serbia, such as *Pravda*, *Vaseljenska*, *SRBski FBReporter*, *Srbin.info*, *Patriot*, *Informer*, and the oldest daily *Politika*. While Dugin had registered his Eurasian Movement as a party in Russia in 2001, his activities in the movement were mainly realized in writing a dozen volumes dedicated to the unleashing of "just" world conflicts to end the "Western" military and capitalist dominance and order, which he calls "Atlanticism," and establish a timeless multicenter old-new Eurasian empire.[8] He has regularly served as a political advisor to several MPs of the ruling party (United Russia), while heading the sociology department at Moscow State University. His formal academic duties ended after he delivered a lecture on the Ukrainian crisis, offering the following solution: "Kill them, kill them, kill them. There should not be any more conversations. As a professor, I consider it so" (UNIAN 2014). Mass student protests ensued, and Dugin was dismissed from the university.

During the same period Dugin's visits to Serbia became more frequent, while his geopolitics, as presented to Serbian audiences, started including more criticisms of the pro-European course of the ruling Serbian Progress Party and more insistence on the fateful role that Serbia must assume as "the Western avant-garde of our Eurasianism." In a lengthy interview entirely dedicated to Serbia, which he gave in 2017 in Belgrade to the Serbian desk of *The News*

---

8 More on Dugin's works can be found on the web site *Geopolitika.ru* (in five languages, including Serbian), run by Dugin's main collaborator, Leonid Savin.

Front agency, a Russian state-backed media outlet based in Crimea, Dugin explained why Serbia occupies a special and historically continuous role in the task of building a Eurasian empire:

> "It was not by accident that the Russian Eurasian White emigres were here in Belgrade. Serbia was not chosen by accident. It is our observation point in the Balkans... We interpret it as a Eurasian mission of Serbia: to become a center of dialogues... In other words, it is not a narrow nationalism, but a profound determination of the Serb identity, with its unique mystical dimensions, its fiery love, a dramatic and bloody, but also beautiful Orthodox history, the history of sacrifice and audacity, wars, defeats, great victories, the creation of the empire of Dušan the Mighty" (Dugin 2017).

In this mission, Serbia will need and get Russian help, posits Dugin. Here, the *Eurasians* pursue a similar, seemingly paradoxical, line to that of Gus'kova. While the current Presidency of Aleksandar Vučić is suspected of "selling" Kosovo, simultaneously, the support that Putin's government is providing to Vučić is considered beneficial, as it supposedly guarantees the *internal* legitimacy of Vučić and his coalition partners who are dealing with the vague promises of prosperity of the European Union.

> "Perhaps, Europe can offer some economic support. However, the people will not see it, but will get only debts, as it was in Greece... And, on top of it, they will have to give Kosovo in return... What can we do? Those who want to preserve their territorial sovereignty, like Assad, what does he do: 'Vladimir Vladimirovich, I am making an alliance with you.' Vladimir Vladimirovich replies: 'We will fly to you.' It is a fact. But the U.S. does not guarantee territorial integrity to its allies. It is a rule that has nothing particular vis-à-vis Serbia. But if Mr. Vučić evaluates this tenet correctly, if he understands what will happen with his government headed by such a progressive lady (sic)[9] if Kosovo will get its independence from Serbia. I think that Americans have it in their plans — the new wave of civil riots, protests, and the disintegration of Serbia... At some point (Vučić) will confront the decision of how he will go down in history: as a miserable traitor, who betrayed the interests of his state, to be cursed for centuries (and to Serbs, it is important!), or he will join the Eurasian union. It is, of course, a radical step, but it means saving the state... Russia today is in such shape that this decision is not as risky as it would have been before" (Dugin 2017).

---

9 He means (imputing his own style of sarcasm) Ana Brnabić, an openly gay Serbian prime minister.

Since 2017, Dugin and his associates began building a new (para-) academic niche in Serbia. Upon the invitation of the Dean of the Faculty of International Politics of the private university "Union Nikola Tesla," Dugin and his associates held a conference in Belgrade in June 2017 entirely dedicated to Eurasianism. The conference became a building block of the new Belgrade School of Geopolitics, initiated and staffed by the Center for Strategic Prognoses from Belgrade and the International Eurasian Movement from Moscow (both organizations are NGOs). The new School, according to Dugin, aims at "building new sovereign and independent Balkan elites, who will not be pawns in the hands of mighty states" (Bilbija 2017). The main Belgrade daily *Politika* introduced Dugin as an influential advisor to Putin. However, when asked to comment on this attribute, Dugin vaguely replied:

> "Officially it is not so. If you observe the relationship between my philosophical and political thought and Putin's actions, you can see that they are in a state of mutual correspondence, they follow one another. How this is happening, I do not wish to talk about. I make efforts to reflect the positions of our nation and give them an intellectual form" (Bilbija 2017).

Between the fall of 2017 and February 2018, there were four cycles of lectures held in Belgrade as part of the School of Geopolitics. The participating institutions included, apart from the stated "Union Tesla" University whose dean gave a keynote address, faculty from the Law and Political Science Faculties of Belgrade State University. While the main topics of the lectures dealt with the "organization of ideas" (of the geopolitical system) and the structure of thought within their traditional and culturological frameworks, as well as the conflicts between them, Dugin also gave interviews to various papers and portals about the role of Serbia in the new geopolitical order:

> "Serbia, for me, is not only solar; it is also made of fire and flames. The Spiritual Serbia is eternal.... It cannot be defeated because Serb people are unique. (In) the case that Serbia would ask to become a member of the Eurasian Economic Union and the Collective Security Treaty Organization, Russia would have to consider this request, given the will of the people" (Dugin 2017).

The ties of far-right activists

As presented above, since the late 2000s, Aleksandr Dugin's ideas of the "post-Western" empire(s) acquired a special "Serbian twist," and subsequently became popular in a range of Serbian media and, gradually, in a segment of local academia. While it cannot be claimed that Dugin and his associates have *directly* collaborated with members of Serbian far-right nationalist groups, the fact remains that the gist of "Eurasianist" ideas about "race/ethnicity," territorial integrity, "Eastern" versus "Atlanticist" (NATO) civilizations, and the role of the Orthodox Church in the "defense" of traditional "timeless" identities are imported in the value system of most Serbian far-right groups. Most importantly, the message that Russia legitimizes and that it will support Serbia's "natural" right to keep Kosovo in its state jurisdiction, in complete disregard of the context in which Kosovo Albanians had pursued their new state since the late 1980s, presents a principal and refurbished primordial basis for the mobilization of the far-right in Serbia. The final important objective that Dugin's geopolitics offers to the Serbian far-right is that it must search for a new continuation with the wartime ideology and activities of the Serbian Radical Party, after the fading of Šešelj's charisma and the apparent betrayal of his former main hardline disciples and ethnic hatred-mongers, now Euro-centrists, Vučić and Nikolić. The ambiguity running through Dugin's (and Gus'kova's before him) opinions of the position of Aleksandar Vučić is replicated in the stances of many new far-right radical groups, who condemn Vučić's pro-European policies, while, for the most part, considering him (still) a devout and aggressive nationalist who would not "sell" Kosovo. The proof of this double game of Vučić they find in the support that he receives from "mother Russia," strong and confidently anti-American under Putin.

The activists' ties

The history of close ties between the Russian and Serbian far-right groups commences with Ilya Goryachev, a one-time assistant in the Russian Duma to Vladimir Zhirinovsky, the less violent Russian counterpart of Šešelj. In 2002, Goryachev, still a history undergraduate, came to Belgrade to study the crimes of the ustaša regime in the WWII Independent State of Croatia. While still studying in Moscow, Goryachev was a member of the far-right parliamentary party *National Alliance*, which had close ties with a mix of right-wing intellectuals and party figures in Serbia, mostly around the International Committee for Truth about Radovan Karadžić. This circle of Serbian friends was most likely his prime host once he landed in Serbia, which then introduced him to the leader of one of the oldest far-right groups in Serbia, *Otačastveni Pokret Obraz* (Fatherland Movement Honor), and its leader Mladen Obradović. The meeting with the latter inspired Goryachev to such an extent that, upon returning to Russia, he started the Russian faction of Serbian *Obraz*. As is the case with Russian ideologues of the "special place of Serbia in Russian and world geopolitics," for Goryachev, too, Vojislav Šešelj was the most promising politician of the Serbian political spectrum in the early-to-mid 2000s (until his departure for the ICTY). Upon Goryachev's initiative, Šešelj became an honorary citizen of Moscow. During one of his visits back in Serbia, in 2012, Goryachev, along with the leader of the far-right Italian *Forza Nuova* Roberto Fiore, and a member of the banned neo-Nazi Serbian group National Alignment (*Nacionalni stroj*), made a ceremonial visit to the Serbian Parliament, as a guest of the Serbian Radical Party. The concrete proof of the fact that Russian *Obraz* has close ties to Russian authorities is its connections with Maksim Mishchenko, a one-time Deputy of the president of the Russian Duma, who was invited to Belgrade in 2009 as a guest speaker at the mass gathering in the center of the city, commemorating the tenth anniversary of the NATO bombing (Byford 2010).

The Russian branch of *Obraz* followed its Serbian model in a number of ways. Goryachev started a newsletter patterned after the Serbian *Obraz*, where its first issue featured a Benetton company advertisement showing a bunch of young people of different ethnicities embracing, with a slogan written over it: "This is genocide, too." The Serbian *Obraz* was formally banned by a Serbian court in 2012, following the violence that its members incited and took part in during the Belgrade Pride Parade in 2010. Its leader, Mladen Obradović, was sentenced to two years in prison for violent threats and hate speech (the sentence was suspended a year later, and a new *Obraz* later resurfaced with a different name, with no legal action taken against them). The Russian *Obraz* continued its activities, with Goryachev and his comrade Nikita Tikhonov (also a one-time visiting student in Belgrade) founding in 2012 the Right-Conservative Alliance (*Pravo-konservativny al'yans*). The founding conference of the movement in Moscow was greeted by a number of radical right, racist and anti-immigrant groups from around Europe, including the Serbian Radical Party, the Greek Golden Dawn, and English Democrats (Evgeny Valyaev 2012). In the same year, Ilya Goryachev fled to Serbia after a warrant was issued by a Russian court, charging him with a conspiracy to murder. In 2013, Goryachev was extradited to Russia and sentenced to life imprisonment for his involvement in five murders on ideological grounds (the victims included journalists, antifascist activists, and people who "looked non-Russian" (BBC World 2015). Undoubtedly, Goryachev and his associate Tikhonov (who was also sentenced to life) took some inspiration in the far-right milieu of Serbia, where a thirteen-year old Roma boy was killed by neo-Nazi skinheads in 1997, and then, in 2000, a Serbian actor was beaten unconscious for "looking Roma," and subsequently died from injuries (Beta 2017).

To illustrate the connections between Serbian far-right groups and (Russian) authorities, it is worth pointing to a photo that the Serbian *Obraz* pinned on its web site in 2010, the same year they staged violence and vandalism on the streets of Belgrade in protest against the Pride Parade. Following the festivity celebrating the Kosovo Battle Day/Saint Vitus Day at the Gazimestan field in the northern part of Kosovo, a dozen *Obraz* members took a picture with the Russian Ambassador to Belgrade, Aleksandr Konuzin, in a brotherly embrace. It is difficult to imagine that Ambassador Konuzin did not know that the counterparts of the Serbian *Obraz* in Moscow were at the time already charged with brutal murders (Byford 2010).

After the outlawing of *Obraz,* the most prominent far-right group in Serbia became the Serbian National Movement *Naši*

(Ours), which was modelled after its Russian far-right original counterpart.[10] Both the Russian and Serbian *Naši* programs are evidently inspired by Aleksandr Dugin's Eurasianism, as they advocate an Euro-Asian "civilizational axis" of several capital cities, which include Belgrade, Saint Petersburg, Kyiv, and Almaty. Like the other far-right group that achieved prominence after the banning of *Obraz*, the Serbian National Movement *1389* (founded in 2004), *Naši*'s principal goal is "liberating and uniting all Serbian territories," "occupied in the 1990s wars," and including Northern Albania and Macedonia. The principal enemies of the movement, and the "civilizations" that they represent, are, predictably, the U.S., NATO, the European Union, LGBTI people, and "gay lobbies" (SNP 1389, various program texts on the portal).

In 2013, the Serbian *Naši* visited Moscow as guests of the Russian group called the *Kosovo Front*, whose leader, Alexander Kravchenko, took part in the war in Bosnia-Herzegovina as part of a Serbian paramilitary unit. As their Facebook page narrates, the *Kosovo Front* extols the might of the Russian Army, its engagement in Syria, and celebrates prospects for military exercises with their "Serbian brethren" with occasional photos of some joint sport or army-like training, with or without weapons.[11] During the visit, the *SNP Naši* sought to meet with Russian conservative policy experts to seek help for their plan to prepare a law that would ban foreign-funded non-governmental organizations (as "Western agents"), and install a one-hundred year ban on LGBTI public activities, modeled after the Russian law that prohibits Pride parades as examples of "gay propaganda."[12]

The SNP *Naši* delegation was counseled by a Russian Orthodox priest in the Trinity Lavra of St. Sergius, the largest pilgrimage and monastic center in Russia (located near Moscow), who introduced them to a special blend of spiritual and military survival exercises practiced on the temple premises. Upon learning that there

---

10   Ivanović's chapter in this volume provides a useful summary of these various groups in Serbia, in the context of their online activity.
11   https://www.facebook.com/kosovski.front.ru/
12   Most of these actions are recounted at the web site of *Naši*: https://nasisrbija.org/ and their Facebook page https://www.facebook.com/snpnasi/

were around three thousand such church-military societies in Russia, gathering teenage and older youth, the Serbian *Naši* vouched that they would establish such clubs in Serbia as well. The remarkable detail of the Russian *Naši* is that they became part of the Russian Federal Agency of Youth Affairs (*Rossmolodezh*), state-funded and officially endorsed by President Putin. Another sociological peculiarity of the Russian *Naši* is that their leader Vasiliy Yakemenko was a member of the infamous *Lyuberi* street gang, active in the late eighties. The Russian *Naši* have now added "antifascist" to their name, to align themselves with the standard Russian WWII patriotic frame, while their most visible activities include patrolling the streets in search of "too Western" looking youth (in their clothing or the manner of speech and behavior) whom they verbally and physically attack in the name of preserving the "local ways." They are also known for fighting the real and suspected opponents of the Russian regime during street demonstrations (Ninković 2013).

Among the recent arrivals at the Serbian right-wing nationalist scene is *Zavetnici* (Oath Bearers) (whose name refers to the oath of preserving Kosovo as the Serbian heartland), which became visible in the media in June 2017, when a dozen of their members (plus *Mlada Srpska Snaga*/Young Serbian Power) gathered in Novi Sad and then in Belgrade, shouting in protest against the screening of the antinationalist documentary film "Kosovo... Nazdravlje! Gezuar!"[13] They succeeded in making the screenings impossible, while their leader Milica Đurđevic explained their protest in the following manner:

> "We deem that it is unthinkable to allow that in the center of Belgrade we have a festival organized for the fourth time that promotes the independence of Kosovo, and which represents some sort of an autochthonous Kosovo culture, which does not exist, and which had never existed... (T)he only cultural trait that Albanians left are the Serbian sacred sites which they destroyed" (Živanović 2017).

The links between *Zavetnici* and Russian state officials are well documented, as the group members are proud to publicize them. On

---

13 *Nazdravlje* is "cheers" or "to your health" in Serbian; *Gezuar* means the same in Albanian.

one occasion of their frequent visits to the Russian Duma, where they were received by the representatives of the ruling party United Russia, they presented the platform of their movement and expressed their gratitude to the hosts for the "great efforts that they are making to create a Serbian lobby in the Duma of the Russian Federation" (In4s 2017).

Armed connections

The evidence of the participation of Serb volunteer fighters in Donbass, in the separatist statelets of Lugansk and Donetsk, is abundant, but comprehensive reporting of their engagement is rather rare. One such story came on RuSerbia.com around the same time that the School of Geopolitics took place in Belgrade in early 2018. One of Aleksandr Dugin's principal associates, Aleksei Gintovt, spoke during his lecture about the numerous Serbs he had welcomed in his home while they were on their way to Donbass to assist their Russian "brethren." During the same week, RuSerbia.com published a lengthy interview with "Deki," a certain mayor Dejan Berić, volunteer fighter of the Donetsk People's Republic (DPR), the most celebrated and awarded "foreigner" in the DPR. While Deki is accused of terrorism by Ukrainian authorities, NATO, and the Western press, he is famous with his Russian hosts, and was awarded the medal, "For the Return of Crimea" by the Russian Defense Minister Sergei Shoigu. Deki is running a school for sniper fighters, and is in charge of security for the DPR president Aleksandr Zakharchenko,[14] who told the portal interviewer the follow-

---

14 On August 31, 2018, Zakharchenko was murdered in a Donetsk café "Separ" (a jovial slang word in Russian for "separatist") in an explosion of a planted device. While he was not the first on the list of Donbass separatist leaders killed in recent years, his death prompted a customary exchange of accusations between Kiev and Moscow. The media in Serbia, Croatia and Bosnia and Herzegovina dedicated ample space to reporting on Zakharchenko's assassination and the support that Vladimir Putin expressed for the Donbass people on this occasion, also mentioning that there were plans in Russia of replacing him with a leader more presentable to the West, and the possibility that he was a victim of infighting among the Donbass strongmen.

ing about Deki and his compatriots: "Serbs made a massive contribution to our struggle, and we will never forget it. Deki is a legendary person. Thank you for your prayers, it all means a lot to us." Mayor Deki complained to the interviewer that Ukrainian officials accused him and the DPR leadership of recruiting a group of Serb volunteers, who, as Deki explained, were possibly enlisted by "our treacherous rulers in Belgrade," (he meant Aleksandar Vučić's Serbian Progress Party), in order to compromise our cause here (Savićević 2018).

Echoing the mentioned ambivalent and shifting stances of Yelena Gus'kova, starting from the mid-2000s mayor Deki has also shown his respect for the leader of the Republika Srpska statelet, Milorad Dodik, whom he sees fighting a similar struggle as the Donetsk and Lugansk Russians. No respect seems to be left for the "Westernized" authorities in Belgrade when the situation in Ukraine is considered, despite the fact that friendly ties between Russia and Serbia are acknowledged as an eternal and sacred matter — that awaits a more pro-Russian (or Eurasian) leader than Vučić.

The most recent instance of a potentially violent group radicalization with ties to Russia was observed during the celebration of the unconstitutional "statehood day" of Republika Srpska in Banja Luka on January 9, 2018. Around thirty men dressed in full fatigues with the insignia "*Srbska čast*" (Serb Honor) appeared on the streets of Banja Luka throughout the day, posing for a photo with a billboard and official logo of the Russian veterans' association "Inheritors of victory" (*Nasledniki pobedy*) in the background (Er. M./Klix.ba 2018). Responding to accusations launched from the side of the Bosnian Federal Security Minister Dragan Mektić that they were preparing a paramilitary unit in Republika Srpska, being trained in the Russian military camp in the Serbian city of Niš (officially — the Russian Humanitarian Aid Center), the leader of the group, Bojan Stojković replied that *Srbska čast* was a humanitarian organization, while posting a photo of himself with a machine gun on his Instagram profile. There, he wrote under a photo of Vladimir Putin: "For such a president, it is worth it to give one's life," and under Milorad Dodik's photo, a rhyme from a popular Serbian (pseudo-) folk song: "Nobody can do us any harm, we are stronger than destiny" (Borger 2018).

In lieu of conclusions: preliminary policy recommendations

The contacts between Serbian and Russian far-right organizations pose a number of important questions, particularly concerning their relationships with respective state agencies and the evaluation of the degree of threat they may carry. This study aims to present a sociological actor-centered (rather than security-oriented) picture of the connections between the far-right groups in Russia and Serbia, arguing that in order to understand how and why a number of radical nationalist and violent right-wing groups in Serbia develop ties with Russian like-minded organizations, one must look at the specific historical, ideological and political contexts over the past quarter of a century.

Following in the footsteps of Jovan Byford and Jovo Bakić's analyses, one can conclude that a main reason for the affinity and cooperation between the far-right groups in Russia and Serbia lie in their shared "freedom" to articulate and instrumentalize their connections with hooligan sport fan clubs and various neo-Nazi organizations (Byford 2010; Bakić 2013). Their liberty and ability to engage in racist, nationalist, and homophobic violence, which spans a wide range of activities, from interrupting film screenings to beating or launching racist slurs at Roma and African American football players, to volunteering in the Donbass separatist war, stems from the fact that they are fully aware of the protracted proceedings in Serbian courts that often end in acquittals or lenient rulings for the perpetrators. The case of *Obraz*, which was banned and was then able to regroup and rename itself, is quite indicative. The atmosphere of lenience and the "relaxed" approach of the judiciary and mainstream political parties also explain why Serbia has become an attractive destination for gatherings and possible joint activities of far-right xenophobic, racist, and anti-immigrant groups from Britain, Italy, and Greece. (See also Rečević's contribution in this volume.)

Recent examples illustrate the state of the grey zone between mainstream Serbian politics and extremism. In her interview to the Belgrade daily *Danas*, analyst Isidora Stakić shows that Serbian state organs use different standards to prosecute Serbian citizens who participate in combat abroad: those who fight in Syria are being accused of "taking part in terrorist activities," while the combatants caught upon returning from Ukraine (Donbass) are charged with "participating in an armed combat on the territory of a different state". While four Serbian ex-fighters from Syria are serving sentences, not a single returnee from Ukraine has been imprisoned (Živanović 2018). Hence, one of the main recommendations for future reforms would be to create mechanisms for unraveling and progressively eradicating the current grey zone between Serbian mainstream politics and extremism.[15] The goal would be to stimulate changes in the role and tasks of the state, which is currently being usurped by one political party, and which has created a shadow system of rule. In this constellation, the growing and radicalizing far-right seems to loyally serve that party-state, while occasionally, when necessary, acting as its controlled opposition. Rebuilding the system of the functioning state and its institutions, including a properly functioning parliament, would be crucial for diminishing the capacity for violent and disruptive action of radical right groups.

As for international efforts, mainly coming from the European Union, it is discouraging to see that not much has been done so far, and hence, local (progressive) civil society activists are not very hopeful. Considering legislation on ethnic, racist, or gender discrimination, EU regulations are not very specific, and much is left to national legislatures to formulate and monitor. For example, only Germany of all EU states severely punishes all forms of race and ethnic discrimination, including public denials of the Holocaust. Hence the fate of neo-Nazi groups, e.g., the National Alignment (*Nacionalni stroj*) in Serbia would be quite different there. But there

---

15   To give an example: in March 2018, an MP of the ruling Serbian Progressive Party attended the second congress of the new and consolidated Serbian Right, whose leader was previously jailed for hate speech crimes and incitement to violence.

is one set of reforms where the EU could and should push for more vigorously, and that is the reform of the judiciary, media freedom, and media openness. The protracted trials of people and organizations which disseminate ethnic and religious hatred and homophobia create an atmosphere of obliviousness and a frivolous general attitude in the society that seem to actually tolerate such values and behaviors, while at the same time undercutting trust in these institutions. The media scene in Serbia since 2012 has been marked by a consolidation of the pro-ruling party block of television channels (private and public) and newspapers, where cases of ethnonational discriminatory speech and denials of war crimes are systematically neglected, while concrete activities of the anti-nationalist groups are simply never covered.

The paradigm that links all far-right ideologies and actions in Serbia, Russia, and Croatia (and in much of the post-socialist realm) is selective and exclusive revisionism of the histories of World War II and the socialist period. The massive political elite-led actions of renaming streets, towns, and various cultural *topoi* in the last 25 years—deleting the memories of antifascist communist fighters, and replacing them often with those of fascist and Nazi collaborators (as "neglected Serbian patriots") has never met with any condemnation from EU officials. The EU should insist on a new approach to legislation in Serbia (and the other states of the Dayton Triangle, Bosnia and Herzegovina, and Croatia, plus Kosovo) that sanctions denials of war crimes committed during the 1991–1999 wars. In relation to this, what has been much needed for a quarter of the century is change in the school curricula, promoting critical thinking, exposing the hate and nationalist speech of the authorities with a specific focus on the period since the disintegration of Yugoslavia, and combatting the rampant historical revisionisms of WWII, which diminish and even seek to co-opt the legacies of antifascism as a shared universal set of values and action.

It could be pondered that the EU officials dealing with Serbia may be silent about the influence of Russian right-wing "geopolitical" activists and scholars because they do not wish to rock the boat with Russia over Serbia, while they may be fully aware that people like Dugin, Sergey Baburin, or Stanislav Byshok (a recent invited speaker in *Matica srpska*, the oldest cultural institution in the Serbian Autonomous Province of Vojvodina), [16] are backed by Russian state support. A depressing and more general diagnosis is that the EU is insufficiently interested in the political culture of Serbia, cultivating the view that a diplomatic and top-down approach — rather than a values-based approach — is paramount in the EU accession agenda. The local liberal civil society is, thus, left on its own, marginalized by a tabloid media loyal to the ruling party, and ridiculed even more than during the dark Milošević era by a seemingly ascendant illiberal, and often extreme, movement.

References

BBC World. 2015. Russia Nationalist Leader Jailed for Life over Hate Crimes," *BBC World News*, July 24, 2015, http://www.bbc.com/news/world-europe-33657409.

Beta. 2017. "Ubicama dečaka Dušana Jovanovića smanjena kazna" ("Murderers of the boy Dušan Jovanović Got Their Sentence Reduced".) *Blic*, October 17, 2017. https://www.blic.rs/vesti/hronika/ubicama-decaka.../6d2hene.

Bakić, Jovo. 2013. Right-wing extremism in Serbia. Belgrade: Friedrich Ebert Stiftung.

Bilbija, Bojan. 2017. "Aleksandr Dugin, intervju: Srbi su isti kao Rusi, samo bolji" ("Aleksandr Dugin, Interview: Serbs are Just Like Russians, Just Better.") *Politika*, June 30, 2017. http://www.politika.rs/scc/clanak/384031/Srbi-su-isti-kao-Rusi-samo-bolji.

Biserko, Sonja. 2008. "Uloga Rusije i njen uticaj na Balkanu" ("The Role of Russia and Its Influence in the Balkans"), *Helsinki Committee for Human Rights in Serbia, special issue*. https://www.helsinki.org.rs/serbian/doc/Rusija2.doc.

---

[16] Stanislav Byshok, currently an analyst with the pro-Kremlin CIS-EMO (Commonwealth of the Independent States Election Monitoring Organization) is a former member of the Russian "Russkiy obraz" and a follower of Ilya Goryachev. Byshok was also once close to the BORN (Boevaya Organizatsiya Russkih Natsionalistov – Military Organization of Russian Nationalists). Being currently focused on the topic of denying legitimacy to the Ukrainian claims on Crimea and Donbass, his lecture in Novi Sad was on "new and old" national identities in the post-Soviet space, using Ukraine as an example.

Biserko, Sonja. 2014. "Extremism: Recognizing a Social Evil." *Helsinki Files*, 34. Belgrade: Helsinki Committee for Human Rights in Serbia. https://www.helsinki.org.rs/doc/files34.pdf.

Blic. 2008. "Ruska državna televizija podržala ubistvo Đinđića" ("Russian State TV Endorses the Murder of Đinđić.") *Blic*, February 23, 2008. https://www.blic.rs/vesti/tema-dana/ruska-drzavna-televizija-podrzala-ubistvo-djindica/3psjs94.

Borger, Julian. 2018. "Russian-trained mercenaries back Bosnia's Serb separatists." *The Guardian*, January 12, 2018. https://www.theguardian.com/world/2018/jan/12/russian-trained-mercenaries-back-bosnias-serb-separatists.

Bulatovich, Liliana. 1996. "Serbskiy general Mladich. Sud'ba zashchitnika otechestva. Moi voennye vstrechi s Radovanom Karadzhichem i generalom Ratko Mladichem. Vospominaet doktor istoricheskikh nauk Yelena Yur'evna Gus'kova" ("Serbian General Mladić: The Destiny of a Fatherland's Defender. My War Encounters with Radovan Karadžić and Ratko Mladić. History PhD Elena Yur'evna Gus'kova Remembers."). https://biography.wikireading.ru/262840.

Bulatovich, Liliana n.d. "Мои военные встречи с Радованом Караджичем и генералом Ратко Младичем. Сербский генерал Младич. Судьба защитника Отечества." https://biography.wikireading.ru/262840 (accessed 10.27.18).

Byford, Jovan. 2010. "Drugi Obraz (The Other 'Obraz.')" *Peščanik*, November 25, 2010. https://pescanik.net/drugi-obraz-2/

Deretić, Jovan I. 2013. "*Serbi: narod i rasa*" ("Serbs: People and Race.") Belgrade: Ganeša.

Dizdarević, Raif. 1999. *Od smrti Tita do smrti Jugoslavije: svjedočenja (From the Death of Tito to the Death of Yugoslavia.)* Sarajevo: OKO.

Dugin, Aleksandr. 1997. *Osnovy geopolitiki (The Foundations of Geopolitics).* Moscow: Arktogeya.

Dugin, Aleksandr. 2008. "Krupny povorot v serbskoi politike; Aleksandr Dugin prizval golosovat za Serbskuyu Radikal'nuyu Partiyu" ("A Major Turn in Serbian Politics; Aleksandr Dugin calls for Casting Votes for the Serbian Radical Party.") *Srpska.ru*, April 11, 2008. http://www.srpska.ru/article.php?nid=7968.

Dugin, Aleksandr. 2017. ''Serbiya – eto samy zapadny avangard nashego evraziistva" ("Serbia – it is the Westernmost Avant-Garde of Our Eurasianism.") *Maxpark*, July 4, 2017. http://maxpark.com/community/13/content/5901737.

Đorić, Marija. 2012. *Huliganizam: nasilje i sport (Hooliganism: Violence and Sport).* Belgrade: Udruženje nauka i društvo Srbije.

Er.M./Klix.ba. 2018. "Udruženje 'Srbska čast' radi na formiranju paravojne formacije u Republici Srpskoj" ("The association "Serbian honor" is working on establishing a paramilitary formation in Republika Srpska.") *Klix.ba*, January 12, 2018. https://www.klix.ba/vij esti/bih/udruzenje-srbska-cast-radi-na-formiranju-paravojne-forma cije-u-republici-srpskoj/180112086.

Gus'kova, Elena. 2004. "Agresija NATO na Jugoslaviju i pozicija Rusije" ("The NATO Aggression Against Yugoslavia and the Position of Russia.") paper presented at the conference of the Forum for the Peace of Equals. http://www.guskova.info/lat?doc=/w/wars/2004-03-24.

Gus'kova, Yelena. 2007. *Nashy mirotvortsy na Balkanakh* (*Our Peace-Makers in the Balkans*), Moscow: INDRIK.

Gus'kova, Elena. 2017. "NATO khochet okonchatel'no dobit' Serbiyu" ("NATO Wishes to Finish Serbia Off.") *Svobodnaya pressa*, June 29, 2017. https://svpressa.ru/politic/article/126228/%22/.

Gus'kova, Elena. 2018a. "Respublika Serbskaya mozhet stat' oplotom Rossii na Balkanakh" ("The Republika Srpska can Become a Bastion of Russia in the Balkans.") *Russkaya narodnaya liniya*, June 15, 2018. http://ruskline.ru/politnews/2018/iyun/15/respublika_serbskaya _mozhet_stat_oplotom_rossii_na_balkanah_eguskova/.

Gus'kova, Elena. 2018b. "Vučić će biti upamćen kao predsednik koji se odrekao zemlje predaka" ("Vučić Will Be Remembered as a President Who Gave Up the Ancestral Land.") *Pravda*, May 18, 2018. http://www.pravda.rs/lat/2018/5/18/jelena-guskova-Vučić-ce-b iti-upamcen-kao-predsednik-koji-se-odrekao-zemlje-predaka/.

Halimović, Dženana. 2016. "Radovan Karadžić, od poete do ratnog zločinca" ("Radovan Karadžić, from Poet to War Criminal.") *Radio Free Europe*, March 26, 2016. https://www.slobodnaevropa.org/ a/radovan-karadzic-od-poete-do-ratnog-zlocinca/27636894.html.

Huseinović, Samir. 2011. "Desni ekstremizam prijeti Zapadnom Balkanu, Intervju sa Dušanom Janjićem" ("Right-Wing Extremism, Interview with Dušan Janjić"). *Deutsche Welle*, November 18, 2011. http://w ww.dw.com/bs/desni-ekstremizam-prijeti-zapadnom-balkanu/a-1 5540466 2011.

In4s. 2017. "Platforma Zavetnika o KiM predstavljena u Moskvi." *In4s*, December 12, 2017. https://www.in4s.net/platforma-zavetnika-kim-predstavljena-moskvi/?lang=lat.

Kuljić, Todor. 2018. "Kapital bi da menja kolektivno sećanje." *Danas*, March 1, 2018. https://www.danas.rs/drustvo/kapital-bi-da-menja-kolek tivno-secanje/.

Kraske, Marion. 2017. "State capture in the Balkans: l'état c'est nous!" https://www.boell.de/en/2017/11/08/state-capture-balkans-letat-cest-nous).

Limonov Eduard. 2011. "Punk and National-Bolshevism, Article invited to write for Attack the System: Pan-Anarchism Against the State, Pan-Secessionism Against the Empire." https://attackthesystem.com/2011/06/09/punk-and-national-bolshevism/.

Milosavljević, Olivera. 2007. "'Dobri' nacionalizam" ("The 'Good' Nationalism.") *Peščanik*, March 19, 2007. http://pescanik.net/dobri-nacionalizam/.

Ninković, Vladimir. 2013. "Serbia and Russia—far right friendships?" *Transconflict*, May 8, 2013. http://www.transconflict.com/2013/05/serbia-and-russia-far-right-friendships-085/.

Pešić, Vesna. 2007. "State Capture and Widespread Corruption in Serbia." *CEPS Working Documents* No. 262. https://ssrn.com/abstract=1338021.

Savićević, Vanja. 2018. "Mayor Deyan Berich: Vse otlichno, a budet eshche luchshe" ("Mayor Deyan Berich: All is Superb, and Will Get Even Better.") *RuSerbia.com*, February 18, 2018. http://ruserbia.com/society/major-dejan-berich-vse-otlichno-a-budet-eshhe-luchshe/.

SNP 1389. "Osnovni ciljevi SNP 1389" ("Main Goals of SNP 1389"); http://www.snp1389.rs/index.php?option=com_content&view=article&id=264&Itemid=85; SNP 1389: »Mladi protiv režimske politike« ("Youth against Regime Policy"); http://www.snp1389.rs/index.php?option=com_content&view=article&id=712%3A2012-05-31-11-58-4&catid=36%3Avesti&Itemid=69; "SNP Naši: 'Program'"; http://nasisrbija.org/program-3/

Stakić, Isidora. 2016. "Serbian Nationalism and Right-Wing Extremism." In *Proceedings of the 31st workshop of the Study Group Regional Stability in South East Europe Violent Extremism in the Western Balkans* edited by Filip Ejdus, and Predrag Jurekovic, 133–147. Available at http://www.filipejdus.com/Public/Uploads/Attach/jurekovic_and_ejdus_2016_violent_extremism_579f5bba2729b.pdf.

Stojanović, Gorčin. 2017. "Dve parade dokaz da nema demokratije" ("The Two Parades Prove that There is No Democracy.") *N1*, September 18, 2017. http://rs.n1info.com/a318729/Vesti/Vesti/Gorcin-Stojanovic-o-Paradi-ponosa-i-novinarskim-udruzenjima.html.

UNIAN. 2014. "V Rossii sobirayut podpisi za uvol'nenie professora MGU prizvavshego ubivat' ukraintsev") ("In Russia, Signatures are Being Collected for Firing the Professor who Called on to Killing Ukrainians.") *Ukrainian Independent Information Agency*, July 15, 2014. https://www.unian.net/politics/928851-v-rossii-sobirayut-podpisi-za-uvolnenie-professora-mgu-prizvavshego-ubivat-ukraintsev.html.

Vasić, Miloš. 2005. "Anatomija zločina" ("The anatomy of a crime.") *Republika*, nos. 354–355, April 1–30, 2005. http://www.republika.co.rs/354-355/21.html.

Vignjević, Vojislava. 1997. "Portret Borisa Jeljcin, predsednik Rusije: Tačerizam po ruskom" ("A portrait of Boris Yeltsin, Russian President: Thatcherism the Russian Way.") *Naša borba*, June 21, 1997. http://www.yurope.com/nasa-borba/arhiva/Jun98/2106/2106_11.HTM.

Valyaev, Evgeny. 2012. "Sozdan Pravo-Konservativny Al'yans" ("The Right-Conservative Aliance is Founded.") *Slav Anthropology*, April 13, 2012. http://slavanthro.mybb3.ru/viewtopic.php?t=9807.

Živanović, K. 2018. "Za ratovanje u Siriji optužba za terorizam, za Ukrajinu uslovna" ("For Fighting in Syria one is Charged with Terrorism, for Ukraine — Probation.") *Danas*, 26 August, 2018. https://www.danas.rs/drustvo/za-ratovanje-u-siriji-optuzba-terorizam-za-ukrajinu-uslovna/.

Živanović, Maja. 2017. "Kosovo Film Ignites Controversy in Serbia." *Balkan Insight*, June 14, 2017. http://www.balkaninsight.com/en/article/kosovo-is-still-controversial-theme-in-serbia-movie-author-06-13-2017.

(Non)violent Extremism Online: How Opinion Leaders Use Online Channels to Disseminate Radical Messages and Intolerance

Davor Marko

Introduction

The roots of violent extremism, combined with the instrumentalization of religion, can be found in the recent war-torn history of the former Yugoslavia, subsequent weak institutions, and the economic regression that has left many people, especially youth, feeling like they have no hope. According to recent research, vulnerabilities in Serbia also include

> "societal fragmentation along ethnic lines, lack of possibilities for young people and especially the role of global and regional politics, which contributes to the conflict potential and represents one of key identified drivers of radicalization" (CeSID 2016, 2).

In addition, ethnic and religious minorities—especially young Bosniaks and Albanians—see themselves as victims of injustice and discrimination (Ibid.). Young people are, consequently, a fertile group for propaganda and indoctrination. While terrorism is widely covered and presented in the Serbian media as a threat, terrorist, extremist, and radical groups have limited direct access to traditional media and rather intensively use the Internet to spread their ideology (Balkan Insight 2016). There is a growing interest in understanding the causes, drivers, and impact of extremist voices in the online sphere in Serbia, but this field generally remains under-researched. The main stakeholders in the field, including the research community, face at least four problems:

- The lack of interdisciplinary scholarship and expertise — the most engaged in the field are researchers in think tanks specialized in security, partly CSOs, academic institutions and international organizations.
- There is no evidence-based research produced on a continuous basis to understand contextually the main drivers of radicalization.
- There is little empirical evidence on the precise role of online media and social networks in the process of radicalization in Serbia and the region of the Western Balkans. There is also limited explanation on how extremist materials influence youth. It remains unclear how online radicalization, in combination with other "offline" factors, affects one's decision to accept/adopt/join radical ideals/groups.
- There is a substantial gap within the research community on new and applicable research methods that can help to assess the role of online channels in violent extremism.

Therefore, this study aims to begin to fill the gap by examining the way two selected influential persons with ideas and viewpoints that can be considered radical or extreme use online channels and social media to disseminate their messages targeting (primarily) youth in Serbia. This analysis includes examples of the ultra-nationalist and far-right, and of a conservative, fundamentalist Muslim voice in Serbia. In order to narrow down the scope of analysis, a limited and targeted set of online activities of these two selected public figures, considered as opinion leaders, will be examined.

As a personification of the ultra-nationalist Serbian far-right, Goran Davidović (known as Firer/Führer) has been selected. He was the founder and leader of *Nacionalni stroj* (National Guard), an organization that was banned in Serbia in 2011 by the Serbian Constitutional Court. Davidović is best known for being involved in two incidents: in 2005, his group disrupted an anti-fascist forum on International Day Against Fascism and Anti-Semitism in Novi Sad, while in 2007 the group attacked an anti-fascist rally, also in Novi Sad. At least 26 persons were arrested, some of them members of the neo-Nazi group *Nacionalni stroj*, led by Davidović (BBC 2017).

The Supreme Court in Serbia issued a one-year sentence to Davidović for inciting racial, religious and national hatred and intolerance.¹ Instead of going to jail, Davidović went into exile. He currently legally lives in Trieste, with Italian documents (Blic 2009), and has a web page and a very active Twitter account. He is considered an informal leader of a newly established ultra-right organization—*Nacionalni srpski front* (*National Serbian Front*). He is also editor in chief of their quarterly bulletin (Insajder 2017).

Sead Islamović was the founder of the pro-Salafi organization *Put sredine* (The Middle Path) who currently leads a community centred around the Hadži Mehova mosque in Novi Pazar, and is considered in this study as an example of an influential, conservative Muslim leader. *Put sredine* was considered to be a recruitment centre for jihadists during 2013 and 2014 (Sandžak press 2013; RTS 2013; Danas 2014). There is no proof that Islamović was involved in this process. Several sources indicate that he gave speeches and showed videos related to the war in Syria in 2014; such videos are no longer available online. Preliminary analysis indicates that Islamović and his community intensively use online platforms and channels, including YouTube and Facebook, to complement their offline activities. Compared to other people who can be more definitively considered as extremist, radical voices (such as Muhamed Porča, Bilal Bosnić, Nusret Imamović, and Nedžad Balkan), Islamović is considered rather more conservative or fundamentalist than a violent or extremist leader. Islamović was born in Sandžak, lived and studied in Medina, Saudi Arabia, and adheres to Salafism, a conservative school of Islamic thought, as do Elvedin Pezić from Sarajevo or Safet Kuduzović who lives in Montenegro. Islamović's current lectures and speeches could be labeled as moderate with some very fundamentalist interpretations (on the position and rights of women, for example). Islamović is the imam of the Hadži Mehova mosque—the biggest mosque in Novi Pazar, in

---

1 The most comprehensive documentation on far-right activities, incidents and trials has been produced by Radio-Television Vojvodina and its journalist, Darko Šper (see the list of online video sources at the end of this document).

terms of structure and size, with more than 3,000 members, mostly young people.

It is worthwhile mentioning the context in which Islamović and organizations affiliated to him operate. According to dominant and sometimes stereotyped narratives, the region of Sandžak in Serbia's southwest is highly polarized and divided, with several main contesters for power and influence — politicians or other public or religious figures — striving to pursue their own interests. These actors, many of whom have been publicly active since the beginning of the 1990s, include political parties and leaders as well as an Islamic community that is institutionally divided. The situation with the two Islamic communities is even more complex. The official narrative declares that the Islamic community in Serbia has been split since 2007 between the similarly-named Islamic Community *of* Serbia [IZS] represented by Hamdija Jusufspahić and Adem Zilkić and with its seat in Belgrade, and the Islamic Community *in* Serbia [IZuS], personified by Muamer Zukorlić and his allies, and headquartered in Novi Pazar and under the jurisdiction of Sarajevo. In fact, both communities have lacked legal recognition dating to changes from 1994, when, during the war in neighboring Bosnia and Herzegovina mufti Hamdija Jusufspahić of Belgrade declared the IZ in Serbia separate from that in Sarajevo, and established an independent institution in Serbia, supported by the Serbian regime. The status of the two Islamic communities remains unresolved (Kostić 2015).

A mixed method approach was used in data collection, relying primarily on qualitative analysis. Social Network Analysis (SNA) was applied to better understand the dynamics and communication flow between Davidović and his followers on Twitter. SNA provides an in-depth analysis of the social structure and network built around his Twitter profile (either using @name or #hashtag). SNA was combined with content analysis in order to detect main narratives, the most salient motifs and buzzwords, and also the tone of communication. For the analysis of Islamović's sermons content analysis was applied, taking into account available video content of two YouTube channels (*Hadži Mehova džamija* and *Put sredine*), their popularity (number of views), the themes Islamović addresses and the timeframe. Special attention is paid to analysis of videos related to women and their rights.

Since this analysis applies various methods of content and social network analysis to a new topic, it can be considered a pilot exercise, particularly in the region. The advantages and limitations, as well as opportunities, challenges, and possibilities for improvement and modification, will be acknowledged and further elaborated to serve as guidance for further research. Several policy implications and recommendations are provided at the end of this chapter.

Conceptual framework/literature review

Violent extremism online

Etymologically, extremism intersects with the notion of limits and boundaries, and when applied to human relations it describes behaviour that tends to cross the boundaries of tolerance and acceptance (Đorić 2012, 45–46). Extremism is a complex social phenomenon that is characterized by an over-emphasized need for self-protection and xenophobic identity politics, attitudes, and expressions (Keveždi 2013, 33–49; Keveždi 2015, 276). It has multiple meanings, can take various forms and refers to ruthless methods by which political ideas are realised that disregard life, liberty and the rights of others (Neuman 2017, 15). Violent extremism has attracted wide research attention only recently and is linked with the lack of general consensus on the definition of terrorism. It is a broader term,

> "covering [the] whole range of violent actions that extremist groups have been responsible for—including politically inspired riots, hate crimes, and even more conventional military-style operations, which many definitions of terrorism failed to capture" (Neumann 2017, 14–15).

The literature on violent extremism falls into two dominant camps—one related to the far-right, while the second considers extremist Islamism or the global violent jihad movement; there is also a body of literature discussing the radical left as a form of extremism (Đorić 2016). The second camp has attracted much more attention recently due to the high profile emergence of ISIS. The topic itself is highly interdisciplinary and envelops a wide array of disciplines, methodological approaches and data (Meleagrou-Hitchens and Kaderbhai 2017, 8).

According to Neumann, radicalisation is the process that leads people to extremism (Neumann 2017, 17). There is no agreement on the definition of radicalisation. Recently, the term and concept has been infused by new meanings and interpretations. What most scholars agree upon is their reference to violence as a central feature of radicalization, or as a tool for reaching political goals or generating political conflict (Neuman and Rogers 2007; McCauley and Moskalenko 2011). Some authors make a distinction between violent radicalisation and non-violent forms of extremism, or cognitive and behavioural radicalisation (Neuman and Stevens 2010, 10), which also take into account activities other than recruitment and explicit calls for violent acts.

The most cited drivers of radicalisation in the literature include physical or face-to-face interactions within "real world" social networks; the process of socialization which implies a gradual adoption of norms, ideologies, and customs; and the role of ideology, identity, leadership figures, and propaganda (Meleagrou-Hitchens and Kaderbhai 2017, 14–15). In the era of social media, the role of the Internet has been increasingly considered. There is no definite answer or understanding of how online platforms and social media contribute to radicalization, but there is some existing research indicating their growing influence in this process (Awan et al. 2011; O'Loughlin et al. 2013).

Hoffman and Sageman provide two opposite understandings of the role of the Internet in the process of radicalization. For Hoffman, who presents a *top-down* description of the phenomenon, the emphasis is on the role of individuals and external recruiters in the real world, with the Internet perceived as a powerful communication tool with which extremists can spread their propaganda, provide training materials as well as distribute a variety of open source materials that could be used for planning and implementing attacks

(Hoffman 2006, 5). Sageman describes a *bottom-up* approach, applying social network analysis and using the case of al-Qaeda to argue that they are a network consisting of personal relationships. According to Sageman, the Internet decreases the role and importance of ideology and leadership, providing a basis for a deliberative process and creation of a "leaderless jihad." For him, such a virtual constellation presents a form of a marketplace in which coordination is spontaneous, from the bottom up and — as liberal theory would emphasize — led by the "invisible hand" of the market (Sageman 2008, 144–145).

Some authors, like Benson, criticize the tendency to over-emphasize the importance of the Internet. Benson argues there is no empirical proof that the Internet has essentially affected the way terrorists operate today, claiming they use the Internet the same way they have used other traditional communication tools, such as phones or the postal service earlier. Benson further makes a crucial methodological critique, arguing that existing studies lack the independent and dependent variables needed to determine the net effect of the Internet on radicalization (Benson 2014, 32). He does not believe that cyberspace has fundamentally altered terrorism. Instead, the growth of the Internet has been even more of a help to security agencies and other actors in fighting global terrorism (Ibid., 293). Benson calls for a more rigorous methodological approach and further study.

This chapter combines both Hoffman's top-down approach and Sageman's deliberative approach, in which an important role in spreading extremist narratives online is played by individuals who are considered non-formal leaders (or influencers) within their communities. Such persons possess a kind of charisma and authority to share their views and impose them upon a community of the like-minded without restraints. Some authors (Neumann 2013, 58–59; Brachman 2009, 19) coined the term "Jihobbysts" when referring to ISIS-related propaganda, nomenclature that could be applied to other types of extremism in which influential persons use the advent of new technologies to spread their ideas. In this regard, the classical theory on opinion leadership provides a useful framework to explain the role of these persons and their online activities.

The "two step flow of communication," a theoretical approach developed by Lazarsfeld and Katz, considers the important role of opinion leaders as mediators who essentially intervene between mass media messages and the way in which they are interpreted by the audience. The authors describe the opinion leader as "the agent who is an active media user, and who interprets the meaning of media messages or content for ordinary media users" (Lazarsfeld and Katz 1955, 32). Such persons enjoy a high reputation among their peers and in their community. Katz outlines three aspects of opinion leadership, including personification of his/her values (who one is), competences (what one knows), and reputation based on networking (who one knows). The groups or (virtual) communities in which leaders are embedded are important as a source of their legitimacy for several reasons. First, people belonging to a certain group benefit from sharing the opinions, attitudes, and behaviours of those with whom they want to be identified. This is especially typical for societies with a high level of authoritarianism (Almond and Verba 1989, 19) as is the case with Serbia (Podunavac 2006; Vladisavljević 2008; Vladisavljević 2014). Second, primary groups represent and reproduce their social reality and, as such, conduct themselves in validation of their own interpretations and evaluations. Finally, these groups can serve as channels for mass media transmission where opinion leaders are acting as gatekeepers (Marko 2011, 171–173).

Extremism online: the case of Serbia

Most authors writing on this topic in Serbia (Ilić 2013; Bakić 2013; Kevieždi 2013; 2015) have been focused on the far-right and ultranationalists while analysing their online activities. Bakić (2013) analysed activities of far-right organizations in Serbian cyberspace with a focus on *Obraz, SNP Naši, SNP 1389,* and *Srbska akcija*[2] — or-

---

2   *Obraz*, which literally means *cheek*, in the sense of "face," and in this context conveys "honour" in a metaphorical sense, is a Serbian far-right organization that was banned for its violent activities and anti-human ideology. *Naši* or *Ours* is a right wing political movement characterized by nationalism and Euroscepticism. *1389* is a Serbian far-right group identified with a youth facsist ideology (the number stands for

ganizations considered to be the main players on the far-right spectrum. They are not ideologically, nor organizationally, homogeneous. In spite of being forbidden in its organizational form, *Nacionalni stroj* and its extremist ideology continues to live through individual online activities, and in particular through its leader Goran Davidović who as noted is active on Twitter and is a key subject in this study (Bakić, in Ilić 2013, 113–117).

Keveždi (2015) analysed the promises of far-right options as expressed on their web pages on the eve of parliamentary elections in Serbia in 2014. His research showed that *Dveri*—which offered a clear policy platform as a party participating in the elections—had the most sophisticated campaign including promises in the domains of politics, healthcare, education, identity, position and participation of women, the economy, etc. *SNP Naši* had the highest amount of promises, followed by *Srbski Obraz* and the Serbian Radical Party. The common motif of their pre-election narrative could be formulated as follows—"Russian Federation and Euro-Asian integration" (Keveždi 2015, 272–290). Both Ivanović and Dević provide further insights that flesh out this survey in their contributions to this volume.

The online activities of extremist individuals and organizations linked to Islam and the misuse of that religion for the sake of radicalization, still lacks solid research and field-based evidence. Petrović and Stakić (2018) have begun to analyse this phenomenon in a more detailed and nuanced way. Prior to this, Kladničanin analysed the activities of Wahhabis in Serbian cyber space. He provided several useful examples of how followers of this movement use online channels to spread their ideas, such as the Facebook page *Poziv u raj/dženet* (*Call to Heaven*)[3]; the Facebook page *Eldar Kundaković*, dedicated to a young person from Novi Pazar who died in

---

the year of the notorious Kosovo Battle, which has a highly symbolic meaning for Serbian nationalistic discourse. *Srbska akcija* or *Serbian action* is neo-fascist movement which references Orthodoxy and Serbian nationalism.

[3] Link for Facebook page: https://www.facebook.com/groups/359650540043/about/

Syria in 2013;[4] or the Facebook page *hfz. Jusuf Barčić*, which is dedicated to this non-formal leader of Wahhabis who died in 2007, and is full of comments that call for the liberation of the Balkans from non-believers and religious "novelties."[5] Kladničanin's analysis also included portals such as *Islambosna*, *Put sredine*, and *Sandžakpress.net*. *Islambosna* has several discussion forums through which visitors propagate hate speech and intolerant speech against "religious" and "ideological" others.[6] *Putsredine* is the formal web site of the community gathered around Sead Islamović.[7] *Sandžakpress.net* is under the control of the Islamic Community of Serbia and its non-formal, long-time leader Muamer Zukorlić.[8] It promotes radical political views and spreads hate speech against Serbian politicians, politicians and NGOs from Sandžak who criticize Zukorlić (Kladničanin in Ilić 2013, 131–133).

Research approach, design, and methods

This paper analyses two cases that represent two types of extremis, far-right and conservative Islamist, as well as the way they use online platforms, channels and social media to spread their ideas and interact with their communities. The cases are focussed on two individuals who represent opinion leaders among their communities/networks, either as informal (Goran Davidović) or formal leaders (Sead Islamović). Since access to reliable and useful data represents the biggest obstacle, this research is reliant primarily on open source data, rather than closed-sourced data (for example police or intelligence service databases, as well as content of closed social media groups). Twitter and YouTube — the two online tools used by the two target influencers — present a good source for such open data.

---

4 This page was no longer active at the beginning of 2018.
5 This page has more than 8,000 followers and is available on: https://www.facebook.com/jusuf.salih.barcic/
6 Web page link: http://www.islambosna.ba
7 *Put sredine* has a web page: https://putsredine.com and a Facebook page with more than 18,000 followers: https://www.facebook.com/NVOPutSredine/?ref=br_rs, and an active YouTube channel.
8 Web page link: http://sandzakpress.net

Initial research of their online activities indicates that they use very different online tools to spread their views and ideas. While Davidović relies on Twitter, Islamović and his community use YouTube to augment their offline activities and closed (moderated) Facebook group. Therefore, the focus is on Davidović's activities on Twitter, and on Islamović's use of YouTube. More detailed justification is provided in a separate section below (see Figure 1).

Social Network Analysis (SNA) was used to analyze Davidović's Twitter presence. Free online software and manual analysis of his online activity were applied for a selected period of two months — November and December 2017. To analyse networks and the most active nodes (actors) around his profile, free tools such as Bird Song analytics,[9] Foller.me,[10] and Mentionmapp[11] were used. Content analysis was used to analyze his narratives.

The content of Sead Islamović's speeches on YouTube was analysed to detect the main motifs, narratives, and language used in his speeches. Based on the general review of videos posted on the Hadži Mehova mosque YouTube channel a preliminary selection of videos for in-depth analysis was made. Selection criteria included their popularity, number of interactions, number of views, and the amount of controversy on the topic chosen. The analysis took into account the entire content of this YouTube channel — since its inception and until the end of January 2018 — with a special focus on November and December 2017.

---

9   This platform provides social media analytics tools that are easy to use and can provide users the needed data. It is useful for initial review of online platforms and social networks. At the advanced level, it runs reports on any public Instagram or Twitter account, Facebook or YouTube channel for the latest insights. Regrettably, it was closed in autumn 2018. Link: https://www.birdsonganalytics.com
10 Foller.me is an online free tool. This tool is excellent for getting an understanding of an individual's Twitter account. Link: www.foller.me
11 This web service maps Twitter user networks and the network of others linked to an account. Mentionmapp builds a visual map of hashtags and username mentions based on the people engagement. Link: http://mentionmapp.com

Additionally, available studies, research, and surveys have been used as secondary sources. Fifteen background interviews enabled the collection of additional data and different perspectives.[12] Previous research work related to media, language, fear, and the role and impact of religious leaders and their public statements affecting youth attitudes also informed these findings (Marko 2011; Marko 2013a; Marko 2013b; Marko 2016).

As evident from the figure below, Davidović uses his Twitter account the most, and other platforms modestly (Facebook or Instagram) or not at all (YouTube). Islamović does not have his own personal website, profile, or channel that can be easily contrasted to Davidović's individual profile, and therefore two organizations (*Put sredine* and the community gathered around *Hadži Mehova* mosque) linked with him have been analysed as well. Both use YouTube and Facebook extensively, Instagram modestly, and Twitter not at all. When it comes to organizational affiliation, Davidović is linked with the National Serbian Front (NSF), whose activities online can be considered as modest. Therefore, there is an admitted asymmetry in terms of case selection.

---

12   Respondent backgrounds include the following: an Islamic scholar, an intelligence service employee (who asked to be anonymous), a scholar on the far-right and hooliganism, a researcher familiar with high tech and innovative methods for online research, a journalist who covers extremism and the far-right, a researcher dealing with the far-right and extremism in media and the online sphere, NGO representatives, and a security expert.

Figure 1: Overview of online platforms and social networks used by Davidović

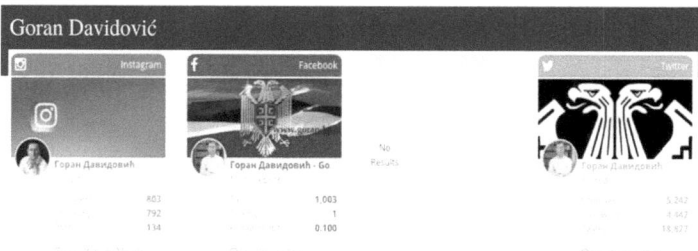

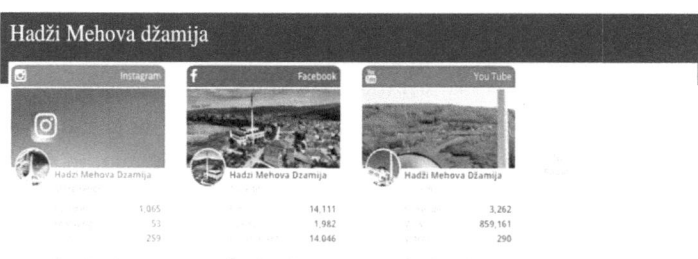

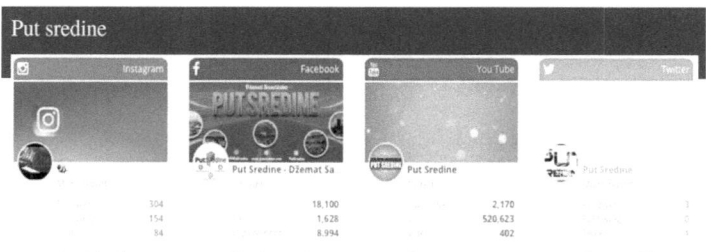

Source: https://insights.birdsonganalytics.com

The rationale for the selection of YouTube to study Islamović lies in the fact that his appearances are mostly oral, in the form of lectures or one-way speeches, with almost no direct interaction with his audience. His speeches and lectures are all examples of original content, and are available on the YouTube channels of both the *Hadži Mehova džamija* and *Put sredine*, where Islamović was a dominant voice until 2014.

Analysis of findings: a far-right influencer online

In this section, the main findings are presented and analyzed to better understand the selected opinion leader's activities, the channels they use and the main narratives they employ in their online communications. It also provides a snapshot of some of the data that can be captured through various analytical tools.

The far-right online: Goran Davidović and the NSF

This study shows that Davidović, who has lived outside of Serbia for years, is very active online, through his web page (www.gorandavidovic.com) and on his Twitter account (@GoranDvd). He is linked with the National Serbian Front (NSF), a growing movement of Serbian radical right ultranationalists. According to Davidović, who is considered to be an informal leader, NSF is "a political association registered on the territory of the Republic of Serbia, in spite of the fact that the idea has appeared in emigration and in the Republika Srpska" (Nationalist 2017). The main goal of the NSF, according to Davidović, is to "unify Serbian nationalists or to foster collaboration among them, and currently it works to merge several nationalist organizations into one association" (Ibid.).

Goran Davidović and Twitter

Davidović's Twitter account has been active since August 6, 2011, and as of the end of January 2018, he has posted more than 18,000 tweets. Taking into account the dynamics of his Twitter activity, Davidović could be considered an active user. As shown in the Table below, Davidović replies to tweets more than 50% of the time (57 out of 100) and while he often posts tweets with @mentions, he very rarely uses #hashtags; a trend which could be considered to reflect his intention to have direct communication and interaction with his followers, as well as his opponents.

Table 1: Some features related to Davidović's tweets (from its inception in 2011)

Replies	57/100
Tweets with @mentions	74/100
Tweets with #hashtags	4/100
Retweets	17/100 (retweets by @GoranDvd)
Tweets with links	31/100
Tweets with media	11/100

Source: Foller.me (2018)

According to the same tool (Foller.me), Davidović is most active during his working hours, and especially in the afternoon, between 15:00 and 17:00, and until 21:00 with some lower intensity. On average, Davidović posts around 10 tweets around 11:00, 20 to 25 tweets between 15:00 and 17:00, and up to 30 in between 17:00 and 21:00.

Figure 2: Frequency of Davidović's tweets

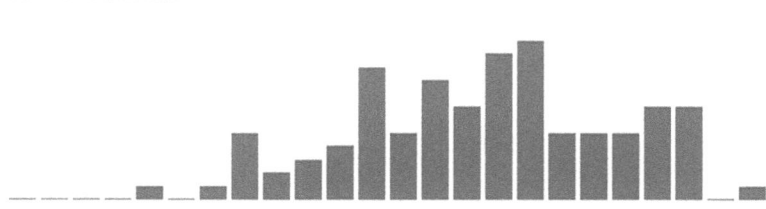

Source: Foller.me (2018)

A manual analysis of Davidović's Twitter activity during November and December 2017, provided additional insight into some trends, including the content of his tweets and the narratives and ideas he promotes among his network (described more below). In this period, Davidović posted a total of 135 tweets and retweeted 88 times.

Structure of Davidović's online network

In January 2018, Davidović had more than 5,200 followers on Twitter, while he followed more than 4,200 profiles.

According to Mentionmapp, a free online tool for Twitter analysis, this is how Davidović's network looks according to the number of @mentions (Figure 3) and retweets (Figure 4):

Figure 3: Davidović's network – defined by mentions

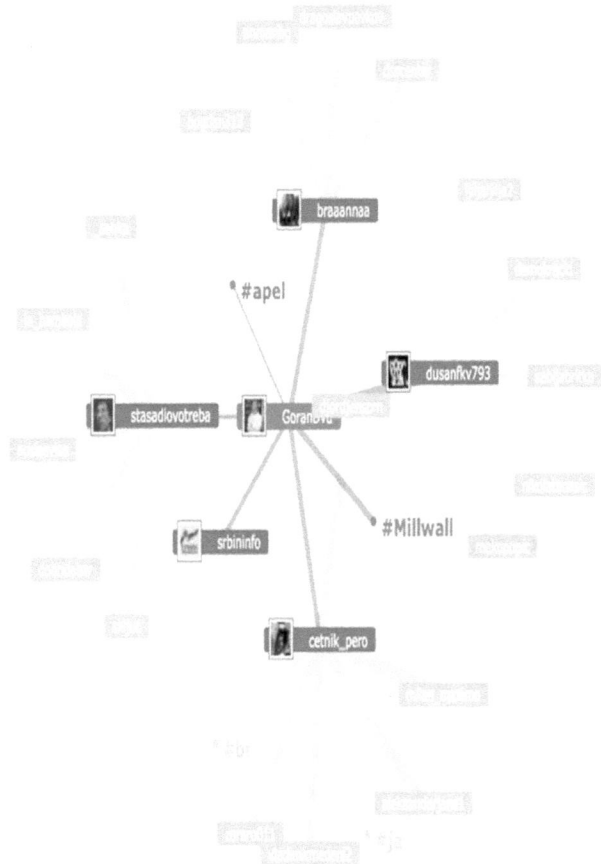

Source: https://mentionmapp.com

Figure 4: Davidović's network — defined by retweets

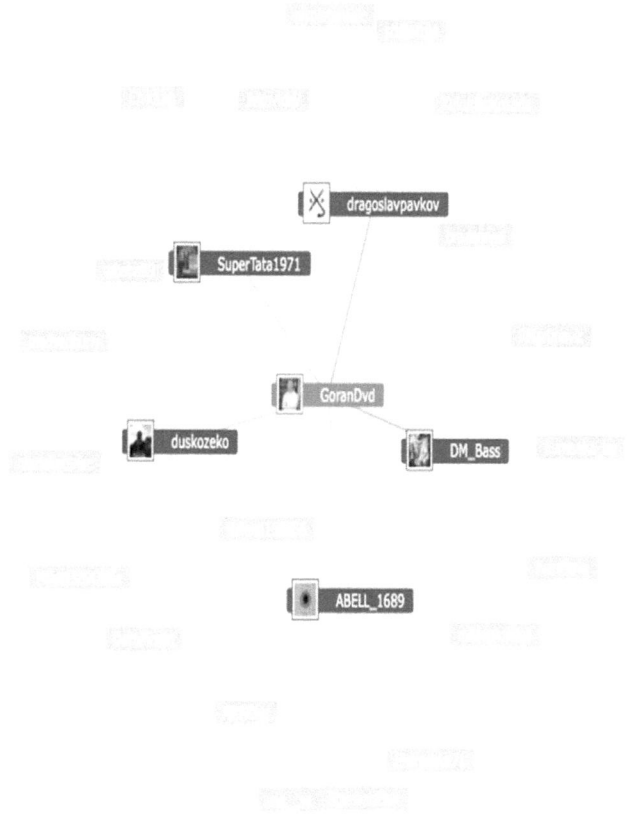

Source: https://mentionmapp.com

Manual analysis that includes tweets from November and December 2017 identified the most active members of his network using the "retweeting" activity as a main indicator. In this period Davidović posted 135 tweets, while the most active members include Dejan (or Дејан in Serbian Cyrillic) (@Bloknalog_z), who retweeted 50.4% of his tweets; Stepa Stepanović (Степа Степановић) (@SlobodaSrbiji) with 24% retweets; and petar petrovic (@placacporeza) with 13.3%. Most of these follows seem to be ordinary people, with some of them expressing their nationalism explicitly. There is reason to speculate that some of the profiles are fake, due to the lack of personalized information and usual dynamic activity common in real profiles. None of these profiles attract a significant number of followers and, therefore are not considered as real influencers. Table 2 provides a summary of his most active followers:

Table 2: The most active followers, per retweet (November–December 2017)

Name & Twitter ID	% of Retweets	Followers	Twitter Profile Description	Location
Dejan or Дејан (@Bloknalog_z)	50.4 %	880	SRS – P.F.C. new account, previous suspended! Maybe this one survives? (СРС - П.Ф.Ц нови налог, предходни суспендован! можда овај преживи?)	Loznica, Serbia
Stepa Stepanović or Степа Степановић (@SlobodaSrbiji)	24 %	1.830	n/a	n/a
petar petrovic (@placacporeza)	13.3 %	4.116	DEAR SNS BOTS, BIA SPIES AND OTHER SIMILAR S**THEADS YOU CAN KISS MY … (DRAGI SNS BOTOVI,BIA ŽBIROVI I OSTALI SLIČNI G**NARI POLJUBITE ME U ….)	P***A M*******A (expletive related to female body part)
Đorđe Marinković or Ђорђе Маринковић @DS_Djole	11.8 %	59	n/a	n/a
Misa Vacic @MisaVacic	11.1 %	1,180	Idealist, modest man, nationalist, fan of history, justice and truth. President of Serbian Right (Идеалиста , скроман човек , националиста , љубитељ историје , правде и истине. Председник Српске Деснице)	Prirodna Srbija (Natural Serbia)
@Gosteljski	11.1 %	811	n/a	Serbia

Žika Pavlović or Жика Павловић @nacionalistaRS	10.4 %	141	Serb.Nationalist. Anti-globalist. (Србин. Националиста. Антиглобалиста.)	n/a
ГУБЕРИНИЋ БОРИС @GUBERINI	10.4 %	1,318	I am not a colonel, you can write me freely (Нисам пуковник,слободно ми пишите)	n/a
Б. М. @Boris_M_75	8.9 %	2,728	La rage de mentir et de croire, s'attrape comme la gale. CELINE. Serblos Tryballos, autem gentem esse totius orbis antiquissimam et maximam, compertum habeo	n/a
@ABELL_1689	8.1 %	801	n/a	n/a
Vladimir Dragićević or Владимир Драгичевић @VDragicevic	8.1 %	837	And you are a revolution, you mother**kers? (Мајку вам сељачку, и ви сте ми револуција!?!)	Serbia
Milovan Stosic @StosicMilovan	8.1 %	298	n/a	n/a

Manual analysis also led to the identification of some influential members of Davidović's network. Some are declared nationalists (Миша Вацић — leader of newly founded "Serbian right," Др Орао Небески) or anti-globalists (for example, Драган Ђорђевић). Yet most are seemingly ordinary persons who are not declared nationalists, and who do not explicitly express radical or extremist views or ideas. The scope of this analysis was too limited, especially in terms of the timeframe, to tackle and examine the issue of their motivation to be part of his network.

Table 3: Influencers in Davidović's Twitter network

Name & Twitter ID	Followers	Tweets	Twitter Profile Description	Location
Đurđijina mama @miljanarad	22,432	23,567	Mother, happy women, lawyer, former Secretary General of the Ministry. Addicted to love, work and hedonism.	Belgrade, Serbia
Maja Vukas @M2aja	17,328	43,025	Account opened without reason. I am here, nobody's daughter, wife, spokesperson. Gained followers thanks to the	Belgrade, Serbia

				hard tweeting and to those who wanted me to withdraw. (Nalog otvorila bez veze. Ovde nisam ničija ćerka, žena, portparol. Za pratioce se izborila zahvaljujući napornom tvitovanju i onima koji su hteli da odustanem.)	
Dr Orao Nebeski or Др Орао Небески @sasakzk	13,618	94,726		Aleksandar cpt. Koprivica For Healthy Serbia (Za zdravu Srbiju)	Belgrade, Serbia
Dragan Đorđević or Драган Ђорђевић @georgijemn	12,982	119,027		Graduated economist and anti globalist, enthusiast who likes to read about Atlantis and talk with well-intentioned people. (дипломирани економиста и антиглобалиста, занесењак који воли да чита о Атлантиди и воли да прича са добронамерним.)	Niš, Serbia
Ivan Miljanski @TalkingFlash	12,676	79,119		Admirer of real values and critic of everything bad. (Poštovalac pravih vrednosti i kritičar svega što je loše.)	Novi Sad, Serbia
Mita Segedinac or Мита Сегединац @msegedinac	8,579	2,286		Honest criminal. All for nature – Nature for all! (Поштени... кри во лац Сви за природу – природа за све!)	Novi Sad, Serbia
Bucili @buci_buc21	8,478	68,803		Proud mum… perfectionist, book lover and eternal dreamer. P.S. a little bit eccentric (ponosnamama...perfekcionista,zaljubljenik u knjige i vecita sanjalica.P.S.pomalo ekscentrik :))	Belgrade, Serbia

Spalesrbija1 @spalesrbija11	8,281	54,149	And the word is touch… if you know… And touch is the word… if you know… I gave and I do not regret, I regret that I did not get more! (I rec je dodir....ako znas...... I dodir je rec...ako znas.... Davao sam i ne zalim, zalim sto nisam dobijao vise!)	Belgrade, Serbia

During November and December 2017, Davidović retweeted others 88 times. The most retweeted posts originated from the National Serbian Front (41% of his retweets), Акакије (Akakije, 11.3%) and Milwall, a football club known for the most notorious hooligan gangs in England (8%). When it comes to #hashtags, Davidović mostly used those related to the National Serbian Front (6 times), its program and principles (21 times) and mission (5 times).

Table 4: The most frequent sources for retweets and the most used #hashtags (November–December 2017)

Retweets		Hashtags	
Национални српски фронт (НСФ) - National Serbian Front (NSF)	36	#циљеви_начела (#goals_principles)	21
Акакије	10	#НСФ (#NSF)	6
Milwall, FC	7	#историја (#history)	6
Arno Gujon	2	#за_шта_се_боримо (#what are we fighting for)	5
Mirjana Bobić Mojsilović	2	#православље (#orthodoxy)	5

To provide some additional context, he also twice retweeted Стојановић Јелена, a member of the Serbian Radical Party in the city of Niš, and Arno Gujon (@arnogujon), a French humanitarian who provided help for Serbian communities in Kosovo, but was linked with the far-right in his home country as well as in Serbia. Gujon appeared on N1 TV in Serbia, and when a journalist asked him about this connection, Davidović and members of his network reacted with evident outrage (see Figure 5). He himself called the journalist (Marija Antić) "mercenary scum" and she subsequently received threats via various online profiles and pages.[13]

Figure 5: Davidović's tweet after Gujon's appearance on N1[14]

Source: https://twitter.com/GoranDvd/status/936677182470066176

Dominant narratives, buzzwords and principles

Davidović's ideology combines strong anti-EU sentiment, radical views regarding Serbian nationhood and statehood (current Serbia is "occupied" and is not within its traditional borders), and the notion of Serbian unity (especially in a territorial sense in which he advocates for the abolishment of the Province of Vojvodina, and unification with Kosovo and with other "occupied Serbian territories" such as the Republika Srpska in neighboring Bosnia and Herzegovina). A tweet from 15 November 2017, illustrates these territorial aspirations:

---

13 http://rs.n1info.com/a346953/Vesti/Vesti/Gujon-precutao-da-je-znao-teme-razgovora.html
14 "Serbs, remember who helped, but also remember the mercenary scum who call themselves journalists. Who cannot remember, let them write it down. It will be important for history, but also for courts when freedom arrives..."

"The River Drina is the backbone of Serbianhood. It passes through the center of our **occupied and scattered Fatherland**. The Drina will never be a border!" (15 November 2017).

Freedom is a frequent principle to which Davidović refers in his tweets in the period under study. As an illustration, in his tweet on December 15, 2017, he states that, "freedom and justice are the ultimate ideals." Taking into account his references to "occupied Serbia," a term he uses regularly, "freedom" is something to which all Serbian people should strive. In several tweets he mentions freedom of speech specifically, highlighting the fact that *he* is the one who is deprived of such a freedom. (Such cases are indicated in his tweets on December 13, 18 and 23, 2017.)

Some of his tweets have a strong humanitarian content, such as one from December 21, 2017 when he called on his community to imagine one year without spending money, directing it instead to assist sick children and children without basic care. In this tweet, he did not direct followers to any specific aid organization, but made a general appeal. One could argue that this kind of "soft touch" appeal helps to soften and normalize his voice.

Figure 6: Davidović's tweet with a humanitarian tone[15]

Source: https://twitter.com/GoranDvd/status/944100633178787841

Davidović does not use explicit language to portray, insult, or dehumanize those who do not share his ideas or attitudes. He occasionally

---

15 "Imagine in Serbia a year without public celebrations and "New Year" parties, illumination, decorations, paying for concerts, financing EXIT [note: a festival], paying agencies and other kinds of tossing around national money. How many sick children could be medicated, fed, dressed… Only for one year."

uses repeated and specific phrases to describe and label the country ("occupied Serbia"), the Autonomous Province of Vojvodina ("bureaucratic monster," "Titoistic creation"), international organizations ("Soros' bullies" and "Soros' vultures;" "the stinky EU"), and journalists ("mercenary scum"), etc. But while analyzing Davidović's tweets during November and December, no direct or explicit calls for violence were noticed. He mainly uses subtle and indirect formulations to make members of his network react ("Say what you think..." on December 10, 2017; "Remember that, to acknowledge when the time of freedom arrives," on November 22, 2017).

Figure 7: Davidović's tweets with a call for action[16]

Sources (beginning top-left, then clockwise): https://twitter.com/GoranDvd/status/939907037911306240; https://twitter.com/GoranDvd/status/935867459885830145; https://twitter.com/GoranDvd/status/931108722704830465; https://twitter.com/GoranDvd/status/933378787143806976

---

16 On the left, from top to bottom:
    @GoranDvd: #when Montenegrin Ustasa from Andrijevica @CulaficGorann shows his true nature. Tell him what you think of his nastiness
    #phew your father eat s*it
    @CulaficGorann: Goran Davidovic The Firer is not killed he escaped to Italy and Gujon works for him, so there's no similarity.

It is also interesting to note that his calls to followers to take action are sophisticated and subtle. Instead of suggesting specific actions that might be considered to be a targeted call for mobilization, Davidović uses provocative and suggestive messages. "Tell them what you think…"; "Remember this…" or more explicitly, "Spread your anger…" — all examples of phrases he uses to activate his network and followers to react to something.

Research findings: an example of conservative Islam in cyber space

This section provides an overview and analysis of how one conservative Muslim leader uses online channels to disseminate his messages, with a focus on how Sead Islamović, Imam of the *Hadži Mehova* mosque from Novi Pazar, in addition to his regular offline activities, lectures and sermons, uses online platforms to further disseminate his messages and ideas. Some brief background provides needed context.

Why *Put sredine* matters

The research confirms that Islamović was a dominant voice and public protagonist of *Put sredine* until 2014, when this NGO was considered a "recruitment center" for the battlefield in Syria.

Islamović and *Put sredine* received media attention following police actions and the arrest of Sead Plovović and Izudin Crnišanin based on allegations of their involvement in terrorist activities and recruitment of young people for Syria. Both were considered Salafists and were members of the organization *Furkan*, a local NGO that served as a place for prayer and where Plovović served as Imam. *Furkan* and *Put*

@GoranDvd: in its announcement the Democratic Party has greets the verdict on general Mladic. Remember that so when the time of freedom comes we have that in mind.
On the right, from top to bottom:
@GoranDvd: All Croatian Ustasa should follow Praljak's example!
@GoranDvd: Do you know that children in Serbia and children in so-called Vojvodina have spring break/holiday in different times? As if there are two states? You don't know? Or you don't care? If you care spread your anger further. AP Vojvodina must be abolished if Serbia wants to live!

sredine, led by Islamović at that time, have been mentioned as recruitment centers (Danas 2014; Radio Free Europe 2015; Politika 2016). Plovović and Crnišanin remain imprisoned as the trial against them has been delayed several times, and has been considered as problematic and unfair (Voice of America 2018).

Multiple sources, mostly from interviews conducted during field research, indicate that *Put sredine* and Islamović himself used videos in 2014 that included content explicitly related to Syria, to raise awareness among Muslim youth in Sandžak about what was happening there. Respondents note that videos were shown during lectures and sermons in various places, including mosques. Content was also promoted through various online platforms on Facebook, including the portals *Islam Bosna*, *Put vremena*, *Minber.ba* or *Essune*. However, these videos were removed and are no longer available on YouTube.

However, some persons linked with Islamović respond that these allegations are baseless and tendentious. They say the roots of such allegations can be found in the bad relation between IZuS, led by Zukorlić, and Islamović himself (RTS 2013). Other sources, and this analysis, describe the split between Islamović and *Put sredine* that occurred in the last three to four years. A review of videos available on the YouTube channel of *Put sredine* shows that Islamović was the dominant voice until 2014, when other people (mainly Esad Mahmutović) replaced him as the main protagonist. It is worthwhile mentioning that the last video with Islamović as the main protagonist on *Put Sredine*'s YouTube channel was published in 2015.

Table 5: Dominant voices/topics on YouTube channel of "Put sredine" (through end January 2018)

Name	Views
Esad Mahmutović	26 %
Sead Islamović	16 %
Activities	11 %
Elvedin Pezić	8 %
Promo	6 %
Educational	5 %
Others	28 %

On the other hand, Islamović dominates the YouTube channel of the *Hadži Mehova* mosque, where 83 % of published videos contain him as the main, and sole, voice.

Table 6: Dominant voices/topics on YouTube channel of *Hadži Mehova džamija* (through end of January 2018)

Name	Views
Sead Islamović	83 %
Others	6 %
Activities	6 %
Promo	4 %
Safet Kuduzović	1 %

The fact that Islamović is no longer present on Put sredine's YouTube channel confirms what respondents, as well as other public sources (Sandžakpress 2017) have indicated — that there was a split between the NGO *Put sredine* and Islamović and his community, in spite of the fact that membership of both partly overlap. Therefore, these online channels and activities should be treated and analyzed separately. The focus of this research is on Islamović and activities related to his community around *Hadži Mehova*.

The *Hadži Mehova* mosque and its online activities

This mosque is formally under the jurisdiction of the IZuS (the one established by Zukorlić, with its base in Novi Pazar), but there are many problems in practice when it comes to collaboration and communication between the mosque and Zukorlić. The communities gathered around his *Hadži Mehova* and *Put sredine* are not the same, but many individuals are members of both.

The community gathered around *Hadži Mehova*, the biggest mosque in Novi Pazar, is very active in the online sphere. This research suggests that Islamović is not only active as an individual in this domain, but has support of technically savvy and information-literate people working on his behalf. The community is especially active on Facebook (more than 14,800 followers), and to a lesser extent on Instagram (more than 1,000 followers and 250 posts by the end of January 2018), while their core content — including lectures and speeches provided by Islamović—are available on the mosque's YouTube channel. Islamović also has his own personal Facebook profile with more than 7,000 followers. His profile is active and has at least one post per day. This personal page content partly overlaps with the Facebook page and You Tube channel run by *Hadži Mehova*. The following tables compares and contrasts some of the most general data related to the online activities of Islamović, *Hadži Mehova* and *Put sredine*.

Table 7: Overview of online channels and social networks

Name	Facebook	Instagram	Twitter	You Tube
Sead Islamović	>> 7,000 followers	n/a	n/a	n/a
Hadži Mehova džamija	>> 14,800 followers	>> 1,000 followers	n/a	>> 3,400 subscribers
Put sredine	>> 18,200 followers	>> 800 followers	n/a	>> 2,200 subscribers

Table 8: *Put sredine* and *Hadži Mehova džamija* (YouTube channels)

Hadži Mehova džamija	vs.	Put Sredine
21 April, 2014	Started	1 March, 2012
3,400+	Subscribers	2,200+
900,000+	Views	500,000+
290+	Videos	402+

Hadži Mehova YouTube channel

As can be observed from Tables 7 and 8, this YouTube channel has more than 3,200 subscribers, and has posted more than 290 videos since its establishment in 2014. The most popular video—"Djela koja uvode žene u dženet" ("Deeds that open heaven's door for women") was published in August 2015, and has had more than 93,000 views.

Table 9: The most popular videos on *Hadži Mehova* YouTube channel

Name	Views
Djela koja uvode žene u dženet (Deeds that open heaven's door for women)	93,000
Pojava Jedžuža i Medžuža (Advent of Yajuj and Majuj)	37,000
Pojava Dedžala (Advent of Dajjal)	34,000
Silazak Issa alejhi selam (Descent of Jesus)	27,000
Pojava Dedžala, II deo (Advent of Dajjal)	22,000
Rušenje časne Kabe (Destruction of the Honorable Kaaba)	19,000

During November and December 2017, the *Hadži Mehova* YouTube channel published 18 videos of Islamović's speeches — 9 in November, and 9 in December. The frequency of publishing is quite dynamic — one video is uploaded on every 3rd or 4th day. These 18 videos attracted more than 87,000 views (68,000 in November, and 19,000 in December 2017), 877 likes, 55 dislikes, and 44 comments. On average, there were 4,800 views, 48 likes/3 dislikes, and 2.4 comments per video. Not all videos have been equally popular; videos on the theme of human virtues were the most popular and attracted the most interaction. For example, the video "Zar majka to zaslužuje" ("Does a mother deserve that") from November 16, 2017 attracted more than 43,000 viewers (by the end of January 2018), had 471 likes, 32 dislikes, and 23 comments — all with positive reactions. Literally all of the 44 comments during this period were positive, glorifying the speaker (Islamović) and calling on God to reward him ("Allah will reward you"[17] was the most common comment).

The most salient topics Islamović addressed in this period were about marriage (33%), human virtues (28%) and the Qur'an and Islam (11%), as shown in Table 10 below.

---

17 "Allah te nagradio" in the local language.

Table 10: Topics/themes of Islamović's speeches in November–December, 2017

Topic/theme	Percentage
Marriage	33 %
Human virtues	28 %
Qur'an and Islam	11 %
Other (Prophet Mohammad, animals, Life, smart phones, women)	5 % each

Due to time constraints, this analysis didn't take into account the entire content of Islamović's speeches published on the *Hadži Mehova* YouTube channel. Instead, for the purposes of this research, I focused on those that have been the most popular, and that deal with the topic of women and their status, role and position within society and the family. These themes were selected in order to better understand whether his language and stances could be considered to be conservative, fundamentalist, or otherwise outside of mainstream European practice.

Dominant narratives and motifs in Islamović's speeches

In this section, some excerpts from Islamović's speeches are presented in order to show his tendency to include comments on and portrayals of women while addressing different topics (marriage and human virtues), including in two of his most popular speeches—"Does a mother deserve that" and "Deeds that make women enter paradise," which, at the time of this writing, is the most watched video with Islamović as main protagonist.[18] In all cases, the author added bold for emphasis.

When it comes to women's rights and obligations, Islamović nominally advocates the equality between males and females, but highlights this equality in terms of obligations. It is perhaps notable that in all of his lectures and speeches, Islamović begins with "Dear brothers," not noting "sisters," as is common by moderate and modern imams.

---

18 By the end of this research timeframe, the video had more than 90,000 views.

On marriage[19]

When addressing marriage and its importance, Islamović points to the roles of males, either husbands or fathers:

> "It is not a shame that a **father offers his daughter** to those he considers as worthy."[20]

Several times during his speeches he indicates that the role of women has been mostly passive throughout history, even presenting it as a rule, not as an exception:

> "A woman was shy, in the time of Muhammad, and during history she was mostly silent. The Prophet knew it, and he said that it is enough for women **to accept silently the offer** for marriage… Silence means acceptance. This is what the Prophet said. This was wise, and he did it to get them out of that shame."[21]

On human virtues[22]

Islamović has a tendency to compare males and females and to draw conclusions based on traditional gender roles. For him, there is an essential biological differentiation between genders that determines their main characteristics. While explaining what "being human" means, Islamović implies that it used to be a mostly male characteristic, but noting that throughout history women managed to reach this "human" level as well. In history of Islam, Islamović said, only four women could be considered as "complete" and completeness, according to his interpretation, refers to essential human virtues. Those women were Asiya, the wife of Pharaoh who reigned

---

19 This is from an Islamović sermon, "Importance of marriage," published on 31 October 2017. Video available on the following link: https://www.youtube.com/watch?v=7Q7nBzFLL0c&t=321s

20 "Nije stid da babo ponudi svoju kćerku za onoga koga vidi da je dobar…" (5:55)

21 "Žensko je do te mjere bilo stidljivo u vrijeme Allahovog Poslanika ili dalje kroz istoriju Isama, da kad bi je pitali hoćeš li šćeri da se udaš ona bi prešutjela. Ne bi imela snage da odgovori… Znajući da su djevojke stidljive, Allahov Poslanik, pa da ih izvučeš iz toga stida, rekao je dovoljno da to prećuti… Vidite kakva je to mudrost njegova, da je izvuče, da je ne posrami... Kada prećuti, kada je babo pita, to je saglasnost" (2:25)

22 This is from the videos, "Too many people, too little humanity," November 3, 2017, available at: https://www.youtube.com/watch?v=NfxE-13ut4w&t=54s; and, "Does a mother deserve that," November 16, 2017, available at: https://www.youtube.com/watch?v=4F-RfJDwCuw&t=307s

during the time of Moses, Aisha and Khadija, two of the Prophet's wives, and Fatimah, the Prophet's daughter.

In one of his most popular speeches on YouTube, Islamović prizes mothers and asks for more recognition of their role. He contrasts this to more liberal conceptions of women in society:

> "When we look at Europe and the West, they are advocating for women's rights… But, **what kind of women** are those? Those are women who are young, beautiful, who are not over 40 years… These women are **instrumentalized for different purposes**, you can guess what purpose… But, what about mothers' rights? There is no longer a woman's right there …"[23]

On women's obligations

In spite of the fact he is talking about women, their rights and obligations, he is addressing males directly since attendees in his mosque are males, and he always opens his speeches with the words: "Dear brothers." This is not the case with any particular speech, but with most. In his speech "Deeds that enable women to enter paradise," (August 2, 2015), Islamović highlights women's obligations as Muslims:

> "Only those women who pray five times per day, who fast during the month of Ramadan, who **protect her body and intimate places, who is not immoral, and who is submissive to her husband** will enter paradise."[24]

He highlights that some of these obligations are applicable to men, but some are particularly important for women. When it comes to "protection of intimate places," Islamović explicitly insist that true female believers need to be covered.

---

23 Excerpt from his speech "Does a mother deserve that," in the local language: "Kad pogledamo Evropu i Zapad traže se neka prava žena. Govore oni ženama treba dat neka prava, treba se brinuti o ženama… Razmislite, tako vam Allaha, o kojim ženama oni govore… To su žene koje su mlade, koje su lijepe, koje nisu preko 40 godina. To su žene koje se mogu koristiti u znate vi koje svrhe. A gde su tu prava majke? Tu više nema prava žena..." (4:03)
24 "Samo ona žena koja bude klanjala 5 dnevnih namaza, koja bude postila mjesec ramazan, koja bude štititila svoja stidna mjesta, koja ne bude nemoralna, i koja bude pokorna svome mužu ući će u dženet" (3:50)

"They should protect all that Allah forbids to be explicitly seen..."[25]

Women need to enter into marriage the "halal" (clean, proper…) way, Islamović stressed, and once they enter marriage they have additional obligations related to the afterlife:

> "Only those that are **submissive to their husbands** will enter paradise, choosing the door by themselves…"[26]

Islamović represents submission to the husband as an obligation of every female Muslim, or—in his interpretation—something given by God. To support his position, Islamović notes what women *do not* need to do—compared to males:

> "Allah didn't say women need **to go to jihad, to fight, to invest their property...** females don't even need to make the pilgrimage to Mecca if it is the case that **they don't have male company**, either a husband, brother, cousin…"[27]

In his speech "Hidžab" from July 2014,[28] Islamović repeatedly interpreted the female's obligation to be covered as part of their duty towards Allah. For him, praying is not enough:

> "Once they finish with prayer, a female walks the streets not uncovered, but almost naked… they think this is not a dangerous thing. They pretend they don't know this is a 24-hour haram, a big sin."[29]

He cited the Prophet's hadith in which Muhammad addressed two types of people that will be punished on Judgment Day:

---

25 "…da žena čuva svoja stidna mjesta... da čuva sve ono što je Allah zabranio da se vidi na njenom tjelu..." (6:35)
26 "Samo ona koja bude pokorna svome mužu ući će u dženet na vrata na koja ona bude htjela" (8:20)
27 "Nije Allah rekao da žena mora ići u džihad, da se bori, da ulaže imetak... čak sa žene spada obaveza da obavi hadžž ako nema pratioca, muškarca... muža, rođaka, brata... to je opet privilegija po njemu!" (8:50)
28 This speech is available on the following link: https://www.youtube.com/watch?v=XsBsQ15JRPY
29 "Imamo slučejava gdje su naše sestre, majke, kćerke pokorne u velikom broju tih ibadeta… Dolaze na namaz… Nakon što osvanu idu otkrivene ulicom, ne samo otkrivene već u velikoj meri razgolićene. Pa, možda one ne znaju koja je obaveza hidžaba. Ne znaju koja je naredba. Dosta njih govori nije to opasna stvar. Isto kao što ne znaju koja opasnost da ona 24 sata čini haram, i to veliki haram. Veliki grijeh…" (3:05)

> "The second category are women that are covered but uncovered... with tight, transparent clothing ... on their heads are haircuts similar to a camel's tail... they will not taste the smell of heaven." [30]

Compared to the period before (when he formally represented *Put sredine* and his speeches were regularly published on its YouTube channel) Islamović's rhetoric and language is actually less direct and explicit. A lecture on female believers ("Odlike vernica I" — "Features of female believers I") that was published on February 13, 2013, is a good illustration.[31] In his lecture, Islamović explicitly accused women of destroying earlier civilizations and peoples.

> "The first civilizations have fallen into immorality when they gave advantage to women instead of to their life goals..."

He further described women as a "weapon" of non-believers...

> "Infidels realized that a woman is a weapon that can destroy Muslims, and they succeeded..." [32]

In the sermons and speeches studied, a lack of morals, which he linked with women exclusively, is what destroyed the first Muslim community, the early Caliphate, and made Muslims blind to many moral and just things.

> "Neither wars, nor hunger are more dangerous than women!"[33]

He also provided several examples of women from the history of Islam and Muslims, noting that they should serve as role models for every female believer, including Hatidža ("first to embrace the Allah's faith, after the Prophet"), Sumeja ("first who gave up her soul on the Allah's path...") and Aisha ("the beloved one").

---

30 "Druga kategorija ljudi su žene koje su pokrivene otkrivene. Otkrivene, utegnute, providna odjeća... Kaže Poslanik na njihovim glavama su frizure kao kamilji repovi. One neće osetiti miris dženeta". (6:15)
31 This speech – "Characteristics of female believers" is available on the following link: https://www.youtube.com/watch?v=d6Hlt2aH1GA&t=903s
32 "Žena je stvar koji uništava narod i koji podiže narod... koja je uspjela da uništi prve civilizacije i narode... prve civilizacije su pale u nemoral kada su prednost dale žena nego svojim životnim ciljevima... " (1:40); "Nevjernici su skontali da je žena oružje kojim mogu da unište muslimane i to im je uspjelo..." (1:40)
33 "Ni ratovi, ni glad ništa nije opasnije od žena!" (6:40)

According to Islamović, the Western culture and way of life brought immorality and are to blame for the improper practice of Islam:

> "Non-believers, prevent our women from giving birth to new Omars... Today, women are occupied with different things they aren't supposed to be... Movies, series, different ways of life that are imported from the West... this produces disorder."[34]

This analysis of his narratives related to women and their rights and status showed that Islamović has applied very explicit and discriminatory rhetoric prior to 2014, when he was a dominant voice on the *Put sredine* YouTube channel. Following the split in 2014 and his shift to *Hadži Mehova* solely, his comments were marked with more sophisticated and less explicit rhetoric, but can still be viewed as problematic when it comes to certain perceptions and interpretations. Taking into account his authority and the lack of deliberation within the community he leads, such interpretations can at minimum be viewed as fundamentalist, and could be viewed as extreme in and for a country with EU aspirations.

Discussion of main findings

Research findings suggest that the selected protagonists of the far-right and rather conservative or even fundamentalist interpretations of Islam significantly use online channels to disseminate their ideas and strengthen their potential influence among targeted audiences. The findings also suggest a substantial difference between these two camps—far-right representative (Davidović) and the organization close to him (National Serbian Front) use Twitter the most, while the Muslim community around Sead Islamović relies on YouTube and Facebook. Being by nature a deliberative platform, Twitter enables Davidović to establish and generate his own virtual structure. This can be described as a democratized but hierarchized network of loose relations among the main generator or opinion

---

34 "Ćafiri, nevernici, sprečavaju našim ženama, hanumama da rađaju nove Omere... danas su hanume zaokupljene raznim stvarima kojima ne bi smele... filmovi, serije, raznim načinima življenja koji su uveženi sa Zapada... stvara se poremećaj!" (11:40)

leader (Davidović) and its members (followers or other influencers). These influencers, as analysis showed, come from different backgrounds, with diverse motivations and rationale, which result in complicated relationships with each other. This is definitely a field that deserves more research attention in the future.

Reflecting the language presented in the conceptual background at the beginning of this paper, Islamović's practice is closer to what Hofman explained as a top-down approach, in which real world individuals and leaders use the Internet to upgrade their offline activities and strengthen their message. On the other hand, Sageman's account of deliberative communication within the online social network suits Davidović's practice. In his practice, the Internet is a crucial generator of his online network in which he serves not as a formal leader, but enjoys a position as a facilitative influencer.

Structures

While online interaction is dominant in the case of Davidović's community, physical and real life communication and interaction is much more relevant for Islamović's community. Davidović is highly dependent on such a network, since he lives outside of Serbia and has no direct or physical contact with the majority of his followers. When it comes to interaction, Davidović prefers interaction with his followers and nodes within his online network (he is even open for criticism and discussion), and his community and interactions within are more dynamic and interactive. On the other hand, Islamović's virtual community is a replication of the real life community he leads, and he uses online channels only to further support his basic activities and strengthen his message. Interaction within Islamović's community is limited and moderated, in which one-way flow of information dominates (sermons, speeches, lectures).

Narratives

When it comes to narratives, both protagonists emphasize the need for self-protection in their speeches, posts, comments, etc., and while their subtle and sophisticated language doesn't explicitly employ xenophobic statements towards "the others" or "enemies," some indications of a tacitly exclusionary view are noticed. There is no (at least no direct) relationship between the discourses produced by these two leaders; they are not intentionally mentioning or feeding off one another. Davidović applies moderate language, relying on statements of democratic principles (such as freedom and justice) to express his ideas, and applying a fairly moderate tone while disseminating ideas that are in fact often not liberal in their intent. Islamović mostly applies "Islamic narratives," interpreting the Quran and Hadiths, using the language of ordinary people and illustrating his stance with examples from everyday life. Islamović is primarily targeting members of his community of Muslims, while Davidović has a potentially bigger audience (he targets both those who agree with him but also those with whom he disagrees and whom he criticizes or attacks). Topics that dominate Davidović's narratives include Serbia ("occupied"), Serbian nationalism, orthodoxy, but also social injustice and human causes (help to children or people in need, etc.).

Are Davidović and Islamović opinion leaders? Why?

While differently structured, their communities, either real or virtual, play an important role as a source of their legitimacy as informal (Davidović) or formal (Islamović) leaders. The *Hadži Mehova* mosque community has a structure, organization and hierarchy in which Islamović is an indisputable leader and influencer. On the other side, in Davidović's virtual community bonds are more flexible, and there is more than one influencer besides him.

In both cases, members of each community benefit from engaging and sharing opinions, ideas, and attitudes with like-minded others, in a way that is similar to their leaders. In the case of the community around Islamović, deliberation is mostly organized in an *ex cathedra* way and as a one-way communication channel, while within Davidović's community all virtual members of the network actively discuss the ideas presented. In the wider context (Serbia, Sandžak, the Islamic communities), Islamović is not considered as a leader, but within his community he is considered to be the main authority for all its members.

For both Davidović and Islamović, their communities, either real life or online, represent a type of social reality in which they and their followers seek confirmation and validation of their own interpretations and ideas. And they represent, accordingly, role models for their followers. Their communities serve as a channel for transmission of ideas and narratives. The gatekeeping role is much more present in the case of Islamović who is the person that ultimately decides what will be on the agenda, while the discursive nature of Davidović's network, generated around his Twitter account, allows others to comment, discuss, and delegate topics.

Conclusion and ideas for further research

This chapter analyzed the way two selected influential persons with ideas and viewpoints that can be considered radical or extreme use online channels and social media to disseminate their messages targeting in particular youth in Serbia. This analysis includes examples of the ultra-national and far-right (Goran Davidović), and of a conservative, fundamentalist Muslim voice in Serbia (Sead Islamović).

Efforts to analyze and detect trends in the use of online platforms and tools to disseminate extremist and radical ideas are similar to those tackling the widespread production of disinformation and "fake" news. In both cases, virtual structures generated in online space provide a powerful architecture through which influencers expose "problematic" and dangerous content to potentially vulnerable consumers.

Therefore, future research efforts should provide a nuanced analysis of the role of the Internet in the process of radicalization and its growing influence in spreading extremist ideas. On the level of methodology, there is a need for a more flexible and innovative approaches and designs to deepen our understanding of the operations of the networked flow of information. As an example, online participant observation could be employed and established as a regular practice to examine the content and visual aesthetics of posts crafted by influencers, and follow their digital trail across platforms.

Additional research also could consider an in-depth content analysis in order to detect potentially dangerous narratives, as well as to compare content across different platforms. At the level of network/community structure, there is a need for more in-depth analysis of the online structures around the Davidović and Islamović communities, since this small scale research only indicates the potential such an approach could bring to research on other influences in terms of their relationships with their followers online and in the real world.

References

Almond, Gabriel and Sidney Verba, eds.. 1989. The Civic Culture: Political Attitudes and Democracy in Five Nations. Thousand Oaks: Sage Publications.

Antonić, Slobodan. 2007. "Savremeni politički ekstremizam." *Hereticus*, 2: 23–30.

Awan, Akil N., Hoskins, Andrew, and O'Loughlin, Ben. 2011. *Radicalisation and Media: Connectivity and Terrorism in the New Media Ecology*. London: Routledge.

Balkan Inisight, "Mapping radicalization online, Resonant Voices Initiative, 2016." Retrieved on December 20, 2017. http://www.balkaninsight.com/en/page/mapping-radicalisation-online.

BBC. 2018. "Serbian police arrest neo-Nazis." *BBC News*, October 8, 2007. Retrieved on January 20, 2018. http://news.bbc.co.uk/2/hi/europe/7033156.stm.

Benson, D.C. 2014. "Why the Internet is Not Increasing Terrorism." *Security Studies* 23 (2): 293–328.

Blic. 2009. "Goran Davidović: Ostajem da živim u Trstu." *Blic*, April 16, 2009. Retrieved on March 5, 2018 https://www.blic.rs/vesti/hronika/goran-davidovic-ostajem-da-zivim-u-trstu/vwhs75p.

Brachman, Jarret. 2009. *Global Jihadism: Theory and Practice*. London: Routledge.

Čarnić, Dprotea. "Svedok: Išao sam u Siriju da ratujem za ID." *Politika*, 15 November 2016. Retrieved on February 15, 2018. http://www.politika.rs/sr/clanak/367886/Svedok-Isao-sam-u-Siriju-da-ratujem-za-ID.

CeSID. 2016. "Survey of the drivers of youth radicalism and violent extremism in Serbia," Completed in Cooperation with the UNDP Serbia Country Office, November.

Davidović, Goran. 2017. "Vojvodina se mora ukinuti ako Srbija želi da živi." 25 November, 2017. Retrieved on December 22, 2017 http://www.nacionalist.rs/2017/11/25/goran-davidovic-vojvodina-se-mora-ukinuti-ako-srbija-zeli-da-zivi/.

Đorić, Marija. 2014. *Ekstremna desnica: Međunarodni aspekti desničarskog esktremizma*, Beograd: Nauka i društvo Srbije.

Đorić, Marija. 2012. "Teorijsko određene ekstremizma," *Kultura polisa*, god. IX, 17: 45–62.

Đorić, Marija. 2016. *Ekstremna levica: ideološki aspekti levičarskog ekstremizma*. Beograd: Institut za političke studije.

Gill, Paul, Horgan, John, and Deckert, Paige. 2014. "Bombing Alone: Tracing the Motivations and Antecedent Behaviors of Lone-Actor Terrorists." *Journal of Forensic Sciences* 59 (2): 425–435.

Gill, Paul, Conway, Maura, Corner, Emily, and Thornton, Amy. 2015. "What are the Roles of the Internet in Terrorism? Measuring Online Behaviours of Convicted UK Terrorists." http://voxpol.eu/wp-content/uploads/2015/11/DCUJ3518_VOX_Lone_Actors_report_02.11.15_WEB.pdf.

Ibrović, Enes. "Poruka braći iz 'Puta sredine.'" *Sandžak press*, September 2017. Retrieved on January 25, 2018. http://sandzakpress.net/poruka-braci-iz-puta-sredine.

Insajder. 2017. "Ćutanje države na ekstremizam u odelu 'umerene desnice.'" *Insajder*, February 4, 2017. Retrieved on February 22, 2018. https://insajder.net/sr/sajt/tema/2959/.

Jelinčić, Jadranka and Ilić, Snežana, (eds.) 2013. *Politički ekstremizam u cyber prostoru Srbije*. Zrenjanin: Centar za razvoj civilnog društva.

Katz, Elihu. 1957. "The two-step flow of communication: An up-to-date report on an hypothesis." *Public Opinion Quarterly*, 21: 61–78.

Katz, Elihu and Lazarsfeld, Paul. 1955. *Personal Influence: The part played by people in the flow of mass communication*. New York: The Free Press.

Komarčević, Dušan. 2015. "Počelo suđenje organizatorima odlaska na sirijsko ratište." *Radio Free Europe*, March 2015. Retrieved on February 14, 2018. https://www.slobodnaevropa.org/a/beograd-pocelo-sudjenje-organizatorima-odlaska-na-sirijsko-ratiste/26904028.html.

Kostić, Stevan. "Sandžačko-sirijska vežba," *RTS*, 27 June, 2013. Retrieved on February 14, 2018. http://www.rts.rs/page/stories/sr/story/125/drustvo/1350266/sandzacko-sirijska-veza.html.

Hoffman, Bruce. 2006. "The Use of the Internet by Islamic extremists," Testimony presented to the US House Permanent Select Committee on Intelligence. https://www.rand.org/content/dam/rand/pubs/testimonies/2006/RAND_CT262-1.pdf.

Hoffman, Bruce. 2008. "The MYouTubeh of Grass-roots Terrorism." *Foreign Affairs* 87 (1).

Kostić, Ivan Ejub. 2015. "Serbia," In *Yearbook of Muslims in Europe* edited by Oliver Scharbrodt, 7: 503–514. London: Brill.

Marko, Davor. 2011. "Alterization of Islam: Borders between Islam and other Faiths, defined by Media." In *Spaces and Borders. Young Researchers about Religion in Central and Eastern Europe*, edited by András Máté-Tóth and Cosima Rughinis, 191–206. Berlin: De Gruyter.

Marko, Davor. 2013. "Power Constellation(s), Symbolic Divisions and Media: Perception of Islam as a Personalized, 'Minorized' and Subordinated Part of Serbian Society." In *Us and them: Symbolic division in Western Balkan Societies*, edited by I. Spasić and P. Cvetičanin, 179–198. Niš: Centre for Empirical Cultural Studies of SEE.

Marko, Davor. 2011. "The Role of Opinion Leaders in the Dissemination of Media Messages During the Re-Election Period: The Case of Bosnia and Herzegovina," *CEU Political Science Journal*, 6, no. 2: 167–191.

McCauley, Clark and Moskalenko, Sophia. 2011. "Individual and Group Mechanisms of Radicalization." In *Protecting the Homeland From International and Domestic Security Threats*, Fenstermacher, L., Kuznar, L., Rieger, T., and Speckhard, A. (eds.), 81–92. Washington D.C.: Air Force Research Laboratory.

Meleagrou-Hitchens, Alexander and Kaderbhai, Nick. 2017. "Research perspectives on online radicalization." International Centre for the Study of Radicalisation (ICSR), King's College London/VOX Poll center of excellence. https://icsr.info/wp-content/uploads/2017/05/ICSR-Paper_Research-Perspectives-on-Online-Radicalisation-A-Literature-Review-2006-2016.pdf.

Neumann, Peter. 2013. "Options and Strategies for Countering Online Radicalization in the United States." *Studies in Conflict and Terrorism* 36 (6): 431–459.

Neumann, Peter. 2017. "Countering Violent Extremism and Radicalisation that Lead to Terrorism: Ideas, Recommendations and Good Practices from the OSCE region." report. https://www.osce.org/chairmanship/346841.

Neumann, Peter and Stevens, Tim. 2011. *Countering Online Radicalisation: A Strategy for Action*, London: International Centre for Study of Radicalisation.

Neumann Peter, and Rogers, Brooke. 2011. *Recruitment and Mobilisation for the Islamist Militant Movement in Europe*, London: King's College London.

Novosel, Slađana. "Povezanost vehabija sa Al Kaidom," *Danas*, 16 March, 2014. Retreived on February 15, 2018 https://www.danas.rs/drustvo/povezanost-vehabija-sa-al-kaidom/.

O'Loughlin, Ben, Boudeau, Carole, and Hoskins, Andrew. 2011. "Distancing the Extraordinary: Audience Understandings of Discourses of "Radicalization."' *Continuum* 25 (2): 153–164.

Petrović, Predrag and Stakić, Isidora. 2018. *Estremism Research Forum: Serbian Report*. Belgrade: British Council.

Podunavac, Milan. 2006. *Revolucija, legitimitet i poredak: slučaj Srbije*. Beograd: Čigoja.

RTV Novi Pazar. 2018. "Muratović kritikuje 'Put sredine' pa posećuje skupove." Retrieved on January 20, 2018. https://www.youtube.com/watch?v=EmnJ5zt-iQE.

Radio-televizija Srbije. 2013. "Sandžačko-sirijska veza," *Radio-televizija Srbije* June 27, 2013. Retrieved on February 15, 2018. http://www.rts.rs/page/stories/sr/story/125/drustvo/1350266/sandzacko-sirijska-veza.html.

Sageman, Marc. 2004. *Understanding Terror Networks*, Philadelphia: University of Pennsylvania Press.

Sageman, Marc. 2004. *Leaderless Jihad: Terror Networks in the Twenty-First Century*. Philadelphia: University of Pennsylvania Press.

Sandžak Press. 2013. "Islamović o odlascima u Siriju za medije." *Sandžak Press* 29 May, 2013. Retrieved on February 15, 2018. http://sandzakpress.net/islamovic-o-odlascima-u-siriju-za-medije-ne-komentarisem-bez-dozvole-predstavnika.

Scharbrodt, Oliver, (ed.) 2015. *Yearbook of Muslims in Europe, Vol. 7*. London: Brill.

Škrgić Mikulić, Elameri. 2018. "Srbija: Četiri početka suđenja godine." *Voice of America*, 12 January, 2018, Retrieved on February 16, 2018. https://ba.voanews.com/a/4204748.html.

Šper, D. "Zovi, samo zovi." RT Vojvodina, https://www.youtube.com/watch?v=JSRJFINJlNw&t=131s.

Šper, D. & F. Vidojević, "Zabranjeni." RT Vojvodina, https://www.youtube.com/watch?v=I7IR2CPeSOE&t=18s.

Šper, D. "Šetnja, strepnja, pretnja." RT Vojvodina, https://www.youtube.com/watch?v=iNbyrW8k5B4&t=1s.

Valić Nedeljković, Dubravka, Knežević, Nikola, and Gruhonjić, Dinko. 2015. *Uloga medija u normalizaciji odnosa na Zapadnom Balkanu*. Novi Sad: Filozofski fakultet, Univerzitet u Novom Sadu/Centar za istraživanje religije, politike i društva.

Vladisavljević, Nebojša. 2008. *Serbia's Antibureaucratic Revolution: Milošević, the Fall of Communism and Nationalist Mobilization*. New York: Palgrave Macmilan.

Vladisavljević, Nebojša. 2014. "Competitive Authoritarianism and Popular Protest: Evidence from Serbia under Milošević." *International Political Science Review*, 37 (1): 36–50.

The Nexus between Online Violent Extremism and Serbian Youth: How Do Young People in Novi Sad, Bor, Zaječar, and Tutin Perceive Online Extremist Narratives?

Kristina Ivanović

Introduction

Over the past few years the topics of radicalization, extremism and terrorism have become an important part of policy discussions in South East Europe, and Serbia is no exception. Existing research suggests that the main reason behind this trend are primarily concerns of ISIS/Daesh-inspired terror occurring outside of Syria and Iraq, the threat of foreign terrorist fighters gaining battlefield experience and then coming back to their home countries, as well as the substantial media attention which surround terrorist activities (Perry 2016). Globalization has made the fight against violent extremism more difficult as violent extremism occurs in many different contexts and takes various forms (Barber 2001; Ebner 2017). Additionally, Internet technologies and social media allow easier connections between groups and individuals, and therefore recruitment and radicalization have become easier (UNDP Serbia Country Office and CeSID 2016).

Various extremist organizations rely on the Internet to promote their rhetoric and to recruit people to their cause, particularly through popular online social media applications. For example, ISIS's social media strategy expanded exponentially from Twitter and Facebook to include dozens of platforms on the open web such as Telegram and various private groups, as well as engaging through some platforms on the dark web (Greenberg 2016). ISIS is self-consciously looking to build a cyber Caliphate, at times referred to as a digital Caliphate (Atwan, Khan and Butter 2015; Greenberg 2016). Far-right groups also view the Internet as an instrument which provides access to new audiences; therefore their strategies include leveraging online resources in order to propagate messages of violence and division (Waldron 2012; Awan and Zempi 2016). Through social media, extremist organizations speak directly to the youth they often target for recruitment, using the medium that works best for these young people.

Generally speaking, while economic factors alone cannot explain radicalization, uneducated, disenfranchised individuals lacking a clear perspective to live up to their true potential are often the most vulnerable to such narratives (OSCE 2015). This is troubling in light of the socio-economic situation in Serbia. Youth unemployment in Serbia is exceptionally high, and this is a pressing issue facing the country. According to official statistics, about 37% of young people were unemployed in the second quarter of 2016. Such a high unemployment rate negatively affects public health and national security as it can lead to increased poverty, crime, mental illness, etc. According to research conducted by the United Nations Development Program in Serbia (UNDP) and the Centre for Free Elections and Democracy (CeSID) these factors alone are sufficient to conclude that young people in Serbia have the potential to become attracted to radical and extremist ideas and ideologies (UNDP Serbia Country Office and CeSID 2016).

Built around the research question ***How do young people in Serbia perceive online extremist messages and narratives,*** this research seeks to contribute to an understanding of the various factors that can influence extremist behavior. Becoming radicalized[1] is a dynamic process and there is no a single pathway that leads into this kind of behavior. Possible drivers of radicalization are different, complex, and can be combined in a unique way in each case as they depend on the social environment as well as on the personal circumstances and psychology of a given man or woman (OSCE 2014). The main findings of the research indicate that while it seems

---

1   In this study, the term "radicalization" is used to refer to the process of developing extremist ideologies and beliefs (Borum 2011).

that young people are minimally receptive to online fundamentalist/Wahhabi[2] and radical right recruiting attempts, some reasons for concern still do exist.

The first part of this research outlines a theoretical framework that consists of relative deprivation theory together with social identity theory. For the methodology, field research and direct engagement with young people in areas often characterized as at risk were necessary in order to learn more about current trends in the way young people perceive and understand the online environment to which they are exposed, and regional differences in these perspectives. Therefore, the focus group method was chosen as most appropriate. First, a targeted content analysis of far-right and Wahhabi narratives online was conducted in order to identify major discourses around which extremist narratives are built. Then, examples of the narratives were used in focus group discussions in order to gain insights on their perceptions of extremist discourses. Finally, based on the focus group findings, conclusions and recommendations are presented.

Theoretical framework

Given the often powerful influence of an individual's attachment to a group, some scholars argue that one key to understanding peace and conflicts in today's world lies in applying a social identity approach[3] (Hennessey and West 1999; Hogg 2001; McKeown, Haji and Ferguson 2016). Analyzing the psychological attachment that one has for a group can be an important step towards understanding extremism, the process of radicalization, and the consequences of both. As argued by Hogg (2014), not every group is problematic and difficulties can occur when people zealously identify with

---

2 Terminology can be difficult on this issue. For reasons of simplicity the interpretation of Islam considered to be extreme when compared to the traditional Islamic practice in the region will be referred to as either fundamentalist, or as Wahhabi – a descriptor used by many of the respondents.
3 In 1979 Henri Tajfel and John Turner introduced Social Identity Theory which argues that various groups such as sports clubs, family, science clubs, etc. are important sources of an individual's self-esteem, and a tool to confirm one's sense of social identity and belonging to a social world.

highly distinctive groups. Extreme groups are usually intolerant of diversity, seek and support strong leadership, and hold ideological and ethnocentric belief systems that dictate group-normative behavior (Hogg 2014). According to Hogg, people are attracted to these groups as they try to reduce uncertainty about their perceptions, attitudes, feelings, and behaviors. In periods of such uncertainty, people identify more strongly with groups which can provide a more clearly defined and directed sense of self (Hogg 2014). The theory adds significant value in explaining the fertile ground for extremism as it also argues that identity validation from the group can be very difficult to obtain. That is why, for example, some individuals decide to employ radical means — potentially including violence — in order to prove their determination to become a group member.

Social identity theory can be applied to the complexities of Serbian society in a study of VERLT; however, this theory alone is not sufficient to provide an adequate understanding of the socio-economic factors responsible for leading some individuals to become engaged in extremist activities. Relative deprivation theory can also be informative, as it links economic disparity with the likelihood of individuals to embrace violent actions. The theory refers to the deprivations experienced (or perceived) when individuals (egoistic deprivation) or a group (fraternal deprivation) compare themselves with others: that is, individuals/groups who lack something compare themselves with the person or group that has it (or which they perceive have it), and in doing so feel deprived (Walker and Pettigrew 1984; Parida 2007; Halevy et al. 2010). Relative deprivation theory[4] argues that feelings such as resentment and anger emerge when a person perceives and acknowledges inequalities that are not necessarily based on objective criteria. The element of comparison is an important element of the theory: individuals who lack something compare themselves with those who have it (Parida 2007). In other words, discontent occurs when a group or a person

---

[4] According to some authors, the nexus between relative deprivation and the onset of conflict is "simplistic" because it fails to explain why some poor people or places do *not* participate in violence (Agbiboa 2015, 16).

wants something and feels entitled to possess the thing they want, but also perceives that another person or a group has the thing they want (Webber 2007; Halevy *et al.* 2010).

In regard to extremism, the notion of what precisely an individual is or is perceived to be deprived of can vary significantly. Literature suggests that in societies where the government is failing to provide elementary justice, security and welfare, individuals tend to feel a sense of deprivation (Parida 2007; Webber 2007; Agbiboa 2015). Parida (2007) further argues that VERLT related dynamics and activities can prosper in societies with a wide discrepancy between rising expectations and declining opportunities for a population—especially among youth (Parida 2007). In this sense, extremist groups may rely on an existing or carefully cultivated sense of egoistic relative deprivation and victimhood in the individual members they seek to recruit. Consequently, this can lead an individual to join the group in order to start a joint effort against a mutual enemy that is perceived to be responsible for their relatively deprived state (Dim 2017).

While generally speaking extremism refers to activities—beliefs, attitudes, feelings, strategies—which are out of the ordinary and outside of the mainstream, it also remains a highly controversial topic. There is no universal definition of this concept, and, for example, Ebner labels anyone "who deliberately incites hatred and fears to exploit existing or provoked tensions for their political agenda" as extremist (Ebner 2017, 13). Extremism as such is a very complex phenomenon which cannot be understood neatly by any single theory, or any single discipline. Hence, this paper argues that social identity theory together with the theory of relative deprivation may provide a useful explanatory mechanism for considering extremism dynamics in Serbia. While poverty makes the population receptive to extremist messages, it is the ideas which individuals choose to adopt that makes them pursue the path of extremism and radicalization.

Youth vulnerability online

Academics and experts worldwide agree that while access to information and communications technologies (ICT) has provided countless opportunities for youth to connect beyond national borders, it has also brought many risks, especially in regard to spreading division, conflict and violent extremism (Geeraerts 2012; Amr 2015; Costello *et al.* 2016; Mughal 2016; Awan 2017). Therefore, the international community and various governmental and non-governmental development initiatives, have recognized the importance of empowering youth with values, knowledge, and capacities to protect themselves against the full range of online threats, including online radicalization to violence (The White House 2013; UNESCO 2015). Abuse that occurs on social networking sites, blogging sites, online chat rooms, and other virtual platforms poses a serious threat not only online. The existing literature suggest that online abuse can also be considered a threat to societal inclusiveness and a potential motivator for hateful acts offline (Awan 2014). Many posts and comments disseminated through social networking sites and similar platforms have an incendiary undertone; therefore some authors argue that online abuse can escalate into attacks in real life (Waldron 2012; Awan and Zempi 2016).

As the Internet has enabled various groups (including extremists) previously incapable of broadly organized actions to amplify their voices, it is important to research the manner in which youth understand these online dynamics. As theory suggests, due to the bad socio-economic situation young people in Serbia can be exposed to particular vulnerabilities that could lead them to embrace radical and extremist ideas and ideologies. The risks of embracing extremist ideas is even more pronounced in light of recent trends in regional and global politics. For example, across Europe and beyond, messages from the extreme right are surfacing with increasing and alarming regularity in both the public and virtual space. Recent elections in the USA, France, Austria, and the Netherlands, and the Brexit referendum in the United Kingdom all have one thing in common: a shift to the populist right including nativist and authoritarian strains (Jekel, Lehner and Vogler 2017).

A Bloomberg analysis of election results across 22 European countries revealed that support for populist radical right parties was higher in 2017 than it has been at any time over the past 30 years (Tartar 2017). Furthermore, global population movements have been contributing to rising mistrust between groups and have deepened existing stereotypes (Džuverović 2016; Rečević this volume). All of these challenges, coupled with the grievances that right-wing movements in Serbia are claiming—such as inequalities when it comes to the treatment of the Serbian Orthodox majority vs. national minorities, the notion of a "stolen" Kosovo, bigotry towards migrants, and hostility towards the spreading of neoliberal values across society—can further boost far-right mobilization in Serbia.

Beside the trends of growing right-wing extremism, ISIS/*Daesh*-inspired extremism also plays an important role in radicalization trends across the Western Balkans, including Serbia. For example, the Islamic State has invested in online campaigns targeting audiences in the Western Balkans. In June 2015 they released a video in which they invited Balkan Muslims to "either join, or kill over there" (Ejdus and Jureković 2016). More recently, in summer 2017, they released an article entitled "*The Balkans — Blood for Enemies, and Honey for Friends*" in which they make direct threats to Serbs and Croats over their role in the wars during 90s. Both messages have a strong grievance component, and it seems that the more Western countries are involved militarily in the Islamic world, particularly in a way that kills civilians, the more young Muslims are likely to see defending their coreligionists as a legitimate goal (Shaffer 2016). A local study published by the Helsinki Committee had similar conclusions. Even though the study does not provide a comparative perspective of different regions and religions, it concluded that Sandžak[5] youth are potentially or even actually open to Islamist extremism and that a not insignificant part of Sandžak youth considers defending their religion with violence as justified (Ilić 2016).

---

5   Sandžak is a part of Serbia in the southwestern part of the country, where a majority of the country's Muslims have lived since the time of the Ottoman empire.

Mapping right-wing movements in Serbian cyber space

There are strong movements at the far-right of the political spectrum in Serbia (Bakić 2013; Jarić 2015) and young people who are often unemployed and generally not well-educated serve as their recruiting base. Examples of far-right nationalist inspired extremism are expressed through hooliganism and serious incidents of street violence where, for example, they get into fights with the fans of opposing teams and the police. According to Bakić (2013) due to social frustrations the generation that grew up during the 1990s and reached adulthood after 2000 became easy prey for the old and the newly emerging far-right movements such as *Obraz*, *Nacionalni stroj*, *Krv i čast*, *Srpski narodni pokret (SNP) 1389*, *Srpski narodni pokret Naši*, and *Srbska akcija* (Bakić 2013). The tables below summarize some of the most influential right-wing movements and their online presence, as well as basic outlines of their ideology.[6]

Table 1: Serbian right-wing movements and their cyber activities

Organization	Website	Facebook	Twitter	Blog/YouTube	Organization Head
Nacionalni Srpski Front (National Serbian Front)	http://nsfront.org/za-sta-se-borimo/?lang=lat	https://www.facebook.com/goran.davidovic.79	https://twitter.com/NSF_Srbija	https://gorandavidovic.com/category/goran/blog/	Goran Davidović
Krv i čast (Blood and Honor)[7]	http://28serbia.blogspot.rs/	No FB page	No Twitter page	https://www.stormfront.org/forum/t893766/; http://combat18.blogspot.rs/2016/04/combat-18.html	Leaderless Resistance[8]

---

6 All noted web sites were last accessed/confirmed on November 6, 2018.
7 This is a Neo-Nazi movement.
8 Leaderless resistance offers an alternative to a classical movement organization which consists of leader, members, and activists. Leaderless resistance operates without an hierarchal command; structure is made from small cells (around 5 people) that work independently. They do not have a leader, but they are guided by the same goal. They can also have a solo actions referred to as "Lone Wolf" actors. Read more at: https://www.stormfront.org/forum/t893766/

Srbska akcija (Serbian Action)	https://akcija.org/	No FB page	https://twitter.com/srbskaakcija	https://akcija.org/blog/	Data not available[9]
SNP 1389 (Serbian People's Movement)	http://www.snp1389.rs/	https://www.facebook.com/SNP1389/	No Twitter page	https://www.youtube.com/user/SNP1389TV	Miša Vacić (until 2014)
Obraz (Honor)	http://www.obraz.rs/	https://www.facebook.com/mladen.obraz	https://twitter.com/PokretOBRAZ	https://www.youtube.com/user/OBRAZinfo/videos	Mladen Obradović

Table 2:   Serbian right-wing movements and their ideology

Right-wing organizations' ideology	
National Serbian Front/*Nacionalni Srpski Front*[10] (NSF)	National freedom Greater Serbia ideology: Unity of all Serbian people and Serbian territories Ideology aimed at all Serbs—regardless of religious or ethnic convictions Social justice—everyone has the right to be employed, to have a house and no one should be hungry Against Euro-Atlantic integration—in favor of a "Europe of Nations" Against neoliberal capitalism Both males and females have the right to serve the army and defend the country Official program does not address women's rights Against LGBT rights
Serbian action/*Srbska akcija*[11] (SA)	Against capitalism and neo-liberalism Community more important than the individual Advocating for monarchical rule: God - King - Head of Household Specific social structure that is built by the "authentic" Serbian spirit and Serbian interests Greater Serbia Limited emancipation, and traditional gender roles Relies on tradition, social welfare and spiritual (Orthodox) discipline
Serbian National Movement 1389/*SNP 1389*[12]	Greater Serbia Social justice Orthodox faith Family values Against Euro-Atlantic integration, in favor of integration with countries like Russia, China, Brazil

---

9   However, additional context can be found at http://www.blic.rs/vesti/hronika/otkrivamo-pravnik-na-celu-nacistickog-stroja/pmrg5wp
10 See more directly on NSF website: http://nsfront.org/za-sta-se-borimo/?lang=lat
11 https://akcija.org/o-nama/
12 http://nsfront.org/za-sta-se-borimo/?lang=lat

	Fight against any type of "deviant" behavior (drugs and LGBT)
Honor/*Obraz*[13]	Nationalism based in the Orthodox faith
	Against Euro-Atlantic integration
	Serbian traditional domestic order ("*domaćinski poredak*")
	Limited emancipation; support for traditional gender roles
	Christian morality will lead to a healthy and wealthy society
	Greater Serbia
Movement Blood and Honour Serbia/*Pokret krv i čast*[14]	Ideology based on white race superiority and national-socialism
	Against abortion — the white race is in decline
	Aryan order (racial ideology)
	Against religion, capitalism, communism, human rights, in favor of paganism

Mapping fundamentalist/Wahhabi narratives in Serbian cyber space

Two Islamic communities have been actively operating in Serbia since October 2007, and both claim to represent all of the Muslims of Serbia: the Islamic Community *in* Serbia (IZuS) and Islamic Community *of* Serbia (IZS). While IZS is more oriented towards political leadership in Belgrade, by contrast IZuS is oriented towards Sarajevo, with its Serbian focal point in Novi Pazar. The differences between these two communities are mostly political and less religious; however the division has sparked some intolerance between these groups and the Bosniak population has become internally divided (King Savić 2017). Furthermore, the schism has created a gap which has the potential to contribute to the process of extremism and radicalization. Individuals who do not want to side with either of the two groups, or who feel this earthly split reflects the corruption of the faith as it has been practiced in the region, could seek other interpretations of the faith viewed as more conservative, pure, or fundamentalist.

There are individuals and groups that are trying to present different interpretations of Islam that are not traditional in the region. Fundamentalist Salafists, sometimes referred to as Wahhabis,

---

[13] http://www.obraz.rs/o-nama/
[14] http://28serbia.blogspot.rs/search/label/%D0%98%D0%B4%D0%B5%D0%BE%D0%BB%D0%BE%D0%B3%D0%B8%D1%98%D0%B0

represent one such group.[15] Recent research showed that the movement has not only challenged the moderate practice of Islam across the Western Balkans, but that it has also become well-organized and is supported with a significant amount of money from abroad (Racimora 2013; Bećirević 2016). More importantly, members of the Wahhabi community have become quite active in the cyber space of Serbia (Kladničanin 2013; Marko this volume). Even though there have been no major recent incidents among Wahhabis in Serbia,[16] this movement is connected with some very controversial individuals, such as Mevlid Jašarević, who was born in Novi Pazar and who shot at the American embassy in Sarajevo in 2011, or Nedžad Balkan from Tutin (about 90 minutes from Novi Pazar), who was arrested in Austria in 2017 under charges of recruiting for the Islamic State (Blic 2017).

Due to religious and geographical proximity and the fact that a significant number of Muslims that live in Serbia see Sarajevo as their spiritual center, it would be incomplete to analyze radicalization trends in Sandžak without understanding trends in Bosnia. Some Wahhabis are popular in both Serbian and Bosnian Muslim communities, including Safet Kuduzović[17] – viewed as the "ultimate

---

15 Wahhabism is a conservative religious branch of Sunni Islam, named after the 18th century reformist scholar Muhammad ibn Abd al-Wahhab, who advocated restoration of the earliest Islamic beliefs and practices. Wahhabism is the official doctrine of Saudi Arabia. The Salafi movement and the doctrine of Salafism promote an interpretation of Islam that emulates the Salaf as an eternal model for Muslims and rejects later innovations to the religion (bid'ah) . In neighboring Bosnia, in mainstream Bosnian society, the terms "Wahhabi" and "Salafi" are often used interchangeably; but Salafi adherents find the term Wahhabism offensive (Bećirević 2016).
16 In 2005, a few Wahhabis caused an incident in Novi Pazar, disrupting a music concert by jumping on the stage and breaking instruments. Additionally, they told people that came to go home, as the concert is an affront to Allah. Read more: https://www.b92.net/info/vesti/index.php?yyyy=2006&mm=06&dd=05&nav_category=12&nav_id=199956
    Also, in 2014 two fundamentalists were arrested under charges of terrorism. They were the leaders of the NGO Furkan, and were recognized to be leaders of a local movement that recruited fighters for Syria. http://www.novosti.rs/vesti/naslovna/hronika/aktuelno.291.html:481904-Vehabije-umesto-u-Siriju-stigle-u-zatvor
17 "Should a woman go to university?" Kuduzović's answer is that a woman has a right to a job or education but only in "appropriate" professions that allow her to contribute to the good of Muslim society. He specifically bans women from studying criminal justice, engineering, or any other profession in which they are likely to mix

authority" among adults adhering to this faith interpretation, and Elvedin Pezić, who is popular among the younger population. The rhetoric of both is in line with the narratives of Imad el-Misri. El-Misri presented the 1992–1995 war in Bosnia as a lesson for Bosnian Muslims who were not on the "true path." He implies that Bosnian Islam has led Bosnian Muslims into becoming "bad Muslims" who were punished during the war for walking the wrong path (Bećirević 2016). Also very popular in Sandžak is Sead Islamović, who was connected to the controversial NGO *Put Sredine* from Novi Pazar that media reports note was involved in recruitment for the Syrian war (Teodorović 2013), and who now leads a large mosque in the city. (Marko studies some of his online sermons in this volume.) Furthermore, media often points out the strong connection between Wahhabis in the Western Balkans and Bosniak diaspora clerics living in Austria such as Nedžad Balkan (originally from Tutin) and Muhamed Porča (born in Sarajevo). Another Austrian based extremist whose online reach is targeted at the Western Balkans is Nusret Imamović who stands behind the website *putvjernika.com*, which glorifies jihad (Blic, 2017).

Influential Wahhabi narrative creators in Serbia mostly use YouTube channels to propagate their messages. The table below summarizes some of their online activities.

Table 3: Wahhabi cyber activities — some highlights

Name	Affiliated with	Facebook	Blog/Youtube
Nedžad Balkan	*Al-Sahaba* mosque in Vienna	n/a	Ebu Muhammed https://www.youtube.com/watch?v=7EhYgBJnE-M
Mohamed Porča	*Al-Tewhid* mosque in Vienna	n/a	https://www.youtube.com/results?search_query=Mohamed+Por%C4%8Da

---

with men in the course of doing their job. See video: https://www.youtube.com/watch?v=_DY9gb7541I

Elvedin Pezić	Often guest lecturer at the NGO *Put Sredine*	https://www.facebook.com/pezicelvedin/	https://www.youtube.com/results?search_query=Elvedin+Pezic
Safet Kuduzović	https://s-d-o.org/ *Švedska Dawetska Organizacija*	https://www.facebook.com/Safet-Kuduzovi%C4%87-1819196525023053	https://www.youtube.com/channel/UCjPYKNcScum3kvQhV63YbiA/videos
Sead Islamović	*Hadži-Mehova mosque*	https://www.facebook.com/HadziMehovaDzamija/	https://www.youtube.com/user/HadziMehovaDzamija/videos

Research methodology

For the purpose of this study a qualitative methodology was chosen as most appropriate, including desk research, fieldwork focus group research and field observation. Research and data collection were carried out in a few stages from November 2017 to February 2018.

Desk research was done during the preparatory phase of the study, which consisted of a survey and in-depth review and analysis of literature on the nexus between extremism, radicalization, and youth. The next step was to identify primary sources such as the most important far-right movements' and Wahhabi narrative creators' portals, social networks, and YouTube channels. A brief and structured content analysis of the identified websites served as a basis and reference for developing the focus group questionnaire. The fieldwork phase was carried out in January 2018 and consisted of nine focus groups in geographically different parts of Serbia. A creative sampling strategy in terms of location was used, with the intention of gathering a wide view of perspectives in spite of the limited research timeframe; therefore, two cities (Novi Sad and Zaječar) and two municipalities (Bor and Tutin) were chosen as a small but diverse sample that includes communities in Vojvodina, south western, and eastern Serbia. The very different ethnic structure of the local populations (see Table 4) made these locations interesting and relevant to the research subject. The author contacted local non-governmental youth-related organizations that helped in recruiting relevant participants. This selection has limitations in terms of the relations to the contacted NGOs; however it was necessary in the absence of extended field time in each community. A total of 63 young people (29 female and 34 male), from 18–28 years of age, participated in nine discussions. Each focus group lasted approximately 90 to 120 minutes depending on the number of participants.

Each focus group started with opening (icebreaker) discussion points followed by a discussion built around a number of examples of extremist content, then leading to closing discussion opportunities for reflections and recommendations. General icebreaker questions were related to Internet habits such as the time that young people spend online, if they engage in online discussions, if they follow the news, which sources do they prefer to follow and if they tend to trust the information they get. Then, the group conversation continued based on the various examples of content posted by groups described as extremist.[18] Finally, closing topics consisted of summarizing participants' thoughts on extremist organizations, their messages and methods (for example, if these narratives are relevant for their particular environment), if there is a difference between religious and far-right extremist groups, and what would they say in general to the people who are studying or working on this issue. All of the focus group discussions followed the same structure; however depending on the location, certain elements resulted in longer or richer conversations than others.

The main thematic discourses for focus group discussions were developed based on the content analysis of some selected websites/portals/social networks of right-wing and Wahhabi

---

18 Examples are described below, and are available on the following links: https://twitter.com/hashtag/%D0%A6%D0%B8%D1%99%D0%B5%D0%B2%D0%B8_%D0%BD%D0%B0%D1%87%D0%B5%D0%BB%D0%B0?src=hash&lang=en; https://www.facebook.com/Islamovickanal/photos/a.746628225477584.1073741835.357737221033355/1040832876057116/?type=3&theater; https://www.google.com/url?q=http://www.nacionalist.rs/2017/11/25/goran-davidovic-vojvodina-se-mora-ukinuti-ako-srbija-zeli-da-zivi/&ust=1530258540000000&usg=AFQjCNE8nQelCg01eQuqCLeZmhjY4kLJkw&hl=sr&source=gmail; https://www.blic.rs/vesti/svet/jeziva-pretnja-isis-a-dzihadisti-objavili-mapu-srbije-uz-poruku-srbi-nismo-vas/vw1fypw; https://videopress.com/v/01Lo9Rce; https://putsredine.com/civilizovana-porodica/

movements. Analysis of the right-wing sites led the author to conclude that their most recent narratives and activities include stridently anti-immigrant rhetoric. Interestingly, both the Wahhabi and the right-wing organizations are constantly very vocal on the role of women in society. Furthermore, as these types of organizations challenge mainstream society it was important to discuss their discourses on the kind of alternative lifestyle or vision that they offer. Finally, discourses on explicit religious manifestations of extremism were discussed. Only extremism related to interpretations of Islam was discussed in focus groups, due both to the limited scope of this research, as well as the observation that radical religious organizations are more popular among Muslim youth, while Serbian young people are more influenced by right-wing nationalist organizations. While extreme right movements do include some Christian religious references in their ideology, they are more political and less religious or doctrinal in terms of organization and content.

Figure 1: **Identifying main thematic discourses**

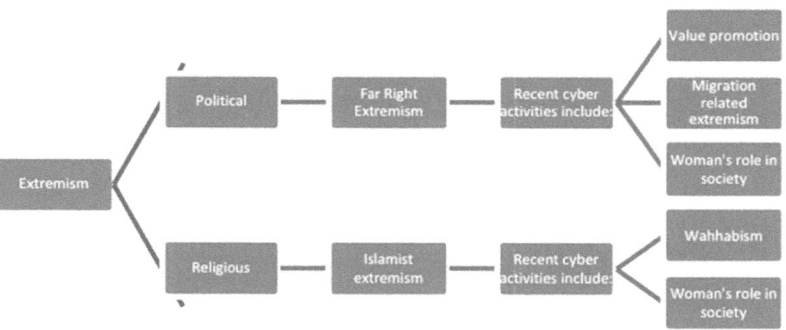

After thematic discourses were identified, the author randomly selected examples of each theme, as it was determined that concrete practical examples would lead to more fruitful and targeted discussions. Discussions were recorded, then summarized in notes, and finally were analyzed according to the main research question, *How do Serbian young people perceive online extremist messages/narratives*. The written notes were thematically coded to identify themes, and particularly relevant quotes were identified and highlighted. To structure this analysis, and in light of time and word count constraints, the following five themes were identified as particularly relevant, and shaped the findings summary and analysis that follows: media awareness and literacy; appeal of extremist content; migration; gender issues/the role of women in society; and Islamist extremism.

Table 4: Basic info on selected cities and municipalities

City	Novi Sad	Zaječar	Bor	Tutin
Location details	Capital of autonomous province of Vojvodina (North)	Administrative center of Zaječar District (East)	Administrative center of Bor District (East)	Municipality in Raška District/Sandžak
Main industry	Oil industry ICT industry Agriculture Chemical industry	Agriculture (beer, milk) Cable industry - TF KA-BLE Cable Factory	Mining industry - Mining and Smelting Combine Bor Agriculture Process manufacturing	Agriculture Small enterprises (wood, process manufacturing)
Average salary (2017)	55,383 rsd[19]	44,348 rsd[20]	51,414 rsd[21]	40,394 rsd[22]
Poverty rate (2016)[23]	15.7%	26.5%	23.1%	66.1%

---

19 http://www.021.rs/story/Novi-Sad/Vesti/178678/Porasla-prosecna-plata-u-Novom-Sadu-dzepovi-deblji-za-2000-dinara.html (Radio 021, 2017)
20 http://www.bor030.net/prosecna-plata-u-boru-septembru-51414-dinara (Mitrović, 2017)
21 http://www.bor030.net/prosecna-plata-u-boru-septembru-51414-dinara (Mitrović, 2017)
22 https://www.b92.net/biz/vesti/srbija.php?yyyy=2018&mm=01&dd=25&nav_id=1351231 (BETA, 2018)
23 According to Poverty Map of Serbia Report, jointly conducted by World Bank and Statistical Office of the Republic of Serbia http://pubdocs.worldbank.org/en/859541477472336209/Poverty-Map-of-Serbia.pdf (Statistical Office of the Republic of Serbia, 2016)

| Natural population increase (2013)[24] | 538 | -598 | -258 | 247 |
| Ethnic structure[25] | Serbs Hungarians Slovaks Rusyns/ Ruthenes Croats | Serbs Vlachs Roma Romanians Bulgarians | Serbs Vlachs Roma Romanians Bulgarians | Bosniaks Muslims[26] Serbs |

Table 5:   Focus groups in Novi Sad

Novi Sad		
Participating Organizations	Total number of participants	
BalkanIdea	25	
Opens2019	Male	Female
Prevent	12	13

Table 6:   Focus groups in Zaječar

Zaječar		
Participating Organizations	Total number of participants	
Zaječarska Inicijativa/Zaječar Initiative	12	
Timočki omladinski centar/Timok Youth Center	Male	Female
Društvo Roma/Roma Society	5	7

Table 7:   Focus groups in Bor

Bor		
Participating Organizations	Total number of participants	
Mladi u Centru/Youth in the Centre together with *Srbija u pokretu*/Serbia on the move	15	
	Male	Female
	11	4

---

24 More info available at http://www.stat.gov.rs/WebSite/repository/documents/00/01/43/42/SN40_163_srb-2013.pdf (Statistical Office of the Republic of Serbia, 2012)

25 More info available at http://www.stat.gov.rs/WebSite/repository/documents/00/01/43/42/SN40_163_srb-2013.pdf (Statistical Office of the Republic of Serbia, 2012)

26 According to the Serbian Constitution, national affiliation may be expressed freely, leading to both Bosniak and Muslim categories of respondents.

Table 8:   Focus groups in Tutin

Tutin		
Participating Organizations	Total number of participants	
Tutinska inicijativa mladih/Tutin Youth Initiative	11	
Impuls	Male	Female
	6	5

Focus group study findings

Media literacy

Each focus group started with opening questions to better understand participants' media consumption habits, critical thinking abilities and level of trust in everyday news. This is considered to be of crucial importance as it sets the foundation for contextual background and gives an overview of how young people understand critical thinking, and their approach towards what is being presented via various traditional and modern media. Additionally, these questions provided valuable information on the level of media literacy among participants and provided insights into their engagement with different media outlets.

All participants, regardless of their gender or region/location, reported that they obtain information through a variety of sources. The preferred choice of media is sometimes based on convenience such as social media, and sometimes based on family preferences: "It is our family tradition that we first watch *Slagalica* quiz and then continue with *RTS Dnevnik*."[27] Additionally, N1 and RTS news channels came out as very popular among the different groups across all locations. As RTS is a public channel, it was generally considered more trustworthy, while N1 is considered to provide a more critical/opposition approach.

Despite the fact that the majority of participants are exposed to different online and offline media sources, the key observation that was noted at the beginning of each discussion was that the majority of participants believe that there is no such thing as objective

---

27   Male participant from Tutin.

reporting. They were expressing general scepticism towards the media, implying a lack of trust: "We can only trust some facts like state visits or the weather forecast, any other news we do not trust immediately. Conclusions should be made only after comparing diverse information."[28] For example, one participant said that he always reads news first from the N1 portal and then from the Sputnik portal because according to him, "the truth is in the middle."[29] While the majority of respondents are willing to invest time and energy in finding good information, a minority of participants chooses *not* to follow political news and events. This was usually heard from some youth in the final year of high school, preoccupied with plans after high school graduation. As their reason for not being interested in political news, other participants mentioned either lack of time or the perception that too much "fake news" is being presented.

Regardless of the region studied, participants spend a day without the Internet only if they are out of town, camping, or on vacation, which means that they are constantly exposed to different kinds of online content. However, across all locations, a deep-seated sense of frustration with the media was expressed, either because of sensational news reporting, selective reporting, the politicized nature of media ownership, or the lack of constructive debates. Online media portals are not perceived as places that are open for sharing different opinions. Participants try to seek a personal understanding of current events by engaging in discussions and debates, but only with people already close to them. A minority of participants reported they sometimes take part in online discussions. Furthermore, while only one participant expressed the view that engaging in online discussion can provide wider views on issues, others gave negative examples of people who are posting online comments only to start a fight. The prevailing attitude is that "the comment sections are usually full of political bots who are not

---

28 Female participant from Zajecar.
29 Male participant from Novi Sad.

there to discuss different opinions, but they are only using the opportunity for trolling."[30]

Finally, the only regional difference that was visible during the first part of discussions was reflected in a sense that while participants from Novi Sad and Zaječar expressed interest in state politics and news related to different parts of Serbia, participants from Bor and Tutin on the other hand reported that they prefer to be focused on local and regional issues. For example, the pressing issue in Bor municipality is the management of the Mining and Smelting Combine Bor factory, as a majority of residents works for the company. Therefore, respondents from Bor agreed that any news that does not concern Mining and Smelting Combine Bor will have a limited reach and short momentum after it is forgotten.[31] On the other hand, 10 out of the 11 respondents from Tutin are high school graduates, thus their primary concern is news related to their future and prospects, and state politics seems distant to them due to their age and current life priorities.

Discussing online extremist content

The opening question for the second part of the discussions was, *"What, in your opinion, are extremism and radicalization"*? The trend noticed in every location was that participants at first hesitated to answer, which can be partially explained by their inadequate understanding of the concepts. They tried to make a difference between extremism and radicalization, explaining that extremism usually goes further than radicalization. Their responses included that extremism is a "call for violence," "labelling people with the aim of discrimination," "Islamic extremism," "Serbian radical party," "Obraz," "no tolerance," "Šešelj." Some participants correctly suggested that these concepts are not necessarily negative, but that they usually imply a negative meaning.

When turning their attention to the examples of radical messages, most participants had at some point seen these messages or

---

30 Female participant from Novi Sad.
31 Male participant from Bor.

similar ones presented through a variety of media outlets. The conversations around the messages, their content and the related outcomes were well developed, even though most of the participants did not have the opportunity to discuss issues on this topic before, and the majority of them had never visited extremist websites, but they have heard of extremist organizations when there were incidents that attracted significant media attention. Approximately every sixth participant has visited the *Obraz* website, and some of them mentioned the Instagram profile *Srbska čast* as it had been recently published in the news.

What makes extremist rhetoric appealing to youth?

As suggested by both theory and practice the sense of belonging to a group is important for each individual. Therefore, one of the topics discussed in the focus groups was what makes highly distinctive groups appealing to youth. As examples, participants were presented with tweets of the National Serbian Front such as:

> "Every activist must devote one's self unconditionally to achieve the goals and values of the National Serbian Front" and "The goals and principles of the National Serbian Front must be among the life priorities of our leadership and activists" (Nacionalni Srpski Front 2017).

This was done to prompt a discussion and to get a better understanding of the impact of the language that some extremist organizations employ while speaking to target groups.

The majority of respondents saw these messages either as very violent commands, or as non-violent messages with problematic content. More interestingly, some participants recognized that this type of narrative offers an excellent life strategy:

> "These organizations are offering an easier way for young people that do not want to spend much time deciding what is in her/his best interest. They offer a structure by giving life priorities which otherwise require an extensive process of individual decision making."[32]

While none of the participants saw these messages as appealing, a majority of them agreed that they are attractive to young people

---

32 Female participant from Zaječar.

who still cannot defend their attitudes and opinions; to those who think that these principles and goals are positive; to those who have doubts in their capabilities; to uneducated people who are looking for group acceptance; and finally to people in bad economic situations who are ready to give up their principles if they are getting something in return.

Additionally, the recent historical legacy makes extremist content appealing for some Serbian youth. Serbia is a post-war society and recent wars to a certain extent still shape everyday life; the ongoing discussion on the status of Kosovo is a case in point. Unfortunately, the current political situation across the region, and the lack of meaningful regional dialogue and reconciliation contributes to some extent to the visibility of extremist discourses. For instance, certain organizations tend to target so-called "Great Serbs." The language they use is very specific; for example they use the letter B instead of P in the adjective *srpski* (Serbian), emphasizing the importance of being traditionally and historically Serbian. These organizations try to boost nationalist feelings and ideology and also distribute ambiguous narratives. An example of such a nationalist narrative is that *the war has stopped only for those who died*,[33] which sparked debates in focus groups. Even though a majority of participants perceived this narrative as violent, especially because it was quoted by a Bosnian army general, a significant minority said that this message has positive connotations and inspires nonviolent struggle. Also, participants from Novi Sad, Bor and Zaječar tended to see this message as a negative contribution to the instability in the region, which serves the interests of high level politics, while some participants from Tutin viewed this differently, with one claiming that the war cannot stop because everyone lost someone during the 90s and people still suffer.[34]

---

33 Atif Dudaković, retired Bosnian Army General, narrative available at https://www.facebook.com/Islamovickanal/photos/a.746628225477584.1073741835.357737221033355/1040832876057116/?type=3&theater; Also reported in newspapers http://www.novosti.rs/vesti/planeta.300.html:667885-DAKOVIC-TRAZI-NAORUZAVANjE-Rat-nije-zavrsen-samo-je-prestala-pucnjava

34 Female participant from Tutin.

When asked to whom such narratives would sound acceptable, respondents tended to externalize the problem: "this is relevant for football fan clubs, to those who do not remember wars in the 90s, and to those who are against official state politics". A majority of them neither mentioned examples from their circle of acquaintances nor had they likened it to their own personal experiences. Their overall perception was that war-related narratives do not concern them and their everyday environment at all.

While discussions related to discourses on alternative life structures and war rhetoric did not show any significant regional differences among youth, different views were apparent when discussing the discourses on migration, the role of women, and religious extremism. Additionally, participants were more open to share personal examples on these other topics.

Migration/refugee related narratives

As one of the most common ways for migrants to arrive in the EU is through the Balkan route and thus crossing through Serbia, ever since the migrant crisis started far-right organizations have been very vocal on this issue. Across European and Serbian media, there have been numerous examples of hate speech, including commentary that very often blames immigrants for various local problems. Even though the general public perception is that Serbia has accepted migrants/refugees properly, the perception of migrants varies across the different parts of Serbia. Tijana Rečević explores this dynamic in her contribution in this volume.

When the migration crisis started, one of the most vocal extremists was Goran Davidović (studied as well by Davor Marko), and his following statement was discussed during focus groups:

> "It should not be allowed that illegal migrants can settle in Serbia and thus change the ethnic structure. It is very disturbing to hear some persons from the government openly promote the idea of migrants' integration into Serbian society and their influence in terms of a population increase. That is sick to think about, let alone speak about in public" (Davidović 2016).

Participants from Novi Sad shared that most people felt threatened when the crisis reached its peak in 2015. While they can relate to the difficulties that migrants are going through due to the recent war legacy in Serbia and the region, they also understand the concerns raised by various groups including those in the far-right. For example, one participant said that she felt disadvantaged when her father told her that migrants are selling tooth paste and toothbrushes that they received from the state as humanitarian aid: "It is not fair that they get for free what I have to pay for, and then they sell it on the street."[35] Another participant added that he has at least a hundred friends on Facebook that share the opinion that migrants should not be allowed to settle in Serbia.[36] More interestingly, a respondent who had the opportunity to work with migrants said that she understands those who became scared due to the enormous cultural differences. She mentioned that migrants come from societies where people think that stoning is an acceptable punishment. For her such an example shows significant cultural differences, and she noted that we as a country should have a careful approach when it comes to their integration.[37]

On the other hand, when asked how people have reacted to migrants in Eastern Serbia (Bor and Zaječar), the answer was essentially "lucratively." That was a period of time when some gas stations doubled or even tripled their prices due to the new demand. As a few participants pointed out,

> "everyone was focused on the negative stories about migrants and no one was dealing properly with the fact that we were selling them SIM cards and illegal taxi services for a huge amount of money."[38]

The prevailing perception in Bor and Zaječar is that migrants and refugees do not stay in Serbia for long, therefore they are not considered to be a threat. These respondents believe that it is not in the migrants' interest to settle in Serbia as here they would have limited possibilities for a better life. These participants agreed that wealthier countries should take care of migrants and refugees as they are able to provide for them, unlike poorer Serbia.

---

35 Female participant from Novi Sad.
36 Male participant from Novi Sad.
37 Female participant form Novi Sad.
38 Female participant from Bor.

Finally, in Tutin, due to religious affinity but also due to their own war memories from the 90s, respondents said that the refugees/migrants were welcomed. The participants shared positive stories, such as a marriage between a local young woman and a young male refugee. Additionally, they said they would not have minded if Tutin had received an even larger number of refugees. However, it seems that not so many Serbian respondents assume that they will ultimately leave the country. In a conversation with an NGO worker from Tutin, she shared her personal experience of working with a few families that are currently in Tutin. She said that they do not want to enroll their children in school as they hope to leave soon, even though it is expected that they will in fact stay in Serbia for quite some time.

The role of women in society

Very often far-right groups prescribe clear definitions of roles in a society, based on traditional male/female expectations. According to them, females are destined to be mothers and predominately family oriented, while males are in charge of the economic and physical security for the entire family. Even though the far-right is assumed to be exclusively masculine with limited access for women, the way in which far-right movements frame their gender related messages leaves enough space for certain groups to identify with their assumptions.[39] This space was also seen in some of the focus group discussions. For example, a significant number of participants, mostly from Tutin, did not recognize anything radical about a message published on NGO *Put Sredine* (Middle Way) website, presented to spark the gender related discussion:

> "Nice manners cannot survive outside the family. In other words, when extramarital relations and children from divorced parents become part of society, and relationships between a man and a women are solely based on passion, lust and basic instincts; and tasks in the family are not divided based on the family responsibilities and natural gifts, and when a woman's role is to be physically attractive and seductive, and when she is liberated from her role of taking care of the children, and when she is able to choose

---

39   See for example video *What Right Wing Women Want*, available at https://www.youtube.com/watch?v=MGwskIpnSPg

to be either a stewardess on the plane, in the hotel or on the boat for the sole purpose of gaining material wealth, instead of raising new human beings, and when material gain becomes more important and more honorable compared to the raising a human character—then such a society is a backward society" (Kutb 2017).[40]

According to one respondent, "If a woman wants to be a mother that should be her priority. Women who get a job and go to work every day should realize that their children will become problematic because no one took good care of them."[41] When asked why they referred to the "civilizational" role that women have: "If a woman raises her child correctly, her child will do the same with their own children and that is how we as women can contribute to human kind."[42] When asked what the father's role in family is, the answer was, "the mother is due to provide love, and the father material security."[43] One female participant even said that

> "the woman whose priority is a career and who puts her own needs before everyone else's should not even try to start a family as she is jealous of everyone".[44]

On the other hand, one female participant from Tutin recognized this narrative as problematic. She further elaborated on the additional pressures on women in Tutin, in terms of whether she will be "allowed" to work after getting married, and then also the pressure caused by the custom of blaming mothers for every problem that a family has, especially related to raising children.

Focus groups in other parts of Serbia recognized this narrative as problematic and disrespectful for both genders. However, these participants also referred to the kind of mentality that does not allow society to deal with gender issues properly:

---

40 Available at: https://putsredine.com/civilizovana-porodica/
41 Female respondent from Tutin.
42 Female respondent from Tutin.
43 Female respondent from Tutin.
44 Female respondent from Tutin.

"We live in a contemporary world but unfortunately in most cases a man would not allow his wife to be more successful in business, in the sense that she is the main breadwinner and he is in charge of the children."[45]

Furthermore, "in our environment no one denies a woman the right to go to university, to go to work or have a career"; however if a woman is not married by a certain age they are seen as spinsters. Additionally, if a man does not get married by the age of 30, society starts to question his sexuality, therefore substantial social pressure exists for both genders.[46]

When asked what type of organization stands behind this message, participants from Tutin suggested that it is probably some religious organization, while others mentioned it is likely the same kind of organization that came up with the traditional slogan, *He should defend and she should give birth* (*On da brani, ona da rađa*), or *Dveri* or the Serbian Orthodox Church. It is obvious that the influence of the patriarchy still shapes social dynamics in Serbia, but the Muslim respondents in the southwestern part of the country seem to be more conservative on these matters than their peers in the East and North. In the end, a majority of participants suggested that it should be a personal choice if a woman wants to pursue a career or to start a family or to do both, and traditional roles should not be propagated in the public sphere as they often are.

Islamist extremism in Serbia

The final narrative discussed was related to examples of Islamist extremism that have been present in Serbian cyber space. Participants were presented with the text, *Blood for Enemies, Honey for Friends* (BIRN 2017)[47] and the video *Honour is in Jihad* (Islamic State 2017).[48] They were first asked to briefly read the article and then to share their thoughts. The majority of respondents across all four locations were shocked by the aggressive language in the text and the way in which religion is being manipulated for political purposes.

---

45 Female respondent form Zajecar.
46 Male respondent from Bor.
47 Available at: http://www.balkaninsight.com/en/article/isis-wows-to-wreak-vengeance-on-balkans-in-new-threat-06-08-2017
48 Available at https://videopress.com/v/01Lo9Rce

Even though participants in all four towns can understand the difference between Islam and extremist Islamist-inspired narratives, the main regional difference that stood out was the lack of knowledge on Islam and its various factions by the participants from Novi Sad, Bor and Zaječar—places which have few if any Muslims. Discussions around these questions seemed a bit distant for youth in these towns, and they simply could not believe that Islamic State managed to recruit some of their Muslim fellow citizens. Only a few participants knew it happened before we mentioned it during the discussion. The majority of participants from Bor, Zaječar and Novi Sad said that they do not think that this narrative is acceptable for Muslims living in Serbia, but they could not provide any further explanations. On the other hand, richer discussions were held in Tutin. While she was reading the article *Blood for Enemies, Honey for Friends* a young student said,

> "if I were not a Muslim and if I did not know the basis of Islam I would definitely be afraid of Muslims. This is not Islam; this is evil trying to hide behind religion."[49]

Participants agreed that this type of narrative only harms their religion, as its main goal is to spread fear.

What came across consistently across all four focus groups was the view that Islamic State is just a project of the major world powers:

> "Organizations like Islamic State or Al Qaida are just an excuse for the United States to enter into different states such as Libya, Syria, Iraq, Afghanistan or the Balkans during the 90s."[50]

Another participant added that the quality of video proves that money plays an important role in explaining how Islamic State operates:

---

49 Female participant from Tutin.
50 Male participant form Tutin.

> "This is a high-quality HD video which costs a lot. Maybe IS is getting money from selling oil on the black market, but the major powers story seems to me more realistic".[51]

As some Wahhabi organizations from (relatively) nearby Novi Pazar were publicly connected with IS recruitment, naturally the discussion touched upon Wahhabi movement activities in Sandžak. The group suggested that this movement has become a traded product, as one participant said that people in Sandžak get money if they grow a beard and wear short pants or hijab. According to him, it is easy to buy people's affiliation in the region due to the poverty and lack of opportunities.[52] Another participant shared a personal example of a first cousin who started practicing a Wahhabi interpretation of Islam:

> "He went on scholarship to Saudi Arabia for studies. His parents were not religious, they neither prayed nor fasted. That is why he was an easy target for a change of beliefs. Now my cousin thinks that he is a better Muslim then the rest of the family who have practiced moderate Islam longer."[53]

Participants reported that they know plenty of examples of people who converted to Wahhabism either due to social benefits or due to true beliefs. Additionally, a participant shared a story of a young man from a village near Tutin (Sebečevo) who went to Syria: "he truly believed that he will fight for a bigger cause."[54] However, one participant from Tutin explained that on the path of faith only defensive wars are allowed: "War is allowed only to defend our religion and our people".[55]

When asked to whom these messages are appealing, participants offered a range of responses, from more general answers such as to those who are selling arms, to the more specific answer that the narrative is acceptable for problematic children that are not under their parents' control. Additionally, the focus group in Tutin

---

51   Male participant from Novi Sad.
52   Male participant from Tutin.
53   Male participant from Tutin.
54   Male participant from Tutin.
55   Female participant from Tutin.

suggested that the division of the Islamic community in Serbia contributes to the occurrence of radicalization processes. As an example, they said that unlike today when different mosques are growing across Sandžak without official approval, when the Islamic Community was united the process required its permission and stricter controls.

Discussion

There are multiple reasons why people may come to feel attached to extremist narratives in Serbia. These narratives can be appealing to individuals in search of meaning, identity, and belonging; to the unemployed or those who have someone unemployed in the family leading to economic uncertainty; to youth whose parents were not themselves religious and therefore are unable to recognize extreme practices of religion; or to those who had lost someone during the wars in the 90s. According to the focus group participants, by far the most vulnerable to extremist narratives in Serbia are young people and those worst affected by the country's poor economic conditions. This is in line with theoretical assumptions according to which societies with limited possibilities can be at risk of skillfully tailored extremist narratives aimed at exploiting any disparate treatment, both real and imagined, to inspire conflict. What is additionally worrying is the potential for extremist organizations to manipulate other people's suffering by providing a vision of an alternative life structure. They are perceived as organizations which offer an easy alternative where individual responsibility does not exist.

Even though it seems that the respondents in this research are minimally or not at all receptive to online recruiting attempts by right-wing and fundamentalist/Wahhabi platforms, a few concerns can be noted. First, an important (though not unexpected) finding is that youth tend to not trust the media. Not unrelated, a deep frustration with the media was expressed during focus groups. Only a few participants said that they trust N1 television and RTS. Most of them complained about scandalous headlines, the politicized nature of media outlets, and questionable ethics in reporting. Further, while it was encouraging to hear examples of young people seeking out different views in the news (e.g., from N1 and Sputnik) it was unclear whether they have the skills needed to truly measure and analyze various news sources. However, as truthful and independent media are a very important resource in the fight against violent extremism, and they can be a key mediator in sending out information that can contribute to alternative narratives, it is important to address this issue and improve their trust.

A second important finding regards youth perceptions of migrants. Even though the way the domestic population is presently relating with migrants and refugees is not alarming, some issues will need to be properly addressed in order to prevent any future incidents. For example, while the majority of participants truly believe that migrants/refugees will leave as soon as they get the first chance, there is also a minority very concerned about whether migrants will be ready to make compromises and accept domestic rules and a European lifestyle. Additionally, the way migrants and refugees are perceived cannot be analyzed in a vacuum, without understanding events on Serbia's borders. Communities that live closer to countries that have been more outspoken about migrants (such as Hungary) tend to perceive to a certain extent that migrants are a threat. Such spillover effects can partially explain why communities in Vojvodina feel uncomfortable imagining full integration of a culturally different migrant population. The explicit anti-immigration and anti-Islam campaign in Hungary culminated with Hungary fortifying its borders with Serbia, which has contributed to the anxiety in the region. In the end, only those communities that feel culturally close to migrants and refugees such as the Muslim minority in Serbia, do not have objections to their possible long-term integration into Serbian society.

Discussing the gender related narratives, it was clear that once more women's role in society is often viewed through rather traditional lenses. This is particularly relevant for Tutin in the south-western part of Serbia where respondents noted that women may be denied the right to work when getting married and expressed that her value in society is measured only through motherhood.

What was striking during the research was that even female participants did not show understanding for girls and women who want to pursue a career or to have both a family and a career. These constraints provide substantial food for thought in terms of the way young people are vulnerable. They are vulnerable not just because they are young or undergoing rapid developmental transitions, but more importantly are exposed to unequal treatment, and the interconnection between gender exclusion, inequality, and poverty tend to reinforce one another in a way that according, to theoretical assumptions, can provide potentially fertile ground for a shift towards more conservative, fundamentalist, or even extremist related views.

Finally, this research provides some insights into religious extremism and the targeting of Muslims in Serbia. Field research confirmed that Wahhabis are active in Sandžak; something also seen through the desk research. Their target audience seems to be young people (not exclusively) who identify as Muslims but who have little to no religious background. Participants from Tutin shared various personal examples of people turning towards Wahhabi interpretations of the faith, but they said that they are not violent or insulting towards others. However, previous analysis indicates the need to be aware of any potential negative impact on social cohesion or security. For example, a study on Salafism/Wahhabism by the Directorate-General for External Policies of the European Union argues that "the presence of a small but radical Wahhabi community" raises concerns that the Balkans could become a "logistical and recruiting base of Islamist terrorists and an Islamic bridgehead in Europe" (Racimora 2013, 14).

Further, as an additional layer of complexity, one often hears reports of social assistance that newly converted Wahhabis get from the movement. Some focus group participants in Tutin shared various personal examples of how religious affiliation can be bought across the Sandžak region. This can be explained as related to the poor socio-economic situation in the region, but also to a spillover effect from neighboring Bosnia. For example, Bećirević (2016) in her study showed that after the war in Bosnia the Salafi/Wahhabi movement evolved around the remaining mujahideen and was financed by Islamic charities: "Part of the protocol of some Middle Eastern charities was to condition monthly stipends for the children of fallen soldiers by their mothers' willingness to wear hijab" (Bećirović 2016, 38). She additionally wrote that heightened security measures taken in the region following September 11, 2001, decreased the influence of some Islamic charities, though key influences from outside of the country, notably from the diaspora in Vienna, have continued to shape Wahhabism in BiH (Bećirević 2016). In light of the close ties between Muslims in Sandžak and in BiH, such dynamics merit further research. Finally, another important finding is that focus group participants tend to believe that Islamic extremism is itself a product of the major world powers and that the Islamic State is just a tool of leading international players to get access to Middle Eastern oil and grow the industry of war.

Conclusion

In recent years, violent extremism of all kinds has been on the rise, exploiting technology to spread its ideology. However, this admittedly limited research showed that the respondents are minimally or not at all receptive to online recruiting attempts by right-wing and fundamentalist/Wahhabi platforms in Serbia, which is in line with the existing literature which argues that the Internet has not yet replaced in-person interactions as a necessary step in radicalization and recruitment (Goldfien and Woolslayer 2015). While the Internet can simplify or accelerate individual movements toward extremism it seems that there is a low if any risk of complete online radicalization and extremist recruitment in Serbia. However, the existence of carefully constructed narratives by extremist groups on issues like gender roles, political manipulation of religion and the impact of the migrant crisis have the potential to create fertile ground for extremist activities, particularly if accompanied with real-world activities and outreach. The risk is higher if preventive activities to deter young people from such engagement are not adequately addressed. Therefore, in closing, this study identifies a few areas which should be strengthened in Serbian society in order to properly address extremist challenges.

First, it is important to engage local public servants as prominent people who support moderate and positive voices, and engage innovatively with local communities to deliver an alternative-narrative and provide constructive real-world youth educational and engagement activities. Such activities should aim to strengthen critical thinking to avoid feelings of frustration and marginalization, particularly among the younger generation. Additionally, it is important to empower youth through media literacy as they should be able to analyze, evaluate, and create messages across a variety of contexts, eventually becoming responsible and active citizens and not only symbolic figures in multi-stakeholder VERLT prevention.

As adherence to traditional and often unequal gender roles can be very challenging when it comes to meeting the needs of young people, adhering to gender equality standards and also ensuring freedom of religion and belief would highly benefit VERLT prevention efforts in Serbia. Therefore, gender awareness workshops in the southwestern part of the country are needed to initiate dialogue on these social issues that have an impact on young men and young women alike. As the strong influence of religion is recognized, it will be important to work on this issue with religious teachers (formal and informal) in order to create a customized solution. Furthermore, there is a need to establish open inter-religious space for dialogue and cooperation, and to educate religious teachers and clerics of all faiths to engage in online and real-world campaigns in order to promote messages of peace, tolerance, and respect.

Finally, in order to promote dialogue, reconciliation, and cooperation, young people should be engaged in local and national campaigns that mobilize widespread support and bring together youngsters from different ethnic, educational, and religious backgrounds. This would give more significance to the role of youth in tackling violent extremism, provide more support for refugees and migrants, and generally enhance social cohesion in Serbia as a whole.

To conclude, this small and preliminary study provides useful insight into how young people think about these issues, and their potential risk factors. There is a need for further exploration of the exact role and processes through which the online environment impacts potential radicalization processes. Therefore, deeper qualitative research on the topic is highly recommended.

References

Agbiboa, Daniel Egiegba. 2015. "The Social Dynamics of Nigeria's Boko Haram Insurgency: Fresh Insights from the Social Identity Theory." *World Bank Research Conference*, 1–26. doi: 10.1080/02533952.2015.1100364.

Amr, Mohamed Sameh. 2015. *Youth and the Internet: Fighting Radicalization and Extremism*. Paris: UNESCO House. Available at: http://unesdoc.unesco.org/images/0023/002335/233595e.pdf.

Atwan, Abdel Bari, Khan, S. and Butter, David. 2015. *ISIS: Marketing Terror*. Chatham House: The Royal Institute of International Affairs.

Awan, Imran. 2014. "Islamophobia and twitter: A typology of online hate against muslims on social media." *Policy and Internet*, 6 (2), 133–150. doi: 10.1002/1944-2866.POI364.

Awan, Imran. 2017. "Cyber-Extremism: Isis and the Power of Social Media." *Social Science and Public Policy*, 54(2), 138–149. doi: 10.1007/s12115-017-0114-0.

Awan, Imran and Zempi, Irene. 2016. "The affinity between online and offline anti-Muslim hate crime: Dynamics and impacts." *Aggression and Violent Behavior*, 27 (September 2014), 1–8. doi: 10.1016/j.avb.2016.02.001.

Bakić, Jovo. 2013. Right-wing extremism in Serbia. Belgrade: Friedrich Ebert Stiftung.

Barber, Benjamin. 2001. *Jihad Vs. McWorld*. New York: Ballantine Books.

Bećirević, Edina. 2016. *Salafism vs. Moderate Islam*. Sarajevo: Atlanksa Inicijativa.

BETA. 2018. "Plata skočila im 400 RSD, ali od prosečne 14.000 RSD manja." *B92*, January 25, 2018. https://www.b92.net/biz/vesti/srbija.php?yyyy=2018&mm=01&dd=25&nav_id=1351231.

BIRN. 2017. "ISIS Threatens Terror Campaign in the Balkans." *Balkan Insight*, June 11–12, 2017. http://www.balkaninsight.com/en/article/isis-wows-to-wreak-vengeance-on-balkans-in-new-threat-06-08-2017.

Blic. 2017. "Kako su hapšenja u Austriji 'obezglavila' jednu od najvećih opasnosti na Balkanu." *Blic*, March 10, 2017. https://www.blic.rs/v esti/hronika/kako-su-hapsenja-u-austriji-obezglavila-jednu-od-najv ecih-opasnosti-na-balkanu/y635x3p.

Costello, Matthew et al. 2016. "Who views online extremism? Individual attributes leading to exposure." *Computers in Human Behavior*, 63, 311–320. doi: 10.1016/j.chb.2016.05.033.

Davidović, Goran. 2017. "Vojvodina se mora ukinuti ako Srbija želi da živi." 25 November, 2017. Retrieved on December 22, 2017 http://www.nacionalist.rs/2017/11/25/goran-davidovic-vojvodina-se-mo ra-ukinuti-ako-srbija-zeli-da-zivi/.

Dim, Emeka Eugene. 2017. "An integrated theoretical approach to the persistence of Boko Haram violent extremism in Nigeria." *Journal of Peacebuilding and Development*, 12 (2), 36–50. doi: 10.1080/154 23166.2017.1331746.

Džuverović, N. 2016. "Socio-Economic Roots of Extremism in the Region." in Ejdus, F. and Jureković, P. (eds) *Violent Extremism in the Western Balkans*. Vienna: Republic of Austria, Federal Ministry of Defence, 25–37. doi: 10.1016/S0022-3913(12)00047-9.

Ebner, Julia.. 2017. *The Rage: The Vicious Circle of Islamist and Far-Right Extremism*. London: I.B.Tauris & Co Ltd.

Ejdus, Filip and Jureković, Predrag. 2016. *Violent Extremism in the Western Balkans*. Vienna: Republic of Austria, Federal Ministry of Defence.

Geeraerts, Sanne B. 2012. "Digital radicalization of youth." *Social Cosmos*, 3 (1), 25–32.

Goldfien, Michael. and Woolslayer, Michael.. 2015. *Countering Extremist Speech Online*. Stanford: IPS Stanford. Available at: https://www.cd n.law.stanford.edu/wp-content/uploads/2016/07/Goldfien-and-Woolslayer-Countering-Extremist-Speech-Online-A-Report-to-the-Department-of-State.pdf.

Greenberg, Karen J. 2016. "Counter-Radicalization via the Internet." *The ANNALS of the American Academy of Political and Social Science*, 668 (1), 165–179. doi: 10.1177/0002716216672635.

Halevy, Nir et al. 2010. "Relative deprivation and intergroup competition." *Group Processes and Intergroup Relations*, 13 (6), 685–700. doi: 10.1177/1368430210371639.

Hennessey, Josephine. and West, Michael A. 1999. "Intergroup Behavior in Organizations: A Field Test of Social Identity Theory." *Small Group Research*, 30 (3), 361–382. doi: 10.1177/104649649903000305.

Hogg, M. A.. 2001. "A Social Identity Theory of Leadership." *Personality and Social Psychology Review*, 5 (3), 184–200. doi: 10.1207/S15327957pspr0503_1.

Hogg, M. A.. 2014. "From Uncertainty to Extremism: Social Categorization and Identity Processes." *Current Directions in Psychological Science*, 23 (5), 338–342. doi: 10.1177/0963721414540168.

Ilić, Vladimir. 2016. *Opinion poll conducted among the Sandžak youth: How Susceptible are the Youth to Islamic Extremism?* Belgrade: Helsinki Committee for Human Rights in Serbia.

Jarić, Isidora. 2015. "The Hidden Threat to Official Government Policy: The political discourse of Serbian right-wing extremists on the Stormfront Internet forum about the LGBT community." in *Representation of Gender minority Groups in Media: Serbia, Montenegro and Macedonia*. Belgrade: Fakultet za medije i komunikacije, 225–239.

Jekel, Thomas, Lehner, Michael, and Vogler, Robert. 2017. "Mapping the Far Right: Geomedia in an Educational Response to Right-Wing Extremism." *ISPRS International Journal of Geo-Information*, 6 (10), 1–28. doi: 10.3390/atmos7060078.

King Savić, Sandra. 2017. "Serbia's Sandžak: Caught Between Two Islamic Communities." *Euxeinos*, 23, 32–37.

Kladničanin, Fahrudin. 2013. "Vehabije u Sajber Prostoru Srbije." in *Politički Ekstremizam u Cyber Prostoru Srbije*, 127–135.

Kutb, Seid. 2017. "Civilizovana porodica, Put Sredine." https://putsredine.com/civilizovana-porodica/ (Accessed: 27 December 2017).

McKeown, Shelley, Haji, Reeshman, and Ferguson, Neil. 2016. *Understanding Peace and Conflict Through Social Identity Theory*. Edited by D. J. Christie. doi: 10.1007/978-3-319-29869-6.

Mitrović, Igor. 2017. "Prosečna plata u Boru u septembru 51.414 dinara." *Bor030.net*, October 26, 2017. https://www.bor030.net/prosecna-plata-u-boru-septembru-51414-dinara (Accessed: 12 January 2018).

Mughal, Sajda. 2016. "Radicalisation of young people on social media." https://www.internetmatters.org/hub/expert-opinion/radicalisation-of-young-people-through-social-media/.

Nacionalni Srpski Front. 2017. "Ciljevi i načela, Nacionalni Srpski Front." Available at: https://twitter.com/hashtag/Циљеви_начела?src=hash&lang=en (Accessed: 15 December 2017).

OSCE. 2014. *Preventing Terrorism and Countering Violent Extremism and Radicalization that Lead to Terrorism: A Community-Policing Approach*. Vienna: OSCE.

OSCE. 2015. *Working With Youth for Youth: Protection Against Radicalization.* Belgrade: OSCE. Available at: http://www.osce.org/cio/205211?download=true.

Parida, Pradeep Kumar. 2007. "Globalisation, Relative Deprivation and Terrorism: An Analysis." *India Quarterly: A Journal of International Affairs,* (October), 122–154.

Perry, Valery. 2016. *Initiatives to Prevent/Counter Violent Extremism in South East Europe.* Sarajevo: RCC. Available at: www.rcc.int.

Racimora, William. 2013. *Salafist/Wahhabite financial support to educational, social and religious institutions.* Brussels: Policy Department DG External Policies. Available at: http://www.europarl.europa.eu/RegData/etudes/etudes/join/2013/457136/EXPO-AFET_ET(2013)457136_EN.pdf.

Radio 021. 2017. "Porasla prosečna plata u Novom Sadu." *Radio 021,* December 25, 2017. http://www.021.rs/story/Novi-Sad/Vesti/178678/Porasla-prosecna-plata-u-Novom-Sadu-dzepovi-deblji-za-2000-dinara.html (Accessed: 12 January 2018).

Shaffer, Ryan. 2016. "Jihad and Counter-Jihad in Europe: Islamic Radicals, Right-Wing Extremists, and Counter- Terrorism Responses." *Terrorism and Political Violence.* 2016, 28 (2), 383–394. doi: 10.1080/09546553.2016.1140538.

Srbska akcija. 2017. Facebook post. https://www.facebook.com/pg/sr.akcija/photos/?ref=page_internal (Accessed: 10 December 2017).

Statistical Office of the Republic of Serbia. 2012. *Ethnicity – Data by Municipalities and Cities.* Belgrade: Statistical Office of the Republic of Serbia. Available at: http://pod2.stat.gov.rs/ObjavljenePublikacije/Popis2011/Nacionalna pripadnost-Ethnicity.pdf.

Statistical Office of the Republic of Serbia. 2016. *Poverty Map of Serbia Method and Key Findings Statistical Office of the Republic of Serbia.* Belgrade: Statistical Office of the Republic of Serbia. Available at: http://pubdocs.worldbank.org/en/859541477472336209/Poverty-Map-of-Serbia.pdf.

Tartar, Andre. 2017. *How the Populist Right Is Redrawing the Map of Europe, Bloomberg,* December 11, 2017. https://www.bloomberg.com/graphics/2017-europe-populist-right/.

Teodorović, Miloš. 2013. "Sandžački dobrovoljci na sirijskom ratištu." *Radio Free Europe,* 1 June, 2013. https://www.slobodnaevropa.org/a/sandzacki-dobrovoljci-na-sirijskom-ratistu/25003927.html.

The White House. 2013. *Online Safety for Youth: Working to Counter Online Radicalization to Violence in the United States.*

UNDP Serbia Country Office and CeSID. 2016. *Survey of the drivers of youth radicalism and violent extremism in Serbia*. Belgrade: CeSID.

UNESCO. 2015. "Empowering youth to build peace: a new integrated framework of action." Available at: http://en.unesco.org/sites/default/files/ci_youth-english-web-20150616-082128118.pdf.

Waldron, Jeremy. 2012. *The Harm in Hate Speech*. Harvard University Press.

Walker, Iain and Pettigrew, Thomas F. 1984. "Relative deprivation theory: An overview and conceptual critique." *British Journal of Social Psychology*, 23 (4), 301–310.

Webber, Craig. 2007. "Revaluating relative deprivation theory." *Theoretical Criminology*, 11 (1), 97–120. doi: 10.1177/1362480607072737.

Mapping Extremist Discourse among Serbian 4Chan /pol/ Users

Boris Milanović

Introduction — what is 4chan and what is /pol/?[1]

Starting as a humble board for discussion of anime films and series, 4Chan has morphed, over the 14 years of its existence, into one of the most popular websites on the Internet (Alexa 2018). The board currently draws over 27.7 million users on a monthly basis, with a million posts made daily (4Chan 2018). The posting demographic of 4Chan skews young and male. Self-released estimates place the user base to be 70% male and mostly falling into the 18 to 34-year-old demographic (4Chan 2018).

4Chan consists of 65 "boards," subforums dedicated to discussion on a category of topic. Boards are places for discussing common modern topics like video games and sports, but also range to more niche topics like discussion of Japanese mecha anime. Currently the most active board on the website is /pol/, short for "Politically Incorrect" (Neet.tv 2018). A key distinguishing feature is the potential anonymity when posting. A user is not compelled to register a username/account to post. While other popular social media sites like Facebook, Reddit, and Twitter require maintaining an account, the only barrier to posting on 4Chan is solving a Captcha code. Starting a discussion thread is as easy as posting any text in the content field, with subsequent users just as easily replying to the original post. There is no private communication between two users; all posts are visible to any viewing person.

This much more welcoming approach to anonymity and ease of access has helped generate a unique culture on 4Chan. Users commonly refer to themselves as "Anons," short for anonymous, and often praise the lax demands for participation required. Being

---

1 The author is grateful for the advice and review provided by Valery Perry and Predrag Nikolić.

an Anon often means standing opposite to "normies" — a term describing individuals and groups considered to be well adjusted to the prevailing social norms of behavior. 4Chan can be a refuge for those unable or unwilling to fit in. As such, the user base provided an ample selection of young people potentially vulnerable to radicalization and violence resulting from radicalization. The site and /pol/ in particular have been identified as a source of right-wing radicalization and has been associated with several prominent threats of violence and violent acts (Edwards 2008; Staff 2014; Tait 2017).

4Chan has a long history of political activism. Project Chanology was a movement targeting the controversial practices of the Church of Scientology. The Project birthed the now well-known real life utilization of the Guy Fawkes mask in political protests, taken on by other movements like Occupy Wall Street. The website has recently been associated with creating and popularizing a number of ideological movements associated with more extreme ideology, predominantly on the far-right. Massive swathes of the user base supported the United States presidential candidacy of Donald Trump, forming what some now describe as the alt-right (Wendling 2018). The website has been the source of a bevy of memes containing racist, misogynistic and anti-Semitic content (Schreckinger 2017). 4Chan was the originator of the controversial Gamergate campaign associated by some with targeted online harassment of women and minority figures working in the gaming industry, and Operation Lollipop, a campaign of impersonating feminist activists (Heartfield 2014) to discredit their policy ideas. Users of 4Chan and /pol/ have been involved with online bot operations to sway public opinion on the French Presidential election in 2017, generally supporting the candidacy of right-wing politician Marie Le Pen (Ferrara 2017).

Gaining great infamy in recent times, 4Chan has been identified by some as one of the chief driving forces behind the surge of the alt-right (Nagle 2017). Users of 4Chan and especially of the /pol/ board have launched into political relevance the symbolism of "Pepe the Frog." 4Chan's breakthrough into acknowledged political relevance perhaps reached its peak (or nadir, depending on your perspective) with Donald Trump himself posting a variation of Pepe the Frog in his own likeness on Twitter (Revesz 2016).

The /pol/ board of 4Chan is the biggest and most radical section of 4Chan. With a massive number of daily posts espousing extreme, generally right-wing ideologies like Nazism, along with extensively and successfully intervening in real world politics, it presents ample but unexplored ground for research.

Additionally, and very importantly, /pol/ has a feature that most of 4Chan is missing and that makes it a productive target for research relevant to Serbia—public identification of the IP source country. The country from which the user is posting is visible at the top of each post. This enables the option of monitoring activities of Serbian users on the board. Serbian users have been posting on the website for years and can be sighted posting under their national IPs. Through logging posts made by users with Serbian IPs from 2014 to present day, and systemically reviewing the discourse they espouse, it is possible to chart whether users hailing from Serbia display patterns of discourse that could be cause for concern.

The extent to which /pol/ and 4Chan discourse can influence and drive violent extremism remains unexplored. This paper will contribute to unraveling the potential the discourse propagated on it by Serbian users may have in radicalizing and realizing violent extremism, by breaking down the common basic themes that characterize their unique ideology. After providing an overview of the available literature and elaborating upon my methodological approach I will present my findings on the discourse analyzed through four distinct but connected themes of the discourse that are crucially relevant for understanding and mounting efforts to counter violent extremism in Serbia.

What does posting on 4Chan look like?

Before delving into the topic, I will attempt to explain briefly what posting on 4Chan typically looks like. The figure below illustrates the layout of a 4Chan post in the archive I used. The text boxes and arrows are my own, added onto a post from the archive to explain individual elements.

I have additionally included an original post from the original 4Chan site to display how similar the layouts are for clarity. The only differences are that the poster ID is clickable (to highlight all posts made by the same user in a single thread); the background colors; and an additional "hide post" option omitted from the archive.

Figure 1:   Layout of a 4Chan post in the archive

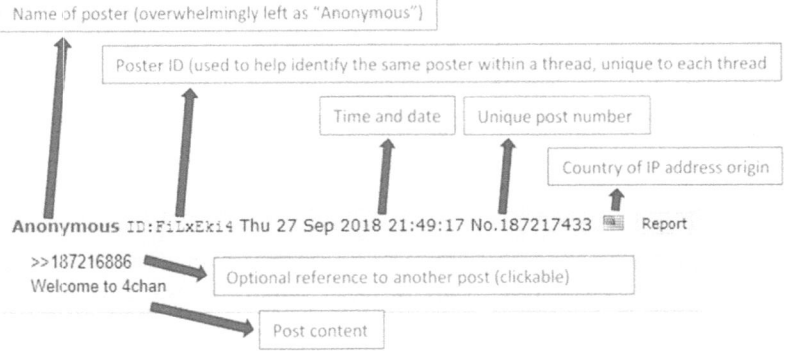

Original post at https://archive.4plebs.org/pol/thread/187561292/#q187562489; graphics added by the author

Figure 2:   What a post looks like on /pol

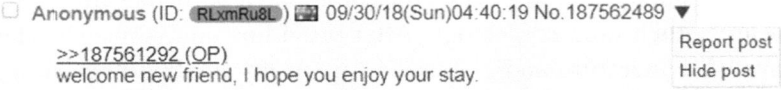

Original post at https://archive.4plebs.org/pol/thread/187216649/#q187217433; graphics added by the author.

Posters have the option of adding one still image, animated image, or brief webm video file to their posts. Such a file would show up immediately under the poster's chosen name. All threads begin with a post containing an image, and all other posting of such files is optional. As previously mentioned, 4Chan culture values anonymity and an overwhelming majority of posters will not input a name in the associated field when posting.[2]

The /pol/ board has 10 active pages, each with 15 conversational and thematic threads at all times. Each new post pushes a thread to the top of the front page until a 310 post "bump limit" has been reached. The same applies when a thread reaches 150 image file submissions. Rarely, some threads are deemed so interesting by the moderating team that they are stickied, fixing them at the top of the front page and removing limits on posts. There is moderation on /pol/ and on 4Chan as a whole, although the moderators have little power granted to them. Posts are removed and posters banned very rarely, and then primarily due to spam.

Threads on /pol/ develop quickly, with users rarely conversing within the same thread for more than 24 hours. Posts are mostly brief, rarely reaching over a couple of hundred words. The pace of /pol/ is frenetic and constant. Content posted on /pol/ keeps current, referencing global news as soon as it comes up. The pace can be so quick that someone simply starts a thread with a link and a screenshot and hundreds of replies pour in within a short timeframe.

Literature review

Academic analysis has insufficiently explored the phenomenon of 4Chan and has especially underexplored /pol/. A significant portion of the earlier work done on 4Chan focused on exploring how the great emphasis on anonymity creates a unique but very popular option for online participation using only ephemeral identities (Bernstein et al. 2011; Knuttila 2011; Stryker 2011). This was an especially relevant aspect of 4Chan as the Internet was being rapidly taken over by social media like Myspace, Facebook and Twitter, all mandating permanent identity construction for participation.

---

2 Posters that choose to use names are frequently frowned upon and referred to pejoratively as "namef*gs."

As some more recent and more numerous (but still sparse) scholarship on 4Chan suggests, a phenomenon as large and as unique as 4Chan offers many interesting focal points for study, and is a phenomenon that is explicitly much more politically relevant than initially posited by social science.

Hine et al. delivered the first large scale study of /pol/ in 2016, broadly confirming several commonly held opinions among the users of /pol/ (Hine et al. 2016). Users are well spread out across the globe, frequently produce original content like memes and infographics, and often behave in an aggressive, harassing manner towards their perceived enemies, engaging with them quickly and directly. Wagener uses 4Chan, through a case study of its hostile treatment of Lauren Mayberry, popular singer of the band "Chvrches," to demonstrate how the most popular Internet communities can be hostile to women (Wagener 2017). Ludemann uses /pol/ as evidence of how the site's unique means and culture of communication can challenge and drive forward developments in discursive theory and, very poignantly, how the immense focus 4Chan places on anonymity shapes how and through which identities its users communicate (Ludemann 2018). Sparby makes perhaps the most practically useful suggestions in how to deal with extremism on 4Chan through analyzing 4Chan's treatment of transwomen, and efforts at constructive dialogue to counteract the hate to which they are subjected (Sparby 2017). Angela Nagle delivered perhaps the most popular recent piece of scholarship on 4Chan with a book exploring how it challenges mainstream interpretations of culture and the political landscape through its fervent and often toxic opposition to them (Nagle 2017).

While the above-cited works offer valuable insight on their chosen focal point of research, the general set of literature on 4Chan remains topically scattered, and devoid of substantial work on its most politically-minded militant aspect, /pol/. It is also worth noting that previous research has not used the opportunity to analyze posts made from specific countries, which provides a more focused lens and more relevant findings.

The need for assessing /pol/ as such has been noted in news media and various mainstream publications[3] especially as the board has gotten much more popular and at the forefront of controversial political campaigns like Gamergate, the QAnon[4] following (Coaston 2018), and the alt-right backing of Donald Trump's presidential run.

The noted immense facetiousness and esotericism of online communication on 4Chan along with the noted general dearth of work examining it deserves wider inquiry into a separate field of relevant literature. Works examining the effects of online anonymity on inhibitions and sincerity can help provide a basis for a more precise understanding of the intent and purpose of posting on /pol/. Disinhibition is a concept developed in psychology indicating that an individual has a lack of restraint in disregarding social convention, impulsivity, and assesses risk poorly. Online communication when participation is anonymous is more likely to feature disinhibited behavior. Lapidot-Lefler and Barak show that anonymous communication, especially when there is no eye contact between participants, generally results in more disinhibition (Lapidot-Lefler and Barak 2012). Santana demonstrates similar results in analyzing newspaper comments online (Santana 2014). Suler provides a basis for distinguishing the factors towards more disinhibition when communicating (Suler 2005). Perhaps most pertinently, Moore et al. (2012) show that the more anonymous a participant is, the more likely he is to behave aggressively in forum posting.

Not all of the literature leads to the conclusion that anonymity drives hostile and violent behavior on the Internet. Cornelius, Gordon, and Harris conducted an experiment in synchronous online play and found that anonymity, if the playing structure is properly rule bound, can bolster the odds of successful communal play (Cornelius, Gordon, and Harris 2011). However, this then places further

---

3   A selection of the most popular articles on this: (Ohlheiser 2016; Herrman 2017; Eordogh 2017; Thompson 2018; Schreckinger 2017; Coaston 2018).
4   QAnon, or just Q, is a supposed Washington insider and Trump diehard supporter, repeatedly posting sensational supposed knowledge of the administration's future actions against targets like illegal immigrants and Hillary Clinton, gaining a massive following in 2018.

focus on understanding that 4Chan has no such rule system in place — users can post pretty much whatever they like, whenever they like. In reviewing existing previous psychological literature and subsequently conducting a series of interviews with young users of the Internet, Davis solidifies the notion that online and offline identities are more aligned than early research and popular perception suggested (Davis 2012).

The referenced papers here briefly serve to help readers take what Serbian 4Chan users say here both seriously and literally. While there has not been enough research of this type done on 4Chan specifically, the body of literature provides a basis for considering that 4Chan with its unique structure and implicit rule set (or lack thereof) is very much an online platform spurring disinhibition in its participants. There does not seem to be much ground for claiming that what one says online is radically different from the views they hold and express as their real life identities. In fact, the disinhibition 4Chan naturally seems to cultivate among its users might just be the perfect opportunity for one to be what they cannot be in reality — as honest as they would like. While posting on 4Chan and on /pol/ often implies layers of irony and inside humor, it does also frequently convey violent extremist sentiment that is very much real.

Methodology

This paper relies on discourse analysis, to dissect and understand the essential tasks of a text. The chosen set of texts is comprised of the archived posts from all Serbian IPs made on 4Chan's "Politically Incorrect" board, /pol/, from December 2014 to September 30, 2018. There are 540,267 posts in the archive as of October 1, 2018. The archive database is owned and operated by an unaffiliated third party, is automatized and shares general rules on what can be removed from this archive of the main 4Chan site (Archive.4plebs 2018). The author of this paper has not had any influence on content saved in the archive. I have only selected *all* of the existing posts from Serbian Internet Protocol addresses made on /pol/ since the

IP display feature[5] was added in 2014. Due to space considerations and reading clarity, only the essential quotable posts are referenced in footnotes. The bibliography section has listed a wider selection of the most relevant posts from Serbian users and has referenced the whole database of analyzed posts for any necessary enquiry. A massive majority of posts made on 4Chan from Serbian IPs are made in English and do not require any translation. Some posts, made in interaction with Serbian speakers or others in the Western Balkans were made in their native language (the language formerly known as Serbo-Croatian) and are a part of this analysis through my translation into English. I have also censored expletives that appear in text through direct quoting.

I have analyzed the content of the archive through literally reading it in its entirety, post by post. I have not used any bulk text processing tools and have relied on my extensive experience of reading and using 4Chan for almost 10 years. I have also read posts from non-Serbian IPs extensively to properly understand Serbian posts in context. Posts do not appear in isolation but in threads where users from across the globe communicate. Additionally, discourse analysis of 4Chan necessitates understanding and elaborating on the subcultural references contained in the texts. This study will primarily explain terms in the main body of text when dealing with concepts that are essential to understanding the main points of analyzed discourse. Otherwise, explanatory sections are noted in footnotes when dealing with concepts that are less essential to the central points being made, but still relevant for understanding 4Chan culture as a whole.

The community of 4Chan operates on a unique discursive context that strongly influences content output. 4Chan has developed a social structure heavily reliant on anonymity. The anonymity of 4Chan posting thus does not permit extensive individual profiling of a discursive author by design, and creates limits on how much insight can be gathered as to why and in what manner an author

---

5   There might be options for users from outside Serbia to spoof IPs through VPNs or similar means for whatever reason. There is no foolproof means of claiming that every single post was made from Serbia but the large number of posts helps make this possibility a minor issue.

has decided to participate in the discourse. I am generally unable to claim definitively that the author of one post is also an author of a different post on /pol/; nor can I provide definitive numbers of total authors. I *do* identify recurring posts from the same author from common signifiers of style and through the user's reference to past posting. It is possible to present a collective framework of what extremist Serbian users of 4Chan are saying as a collective steeped in an engaging and unique environment, structuring behavior as well as bearing a legacy of understating their nation and social environment in a specific way that makes them vulnerable to radicalization.

This analysis accepts and applies the benefits of distinguishing concepts of "Self" and "the Other" in discourse. It applies these concepts to national Serbian identity construction in discourse. This analysis inherits the understanding that this distinction is a complex dialectic with frequent fluctuation in how participants frame their identities and the identities of their counterparts (Hansen 2006). The distinction is susceptible to change, and being purposefully wielded for the pursuit and expression of power. This helps drive the understanding that this paper is an opportunity to analyze through conceptualizing the discourse as a series of discursive encounters, of contrasting "the discourse of the Self with the Other's 'counter-construction' of Self and Other" (Hansen 2006, 68). The arena of /pol/ presents a continuous series of opportunities in engaging and competing *against* users of "opponent" nationalities and *for* the affection and discursive incorporation into a wider, extremist identity of the like-minded. The paper will demonstrate that discourse from extremist Serbian users eventually gains part into a wider, extremist "European" and "Western" self.

This is not to imply that all posts on /pol/ are extremist. It is important to state that, while the extremist discourse analyzed here is predominant amongst Serbian users, it is not the only discourse present. 4Chan is not inherently or exclusively extremist and should not be treated as such. It continues to be an incredibly unique Internet community of immense creativity and camaraderie and brings value to the Internet despite its faults. Posting on 4Chan is not evidence of extremist thought or intention. It frequently features a vast array of voiced opinions and debates falling well outside of the range of extremist thought. However, at least among Serbian users, the type of discourse analyzed here appear so frequently and coherently that it presents the predominant discourse featured, bearing severe implications for peaceful coexistence in a democratic society, and meriting inquiry.

This paper cannot conclusively determine whether this discourse becomes extremist primarily due to the structure and norms of 4Chan and /pol/ themselves, or owes its development more to the conditions in which Serbian users are socialized in their country. There is ground to say the environment of 4Chan itself spurs extremist ideology. The posting culture of 4Chan provides space for extremist viewpoints to be expressed quickly, anonymously and to a receptive audience of extremists worldwide. Being willing to use insulting verbiage and extreme imagery is normalized behavior and opposition to such behavior is considered contrary to the prevailing cultural norms of participation on 4Chan. However, there is also plenty of evidence suggesting Serbian users are bringing in an immense amount of socially conditioned hatred into these conversations online. While I cannot determine the exact ratio of influence these two sources of conditioning bring, I would suggest that both are at play. This remains a relevant question to consider in further research.

In elaborating the theoretical underpinnings of my research, I should note that the analysis featured in the paper uses concepts and frames of reference best elaborated through critical discourse analysis (CDA). For instance, the practices of critical discourse analysis are useful as CDA generally includes the understanding that texts are rarely the product of a single person (Wodak 2002, 11) and is suitable for comprehensively analyzing a vast number of authors contributing to a set of cohesive ideological positions. However, while this paper learns from CDA it cannot complete the lofty demands of critical discourse analysis in full. Critical discourse analysis takes on as a central task the objective of addressing the possible ways of righting and mitigating social wrongs (Fairclough 2013,

11). This analysis does not have the space to conceptualize a working plan towards countering violent extremism on its own and cannot fully elaborate the societal forces driving it. It describes a problem that is woefully underexplored, relevant and timely. This paper is thus the first step towards a more comprehensive approach and (tentative) answer. It is descriptive in character but can also contribute to efforts to prevent and counter violent extremism.

As this paper does engage the idea that the discourse being analyzed is facilitating processes of radicalization into violent extremism it bears elaborating what that means. Conversations on how to define extremism and extremism-adjacent terms are difficult and include a variety of competing, potentially conflicting interests (Hopkins and Kahani-Hopkins 2009). There is no commonly accepted definition. I therefore opt for the simplest posited practicable explanation of these, viewing radicalization into violent extremism as "the processes by which people come to adopt beliefs that not only justify violence but compel it, and how they progress—or not—from thinking to action"(Borum 2011, 8). The other authors in this volume provide their own understanding of extremism and extremism-adjacent terms, providing further context to extremism research efforts in Serbia.

Discourse analysis

The following contains four sections, each explaining a crucial and frequently present theme of the analyzed discourse in an effort to present the findings in as concise and as informative of a fashion possible. Four broad themes of discourse were identified based on this preliminary and qualitative research. I have selected and here outlined these themes due to both the severity of what they convey as well as the frequency with which they appear.

Serbian users of /pol/ develop and promote extremist discourse based on inherited old patterns of extreme nationalism, and seek to change the narrative of their nation into a story of consistent and profound heroism of targeted prosecution of ideological opponents

As is predominantly the case when communicating in an environment where assumption of any kind of group identity is possible, the space of /pol/ has Serbian users creatively attempt to convey a story of their own identity — one conducive to the spread of extremist ideology.

Discourse on /pol/ portrays Serbia as a fallen nation with a virtuous history. As with every country, Serbia certainly has a history that is valuable for its citizens to understand. However, the extremist discourse of /pol/ finds value in something more objectionable: its history is virtuous as its essential value is in militant opposition to Muslims. Putting off the Ottoman invasion of Europe, removing the remnants of Turkish rule after it ended and trying to cleanse the Balkan peninsula of its Islamic inhabitants in the Yugoslavian Wars of the 1990s, are considered equally worthy of pride. The long storied narrative of Bosnian Muslims having betrayed their Slavic origins by converting to Islam is once again a central piece of extreme discourse. The discourse views Bosnians as

> "Serbs/Croats that converted to Islam back when the Ottomans rolled through the area in the 14th/15th century. As such, they deserve hate even today from Catholic Croats and Orthodox Serbs for being traitors, when countless others refused to convert, even when facing the infamous taxes leveled against Christians in the Ottoman Empire" ("/Pol/ - Politically Incorrect » Thread #58132459" 2015).

The discourse generally uses terms like Bosnian, Bosniak, or Muslim, leaving little space for nuanced portrayals of these people. The perceived legacy of Bosnian Muslims as remnants means they are inherently traitorous; they are the "5th column" of the Balkans ("/Pol/ - Politically Incorrect » Thread #122122528" 2017). The essence of their Serbian identity and tradition is imbued in hostility and militancy against Islam:

> "I am here, a Serb, because my ancestors didn't deny their heritage, their people, to live a better life, they died refusing Islam and it took time but managed to come back" ("/Pol/ - Politically Incorrect » Thread #50906710" 2017).

The national, Serbian, Self attempts to constitute the Other through showing that the degrees of difference between the two are much steeper than the rest of the world perceives. Serbian users initially think that they have a barbaric image in the eyes of others, especially Westerners, and seek to swap this perceived position by placing the Muslims of the Balkans as the barbarians. Controversy over rocks being pelted at then Serbian Prime Minister Vučić's official visit to Srebrenica during the anniversary of the massacre offered another opportunity for showing the Westerners that Bosnia remains home to a barbaric group of people ("/Pol/ - Politically Incorrect » Thread #47851193" 2015) with a Serbian users asking:

> "Is this the clash of civilizations coming? Is the West really not going to condemn this?"("/Pol/ - Politically Incorrect » Thread #47839202" 2015)

Similar mechanisms extend to other ethnic and religious groups in the Balkans, like Croatians and Albanians. However, Muslims emerge as the primary Other through which the Serbian Self is presented in the posts of extreme /pol/ users. Radical discourse finds an audience ready for and receptive to a demonization of Muslim people in the Balkans that is congruent to their own extremist understanding of Muslims as a threat to survival. I would speculate this happens as Muslims are the most familiar, and most maligned, category of people living in the Balkans to extremists in Western countries, and a category that Serbian extremists can successfully construct their identities against when communicating with extremists in the West. Extremists in the West draw easy parallels and generalizations between Muslims in their countries and the Muslims of the Balkans.

Figure 3: Meme of a Pepe gleefully looming over the graves of Srebrenica

Source: https://i.4pcdn.org/pol/1427674130362.jpg

Users attempt to introduce their heroes into the collective mythology though specific mechanisms. For example, one mechanism prominent in discourse initiated by Serbian users is the topic of Ratko Mladić currently appealing his conviction of war crimes at the International Criminal Tribunal for the former Yugoslavia (ICTY) at The Hague. Most often, a Serbian user will ask others a neutral opening question like, "What does /pol/ think of this guy?" Then the user will give a short summation of what they feel is the official, incorrect narrative of Mladić's alleged crimes before rejecting these and placing a different narrative. The other narrative generally focuses on portraying a heroic figure where Westerners would have heard otherwise, beloved by his people and now suffering for his deeds unjustly. This narrative selling has been received well on /pol/. Users posting from IPs outside of Serbia describe Mladić as a similarly heroic figure, calling him "the greatest man on Earth," a "major kebab remover you should lend him to western European countries" ("/Pol/ - Politically Incorrect» Thread #42367712" 2015). (It should be noted that this term appears frequently and will be additionally explained later in the paper.) Understanding Mladić as a hero does seem to tie into going against other understandings of Serbia as a state doing wrong. For instance, a user posting through an American IP, posting in a thread celebrating Mladić's birthday issued his best wishes while apologizing for the U.S. led NATO bombing campaign of 1999 ("/Pol/ - Politically Incorrect» Thread #42418076" 2015).

The same process is visible with other figures of influence operationalizing a murderous ideology. The prominent figures of celebration and elevation to heroic status include Serbian fascist Dimitrije Ljotić; Serbian Radical Party President Vojislav Šešelj; former President of Republika Srpska and now convicted war criminal Radovan Karadžić; and former Yugoslavian President Slobodan Milošević ("/Pol/ - Politically Incorrect» Thread #47690088" 2015; "/Pol/ - Politically Incorrect» Thread #58361096" 2015; "/Pol/ - Politically Incorrect» Thread #68656676" 2016; "/Pol/ - Politically Incorrect» Thread #47613849" 2015).

This process is not restricted to figures implicated in the persecution of war crimes. It also extends to more innocuous figures. Serbian Orthodox Bishop and celebrated theologian Nikolaj Velimirović receives praise for being decorated by Adolf Hitler ("/Pol/ - Politically Incorrect» Thread #58361096" 2016).

Asserting your preferred version of Serbia's history comes with asserting your symbolism as part 4Chan's culture. This manifests itself through creating memes to accompany posts. Overall, It leads to enthusiastically asserting your nation's identity as one marked by prosecution of others. It means being proud of being a "kebab remover," a mass murderer of Muslim people. Serbs being kebab removers in essence has, even though it started on 4Chan, expanded beyond 4Chan alone and has become a massively popular meme across a variety of online spaces.[6]

---

[6] A YouTube video of the meme's most popular variation has 8.6 million views alone — https://www.youtube.com/watch?v=ocW3fBqPQkU (Ryuuzakii666 2012).

Extremist Serbs here often feel as though they cannot live this identity fully in the real world. The Serbia of today is beholden to the EU and the West in general and unable to continue the legacy they have constructed. In the words of a Serbian user,

> "let us not forget, today, *(we are)* not so based[7] anymore, we are cucks,[8] we let migrants come and go, we suck Merkel c*** and who knows what is the future, we are nothing today" ("/Pol/ - Politically Incorrect » Thread #74754782" 2016).

Serbian history has a didactic role to play. Serbs feel the need to warn the West of the dangers Muslims pose and motivate them to take a stand. The Westerners are too permissive. One user remarks,

> "I saw how you treat these subhumans -- welcoming them among you with a condescending attitude of protectors. But they don't want your protection, they want your obedience. Your benevolence only rings as weakness in their ears. Over here, we know this instinctively"("/Pol/ - Politically Incorrect » Thread #48045511" 2015).

The West is too permissive towards immigration, especially from predominantly Islamic countries, and is letting its native white population slowly disappear. Serbian users portray their country as immune to these failings, praising that drops in the relative number of white people,

> "Still hasn't happened in my country and wont any time soon. I pray to God every day that my country stays shi**y and people remain hostile towards immigrants so that no immigrant EVER wants to come here" ("/Pol/ - Politically Incorrect » Thread #45306733" 2015).

Compassion as part of Serbia and Europe's new ascension is not an option as,

> "feeling empathy towards these subhumans is like feeling empathy for leeches that suck your blood and will continue to do so until you're dead. Grow some balls. Pray for Muslim deaths" ("/Pol/ - Politically Incorrect » Thread #50939050" 2015).

---

7   "Based" = awesome.
8   Short for cuckold, indicating a subservient, spineless man.

As is evident from these and the following quoted passages, the language of discursive arena combat is immensely dehumanizing and coarse. It is not very precise. For instance, posts will, within the same space, use terms like Bosnian, Muslim, Bosniak and the various associated pejoratives interchangeably when referencing the same roughly conceptualized and generalized group of people. I would speculate that this language is, in great part, styled like this to achieve the most impact. This discourse primarily wants to be noticed and considered appealing rather than be considered absolutely precise or rigorous.

This assertion of narrative coexists with an understanding of what Europe is. Europe was built and made superior through war: "Europe has been molded by constant conflict and go figure, as soon as things settle down, it starts breeding manworms" ("/Pol/ - Politically Incorrect » Thread #94960091" 2016). Serbs, unlike the European of today, can say they make their ancestors proud for maintaining the nation ("/Pol/ - Politically Incorrect » Thread #165192436" 2018). It, along with Serbia, will need to fight to set itself right again.

Serbian identity is thus presented on /pol/ as rooted in opposition to and violent conflict with old enemies—the other groups of the Balkans—and, especially Muslims. The efforts of extremist minded posters to counteract the perceived negative image of Serbs in the West find a receptive, also extremist minded audience. This is especially true due to the perceived common enemies the Serbian identity and the West share.

Serbian users of /pol/ portray themselves and their nation as presently suitable for and susceptible to violent extremism to a great degree

Overcoming perceived negative perceptions of the Serbian self and successfully having the Muslim other understood as a threat that needs to be stopped leads into additional identity construction. Serbs know their ideological priorities and know what to oppose, as "Islam is the biggest threat to western civilization" ("/Pol/ - Politically Incorrect » Thread #111768299" 2017). Misunderstanding the true nature of Islam leads to national devastation, as one Serbian user warned a fellow user with a Canadian IP address: "soon you'll gonna feel on your skin what does it mean" ("/Pol/ - Politically Incorrect » Thread #111691155" 2017). Serbia is much safer than the European Union, "because no Muslim would dare to commit a terrorist attack here" ("/Pol/ - Politically Incorrect » Thread #58225511" 2015). If a terrorist attack were to take place, Serbs would strike back ferociously as "many Nationalist organizations (and my friends) already said we'd burn all the Mosques in the country if we get attacked" (Ibid.). After all, Serbia has been "defending Europe from jihad since 1389" ("/Pol/ - Politically Incorrect » Thread #134058580" 2017), and today this is as needed as ever. They understand Serbia as the type of country that can, with effort, grow into a shining example of a country that can excel at combatting Islam. There is past successful practice and potential for an even more intese renewal and institutionalization of these ideas.

Figure 4: A Kebab Remover pasted over a famous image of a Serbian paramilitary member kicking a dead Muslim woman in Bijeljina

Source: https://i.4pcdn.org/pol/1420818292959.jpg

Attempts to portray Serbia as a haven for the genocide minded seem to have succeeded ("/Pol/ - Politically Incorrect » Thread #47851193" 2015; "/Pol/ - Politically Incorrect » Thread #49898005" 2015). Extremist voices on 4Chan portray the average Serb as already anti-Semitic, anti-globalist, and hateful towards Muslims ("/Pol/ - Politically Incorrect » Thread #118363300" 2017). Serbia is also supposedly more welcoming of overt racism. One "can pretty much be openly racist here. There's a certain layer of the population who will try and fake shock and outrage, but nobody cares about them and considers them pu**ies basically" ("/Pol/ - Politically Incorrect » Thread #59280365" 2017). This worldview sees efforts to promote tolerant societies are no more than cosmetic in Serbia.

There is an understanding that Serbian people are more likely to be socioeconomically stranded and thus more easily recruited for extremist causes. As one Serbian /pol/ user recognizes, "it's really simple. When you have zero career prospects, and fragile states, you are more open to radical ideologies" ("/Pol/ - Politically Incorrect » Thread #105524970" 2017). The added problem here is that Serbian users now comprehend the source of their difficulties from an extremist perspective. A Serbian user understands his inability to earn a living in Serbia as a consequence of global Jewry and advises his fellow users to

> "find the richest Jew around and blow his brains out. Form a group. Kill someone important, start a war. We are economic slaves. It's worse than that because a slave had some chance of running away, but we have literally 0 chance of ever being 1%. It just doesn't happen" ("/Pol/ - Politically Incorrect » Thread #83625550" 2017).

Deeply hopeless situations merit extreme and immediate answers. Displeasure with the administration of Aleksandar Vučić is clear and framed as them being "just kike[9] slaves" ("/Pol/ - Politically Incorrect » Thread #51165782" 2015). The Jews jack up housing prices ("/Pol/ - Politically Incorrect » Thread #96241986" 2016).

---

9   This is a pejorative term for Jewish people.

Having difficulty over getting a date is because "you've been brainwashed by the Jew media into being scared of women" ("/Pol/ - Politically Incorrect » Thread # 181619781" 2018).

Serbia is a state where it is easy to be in a vulnerable position and where it is easy to fall under the influence of extremist messaging.

Descent into radical ideologies comes quick and strong. Users frequently recount how posting on /pol/ turns them into radicals. One Serbian user described a harrowing personal journey when [a] "few months ago I finally became fully red-pilled.[10] I got to the bottom of everything and I went from a libertarian to a Nat Soc[11] within weeks" ("/Pol/ - Politically Incorrect » Thread #113511733" 2017). Taking the red pill left him in a dire state of being "now completely and utterly disgusted of this world and the disgusting creatures that tread it" and contemplating suicide. The thread he started grew into other users trying to avert him from suicidal ideation through advice like getting more active in his nation's politics and spreading his ideals of "the renewal of the nation states of the world and a peaceful world without Jewry" to his girlfriend, friends and family. Another Serbian user was less distressed by the original poster's thoughts of suicide, advising him "if you really decide to kill yourself, could you please kill some of the retarded politicians, like suicide bombing or something first?" with another Serbian IP poster adding that he is "serious about suicide bombing."

Another user bragged about how quickly his political awakening took hold, claiming that he "used to be a pretty cool guy, all it took was a couple of months of /pol/ and all I can do at parties is talk about the race war, Turks, Jews and the rights of the Christian European man" ("/Pol/ - Politically Incorrect » Thread #56906493" 2015). A different Serbian user echoes this sentiment and seeks advice on "where does /pol/ go to meet redpilled people? Preferably girls. I can't do it anymore, pretending like everything is ok" ("/Pol/ - Politically Incorrect » Thread #56916223" 2015). When

---

10 "Taking the red pill" is equivalent to gaining a profound new understanding of the world. The metaphor comes from the film "The Matrix."
11 Short for National-Socialist.

people completely fall into extremist ideology and start spreading the message, they often, surprisingly, find an immensely receptive audience. One user claims they started "advocating genocide at an early age," back in the 4th or 5th grade and was surprised that "most of my class agreed that ethnically cleansing our country was a necessity" ("/Pol/ - Politically Incorrect » Thread #57665487" 2015).

Ideologies that promote tolerance and are opposed to violence against minority groups are presented as having much less support in Serbia than elsewhere. Serbia is portrayed as resilient to the induction of leftist terminology like toxic masculinity into everyday speak ("/Pol/ - Politically Incorrect » Thread #46705843" 2015), and Serbs are able to resist the false promises of Western liberal ideology and "go full 1488[12] anti-f*g nationalist" ("/Pol/ - Politically Incorrect » Thread #176069827" 2018).

This does not mean that Serbia does not require action towards an ideologically acceptable society. The fight for an ideal Serbia is only beginning. As much as Serbian users propagate a narrative of their country as inherently more xenophobic, racist, and nationalistic than other countries in Europe they also malign the perceived growing tolerance towards minorities and foreigners in Serbia. Serbian identity is still splintered and tempted by disruptive outside forces. Serbia's government is not serious about advancing their ideal society. Even worse, the government is frequently kowtowing to the oppressive demands of Western states, pushing Serbia deeper into degenerate structures. Serbian society is now accepting of Western vices to an unacceptable degree. One user narrates their disgust over seeing a black man and a pregnant white woman together on the street in his town, a never before seen sight ("/Pol/ - Politically Incorrect » Thread #120982275" 2017).

I would summarize this worldview as seeing much work still to be done in a society inherently friendly to extremists but currently beset by strong outside forces and slipping away. There is a curious mechanism at work here—users promote a narrative of a

---

12 The term 1488 refers to a quote generally used as an identifier by Nazi enthusiasts, often falsely attributed to Adolf Hitler and actually uttered by American white supremacist organizer David Lane (more detail available at Wikipedia 2018).

nation both immensely resistant and superior to these outside forces but one simultaneously being torn apart by the same forces to which it is resistant. The narrative is thus actionable, requiring vigilance. You need to fight as the threat is immediate and overwhelming but while also knowing that the fight can be easily won as you are fighting alongside and for a people that cannot be beaten. This viewpoint sees the Serbian people as strong due to their supposed inherent support for extremist ideology.

Serbian users of /pol/ create alliances with extremist discourse existing in other countries through adopting new targets of hate and merging their old perceived enemies with a new, wide and encompassing extremist discourse

Serbian extremism recognizes, aligns with, and tries to amplify far-right extremism in the West on 4Chan. Both can and should complement each other's efforts in ongoing combat against ideological enemies. For instance, noticing that North America and Europe have become sources of more hostile ideology against Muslim people goes hand-in-hand with efforts of reviving plots of genocide in the Balkans. Fears of Islamist terror strikes in Europe feed into Serbian pleas for the nations of Europe to "let us cleanse them at least from Balkan" ("/Pol/ - Politically Incorrect » Thread #48204097" 2015). Europe's mistakes in permitting the infiltration of Islam into its national borders has led to a dire state of affairs, "since you liked to play SJW,[13] now you have Bosnia and Kosovo, two main ISIS recruiting centers from EU confirmed even by your government" (Ibid.). Serbia can once again be strong enough to mount a campaign of cleansing as "our army is ready you just need to let us do our business" (Ibid.) and deal with this problem.

---

13 Short for "Social Justice Warrior", usually referring to a zealous, extreme, or disingenuous progressive.

Figure 5: Fusing symbolism though a collage of Serbian Radical Party President Vojislav Šešelj, the Black Sun and Trump's famous catchphrase

Source: https://i.4pcdn.org/pol/1461515104250.jpg

However, these efforts morph to become part of a wider set of priorities aligned with other forms of Western extremism like anti-Semitism and racism. A perfect world is, as one Serbian /pol/ user puts it, a world where we "execute every nonwhite race" ("/Pol/ - Politically Incorrect » Thread #123986794" 2017). Another user advocates for storming Israel as a way of fighting back European native displacement ("/Pol/ - Politically Incorrect » Thread #51215536" 2015). Combatting anti-fa in the streets, so far a marginal movement in Serbia at most, should now be a top priority for Serbian people ("/Pol/ - Politically Incorrect » Thread #121786810" 2017).

The users of 4Chan see women as a common source of issues facing their respective nations and bond over communal hatred of them. Women can be saved however, by a renewed, politically minded generation of men. All they need is "some right-wing c**k to sort themselves out" ("/Pol/ - Politically Incorrect » Thread #

121503298" 2017). Dealing with the failures of modern women will require extreme solutions as "the only way to put sluts in their place is by raping them" ("/Pol/ - Politically Incorrect » Thread #46147395" 2015). Women are also fixable by "beating disobedient women" into "re-indoctrination" ("/Pol/ - Politically Incorrect » Thread #138630629" 2017). Women are especially troublesome as they are the primary supporters of destructive leftist causes ("/Pol/ - Politically Incorrect » Thread #158161298" 2017).

The fears of Islamist terrorism speak and serve to unify towards a common purpose. Muslims "commit 98% of terrorism, they should be exterminated" (Ibid.). These fearful conceptualizations have especially taken hold with the ongoing refugee crisis exacerbated by the Syrian Civil War. Serbia has been at the center of the Europe-bound refugee route (see Rečević in this volume). Most European countries were facing fears by some that the predominantly Muslim refugees posed a threat to their states and societies. Common fears of this nature provide fertile ground for new, potentially violent political options

A recent political campaign has proved to be a focal point for unifying tendencies and serves as a good example of alliance building. Donald Trump has been a rallying force for the reinvention of right-wing subcultures, especially on the Internet. Serbian users have been a strong part of this shift. Serbian nationalism here is able to incorporate and whole-heartedly support the now President of the United States.

Serbs have much to teach their fellow Western users. Serbian experiences of the deposing of Slobodan Milošević are warning signs of what progressive political projects can do to a country. The perceived fraudulent and anti-Serbian 2000 presidential elections threatened to repeat themselves in having similar unpatriotic and destructive forces endanger the presidency of Donald Trump ("/Pol/ - Politically Incorrect » Thread #98575113" 2016).

Figure 6: Donald Trump's face pasted over a famous photo of Serbian paramilitary leader and crime lord Željko Ražnatović ("Arkan")

Source: https://i.4pcdn.org/pol/1460059415593.jpg

The reinvigoration of the extreme fringes of the right-wing due to Trump's campaign had also inspired Serbian users. This reinvigoration comes in the form of an irrational, passionate and masculine energy, a "weird sensation of confidence thanks to Trump" ("/Pol/ - Politically Incorrect » Thread #66824824" 2016). One Serbian uses credits Trump for transforming him from a stereotypical introvert to an "alpha," "far more aggressive when provoked," and to someone who no longer cares what liberals think of him anymore ("/Pol/ - Politically Incorrect » Thread #67403986" 2016). Supporting Donald Trump gave a user the opportunity to get into a confrontation with a group of black people by wearing a "Make America Great Again" hat in his Serbian town ("/Pol/ - Politically Incorrect » Thread #66754704" 2016). Support for Trump from Serbian people on 4Chan goes hand-in-hand with extremist ideology. One user prides themselves on having influenced the political views of their classmates to support Trump over

Hilary Clinton and seeks advice on how to take this influence to its next logical level—having them know the "truth" about the common enemies of extremists on /pol/, Jews and black people ("/Pol/ - Politically Incorrect » Thread #96886556" 2016). Some see the win for Trump as a means of progress towards a new war in the Balkans. Another user praises Donald Trump for being the focal point for his Serbian nationalist reawakening, as they describe themselves as previously being "out of touch with my roots given I grew up in the United States," but, having learned from the terrible events of Islamic terrorism, the user eventually returned to Serbia. The return to the homeland was bolstered by a deep disappointment and hatred of the liberal structuring of society ("/Pol/ - Politically Incorrect » Thread #97622056" 2016).

Donald Trump's victory has been a catalyst for renewed hopes for extreme political projects, regardless of any actual policy in the US. It presents new dangers for the Muslim population of the Balkans, at least by the understanding of Serbian extremists who anticipate support or a carte blanche for Serbian territorial expansion in the future. The rocky foreign relations of the US and the perceived growth of combativeness its foreign policy has can be of great use to Serbian extremist action. If the US were to start World War III, Serbia could "conduct a little genocide while everyone is distracted" ("/Pol/ - Politically Incorrect » Thread #121645754" 2017).

Being part of a wider self, one based on both Serbian nationalism but also on a wide encompassing white, Christian, extremist identity here requires taking on a wider set of concerns and targets. Being racist towards black people becomes a matter of great concern for Serbian participants ("/Pol/ - Politically Incorrect » Thread #48610389" 2015) despite minor numbers of black people living in the country.

All of this contributes to a synthesis of goals and core beliefs of extremists from both Serbia and from outside of it in the 4Chan online space. Extreme nationalism of old takes on a wider set of elements of hateful ideology like anti-Semitism and racism. They also idealize the same set of newly relevant figures, finding reasons to support idealized protagonists. This alliance building does not depend on overcoming old hatred towards Western states. On the contrary, hatred of modern Western society can bind together with people who all hate what the West now is—Western extreme reactionaries. They share appreciation for idealized images of what Europe and the US used to be and communally dream of a better world.

Serbian users of /pol/ demonstrate a strong willingness to commit ideological violence

Violence in dealing with pressing political issues is not to be avoided if possible but to be openly and eagerly embraced ("/Pol/ - Politically Incorrect » Thread #49633684" 2015). Violence as a viable and preferred option is an acceptable consideration for an entire generation of Serbian people who have not received satisfactory answers to

> "why shouldn't you kill your enemies? Why shouldn't you kill the politician who is making your country worse? Why shouldn't you kill those who are financing the ruin of your people and culture and everything else?" ("/Pol/ - Politically Incorrect » Thread #101758764" 2016).

This violence is possible in the real world as it is based on rational preparation. The radicals of 4Chan are very much aware that reaching massive numbers of people required for political action is accomplishable through employing gradual radicalization tactics and methods that are sustainable. Many aspects of society can become intensely politicized and weaponized. One should first start up small, on the surface apolitical get-togethers like boxing clubs, and gradually inject radical politics into their functioning to turn the people attending into violent adherents of ideology ("/Pol/ - Politically Incorrect » Thread #133539458" 2017). Individual self-improvement, while on its own a beneficial idea, is mixed up with a profoundly political and, often, extremist message. For example, one should join a gym not to better one's health but to be strong enough for fighting the Jews ("/Pol/ - Politically Incorrect » Thread #105859256" 2017). Memes are a tool for the gradual radicalization of peers and family within this mindset. One Serbian user asks how they can get his family "laughing about holocaust memes and what not" towards red pilling them completely ("/Pol/ - Politically Incorrect » Thread #145675667" 2017). One Serbian user encourages the stereotypical friendless, traditionally maladjusted other users of /pol/ to integrate into society as to not damage their cause ("/Pol/ - Politically Incorrect » Thread #86981195" 2016). Posting traditional army music is to make one "go genocide mode" ("/Pol/ - Politically Incorrect » Thread #49029247" 2015). Some users encourage each other to learn from one another how to become violent against Muslims. One Serbian user advises,

> "quick, spread propaganda sheets explaining how to torture people by the ways of Pol Pot, we are going to rape them so hard they will beg to be killed, but the torture will be eternal because we will hook them to life support to slow their dying so they can be tortured longer" ("/Pol/ - Politically Incorrect » Thread #48045511" n.d.).

Users also commonly share successes and advice for how to "red pill," how to radicalize, friends, romantic partners, and family ("/Pol/ - Politically Incorrect » Thread #51861195" 2015). These stories often include the twist where the user attempts to propagate his views only to discover that the people he was trying to radicalize were already quite radical themselves.

Very often, investment in /pol/ as a community mirrors attachment to more familiar extremist movements. One loses attachment and contact with family and friends, effectively replacing them with other radical followers of a set of politically actionable ideas that are greater than one's self ("/Pol/ - Politically Incorrect » Thread #101969776" 2016). 4Chan has become the central hub for online activities of Serbian Neo Nazis ("/Pol/ - Politically Incorrect » Thread #111979680" 2017). Discussed potential methods can be projected as massively ambitious genocidal undertakings. There are regular discussions on the methods of effective mass murder, predominantly targeted against Muslim and black people. One Serbian user started a lengthy thread inquiring about the possibility of an "ethnic bioweapon" usable against specific targeted groups of people ("/Pol/ - Politically Incorrect » Thread #130817208" 2017).

A common and relevant connected pattern is that non-violent solutions are not part of serious consideration towards their ideal society as "violence solves everything. Killing solves everything permanently" ("/Pol/ - Politically Incorrect» Thread #54213852" 2015). One user even goes as far to claim they tortured and sexually abused an unidentified group of men ("/Pol/ - Politically Incorrect» Thread #66097781" 2016). These instances of extreme and more credible sounding threats are however difficult to link to actual crimes without assistance from police authorities. Times have become so extreme that

> "now only bullets and bombs can save the white race, pick up a gun, find a first liberal/Jew/billionaire/politician and blow their brains out, that's how we win" ("/Pol/ - Politically Incorrect» Thread #71859326" 2016).

Goading others into doing violence becomes part of a wider discourse. For example, a Serbian user asks "why doesn't someone kill them all? America has school or other shootings every day I guess, why not make it useful for once?" ("/Pol/ - Politically Incorrect» Thread #45524684" 2015). In discussion over British Islamist ISIS supporter and controversial preacher Anjem Choudary a Serbian user laments the lack of radical action from British patriots, threatening that they "personally would slit his throat if he comes anywhere near Serbia" ("/Pol/ - Politically Incorrect» Thread #48225488" 2015). Again, as I mentioned previously, the identities referenced in this discourse are generalized and do not permit much distinction between extreme and moderate Muslims. Threats against the Muslim population of both the Balkans and the EU are explicit. One user threatens that "soon mosques will burn and the invaders will die and be purged. You should be afraid" ("/Pol/ - Politically Incorrect» Thread #64493871" 2016). There is no time to waste - "guys I want to do something before it gets too late, I feel like a f***ing p***y" a Serbian user pleads ("/Pol/ - Politically Incorrect» Thread #51517070" 2015). Serbian users frequently goad users of /pol/ from other, primarily Western, states into violent answers for their political concerns. "Just let me be a Swede for a few days," pleads a Serbian user, "this whole situation is so easily solved. They just have to start beating up muds[14] and prosecuting them" ("/Pol/ - Politically Incorrect » Thread #101898749" 2016).

As much as there is ground to claim that extremist on /pol/ are planning, actively and comprehensively, long-term ways of influencing society and effecting the real world, extremism on /pol/ and its real life manifestations are not complete ideological projects. There is no widespread support for any visible and active political movement in Serbia. They see movements like Obraz as having been suppressed into irrelevance, current parties like *Dveri* and *Zavetnci* are not extreme enough, and Šešelj has embarrassed himself as a political figure ("/Pol/ - Politically Incorrect » Thread #142138454" 2017; "/Pol/ - Politically Incorrect » Thread #119742217" 2017). It remains to be seen if a suitable, public option will appear in the future. The stereotype of 4Chan users as all being socially isolated youths with little connection to real life and no perspective does not entirely hold up, at least concerning Serbian users. The analysis came across posters of various age groups, with many posts featuring users self-identifying as well situated socially and in profitable career paths like law, IT, and political party administration. There is no evidence suggesting that a majority of Serbian users lack the resources or social connections to start their own movements for the pursuit of political goals. This does however raise doubt over whether these existing, more conventionally accomplished users could find enough commonality with the more stereotypical "loser" portions of the user base to function effectively as a real life movement able to push through its political vision

There are numerous differing views on ideal future political setups users prefer that appear when reading the vast number of archived posts. Viewpoints within extremist discourse on several essential points of social structure differ. There is no widespread agreement of issues like choosing an optimal economic system; some want more freedom for capitalist structures while others prefer structures more reminiscent of the Yugoslavian economy or something altogether different. Users of /pol/ have not settled on their preferred way of ordering an ideal society but they seem much

---

14 "Muds" is short for "mudslimes," a pejorative term for Muslim people.

more in agreement that it will require violence. The expressed desire for violence is often very pressing, demanding immediate action but also able to be made a driver of long-term planning for violence.

Conclusion

The discourse of Serbian users on 4Chan has, while deeply rooted in extremist forms of inherited nationalist ideology, been morphing into an all-encompassing ideology of hate towards a wider set of "Other" groups. This discourse clearly shows a great desire for real world action, especially as it can be realized through violence. They understand Serbia and portray it to others as a prime candidate for a revival on extremist terms.

This study was conducted for the primary purpose of familiarizing wider sets of potential readers with the essential elements of Serbian extremism on /pol/ and on 4Chan. It does not aim to and cannot provide a complete set of recommendations on how particular stakeholders can engage with the presented phenomenon. That process requires a wider set of actors with a familiarity of and concern about the subject. I hope that this paper provides the familiarity and causes the concern.

This process of developing answers is important. The future of /pol/ extremism and the consequences that might ensue for Serbia are unclear. This uncertainty is amplified by a personal observation, coming up especially in the last year of archived posts. The extremists of /pol/ are in a state of flux. Many extreme users of 4Chan are clamoring for a new unifying doctrine to guide political action in the future, more universally accepted unifying principles and the means with which to communicate them: "really there needs to be a holy script/book outlining how important race is and IQ, culture. Maybe an online forum or board to spread the message. I see people talking about a new religion all the time, the sentiment is there" ("/Pol/ - Politically Incorrect » Thread #124644867" 2017). More relevantly, the extremism elaborated would need real-life political movements to manifest itself effectively. Currently relevant terms and forms of political organization, at least in Serbia, are not extremist enough to be appealing nor sufficiently politically savvy or strong to affect change. The term "alt-right" has not been warmly embraced by the users of /pol/ ("/Pol/ - Politically Incorrect » Thread #113643285" 2017), who are, ironically enough, often credited as the main force in its entrenchment in mainstream conversation (Wendling 2018; Nagle 2017). While individual reasons for rejecting the alt-right vary, perhaps the most compelling reason seen is the perception that visible leaders of the alt-right movement are inept at being as genuine, as entertaining, as subtle, and as engaging in their radicalism as /pol/ is. Similarly, there is disappointment that Donald Trump, the main idealized vanquisher of enemies, has not and will not go as far as extremists would have hoped. Former prominent figures of Serbian extremism of old and several of their potential heirs have stumbled in suiting the tastes of Serbian extremist 4Chan users. They are looking for more.

We also need to learn more. How does the prevailing culture of anonymity on 4Chan affect the odds of real life violence occurring consequently? Is this specific type of discourse already present in our political institutions and supported by bearers of power in Serbia? What are the present societal drivers guiding Serbian users to behave like this? These are only some of the questions resulting from this analysis requiring contemplation and answers. Here I would make my only explicit recommendation. Regardless of what specific answers stakeholders design and implement, I would urge them to avoid as much as possible repressing citizens' rights of free expression. The potential dangers this type of extremism brings will be difficult to assuage by restrictive measures and seem far too connected to Serbia's historical and ongoing societal difficulties to be dealt with through restrictions, censorship, or other such blunt measures. While the future of Serbian extremism is unclear, what is certainly clear is that Serbian extremist discourse on /pol/ demands attention and comprehensive efforts to counter such violent sentiments, bearing consequences and lessons for security institutions, educational systems, and overall democratic progress.

Post references

(This section includes the bibliography of quoted and footnoted 4Chan posts from Serbian IPs along with a wider selection of essentially relevant Serbian posts as elaborated in the methodology section, grouped under annotated group titles. The grouping is only intended to ease reading. All cited posts are originally from the 4Chan website)

Bibliographical entry for entire 4Chan database

"/Pol/ - Politically Incorrect » Searching for Posts from 'Serbia' and in Ascending Order.," 2014 to 2018. https://archive.4plebs.org/pol/search/country/RS/order/asc/.

Popular image memes

"/pol/ - Politically Incorrect » Searching for Posts with the Image Hash '0QJBhEpLE7scREsrKPRNiw=='." Acc. August 31, 2018. https://archive.4plebs.org/pol/search/image/0QJBhEpLE7scREsrKPRNiw/.

"/pol/ - Politically Incorrect » Searching for Posts with the Image Hash '6I8ZpwDsl8sCRWKEEJIliA=='." Acc. August 31, 2018. https://archive.4plebs.org/pol/search/image/6I8ZpwDsl8sCRWKEEJIliA/.

"/pol/ - Politically Incorrect » Searching for Posts with the Image Hash '6kLV4qPOEsZ5DVApNqkDug=='." Acc. August 31, 2018. https://archive.4plebs.org/pol/search/image/6kLV4qPOEsZ5DVApNqkDug/.

"/pol/ - Politically Incorrect » Searching for Posts with the Image Hash '6sEaWWY0kqUXh8bnuCZaEg=='." Acc. August 31, 2018. https://archive.4plebs.org/pol/search/image/6sEaWWY0kqUXh8bnuCZaEg/.

"/pol/ - Politically Incorrect » Searching for Posts with the Image Hash 'BQPVILN8p5EsP5R0VtgbNA=='." Acc. August 31, 2018. Https://archive.4plebs.org/pol/search/image/BQPVILN8p5EsP5R0VtgbNA/.

"/pol/ - Politically Incorrect » Searching for Posts with the Image Hash 'BxitaXEMwO1j0dwrEG91Ag=='." Acc. August 31, 2018. https://archive.4plebs.org/pol/search/image/bxitaXEMwO1j0dwrEG91Ag/.

"/pol/ - Politically Incorrect » Searching for Posts with the Image Hash 'Cnu3Ankv89IMB/D97UVE0g=='." Acc. August 31, 2018. https://archive.4plebs.org/pol/search/image/cnu3Ankv89IMB_d97UVE0g/.

"/pol/ - Politically Incorrect » Searching for Posts with the Image Hash 'EtjCj5PFan6vSb74sBljJg=='." Acc. August 31, 2018. https://archive.4plebs.org/pol/search/image/EtjCj5PFan6vSb74sBljJg/.

"/pol/ - Politically Incorrect » Searching for Posts with the Image Hash 'FDCSaLbuNj8G0IcYz0JaZg=='." Acc. August 31, 2018. https://archive.4plebs.org/pol/search/image/fDCSaLbuNj8G0IcYz0JaZg/.

"/pol/ - Politically Incorrect » Searching for Posts with the Image Hash 'GsRKV8Ej3Dj7UU+lh0AmFA=='." Acc. August 31, 2018. https://archive.4plebs.org/pol/search/image/gsRKV8Ej3Dj7UU-lh0AmFA/.

"/pol/ - Politically Incorrect » Searching for Posts with the Image Hash 'R/IJlvvvhOJ28/KNAlfnTQ=='." Acc. August 31, 2018. https://archive.4plebs.org/pol/search/image/R_IJlvvvhOJ28_kNAlfnTQ/.

"/pol/ - Politically Incorrect » Searching for Posts with the Image Hash 'TG7yXgmPzF2Ymsp23DINsA=='." Acc. August 31, 2018. https://archive.4plebs.org/pol/search/image/tG7yXgmPzF2Ymsp23DINsA/.

"/pol/ - Politically Incorrect » Searching for Posts with the Image Hash 'UKgsW9LkSVNL21AkppDJkA=='." Acc. August 31, 2018. https://archive.4plebs.org/pol/search/image/UKgsW9LkSVNL21AkppDJkA/.

"/pol/ - Politically Incorrect » Searching for Posts with the Image Hash 'Uo/YCVoy4ugzkH/PEIg7zg=='." Acc. August 31, 2018. https://archive.4plebs.org/pol/search/image/Uo_yCVoy4ugzkH_pEIg7zg/.

"/pol/ - Politically Incorrect » Searching for Posts with the Image Hash 'VN6NwH8JmayUGzhiqULoOw=='." Acc. August 31, 2018. https://archive.4plebs.org/pol/search/image/VN6NwH8JmayUGzhiqULoOw/.

"/pol/ - Politically Incorrect » Searching for Posts with the Image Hash 'ZUQOsAmMlJ/I9T1zrBrtvw=='." Acc. August 31, 2018. https://archive.4plebs.org/pol/search/image/ZUQOsAmMlJ_i9T1zrBrtvw/.

Arguments for attention from primarily Western users through reframing the Serbian identity

"/pol/ - Politically Incorrect » Thread #40450023." Acc. August 31, 2018. https://archive.4plebs.org/pol/thread/40450023/#q40453323.

"/pol/ - Politically Incorrect » Thread #41603209." Acc. August 31, 2018. https://archive.4plebs.org/pol/thread/41603209/#q41614492.

"/pol/ - Politically Incorrect » Thread #49079587." Acc. August 31, 2018. https://archive.4plebs.org/pol/thread/49079587/#q49079587.

"/pol/ - Politically Incorrect » Thread #42900025." Acc. August 31, 2018. https://archive.4plebs.org/pol/thread/42900025/#q42900999.

"/pol/ - Politically Incorrect » Thread #48732530." Acc. August 31, 2018. https://archive.4plebs.org/pol/thread/48732530/#q48732530.

"/pol/ - Politically Incorrect » Thread #49765146." Acc. August 31, 2018. https://archive.4plebs.org/pol/thread/49765146/#q49765958.

"/pol/ - Politically Incorrect » Thread #43545102." Acc. August 31, 2018. https://archive.4plebs.org/pol/thread/43545102/.

"/pol/ - Politically Incorrect » Thread #44227194." Acc. August 31, 2018. https://archive.4plebs.org/pol/thread/44227194/#q44227194.

"/pol/ - Politically Incorrect » Thread #50200062." Acc. August 31, 2018. https://archive.4plebs.org/pol/thread/50200062/#q50204673.

"/pol/ - Politically Incorrect » Thread #49079587." Acc. August 31, 2018. https://archive.4plebs.org/pol/thread/49079587/#q49081205.

"/pol/ - Politically Incorrect » Thread #49029247." Acc. August 31, 2018. https://archive.4plebs.org/pol/thread/49029247/#q49029247.

"/pol/ - Politically Incorrect » Thread #46076777." Acc. August 31, 2018. https://archive.4plebs.org/pol/thread/46076777/#q46076777.

"/pol/ - Politically Incorrect » Thread #51453716." Acc. August 31, 2018. https://archive.4plebs.org/pol/thread/51453716/#q51453716.

"/pol/ - Politically Incorrect » Thread #53157231." Acc. August 31, 2018. https://archive.4plebs.org/pol/thread/53157231/#q53157231.

"/pol/ - Politically Incorrect » Thread #56090393." Acc. August 31, 2018. https://archive.4plebs.org/pol/thread/56090393/#q56090393.

"/pol/ - Politically Incorrect » Thread #58067614." Acc. August 31, 2018. https://archive.4plebs.org/pol/thread/58067614/#q58067614.

"/pol/ - Politically Incorrect » Thread #66662928." Acc. August 31, 2018. https://archive.4plebs.org/pol/thread/66662928/#q66662928.

"/pol/ - Politically Incorrect » Thread #67002929." Acc. August 31, 2018. https://archive.4plebs.org/pol/thread/67002929/#q67006040.

"/pol/ - Politically Incorrect » Thread #69089817." Acc. August 31, 2018. https://archive.4plebs.org/pol/thread/69089817/#q69089817.

"/pol/ - Politically Incorrect » Thread #73504377." Acc. August 31, 2018. https://archive.4plebs.org/pol/thread/73504377/#q73504377.

"/pol/ - Politically Incorrect » Thread #74754782." Acc. August 31, 2018. https://archive.4plebs.org/pol/thread/74754782/#q74761799.

"/pol/ - Politically Incorrect » Thread #80209539." Acc. August 31, 2018. https://archive.4plebs.org/pol/thread/80209539/#q80209539.

"/pol/ - Politically Incorrect » Thread #84085344." Acc. August 31, 2018. https://archive.4plebs.org/pol/thread/84085344/#q84085344.

"/pol/ - Politically Incorrect » Thread #86201772." Acc. August 31, 2018. https://archive.4plebs.org/pol/thread/86201772/#q86201772.

"/pol/ - Politically Incorrect » Thread #90731090." Acc. August 31, 2018. https://archive.4plebs.org/pol/thread/90731090/#q90731090.

"/pol/ - Politically Incorrect » Thread #94812642." Acc. August 31, 2018. https://archive.4plebs.org/pol/thread/94812642/#q94823774.

"/pol/ - Politically Incorrect » Thread #104164372." Acc. August 31, 2018. https://archive.4plebs.org/pol/thread/104164372/#q104164372.

"/pol/ - Politically Incorrect » Thread #105701137." Acc. August 31, 2018. https://archive.4plebs.org/pol/thread/105701137/#q105701898.

"/pol/ - Politically Incorrect » Thread #107249492." Acc. August 31, 2018. https://archive.4plebs.org/pol/thread/107249492/#q107282848.

"/pol/ - Politically Incorrect » Thread #110822721." Acc. August 31, 2018. https://archive.4plebs.org/pol/thread/110822721/#q110822721.

"/pol/ - Politically Incorrect » Thread #116318780." Acc. August 31, 2018. https://archive.4plebs.org/pol/thread/116318780/#q116318780.

"/pol/ - Politically Incorrect » Thread #119609790." Acc. August 31, 2018. https://archive.4plebs.org/pol/thread/119609790/#q119611631.

"/pol/ - Politically Incorrect » Thread #121699854." Acc. August 31, 2018. https://archive.4plebs.org/pol/thread/121699854/#q121721362.

"/pol/ - Politically Incorrect » Thread #122455488." Acc. August 31, 2018. https://archive.4plebs.org/pol/thread/122455488/#q122460973.

"/pol/ - Politically Incorrect » Thread #128407865." Acc. August 31, 2018. https://archive.4plebs.org/pol/thread/128407865/#q128410297.

"/pol/ - Politically Incorrect » Thread #128463728." Acc. August 31, 2018. https://archive.4plebs.org/pol/thread/128463728/#q128464641.

"/pol/ - Politically Incorrect » Thread #128710781." Acc. August 31, 2018. https://archive.4plebs.org/pol/thread/128710781/#q128715465.

"/pol/ - Politically Incorrect » Thread #129183382." Acc. August 31, 2018. https://archive.4plebs.org/pol/thread/129183382/#q129193381.

"/pol/ - Politically Incorrect » Thread #130269412." Acc. August 31, 2018. https://archive.4plebs.org/pol/thread/130269412/#q130271717.

"/pol/ - Politically Incorrect » Thread #133204404." Acc. August 31, 2018. https://archive.4plebs.org/pol/thread/133204404/#q133204404.

"/pol/ - Politically Incorrect » Thread #134058580." Acc. August 31, 2018. https://archive.4plebs.org/pol/thread/134058580/#q134058580.

"/pol/ - Politically Incorrect » Thread #151590431." Acc. August 31, 2018. https://archive.4plebs.org/pol/thread/151590431/#q151590431.

"/pol/ - Politically Incorrect » Thread #165192436." Acc. August 31, 2018. https://archive.4plebs.org/pol/thread/165192436/#q165206281.

Promoting Serbian political figures as heroes of extremist ideology

"/pol/ - Politically Incorrect » Thread #42367712." Acc. August 31, 2018. https://archive.4plebs.org/pol/thread/42367712/#q42367712.

"/pol/ - Politically Incorrect » Thread #42367712." Acc. August 31, 2018. https://archive.4plebs.org/pol/thread/42367712/#42369754.

"/pol/ - Politically Incorrect » Thread #48079871." Acc. August 31, 2018. https://archive.4plebs.org/pol/thread/48079871/#q48080512.

"/pol/ - Politically Incorrect » Thread #48098771." Acc. August 31, 2018. https://archive.4plebs.org/pol/thread/48098771/#q48099381.

"/pol/ - Politically Incorrect » Thread #47613849." Acc. August 31, 2018. https://archive.4plebs.org/pol/thread/47613849/#q47613849.

"/pol/ - Politically Incorrect » Thread #47690088." Acc. August 31, 2018. https://archive.4plebs.org/pol/thread/47690088/#q47701621.

"/pol/ - Politically Incorrect » Thread #42418076." Acc. August 31, 2018. https://archive.4plebs.org/pol/thread/42418076/#q42418076.

"/pol/ - Politically Incorrect » Thread #56522123." Acc. August 31, 2018. https://archive.4plebs.org/pol/thread/56522123/#q56522123.

"/pol/ - Politically Incorrect » Thread #57360744." Acc. August 31, 2018. https://archive.4plebs.org/pol/thread/57360744/#q57365666.

"/pol/ - Politically Incorrect » Thread #58361096." Acc. August 31, 2018. https://archive.4plebs.org/pol/thread/58361096/#q58361096.

"/pol/ - Politically Incorrect » Thread #59929620." Acc. August 31, 2018. https://archive.4plebs.org/pol/thread/59929620/#q59930785.

"/pol/ - Politically Incorrect » Thread #68585265." Acc. August 31, 2018. https://archive.4plebs.org/pol/thread/68585265/#q68588707.

"/pol/ - Politically Incorrect » Thread #68623114." Acc. August 31, 2018. https://archive.4plebs.org/pol/thread/68623114/#q68630914.

"/pol/ - Politically Incorrect » Thread #68638065." Acc. August 31, 2018. https://archive.4plebs.org/pol/thread/68638065/#q68638065.

"/pol/ - Politically Incorrect » Thread #68656676." Acc. August 31, 2018. https://archive.4plebs.org/pol/thread/68656676/#q68664276.

"/pol/ - Politically Incorrect » Thread #75445601." Acc. August 31, 2018. https://archive.4plebs.org/pol/thread/75445601/#q75446789.

"/pol/ - Politically Incorrect » Thread #80360562." Acc. August 31, 2018. https://archive.4plebs.org/pol/thread/80360562/#q80367224.

"/pol/ - Politically Incorrect » Thread #81117818." Acc. August 31, 2018. https://archive.4plebs.org/pol/thread/81117818/#q81117818.

"/pol/ - Politically Incorrect » Thread #94277116." Acc. August 31, 2018. https://archive.4plebs.org/pol/thread/94277116/#q94277116.

"/pol/ - Politically Incorrect » Thread #95694440." Acc. August 31, 2018. https://archive.4plebs.org/pol/thread/95694440/#q95710376.

"/pol/ - Politically Incorrect » Thread #96715292." Acc. August 31, 2018. https://archive.4plebs.org/pol/thread/96715292/#q96715292.

"/pol/ - Politically Incorrect» Thread #97496238." Acc. August 31, 2018. https://archive.4plebs.org/pol/thread/97496238/#q97497558.

"/pol/ - Politically Incorrect» Thread #106672539." Acc. August 31, 2018. https://archive.4plebs.org/pol/thread/106672539/#q106672539.

"/pol/ - Politically Incorrect» Thread #119189508." Acc. August 31, 2018. https://archive.4plebs.org/pol/thread/119189508/#q119196822.

"/pol/ - Politically Incorrect» Thread #122617118." Acc. August 31, 2018. https://archive.4plebs.org/pol/thread/122617118/#q122619580.

"/pol/ - Politically Incorrect» Thread #123239687." Acc. August 31, 2018. https://archive.4plebs.org/pol/thread/123239687/#q123242303.

"/pol/ - Politically Incorrect» Thread #150727889." Acc. August 31, 2018. https://archive.4plebs.org/pol/thread/150727889/#q150728985.

"/pol/ - Politically Incorrect» Thread #154872391." Acc. August 31, 2018. https://archive.4plebs.org/pol/thread/154872391/#q154888221.

"/pol/ - Politically Incorrect» Thread #165811208." Acc. August 31, 2018. https://archive.4plebs.org/pol/thread/165811208/#q165815039.

Discursive arena denigration of competing identities

"/pol/ - Politically Incorrect» Thread #43259299." Acc. August 31, 2018. https://archive.4plebs.org/pol/thread/43259299/#q43269919.

"/pol/ - Politically Incorrect» Thread #47839202." Acc. August 31, 2018. https://archive.4plebs.org/pol/thread/47839202/#q47839202.

"/pol/ - Politically Incorrect» Thread #47851193." Acc. August 31, 2018. https://archive.4plebs.org/pol/thread/47851193/#q47851193.

"/pol/ - Politically Incorrect» Thread #48045511." Acc. August 31, 2018. https://archive.4plebs.org/pol/thread/48045511/#q48045511.

"/pol/ - Politically Incorrect» Thread #50013658." Acc. August 31, 2018. https://archive.4plebs.org/pol/thread/50013658/#q50019837.

"/pol/ - Politically Incorrect» Thread #50906710." Acc. August 31, 2018. https://archive.4plebs.org/pol/thread/50906710/#q50917508.

"/pol/ - Politically Incorrect» Thread #50939050." Acc. August 31, 2018. https://archive.4plebs.org/pol/thread/50939050/#q50939050.

"/pol/ - Politically Incorrect» Thread #52359642." Acc. August 31, 2018. https://archive.4plebs.org/pol/thread/52359642/#q52359642.

"/pol/ - Politically Incorrect» Thread #56175719." Acc. August 31, 2018. https://archive.4plebs.org/pol/thread/56175719/#q56175719.

"/pol/ - Politically Incorrect» Thread #56608587." Acc. August 31, 2018. https://archive.4plebs.org/pol/thread/56608587/#q56609645.

"/pol/ - Politically Incorrect » Thread #58132459." Acc. August 31, 2018. https://archive.4plebs.org/pol/thread/58132459/#q58137175.

"/pol/ - Politically Incorrect » Thread #59876895." Acc. August 31, 2018. https://archive.4plebs.org/pol/thread/59876895/#q59902729.

"/pol/ - Politically Incorrect » Thread #66858800." Acc. August 31, 2018. https://archive.4plebs.org/pol/thread/66858800/#q66876322.

"/pol/ - Politically Incorrect » Thread #67693253." Acc. August 31, 2018. https://archive.4plebs.org/pol/thread/67693253/#q67726870.

"/pol/ - Politically Incorrect » Thread #80590443." Acc. August 31, 2018. https://archive.4plebs.org/pol/thread/80590443/#q80590443.

"/pol/ - Politically Incorrect » Thread #82948127." Acc. August 31, 2018. https://archive.4plebs.org/pol/thread/82948127/#q82977753.

"/pol/ - Politically Incorrect » Thread #98120160." Acc. August 31, 2018. https://archive.4plebs.org/pol/thread/98120160/#q98140278.

"/pol/ - Politically Incorrect » Thread #98309850." Acc. August 31, 2018. https://archive.4plebs.org/pol/thread/98309850/#q98309850.

"/pol/ - Politically Incorrect » Thread #102056256." Acc. August 31, 2018. https://archive.4plebs.org/pol/thread/102056256/#q102062846.

"/pol/ - Politically Incorrect » Thread #106645827." Acc. August 31, 2018. https://archive.4plebs.org/pol/thread/106645827/#q106657112.

"/pol/ - Politically Incorrect » Thread #109398006." Acc. August 31, 2018. https://archive.4plebs.org/pol/thread/109398006/#q109402310.

"/pol/ - Politically Incorrect » Thread #111768299." Acc. August 31, 2018. https://archive.4plebs.org/pol/thread/111768299/#q111768299.

"/pol/ - Politically Incorrect » Thread #115357324." Acc. August 31, 2018. https://archive.4plebs.org/pol/thread/115357324/#q115357324.

"/pol/ - Politically Incorrect » Thread #116861152." Acc. August 31, 2018. https://archive.4plebs.org/pol/thread/116861152/#q116887766.

"/pol/ - Politically Incorrect » Thread #118018846." Acc. August 31, 2018. https://archive.4plebs.org/pol/thread/118018846/#q118018846.

"/pol/ - Politically Incorrect » Thread #119199055." Acc. August 31, 2018. https://archive.4plebs.org/pol/thread/119199055/#q119201696.

"/pol/ - Politically Incorrect » Thread #119609929." Acc. August 31, 2018. https://archive.4plebs.org/pol/thread/119609929/#q119617540.

"/pol/ - Politically Incorrect » Thread #122122528." Acc. August 31, 2018. https://archive.4plebs.org/pol/thread/122122528/#q122127787.

"/pol/ - Politically Incorrect » Thread #122491511." Acc. August 31, 2018. https://archive.4plebs.org/pol/thread/122491511/#q122493825.

"/pol/ - Politically Incorrect » Thread #122752103." Acc. August 31, 2018. https://archive.4plebs.org/pol/thread/122752103/#q122760709.

"/pol/ - Politically Incorrect » Thread #165121630." Acc. August 31, 2018. https://archive.4plebs.org/pol/thread/165121630/#q165130257.

"/pol/ - Politically Incorrect » Thread #165602365." Acc. August 31, 2018. https://archive.4plebs.org/pol/thread/165602365/#q165635613.

"/pol/ - Politically Incorrect » Thread #171196613." Acc. August 31, 2018. https://archive.4plebs.org/pol/thread/171196613/#q171200326.

"/pol/ - Politically Incorrect » Thread #184641271." Acc. August 31, 2018. https://archive.4plebs.org/pol/thread/184641271/#q184669111.

Promoting themselves and their nation as presently suitable for and susceptible to violent extremism to a great degree

"/pol/ - Politically Incorrect » Thread #45306733." Acc. August 31, 2018. https://archive.4plebs.org/pol/thread/45306733/#q45312117.

"/pol/ - Politically Incorrect » Thread #46705843." Acc. August 31, 2018. https://archive.4plebs.org/pol/thread/46705843/#q46706697.

"/pol/ - Politically Incorrect » Thread #51348988." Acc. August 31, 2018. https://archive.4plebs.org/pol/thread/51348988/#q51348988.

"/pol/ - Politically Incorrect » Thread #55171630." Acc. August 31, 2018. https://archive.4plebs.org/pol/thread/55171630/#q55181179.

"/pol/ - Politically Incorrect » Thread #57665487." Acc. August 31, 2018. https://archive.4plebs.org/pol/thread/57665487/#q57675570.

"/pol/ - Politically Incorrect » Thread #57886404." Acc. August 31, 2018. https://archive.4plebs.org/pol/thread/57886404/#q57889677.

"/pol/ - Politically Incorrect » Thread #58225511." Acc. August 31, 2018. https://archive.4plebs.org/pol/thread/58225511/#q58226125.

"/pol/ - Politically Incorrect » Thread #59279833." Acc. August 31, 2018. https://archive.4plebs.org/pol/thread/59279833/#q59280365.

"/pol/ - Politically Incorrect » Thread #64709253." Acc. August 31, 2018. https://archive.4plebs.org/pol/thread/64709253/#q64716780.

"/pol/ - Politically Incorrect » Thread #66694798." Acc. August 31, 2018. https://archive.4plebs.org/pol/thread/66694798/#q66695153.

"/pol/ - Politically Incorrect » Thread #72520500." Acc. August 31, 2018. https://archive.4plebs.org/pol/thread/72520500/#q72520500.

"/pol/ - Politically Incorrect » Thread #72808591." Acc. August 31, 2018. https://archive.4plebs.org/pol/thread/72808591/#q72815918.

"/pol/ - Politically Incorrect » Thread #75478975." Acc. August 31, 2018. https://archive.4plebs.org/pol/thread/75478975/#q75478975.

"/pol/ - Politically Incorrect » Thread #80486931." Acc. August 31, 2018. https://archive.4plebs.org/pol/thread/80486931/#q80486931.

"/pol/ - Politically Incorrect» Thread #85811890." Acc. August 31, 2018. https://archive.4plebs.org/pol/thread/85811890/#q85817789.

"/pol/ - Politically Incorrect» Thread #106064891." Acc. August 31, 2018. https://archive.4plebs.org/pol/thread/106064891/#q106064891.

"/pol/ - Politically Incorrect» Thread #111979680." Acc. August 31, 2018. https://archive.4plebs.org/pol/thread/111979680/#q111995494.

"/pol/ - Politically Incorrect» Thread #118363300." Acc. August 31, 2018. https://archive.4plebs.org/pol/thread/118363300/#q118363300.

"/pol/ - Politically Incorrect» Thread #123757944." Acc. August 31, 2018. https://archive.4plebs.org/pol/thread/123757944/#q123757944.

"/pol/ - Politically Incorrect» Thread #128847988." Acc. August 31, 2018. https://archive.4plebs.org/pol/thread/128847988/#q128858043.

"/pol/ - Politically Incorrect» Thread #130220930." Acc. August 31, 2018. https://archive.4plebs.org/pol/thread/130220930/#q130220930.

"/pol/ - Politically Incorrect» Thread #133115650." Acc. August 31, 2018. https://archive.4plebs.org/pol/thread/133115650/#q133121897.

"/pol/ - Politically Incorrect» Thread #141521989." Acc. August 31, 2018. https://archive.4plebs.org/pol/thread/141521989/#q141521989.

"/pol/ - Politically Incorrect» Thread #162321178." Acc. August 31, 2018. https://archive.4plebs.org/pol/thread/162321178/#q162327024.

"/pol/ - Politically Incorrect» Thread #162847071." Acc. August 31, 2018. https://archive.4plebs.org/pol/thread/162847071/#q162862062.

"/pol/ - Politically Incorrect» Thread #166973953." Acc. August 31, 2018. https://archive.4plebs.org/pol/thread/166973953/#q166973953.

"/pol/ - Politically Incorrect» Thread #175472352." Acc. August 31, 2018. https://archive.4plebs.org/pol/thread/175472352/#q175472352.

"/pol/ - Politically Incorrect» Thread #176404160." Acc. August 31, 2018. https://archive.4plebs.org/pol/thread/176404160/#q176404160.

"/pol/ - Politically Incorrect» Thread #177094847." Acc. August 31, 2018. https://archive.4plebs.org/pol/thread/177094847/#q177098428.

Expanding targets of hate with the Other from Western extremism, taking on their terminology and goals

"/pol/ - Politically Incorrect» Thread #47462894." Acc. August 31, 2018. https://archive.4plebs.org/pol/thread/47462894/#q47473664.

"/pol/ - Politically Incorrect» Thread #48126298." Acc. August 31, 2018. https://archive.4plebs.org/pol/thread/48126298/#q48126640.

"/pol/ - Politically Incorrect» Thread #48204097." Acc. August 31, 2018. https://archive.4plebs.org/pol/thread/48204097/#q48204097.

"/pol/ - Politically Incorrect » Thread #48610389." Acc. August 31, 2018. https://archive.4plebs.org/pol/thread/48610389/#q48612079.

"/pol/ - Politically Incorrect » Thread #51013723." Acc. August 31, 2018. https://archive.4plebs.org/pol/thread/51013723/#q51016596.

"/pol/ - Politically Incorrect » Thread #51089202." Acc. August 31, 2018. https://archive.4plebs.org/pol/thread/51089202/#q51089202.

"/pol/ - Politically Incorrect » Thread #51165782." Acc. August 31, 2018. https://archive.4plebs.org/pol/thread/51165782/#q51167413.

"/pol/ - Politically Incorrect » Thread #51215536." Acc. August 31, 2018. https://archive.4plebs.org/pol/thread/51215536/#q51215679.

"/pol/ - Politically Incorrect » Thread #56380926." Acc. August 31, 2018. https://archive.4plebs.org/pol/thread/56380926/#q56380926.

"/pol/ - Politically Incorrect » Thread #59053079." Acc. August 31, 2018. https://archive.4plebs.org/pol/thread/59053079/#q59057740.

"/pol/ - Politically Incorrect » Thread #63659870." Acc. August 31, 2018. https://archive.4plebs.org/pol/thread/63659870/#q63668420.

"/pol/ - Politically Incorrect » Thread #66754704." Acc. August 31, 2018. https://archive.4plebs.org/pol/thread/66754704/#q66756030.

"/pol/ - Politically Incorrect » Thread #71815271." Acc. August 31, 2018. https://archive.4plebs.org/pol/thread/71815271/#q71815271.

"/pol/ - Politically Incorrect » Thread #71819196." Acc. August 31, 2018. https://archive.4plebs.org/pol/thread/71819196/#q71819196.

"/pol/ - Politically Incorrect » Thread #67114139." Acc. August 31, 2018. https://archive.4plebs.org/pol/thread/67114139/#q67114139.

"/pol/ - Politically Incorrect » Thread #74849737." Acc. August 31, 2018. https://archive.4plebs.org/pol/thread/74849737/#q74853675.

"/pol/ - Politically Incorrect » Thread #74889166." Acc. August 31, 2018. https://archive.4plebs.org/pol/thread/74889166/#q74889166.

"/pol/ - Politically Incorrect » Thread #80747190." Acc. August 31, 2018. https://archive.4plebs.org/pol/thread/80747190/#q80747190.

"/pol/ - Politically Incorrect » Thread #81349957." Acc. August 31, 2018. https://archive.4plebs.org/pol/thread/81349957/#q81350596.

"/pol/ - Politically Incorrect » Thread #81491247." Acc. August 31, 2018. https://archive.4plebs.org/pol/thread/81491247/#q81491247.

"/pol/ - Politically Incorrect » Thread #88381017." Acc. August 31, 2018. https://archive.4plebs.org/pol/thread/88381017/#q88381017.

"/pol/ - Politically Incorrect » Thread #96241986." Acc. August 31, 2018. https://archive.4plebs.org/pol/thread/96241986/#q96253742.

"/pol/ - Politically Incorrect » Thread #97022075." Acc. August 31, 2018. https://archive.4plebs.org/pol/thread/97022075/#q97022075.

"/pol/ - Politically Incorrect » Thread #97797929." Acc. August 31, 2018. https://archive.4plebs.org/pol/thread/97797929/#q97798369.

"/pol/ - Politically Incorrect » Thread #98012611." Acc. August 31, 2018. https://archive.4plebs.org/pol/thread/98012611/#q98013529.

"/pol/ - Politically Incorrect » Thread #98802070." Acc. August 31, 2018. https://archive.4plebs.org/pol/thread/98802070/#q98818938.

"/pol/ - Politically Incorrect » Thread #101969776." Acc. August 31, 2018. https://archive.4plebs.org/pol/thread/101969776/#q101995142.

"/pol/ - Politically Incorrect » Thread #103412123." Acc. August 31, 2018. https://archive.4plebs.org/pol/thread/103412123/#q103412123.

"/pol/ - Politically Incorrect » Thread #104753394." Acc. August 31, 2018. https://archive.4plebs.org/pol/thread/104753394/#q104753394.

"/pol/ - Politically Incorrect » Thread #109811960." Acc. August 31, 2018. https://archive.4plebs.org/pol/thread/109811960/#q109813378.

"/pol/ - Politically Incorrect » Thread #119309891." Acc. August 31, 2018. https://archive.4plebs.org/pol/thread/119309891/#q119313500.

"/pol/ - Politically Incorrect » Thread #128271206." Acc. August 31, 2018. https://archive.4plebs.org/pol/thread/128271206/#q128279877.

"/pol/ - Politically Incorrect » Thread #128747944." Acc. August 31, 2018. https://archive.4plebs.org/pol/thread/128747944/#q128761517.

"/pol/ - Politically Incorrect » Thread #130530848." Acc. August 31, 2018. https://archive.4plebs.org/pol/thread/130530848/#q130530848.

"/pol/ - Politically Incorrect » Thread #136099413." Acc. August 31, 2018. https://archive.4plebs.org/pol/thread/136099413/#q136117618.

"/pol/ - Politically Incorrect » Thread #136102130." Acc. August 31, 2018. https://archive.4plebs.org/pol/thread/136102130/#q136115658.

"/pol/ - Politically Incorrect » Thread #136243519." Acc. August 31, 2018. https://archive.4plebs.org/pol/thread/136243519/#q136247382.

"/pol/ - Politically Incorrect » Thread #149663780." Acc. August 31, 2018. https://archive.4plebs.org/pol/thread/149663780/#q149663780.

"/pol/ - Politically Incorrect » Thread #175292781." Acc. August 31, 2018. https://archive.4plebs.org/pol/thread/175292781/#q175305381.

Threats of and calls for violence

"/pol/ - Politically Incorrect » Thread #44413916 [WWW Document], 2015. URL https://archive.4plebs.org/pol/thread/44413916/#q44415386.

"/pol/ - Politically Incorrect » Thread #45524684." Acc. August 31, 2018. https://archive.4plebs.org/pol/thread/45524684/#q45525116.

"/pol/ - Politically Incorrect » Thread #46271020." Acc. August 31, 2018.
https://archive.4plebs.org/pol/thread/46271020/#q46272223.

"/pol/ - Politically Incorrect » Thread #49633684." Acc. August 31, 2018.
https://archive.4plebs.org/pol/thread/49633684/#49637246.

"/pol/ - Politically Incorrect » Thread #48225488." Acc. August 31, 2018.
https://archive.4plebs.org/pol/thread/48225488/#q48225488.

"/pol/ - Politically Incorrect » Thread #48204097." Acc. August 31, 2018.
https://archive.4plebs.org/pol/thread/48204097/#q48204097.

"/pol/ - Politically Incorrect » Thread #51240163." Acc. August 31, 2018.
https://archive.4plebs.org/pol/thread/51240163/#q51250215.

"/pol/ - Politically Incorrect » Thread #51335839." Acc. August 31, 2018.
https://archive.4plebs.org/pol/thread/51335839/#q51341124.

"/pol/ - Politically Incorrect » Thread #51401750." Acc. August 31, 2018.
https://archive.4plebs.org/pol/thread/51401750/#q51401750.

"/pol/ - Politically Incorrect » Thread #51617003." Acc. August 31, 2018.
https://archive.4plebs.org/pol/thread/51617003/#q51623276.

"/pol/ - Politically Incorrect » Thread #53935649." Acc. August 31, 2018.
https://archive.4plebs.org/pol/thread/53935649/#q53935828.

"/pol/ - Politically Incorrect » Thread #54903854." Acc. August 31, 2018.
https://archive.4plebs.org/pol/thread/54903854/#q54907174.

"/pol/ - Politically Incorrect » Thread #55375279." Acc. August 31, 2018.
https://archive.4plebs.org/pol/thread/55375279/#q55391194.

"/pol/ - Politically Incorrect » Thread #64493871." Acc. August 31, 2018.
https://archive.4plebs.org/pol/thread/64493871/#q64502491.

"/pol/ - Politically Incorrect » Thread #66097781." Acc. August 31, 2018.
https://archive.4plebs.org/pol/thread/66097781/#q66098746.

"/pol/ - Politically Incorrect » Thread #67365439." Acc. August 31, 2018.
https://archive.4plebs.org/pol/thread/67365439/#q67365439.

"/pol/ - Politically Incorrect » Thread #68336412." Acc. August 31, 2018.
https://archive.4plebs.org/pol/thread/68336412/#q68347118.

"/pol/ - Politically Incorrect » Thread #69514428." Acc. August 31, 2018.
https://archive.4plebs.org/pol/thread/69514428/#q69526347.

"/pol/ - Politically Incorrect » Thread #71447839." Acc. August 31, 2018.
https://archive.4plebs.org/pol/thread/71447839/#q71454575.

"/pol/ - Politically Incorrect » Thread #71859326." Acc. August 31, 2018.
https://archive.4plebs.org/pol/thread/71859326/#q71860434.

"/pol/ - Politically Incorrect » Thread #71908793." Acc. August 31, 2018.
https://archive.4plebs.org/pol/thread/71908793/#q71910906.

"/pol/ - Politically Incorrect » Thread #72356252." Acc. August 31, 2018.
https://archive.4plebs.org/pol/thread/72356252/#q72362067.

"/pol/ - Politically Incorrect » Thread #73280575." Acc. August 31, 2018. https://archive.4plebs.org/pol/thread/73280575/#q73280575.

"/pol/ - Politically Incorrect » Thread #73969542." Acc. August 31, 2018. https://archive.4plebs.org/pol/thread/73969542/#q73976070.

"/pol/ - Politically Incorrect » Thread #75344378." Acc. August 31, 2018. https://archive.4plebs.org/pol/thread/75344378/#q75347068.

"/pol/ - Politically Incorrect » Thread #81020430." Acc. August 31, 2018. https://archive.4plebs.org/pol/thread/81020430/#q81021368.

"/pol/ - Politically Incorrect » Thread #81756333." Acc. August 31, 2018. https://archive.4plebs.org/pol/thread/81756333/#q81773520.

"/pol/ - Politically Incorrect » Thread #85376922." Acc. August 31, 2018. https://archive.4plebs.org/pol/thread/85376922/#q85382405.

"/pol/ - Politically Incorrect » Thread #86873039." Acc. August 31, 2018. https://archive.4plebs.org/pol/thread/86873039/#q86873039.

"/pol/ - Politically Incorrect » Thread #88113269." Acc. August 31, 2018. https://archive.4plebs.org/pol/thread/88113269/#q88115109.

"/pol/ - Politically Incorrect » Thread #101758764." Acc. August 31, 2018. https://archive.4plebs.org/pol/thread/101758764/#q101758764.

"/pol/ - Politically Incorrect » Thread #101898749." Acc. August 31, 2018. https://archive.4plebs.org/pol/thread/101898749/#q101899369.

"/pol/ - Politically Incorrect » Thread #111691155." Acc. August 31, 2018. https://archive.4plebs.org/pol/thread/111691155/#q111696827.

"/pol/ - Politically Incorrect » Thread #119742217." Acc. August 31, 2018. https://archive.4plebs.org/pol/thread/119742217/#q119762943.

"/pol/ - Politically Incorrect » Thread #121645754." Acc. August 31, 2018. https://archive.4plebs.org/pol/thread/121645754/#q121652123.

"/pol/ - Politically Incorrect » Thread #122122528." Acc. August 31, 2018. https://archive.4plebs.org/pol/thread/122122528/#q122126094.

"/pol/ - Politically Incorrect » Thread #123255486." Acc. August 31, 2018. https://archive.4plebs.org/pol/thread/123255486/#q123270077.

"/pol/ - Politically Incorrect » Thread #128793039." Acc. August 31, 2018. https://archive.4plebs.org/pol/thread/128793039/#q128793039.

"/pol/ - Politically Incorrect » Thread #132799658." Acc. August 31, 2018. https://archive.4plebs.org/pol/thread/132799658/#q132815938.

"/pol/ - Politically Incorrect » Thread #132898010." Acc. August 31, 2018. https://archive.4plebs.org/pol/thread/132898010/#q132910074.

"/pol/ - Politically Incorrect » Thread #136650566." Acc. August 31, 2018. https://archive.4plebs.org/pol/thread/136650566/#q136662296.

"/pol/ - Politically Incorrect » Thread #136729912." Acc. August 31, 2018. https://archive.4plebs.org/pol/thread/136729912/#q136752547.

"/pol/ - Politically Incorrect » Thread #138523428." Acc. August 31, 2018.
https://archive.4plebs.org/pol/thread/138523428/#q138534497.

"/pol/ - Politically Incorrect » Thread #138630629." Acc. August 31, 2018.
https://archive.4plebs.org/pol/thread/138630629/#q138636171.

"/pol/ - Politically Incorrect » Thread #158161298." Acc. August 31, 2018.
https://archive.4plebs.org/pol/thread/158161298/#q158162346.

"/pol/ - Politically Incorrect » Thread #165451700." Acc. August 31, 2018.
https://archive.4plebs.org/pol/thread/165451700/#q165452013.

"/pol/ - Politically Incorrect » Thread #165584947." Acc. August 31, 2018.
https://archive.4plebs.org/pol/thread/165584947/#q165587839.

"/pol/ - Politically Incorrect » Thread #166004744." Acc. August 31, 2018.
https://archive.4plebs.org/pol/thread/166004744/#q166004744.

Methods of and journeys to radicalization

"/pol/ - Politically Incorrect » Thread #51861195." Acc. August 31, 2018.
https://archive.4plebs.org/pol/thread/51861195/#q51861195.

"/pol/ - Politically Incorrect » Thread #56906493." Acc. August 31, 2018.
https://archive.4plebs.org/pol/thread/56906493/#q56906493.

"/pol/ - Politically Incorrect » Thread #56916223." Acc. August 31, 2018.
https://archive.4plebs.org/pol/thread/56916223/#q56916223.

"/pol/ - Politically Incorrect » Thread #59768498." Acc. August 31, 2018.
https://archive.4plebs.org/pol/thread/59768498/#q59768498.

"/pol/ - Politically Incorrect » Thread #62699495." Acc. August 31, 2018.
https://archive.4plebs.org/pol/thread/62699495/#q62704561.

"/pol/ - Politically Incorrect » Thread #65249756." Acc. August 31, 2018.
https://archive.4plebs.org/pol/thread/65249756/#q65257335.

"/pol/ - Politically Incorrect » Thread #65259103." Acc. August 31, 2018.
https://archive.4plebs.org/pol/thread/65259103/#q65259103.

"/pol/ - Politically Incorrect » Thread #66824824." Acc. August 31, 2018.
https://archive.4plebs.org/pol/thread/66824824/#q66824824.

"/pol/ - Politically Incorrect » Thread #67403986." Acc. August 31, 2018.
https://archive.4plebs.org/pol/thread/67403986/#q67404277.

"/pol/ - Politically Incorrect » Thread #67751047." Acc. August 31, 2018.
https://archive.4plebs.org/pol/thread/67751047/#q67752453.

"/pol/ - Politically Incorrect » Thread #77006906." Acc. August 31, 2018.
https://archive.4plebs.org/pol/thread/77006906/#q77006906.

"/pol/ - Politically Incorrect » Thread #79390974." Acc. August 31, 2018.
https://archive.4plebs.org/pol/thread/79390974/#q79391049.

"/pol/ - Politically Incorrect» Thread #79987097." Acc. August 31, 2018. https://archive.4plebs.org/pol/thread/79987097/#q79987097.

"/pol/ - Politically Incorrect» Thread #81757740." Acc. August 31, 2018. https://archive.4plebs.org/pol/thread/81757740/#q81757740.

"/pol/ - Politically Incorrect» Thread #82164252." Acc. August 31, 2018. https://archive.4plebs.org/pol/thread/82164252/#q82164252.

"/pol/ - Politically Incorrect» Thread #85114167." Acc. August 31, 2018. https://archive.4plebs.org/pol/thread/85114167/#q85114167.

"/pol/ - Politically Incorrect» Thread #85385966." Acc. August 31, 2018. https://archive.4plebs.org/pol/thread/85385966/#q85385966.

"/pol/ - Politically Incorrect» Thread #85412023." Acc. August 31, 2018. https://archive.4plebs.org/pol/thread/85412023/#q85413166.

"/pol/ - Politically Incorrect» Thread #85517844." Acc. August 31, 2018. https://archive.4plebs.org/pol/thread/85517844/#q85527333.

"/pol/ - Politically Incorrect» Thread #86071672." Acc. August 31, 2018. https://archive.4plebs.org/pol/thread/86071672/#q86071672.

"/pol/ - Politically Incorrect» Thread #94675580." Acc. August 31, 2018. https://archive.4plebs.org/pol/thread/94675580/#q94681532.

"/pol/ - Politically Incorrect» Thread #96018655." Acc. August 31, 2018. https://archive.4plebs.org/pol/thread/96018655/#q96018655.

"/pol/ - Politically Incorrect» Thread #96526024." Acc. August 31, 2018. https://archive.4plebs.org/pol/thread/96526024/#q96527812.

"/pol/ - Politically Incorrect» Thread #96886556." Acc. August 31, 2018. https://archive.4plebs.org/pol/thread/96886556/#q96886556.

"/pol/ - Politically Incorrect» Thread #97622056." Acc. August 31, 2018. https://archive.4plebs.org/pol/thread/97622056/#q97622056.

"/pol/ - Politically Incorrect» Thread #102027535." Acc. August 31, 2018. https://archive.4plebs.org/pol/thread/102027535/#q102031706.

"/pol/ - Politically Incorrect» Thread #102730991." Acc. August 31, 2018. https://archive.4plebs.org/pol/thread/102730991/#q102730991.

"/pol/ - Politically Incorrect» Thread #103454821." Acc. August 31, 2018. https://archive.4plebs.org/pol/thread/103454821/#q103480077.

"/pol/ - Politically Incorrect» Thread #105524970." Acc. August 31, 2018. https://archive.4plebs.org/pol/thread/105524970/#q105533660.

"/pol/ - Politically Incorrect» Thread #111899806." Acc. August 31, 2018. https://archive.4plebs.org/pol/thread/111899806/#q111904985.

"/pol/ - Politically Incorrect» Thread #113511733." Acc. August 31, 2018. https://archive.4plebs.org/pol/thread/113511733/#q113511733.

"/pol/ - Politically Incorrect» Thread #116426491." Acc. August 31, 2018. https://archive.4plebs.org/pol/thread/116426491/#q116426491.

"/pol/ - Politically Incorrect » Thread #119626971." Acc. August 31, 2018. https://archive.4plebs.org/pol/thread/119626971/#q119643386.

"/pol/ - Politically Incorrect » Thread #119742217." Acc. August 31, 2018. https://archive.4plebs.org/pol/thread/119742217/#q119749915.

"/pol/ - Politically Incorrect » Thread #120130723." Acc. August 31, 2018. https://archive.4plebs.org/pol/thread/120130723/#q120130723.

"/pol/ - Politically Incorrect » Thread #120305758." Acc. August 31, 2018. https://archive.4plebs.org/pol/thread/120305758/#q120317616.

"/pol/ - Politically Incorrect » Thread #121556787." Acc. August 31, 2018. https://archive.4plebs.org/pol/thread/121556787/#q121556787.

"/pol/ - Politically Incorrect » Thread #122976772." Acc. August 31, 2018. https://archive.4plebs.org/pol/thread/122976772/#q122981233.

"/pol/ - Politically Incorrect » Thread #123677453." Acc. August 31, 2018. https://archive.4plebs.org/pol/thread/123677453/#q123694236.

"/pol/ - Politically Incorrect » Thread #124044565." Acc. August 31, 2018. https://archive.4plebs.org/pol/thread/124044565/#q124044565.

"/pol/ - Politically Incorrect » Thread #125129817." Acc. August 31, 2018. https://archive.4plebs.org/pol/thread/125129817/#q125129817.

"/pol/ - Politically Incorrect » Thread #125192218." Acc. August 31, 2018. https://archive.4plebs.org/pol/thread/125192218/#q125192218.

"/pol/ - Politically Incorrect » Thread #125643635." Acc. August 31, 2018. https://archive.4plebs.org/pol/thread/125643635/#q125643635.

"/pol/ - Politically Incorrect » Thread #126193919." Acc. August 31, 2018. https://archive.4plebs.org/pol/thread/126193919/#q126193919.

"/pol/ - Politically Incorrect » Thread #127202247." Acc. August 31, 2018. https://archive.4plebs.org/pol/thread/127202247/#q127202247.

"/pol/ - Politically Incorrect » Thread #128570475." Acc. August 31, 2018. https://archive.4plebs.org/pol/thread/128570475/#q128581855.

"/pol/ - Politically Incorrect » Thread #130150457." Acc. August 31, 2018. https://archive.4plebs.org/pol/thread/130150457/#q130162328.

"/pol/ - Politically Incorrect » Thread #130817208." Acc. August 31, 2018. https://archive.4plebs.org/pol/thread/130817208/#q130817208.

"/pol/ - Politically Incorrect » Thread #132097111." Acc. August 31, 2018. https://archive.4plebs.org/pol/thread/132097111/#q132102881.

"/pol/ - Politically Incorrect » Thread #132244243." Acc. August 31, 2018. https://archive.4plebs.org/pol/thread/132244243/#q132244243.

"/pol/ - Politically Incorrect » Thread #133539458." Acc. August 31, 2018. https://archive.4plebs.org/pol/thread/133539458/#q133542773.

"/pol/ - Politically Incorrect » Thread #135149182." Acc. August 31, 2018. https://archive.4plebs.org/pol/thread/135149182/#q135196367.

"/pol/ - Politically Incorrect » Thread #137706408." Acc. August 31, 2018. https://archive.4plebs.org/pol/thread/137706408/#137706408.

"/pol/ - Politically Incorrect » Thread #144618614." Acc. August 31, 2018. https://archive.4plebs.org/pol/thread/144618614/#q144618614.

"/pol/ - Politically Incorrect » Thread #145675667." Acc. August 31, 2018. https://archive.4plebs.org/pol/thread/145675667/#q145675667.

"/pol/ - Politically Incorrect » Thread #152477340." Acc. August 31, 2018. https://archive.4plebs.org/pol/thread/152477340/#q152477340.

"/pol/ - Politically Incorrect » Thread #158203529." Acc. August 31, 2018. https://archive.4plebs.org/pol/thread/158203529/#q158203529.

"/pol/ - Politically Incorrect » Thread #162512277." Acc. August 31, 2018. https://archive.4plebs.org/pol/thread/162512277/#q162512277.

"/pol/ - Politically Incorrect » Thread #174486390." Acc. August 31, 2018. https://archive.4plebs.org/pol/thread/174486390/#q174493567.

"/pol/ - Politically Incorrect » Thread #175421342." Acc. August 31, 2018. https://archive.4plebs.org/pol/thread/175421342/#q175421342.

"/pol/ - Politically Incorrect » Thread #175612615." Acc. August 31, 2018. https://archive.4plebs.org/pol/thread/175612615/#q175620138.

"/pol/ - Politically Incorrect » Thread #176069827." Acc. August 31, 2018. https://archive.4plebs.org/pol/thread/176069827/#q176076387.

"/pol/ - Politically Incorrect » Thread #176790736." Acc. August 31, 2018. https://archive.4plebs.org/pol/thread/176790736/#q176795416.

"/pol/ - Politically Incorrect » Thread #182507237." Acc. August 31, 2018. https://archive.4plebs.org/pol/thread/182507237/#q182507237.

"/pol/ - Politically Incorrect » Thread #184992094." Acc. August 31, 2018. https://archive.4plebs.org/pol/thread/184992094/#q185023383.

"/pol/ - Politically Incorrect » Thread #186207406." Acc. August 31, 2018. https://archive.4plebs.org/pol/thread/186207406/#q186209324.

Discussions over how to lead a life congruent to achieving their political aims

"/pol/ - Politically Incorrect » Thread #49091023." Acc. August 31, 2018. https://archive.4plebs.org/pol/thread/49091023/#q49094437.

"/pol/ - Politically Incorrect » Thread #49898005." Acc. August 31, 2018. https://archive.4plebs.org/pol/thread/49898005/#q49898005.

"/pol/ - Politically Incorrect » Thread #79703717." Acc. August 31, 2018. https://archive.4plebs.org/pol/thread/79703717/#q79703717.

"/pol/ - Politically Incorrect » Thread #86981195." Acc. August 31, 2018. https://archive.4plebs.org/pol/thread/86981195/#q86981195.

"/pol/ - Politically Incorrect » Thread #87630751." Acc. August 31, 2018. https://archive.4plebs.org/pol/thread/87630751/#q87643236.

"/pol/ - Politically Incorrect » Thread #88285062." Acc. August 31, 2018. https://archive.4plebs.org/pol/thread/88285062/#q88285062.

"/pol/ - Politically Incorrect » Thread #102343520." Acc. August 31, 2018. https://archive.4plebs.org/pol/thread/102343520/#q102350193.

"/pol/ - Politically Incorrect » Thread #105859256." Acc. August 31, 2018. https://archive.4plebs.org/pol/thread/105859256/#q105859256.

"/pol/ - Politically Incorrect » Thread #124046751." Acc. August 31, 2018. https://archive.4plebs.org/pol/thread/124046751/#q124064223.

"/pol/ - Politically Incorrect » Thread #130147090." Acc. August 31, 2018. https://archive.4plebs.org/pol/thread/130147090/#q130154617.

"/pol/ - Politically Incorrect » Thread #138509654." Acc. August 31, 2018. https://archive.4plebs.org/pol/thread/138509654/#q138518007.

"/pol/ - Politically Incorrect » Thread #139979370." Acc. August 31, 2018. https://archive.4plebs.org/pol/thread/139979370/#q139979370.

"/pol/ - Politically Incorrect » Thread #141164231." Acc. August 31, 2018. https://archive.4plebs.org/pol/thread/141164231/#q141178988.

"/pol/ - Politically Incorrect » Thread #165947101." Acc. August 31, 2018. https://archive.4plebs.org/pol/thread/165947101/#q165947101.

"/pol/ - Politically Incorrect » Thread #175678515." Acc. August 31, 2018. https://archive.4plebs.org/pol/thread/175678515/#q175695491.

"/pol/ - Politically Incorrect » Thread #177573811." Acc. August 31, 2018. https://archive.4plebs.org/pol/thread/177573811/#q177573811.

"/pol/ - Politically Incorrect » Thread #181248349." Acc. August 31, 2018. https://archive.4plebs.org/pol/thread/181248349/#q181248660.

"/pol/ - Politically Incorrect » Thread #181619781." Acc. August 31, 2018. https://archive.4plebs.org/pol/thread/181619781/#q181684344.

Various presented options of future political development, primarily through an extremist ideological lens

"/pol/ - Politically Incorrect » Thread #45345659." Acc. August 31, 2018. https://archive.4plebs.org/pol/thread/45345659/#q45351117.

"/pol/ - Politically Incorrect » Thread #46147395." Acc. August 31, 2018. https://archive.4plebs.org/pol/thread/46147395/#q46147395.

"/pol/ - Politically Incorrect » Thread #49316041." Acc. August 31, 2018. https://archive.4plebs.org/pol/thread/49316041/#q49318637.

"/pol/ - Politically Incorrect » Thread #49486114." Acc. August 31, 2018. https://archive.4plebs.org/pol/thread/49486114/#q49486114.

"/pol/ - Politically Incorrect » Thread #46334488." Acc. August 31, 2018. https://archive.4plebs.org/pol/thread/46334488/#q46334488.

"/pol/ - Politically Incorrect » Thread #51833980." Acc. August 31, 2018. https://archive.4plebs.org/pol/thread/51833980/#q51843246.

"/pol/ - Politically Incorrect » Thread #56585419." Acc. August 31, 2018. https://archive.4plebs.org/pol/thread/56585419/#q56585419.

"/pol/ - Politically Incorrect » Thread #64893122." Acc. August 31, 2018. https://archive.4plebs.org/pol/thread/64893122/#q64893122.

"/pol/ - Politically Incorrect » Thread #81426231." Acc. August 31, 2018. https://archive.4plebs.org/pol/thread/81426231/#q81435007.

"/pol/ - Politically Incorrect » Thread #101191724." Acc. August 31, 2018. https://archive.4plebs.org/pol/thread/101191724/#q101191724.

"/pol/ - Politically Incorrect » Thread #104049137." Acc. August 31, 2018. https://archive.4plebs.org/pol/thread/104049137/#q104049137.

"/pol/ - Politically Incorrect » Thread #112155689." Acc. August 31, 2018. https://archive.4plebs.org/pol/thread/112155689/#q112185259.

"/pol/ - Politically Incorrect » Thread #119451220." Acc. August 31, 2018. https://archive.4plebs.org/pol/thread/119451220/#q119464334.

"/pol/ - Politically Incorrect » Thread #121979723." Acc. August 31, 2018. https://archive.4plebs.org/pol/thread/121979723/#q121983239.

"/pol/ - Politically Incorrect » Thread #122122528." Acc. August 31, 2018. https://archive.4plebs.org/pol/thread/122122528/#q122125110.

"/pol/ - Politically Incorrect » Thread #122122528." Acc. August 31, 2018. https://archive.4plebs.org/pol/thread/122122528/#q122126252.

"/pol/ - Politically Incorrect » Thread #123986794." Acc. August 31, 2018. https://archive.4plebs.org/pol/thread/123986794/#q123986794.

"/pol/ - Politically Incorrect » Thread #128400276." Acc. August 31, 2018. https://archive.4plebs.org/pol/thread/128400276/#q128402753.

"/pol/ - Politically Incorrect » Thread #128642664." Acc. August 31, 2018. https://archive.4plebs.org/pol/thread/128642664/#q128642664.

"/pol/ - Politically Incorrect » Thread #129035062." Acc. August 31, 2018. https://archive.4plebs.org/pol/thread/129035062/#q129035062.

"/pol/ - Politically Incorrect » Thread #138603537." Acc. August 31, 2018. https://archive.4plebs.org/pol/thread/138603537/#q138603537.

"/pol/ - Politically Incorrect » Thread #142138454." Acc. August 31, 2018. https://archive.4plebs.org/pol/thread/142138454/#q142147392.

"/pol/ - Politically Incorrect » Thread #175173133." Acc. August 31, 2018. https://archive.4plebs.org/pol/thread/175173133/#q175220981.

"/pol/ - Politically Incorrect » Thread #186348652." Acc. August 31, 2018. https://archive.4plebs.org/pol/thread/186348652/#q186353794.

Miscellaneous

"/pol/ - Politically Incorrect » Thread #51517070." Acc. August 31, 2018. https://archive.4plebs.org/pol/thread/51517070/#q51543289.

"/pol/ - Politically Incorrect » Thread #51630836." Acc. August 31, 2018. https://archive.4plebs.org/pol/thread/51630836/#q51636462.

"/pol/ - Politically Incorrect » Thread #52007879." Acc. August 31, 2018. https://archive.4plebs.org/pol/thread/52007879/#q52014056.

"/pol/ - Politically Incorrect » Thread #52164178." Acc. August 31, 2018. https://archive.4plebs.org/pol/thread/52164178/#q52164178.

"/pol/ - Politically Incorrect » Thread #52802144." Acc. August 31, 2018. https://archive.4plebs.org/pol/thread/52802144/#q52802144.

"/pol/ - Politically Incorrect » Thread #54213852." Acc. August 31, 2018. https://archive.4plebs.org/pol/thread/54213852/#q54219919.

"/pol/ - Politically Incorrect » Thread #57360744." Acc. August 31, 2018. https://archive.4plebs.org/pol/thread/57360744/#q57365085.

"/pol/ - Politically Incorrect » Thread #57561184." Acc. August 31, 2018. https://archive.4plebs.org/pol/thread/57561184/#q57565996.

"/pol/ - Politically Incorrect » Thread #64439891." Acc. August 31, 2018. https://archive.4plebs.org/pol/thread/64439891/#q64452366.

"/pol/ - Politically Incorrect » Thread #66784911." Acc. August 31, 2018. https://archive.4plebs.org/pol/thread/66784911/#q66790722.

"/pol/ - Politically Incorrect » Thread #71364997." Acc. August 31, 2018. https://archive.4plebs.org/pol/thread/71364997/#q71364997.

"/pol/ - Politically Incorrect » Thread #79621394." Acc. August 31, 2018. https://archive.4plebs.org/pol/thread/79621394/#q79621394.

"/pol/ - Politically Incorrect » Thread #80103215." Acc. August 31, 2018. https://archive.4plebs.org/pol/thread/80103215/#q80111418.

"/pol/ - Politically Incorrect » Thread #81113714." Acc. August 31, 2018. https://archive.4plebs.org/pol/thread/81113714/#q81113714.

"/pol/ - Politically Incorrect » Thread #83625550." Acc. August 31, 2018. https://archive.4plebs.org/pol/thread/83625550/#q83640184.

"/pol/ - Politically Incorrect » Thread #97980139." Acc. August 31, 2018. https://archive.4plebs.org/pol/thread/97980139/#q97980139.

"/pol/ - Politically Incorrect » Thread #98535618." Acc. August 31, 2018. https://archive.4plebs.org/pol/thread/98535618/#q98535618.

"/pol/ - Politically Incorrect » Thread #98575113." Acc. August 31, 2018. https://archive.4plebs.org/pol/thread/98575113/#q98602388.

"/pol/ - Politically Incorrect » Thread #101685575." Acc. August 31, 2018. https://archive.4plebs.org/pol/thread/101685575/#q101685575.

"/pol/ - Politically Incorrect » Thread #113643285." Acc. August 31, 2018. https://archive.4plebs.org/pol/thread/113643285/#q113643285.

"/pol/ - Politically Incorrect » Thread #89617010." Acc. August 31, 2018. https://archive.4plebs.org/pol/thread/89617010/#q89630879.

"/pol/ - Politically Incorrect » Thread #119742217." Acc. August 31, 2018. https://archive.4plebs.org/pol/thread/119742217/#q119753141.

"/pol/ - Politically Incorrect » Thread #121786810." Acc. August 31, 2018. https://archive.4plebs.org/pol/thread/121786810/#q121828201.

"/pol/ - Politically Incorrect » Thread #124323742." Acc. August 31, 2018. https://archive.4plebs.org/pol/thread/124323742/#q124336640.

"/pol/ - Politically Incorrect » Thread #126091548." Acc. August 31, 2018. https://archive.4plebs.org/pol/thread/126091548/#q126094339.

"/pol/ - Politically Incorrect » Thread #127114269." Acc. August 31, 2018. https://archive.4plebs.org/pol/thread/127114269/#q127114269.

"/pol/ - Politically Incorrect » Thread #137329920." Acc. August 31, 2018. https://archive.4plebs.org/pol/thread/137329920/#q137338298.

"/pol/ - Politically Incorrect » Thread #184638895." Acc. August 31, 2018. https://archive.4plebs.org/pol/thread/184638895/#q184650006.

General references

(This section includes all of the other relevant literature used for this paper)

4Chan. n.d. "1385940778786.Gif (160×240)." Accessed August 27, 2018. https://i.4pcdn.org/pol/1385940778786.gif.

4Chan. n.d. "1420818292959.Jpg (629×545)." Accessed August 27, 2018. https://i.4pcdn.org/pol/1420818292959.jpg.

4Chan. n.d. "1427674130362.Jpg (967×807)." Accessed August 27, 2018. https://i.4pcdn.org/pol/1427674130362.jpg.

4Chan. n.d. "1460059415593.Jpg (845×1280)." Accessed August 27, 2018. https://i.4pcdn.org/pol/1460059415593.jpg.

4Chan. n.d. "1461515104250.Jpg (529×367)." Accessed August 27, 2018. https://i.4pcdn.org/pol/1461515104250.jpg.

4Chan. 2018. "Advertise - 4chan." http://www.4chan.org/advertise.

Alexa. 2018. "4chan.Org Traffic, Demographics and Competitors - Alexa." February 17, 2018. https://www.alexa.com/siteinfo/4chan.org.

Archive.4plebs. n.d. "4plebs » FAQ." https://archive.4plebs.org/_/articles/faq/.

Bernstein, Michael S., Andrés Monroy-Hernández, Drew Harry, Paul André, Katrina Panovich, and Gregory G. Vargas. 2011. "4chan and /b: An Analysis of Anonymity and Ephemerality in a Large Online Community." In *ICWSM*, 50–57.

Borum, Randy. 2011. "Radicalization into Violent Extremism I: A Review of Social Science Theories." *Journal of Strategic Security* 4 (4): 7–36. https://doi.org/10.5038/1944-0472.4.4.1.

Coaston, Jane. 2018. "#QAnon, the Scarily Popular pro-Trump Conspiracy Theory, Explained." Vox. August 1, 2018. https://www.vox.com/policy-and-politics/2018/8/1/17253444/qanon-trump-conspiracy-theory-reddit.

Cornelius, Sarah, Carole Gordon, and Margaret Harris. 2011. "Role Engagement and Anonymity in Synchronous Online Role Play." *The International Review of Research in Open and Distributed Learning* 12 (5): 57–73.

Davis, Katie. 2012. "Tensions of Identity in a Networked Era: Young People's Perspectives on the Risks and Rewards of Online Self-Expression." *New Media & Society* 14 (4): 634–51. https://doi.org/10.1177/1461444811422430.

Dibbell, Julian. 2010. "Radical Opacity." *Technology Review* 113 (5): 82–86.

Dockery, Wesley. 2017. "The Balkan Route—Explained." InfoMigrants. March 29, 2017. http://www.infomigrants.net/en/post/2546/the-balkan-route-explained.

Edwards, Geoff. 2008. "Frankston South Student Faces Court over Email -- News | Frankston Standard Leader." 2008. https://web.archive.org/web/20090425195614/http://frankston-leader.whereilive.com.au/news/story/frankston-south-student-faces-court-over-email/.

Eordogh, Fruzsina. 2014. "What the Internet's Most Infamous Trolls Tell Us About Online Feminism." Motherboard. 2014. https://motherboard.vice.com/en_us/article/3dkaz8/trolls-4chan-online-feminism-women-of-color.

Fairclough, Norman. 2013. *Critical Discourse Analysis: The Critical Study of Language*. 2. ed. London: Routledge.

Ferrara, Emilio. 2017. "Disinformation and Social Bot Operations in the Run up to the 2017 French Presidential Election."

Hansen, Lene. 2006. *Security as Practice: Discourse Analysis and the Bosnian War*. The New International Relations. Routledge.

Heartfield, James. 2014. "Operation Lollipop: A Useful Parody." Spiked Online. 2014. http://www.spiked-online.com/newsite/article/operation-lollipop-a-useful-parody/15224.

Herrman, John. 2017. "How Hate Groups Forced Online Platforms to Reveal Their True Nature." *The New York Times*, August 21, 2017, sec. Magazine. https://www.nytimes.com/2017/08/21/magazine/how-hate-groups-forced-online-platforms-to-reveal-their-true-nature.html.

Hine, Gabriel Emile, Jeremiah Onaolapo, Emiliano De Cristofaro, Nicolas Kourtellis, Ilias Leontiadis, Riginos Samaras, Gianluca Stringhini, and Jeremy Blackburn. 2016a. "A Longitudinal Measurement Study of 4chan's Politically Incorrect Forum and Its Effect on the Web." *ArXiv E-Prints*, 1–15.

———. 2016b. "Kek, Cucks, and God Emperor Trump: A Measurement Study of 4chan's Politically Incorrect Forum and Its Effects on the Web." *ArXiv:1610.03452 [Physics]*, October. http://arxiv.org/abs/1610.03452.

Hopkins, Nick, and Vered Kahani-Hopkins. 2009. "Reconceptualizing Extremism and Moderation: From Categories of Analysis to Categories of Practice in the Construction of Collective Identity." *British Journal of Social Psychology* 48 (1): 99–113. https://doi.org/10.1348/014466608X284425.

Knuttila, Lee. 2011. "User Unknown: 4chan, Anonymity and Contingency." *First Monday* 16 (10). http://www.ojphi.org/ojs/index.php/fm/article/view/3665.

Lapidot-Lefler, Noam, and Azy Barak. 2012. "Effects of Anonymity, Invisibility, and Lack of Eye-Contact on Toxic Online Disinhibition." *Computers in Human Behavior* 28 (2): 434–43. https://doi.org/10.1016/j.chb.2011.10.014.

Ludemann, Dillon. 2018. "/Pol/Emics: Ambiguity, Scales, and Digital Discourse on 4chan." *Discourse, Context & Media* 24 (August): 92–98. https://doi.org/10.1016/j.dcm.2018.01.010.

Moore, Michael J., Tadashi Nakano, Akihiro Enomoto, and Tatsuya Suda. 2012. "Anonymity and Roles Associated with Aggressive Posts in an Online Forum." *Computers in Human Behavior* 28 (3): 861–67. https://doi.org/10.1016/j.chb.2011.12.005.

Nagle, Angela. 2017. *Kill All Normies: Online Culture Wars From 4Chan and Tumblr to Trump and the Alt-Right*. Zero Books. http://gen.lib.rus.ec/book/index.php?md5=da9ff47af0c4090ec0c2f413cca84404.

Neet.Tv. 2018. "4chan Statistics." https://catalog.neet.tv/stats.html.

Nissenbaum, Asaf, and Limor Shifman. 2017. "Internet Memes as Contested Cultural Capital: The Case of 4chan's/b/Board." *New Media & Society* 19 (4): 483–501.

Ohlheiser, Abby. 2016. "Analysis | 'We Actually Elected a Meme as President': How 4chan Celebrated Trump's Victory." *Washington Post*, November 9, 2016. https://www.washingtonpost.com/news/the-intersect/wp/2016/11/09/we-actually-elected-a-meme-as-president-how-4chan-celebrated-trumps-victory/.

Revesz, Rachael. 2016. "Hillary Clinton Attacks Donald Trump for Posting Pepe the Frog Meme | The Independent." 2016. http://www.independent.co.uk/news/world/americas/donald-trump-hillary-clinton-pepe-frog-instagram-breitbart-white-supremacist-alex-jones-milo-a7240581.html.

Ryuuzakii666. 2012. *REMOVE KEBAB (Perfect Loop)*. https://www.youtube.com/watch?v=ocW3fBqPQkU.

Santana, Arthur D. 2014. "Virtuous or Vitriolic." *Journalism Practice* 8 (1): 18–33. https://doi.org/10.1080/17512786.2013.813194.

Schreckinger, Ben. 2017. "World War Meme." POLITICO Magazine. 2017. https://www.politico.com/magazine/story/2017/03/memes-4chan-trump-supporters-trolls-internet-214856.

Sparby, Erika M. 2017. "Digital Social Media and Aggression: Memetic Rhetoric in 4chan's Collective Identity." *Computers and Composition* 45 (September): 85–97. https://doi.org/10.1016/j.compcom.2017.06.006.

Staff, WSAZ News. 2014. "Teen Arrested for Threatening to Blow Up School." 2014. http://www.wsaz.com/home/headlines/Teen-Arrested-for-Threatening-to-Blow-Up-School-241452621.html.

Suler, John. 2005. "The Online Disinhibition Effect." *International Journal of Applied Psychoanalytic Studies* 2 (2): 184–188.

Tait, Amelia. 2017. "We Need to Talk about the Online Radicalisation of Young, White Women." 2017. https://www.newstatesman.com/science-tech/internet/2017/08/we-need-talk-about-online-radicalisation-young-white-women.

Thompson, Andrew. 2018. "The Measure of Hate on 4Chan." *Rolling Stone* (blog). May 10, 2018. https://www.rollingstone.com/politics/politics-news/the-measure-of-hate-on-4chan-627922/.

Wagener, Albin. 2017. "Lauren Mayberry vs. 4chan's Online Misogyny: A Critical Discourse Analysis Perspective." *Lodz Papers in Pragmatics* 13 (2). https://doi.org/10.1515/lpp-2017-0015.

Wendling, Mike. 2018. *Alt-Right: From 4chan to the White House*. Fernwood Publishing.

Wikipedia. 2018. "Fourteen Words." August 23, 2018. https://en.wikipedia.org/w/index.php?title=Fourteen_Words&oldid=856126424.

Wodak, Ruth, ed. 2002. *Methods for Critical Discourse Analysis*. Sage.

Violent Extremism and Radicalization in the Context of the Migrant Crisis: Evidence from Serbia

Tijana Rečević

Introduction[1]

The last several years have been marked by the escalation of two global crises—the rise of violent extremism, and unprecedented mass migration—which have largely coincided both temporally and spatially. While the link between migration and violent extremism and radicalization that lead to terrorism (VERLT) has always been embedded in perilous stereotypes often conflating these two phenomena, the ongoing migrant crisis in Europe has only strengthened "a chain of false links" (Maunganidze 2017) drawn between the two. The ongoing hyper-securitization of migrants who arrived on European soil rapidly replaced the mantras of freedom and equality in the rhetoric of leading politicians across Europe, announcing the revival of all kinds of extremist actors at all levels and arousing a dangerous societal security dilemma between them. Unfortunately, the best panacea against such a vicious circle of prejudice and fears among both migrant and host populations—the evidence-based understanding of all the linkages between migration and VERLT—still remains very limited.

As a country through which close to a million migrants[2] transited on their way to Western Europe while the so called "Western

---

1 The author is grateful to Kristina Ivanović, Niké Wentholt, Boris Milanović, and Valery Perry for helpful comments to the earlier versions of the manuscript. In addition, further thanks are owed to multiple anonymous stakeholders who were very responsive during the interview phase.
2 In this research, the term "migrant" was used to encompass asylum seekers, refugees, and economic migrants, and such broad use of the term should not be construed as a commentary on the legal status of the populations and communities described below, or the legal protections that they should or should not be afforded.

Balkans route" was open (Beta 2016), and a country in which approximately 4,000 migrants currently live since the closure of that route prevented them from moving on (UNHCR 2018), Serbia is indeed a case which needs to be considered in discussions on the linkages between the recent mass migration and VERLT risks. The fact that Serbia has crossed from being a "country of origin" via a "transit country" to a potential "destination country" in only two years, created a legal and political "limbo" in which neither the migrants nor the local population want to remain. Even though only a few serious incidents have been recorded in relation to the migrant situation in Serbia since the outbreak of the crisis in summer 2015, the prolongation of such an ambiguous limbo state undoubtedly contributes to the grievances and resentments in both the migrant and local population, making the potential for their radicalization—including "reciprocal radicalization" (Eatwell 2006)—a real and rising concern. The fact that the existing migrant situation in Serbia threatens to last only exacerbates these concerns, therefore urging more attention of both academia and policy makers.

Responding to such a need, this study aims to provide some jumping-off evidence on the potential for radicalization among both the migrant population currently staying in Serbia and the local population in the communities most affected by the inflow of migrants. After a short summary of the ongoing migrant crisis in Serbia, the first section presents a brief overview of the burgeoning literature dealing with migration-related VERLT threats. The second section starts by describing the methods used and continues by presenting the main findings of the study. Finally, the conclusion briefly discusses the implications of the author's main claim—that the current potential for reciprocal radicalization between the migrant and local population in Serbia does not seem to be alarmingly high, but threatens to rise due to insufficient attention devoted to the subject by the relevant stakeholders.

Background: the migrant crisis in Serbia

The first significant increase in the number of migrants in Serbia started in 2011 and then grew steadily until summer 2015, when the whole world faced the largest migration wave since World War II. While the low number of those who applied for asylum in Serbia in the years preceding 2015 showed that Serbia was not really among the preferred countries of destination (Lukić 2016), geography still made it one of the most exposed. Being on the so called Western Balkan route—an informal humanitarian corridor through which nearly a million migrants passed through on their way towards Western Europe by March 2016 (Beta 2016)—Serbia encountered enormous challenges to enable registration and provide food, shelter, medical and other necessary relief to migrants transiting its territory first towards Hungary, and later towards Croatia. Responding to such a situation, in addition to the existing five asylum centers, the government opened several temporary reception centers close to the main entry, transit, and exit points throughout Serbia, where the majority of migrants stayed before leaving Serbia. Nevertheless, in the desire to leave Serbia as soon as possible and reveal as little information about themselves as necessary, hundreds of migrants also stayed in the streets of Belgrade and other cities on the route, mainly in parks near the main bus and train stations.

Eventually, a series of restrictive measures introduced by EU countries in early 2016, culminating in the so-called EU-Turkey Statement from March 2016, announced the closure of the Western Balkans route, leaving approximately 2,000 migrants stranded in Serbia (Al Jazeera 2017). Nonetheless, although this arrangement led to a significant reduction in the number of newly arrived migrants, it failed to completely prevent them from trying to reach the desired countries of destination, which is why the number of migrants in Serbia reached close to 8,000 on the first anniversary of the agreement in March 2017 (UNHCR 2018). Although this number dropped primarily due to the emergence of new smuggling routes, approximately 4,000 migrants today live in 18 centers (5 asylum centers and 13 temporary reception and transit centers throughout Serbia)—unable to continue to Western Europe, unable or reluctant to move back to their countries of origin, and unwilling to apply for asylum in Serbia.

Even though the situation in these centers has significantly improved since the beginning of the crisis, numerous lasting problems make life in them far from good (Boček 2017). Most importantly, since the large majority of migrants have not submitted a formal asylum application but are still allowed to stay in Serbia and receive aid and services in the government centers, their so called "tolerated stay" falls into a grey area under Serbian law, meaning that there is no legal framework governing their status and rights. Hence, after suffering throughout their journey to Serbia, migrants have several suboptimal options to leave this limbo (in which some of them have been living for longer than two years): to apply for asylum in Serbia; to apply for family reunification and assisted voluntary return; to wait to transit to Hungary (which admits approximately 10 persons a day); or to try to illegally cross the Croatian, Hungarian or Bosnian border. As of this writing (mid–2018), the last two options are by far the most popular ones, both contributing to migrants' suffering and frustrations in ways which are further discussed in this chapter.

On the other side, the fact that there are 18 reception centers throughout Serbia currently, in comparison to only one asylum center in 2011, already indicates the extent to which the last migration wave has affected the local population in Serbia. While the initial increase in the number of migrants in 2011 was followed by massive protests, the years of mass influx of migrants—2015 and 2016— were marked by only sporadic and small-scale protests by local populations and right-wing organizations. For that reason, and due to the fact that the Serbian government never closed its borders during the entire crisis, Serbia was often praised by high-ranking UN and EU officials for its humane attitude and solidarity towards migrants transiting its territory. Nevertheless, the expiry of such positive attitudes seemed to be announced by several anti-migrant protests throughout Serbia in the summer of 2017. While still perceiving migrants' stay in their communities as a temporary issue, the local population in the municipalities most affected by the ongoing crisis started to worry that this "tolerated stay" of migrants could become a permanent or at least a prolonged solution. Since the majority of the population in Serbia seems to be opposed to the permanent settlement of migrants in their vicinity (Group 484 2017, 6; TNS Medium Gallup 2017), such changes in prevailing perceptions indeed indicate that a fertile ground for further polarization and potential radicalization among the local population in Serbia might be emerging.

Migration and VERLT: literature review and theoretical framework

Although both violent extremism and mass migration have been at the very forefront of academic and policy discussions in the last several years, the theoretical assumptions which urge further exploration and supporting evidence are those considering migration to be a cause, or at least a catalyst, of VERLT (Cinoglu and Altun 2013; Koser 2015a; Lenos 2016; McKeever and Fink 2017; Koser and Cunningham 2018).[3] Sparking fear, anxiety, and mistrust on all sides, mass migration could create an excellent environment for all types of extremists propagating "us vs. them" ideologies to flourish (Busher and Macklin 2015; Ebner 2018; Lenos 2016, 8), benefiting from their unspoken alliance to destroy the grey middle in between. While the dynamics of such cumulative or reciprocal radicalization (Eatwell 2006, 205) is extremely complex, VERLT risks among migrants, on one side, and VERLT risks among host populations, on the other, undoubtedly represent two main axes.

VERLT and the migrant population

Although the number of cases in which refugees and migrants were radicalized or recruited for violent extremist goals remains low,[4] the evidence from camps in Pakistan, Afghanistan, Iraq, as well as the most recent case of Syria's Yarmouk refugee camp, indeed warns that radicalization of refugees and migrants is a reality that must be addressed (Martin-Rayo 2011; Mc Sweeney, 2012; Sude,

---

3   I attempt to separate the existing literature on VERLT from the literature on counterterrorism, meaning that the focus of this study are the threats of radicalization and violent extremism among "genuine migrants," instead of the threats from already radicalized "fake migrants" who sometimes infiltrate migrant flows.
4   It should be, however, noted that the reluctance of governments to reveal this confidential and sensitive data remains high (Koser and Cunningham 2016, 85).

Stebbins and Weillant, 2015). Nevertheless, since academic consensus on the causes of VERLT is still lacking even in relation to presumed "typical cases," such a consensus could therefore hardly be expected in relation to migrant populations, where complex drivers of VERLT intersect with complex motivations, experiences, and expectations of those fleeing their homes. At least two groups of conditions conducive to allow for VERLT to occur among migrant populations can, however, be noted in the existing literature.

The first group consists of socio-economic and psychological "push and pull" factors. The loss of home, sense of dislocation, thwarted expectations, death of and separation from family members and friends, economic, and other frustrations existent among those fleeing their homes create a pool of grievances and resentments which make migrants particularly vulnerable to extremist ideas (Haider 2014; Koser 2015b, 2016; Lenos 2016; Reitano and Tinti 2017). Differentiating between the causes and natures of migrants' resentments, together with other psychological factors, the literature attempts to further investigate which groups of migrants are the most vulnerable to VERLT, pointing to youth, children and victims of abuse of different kinds (Koser 2015b; United Nations 2015). Nevertheless, while emphasizing the importance of different factors and the vulnerability of different groups, almost all authors agree that VERLT is most likely to occur in protracted conflict and crisis situations, which, unfortunately, describes the majority of migrant crises worldwide today (Koser 2016).

The second and, according to many authors, the most important group consists of factors related to the migration system of host countries. Restrictiveness or openness of their policies regarding the access to asylum procedure, shelter, food, healthcare, physiological support, social benefits, labor market, and other integration measures decisively affect the susceptibility of migrant populations to VERLT. If their basic needs are not met, if they are being repeatedly brutalized and neglected, and if they are ultimately made invisible by migration policies, migrants may be tempted to adopt radical stands and even turn to violent means instead of waiting in despair for years (Koser 2015b; Sude Stebbins and Weillant,

2015; Hakimi 2016; Lenos 2016; Mullins 2016). Among the important factors are living conditions in the camps, which are—by analogy with prisons—often considered "breeding grounds" for radicalization and violent extremism (Koser and Cunningham 2016; Schmid 2016). The location of camps is, for instance, very important since the remoteness of camps from inhabited areas and city centers largely contributes to the migrants' sense of isolation and alienation, thus potentially increasing their vulnerability to VERLT (Sude, Stebbins and Weillant 2015, 2). The type of camps is also significant since open-type camps (unrestricted freedom of movement) seem to be more favorable to the psychological state of refugees and migrants, and therefore less favorable to VERLT than are the closed-type (detention) ones (Schmid 2016). The openness of camps is particularly important when people of different nationalities, ethnicities, and religions are accommodated together, since ethnic and other sectarian tensions imported from countries of origin could be exacerbated in the harsh conditions of camps and then manifested in violence in countries of destination (United Nations 2015). Nevertheless, while open camps are undoubtedly more humane, they also come with risks, since the population living in open camps is often more exposed to smugglers and other criminal, extremist, or even militant groups striving to abuse, exploit, or recruit refugee and migrant populations for their own ends.

VERLT and the host communities

Regardless of the host government's migration policy, the local population in the countries affected by mass inflows of migrants is most likely to remain divided on this issue to a lesser or greater extent. While such disruption in the social cohesion of host communities can be rather mild and temporary, it can also open a window of opportunity for further polarization and radicalization against migrants to take place (Haider 2014; RAN 2016). Two segments of any host society evoke the greatest concern in this regard.

Undoubtedly the greatest risk of radicalization exists among right-wing extremist organizations and political parties who spread xenophobic, anti-immigrant, anti-Islam, and similar extremist views, sometimes calling for the use of violence against migrant populations (Fekete 2009; Lenos 2016, 6). Considering migrants to be a threat to national cohesion, national culture, and a national way of life (Ratković 2017, 48), these groups use ethno-nationalist and xenophobic rhetoric to persuade the majority community to stand up for the "national cause," using all necessary means to fight all "invaders" who allegedly threaten their rule, culture, and values. The speed by which the right-wing scene in numerous European countries has flourished and strengthened primarily due to vocal anti-immigrant populism in the context of the recent crisis, testifies to the huge potential for radicalization which mass arrival of migrants can unleash even in societies with long-lasting liberal traditions and even their own immigrant history (Davey and Ebner 2017). Moreover, the alarming rise in violent attacks against migrants in the period 2014–2016, mainly in Germany, Sweden, Greece, and Finland, warns that a thin line between non-violent and violent extremism has been crossed in many cases, if not permanently destroyed (Institute for Economics & Peace 2018, 57).

While some extremist groups are indeed prone to use violence against migrants, they should be differentiated from groups of "concerned" and "angry" citizens whose opposition to accepting migrants may not stem from harbored ethnic, religious, and other sectarian biases, but can be generated by some more "rational" fears, such as those of an economic nature. Simply labelling angry locals as potential violent extremists can cover some "microradicalizations" (Bailey and Edwards 2017) which, if not identified early and properly addressed, indeed risk feeding polarization in the host society and evoking a self-fulfilling prophecy. A cautious and strategic approach of governments and other actors (academia included) involved in dealing with preventing local resentment among host communities is therefore highly needed, since both underestimating and overestimating locals' negative attitudes can do nothing but exacerbate the potential for their radicalization.

The migrant crisis and VERLT: evidence from Serbia

Research design

Due to the almost complete absence of any previous research or evidence on the linkage between the recent mass inflow of migrants and VERLT in Serbia, this jumping-off research relied on careful triangulation of evidence gathered through desk research and semi-structured interviews. Thorough desk research contributed to an enhanced understanding of the migrant situation in Serbia and the responsibilities of relevant stakeholders involved in migration management (including its security aspects). The first part of desk research included an in-depth analysis of the existing strategic, policy, and legislative frameworks regarding both CVE and migrant/refugee policy, as well as specialized reports and publications published by relevant stakeholders engaged in these matters. The second part of desk research focused on online content about the migration-related activities of the major right-wing organizations and political parties in Serbia, their social media channels, several social media sources dedicated to public discussion on the migration situation in Serbia, as well as existing public surveys on the attitudes of the local populations in the affected communities.

In addition, 23 semi-structured interviews were conducted with two main groups of respondents. The first group consisted of the representatives of the key government agencies (i.e., the Commissariat for Refugees and Migration, Ministry of Labor, Employment, Social and Veteran Issues),[5] local authorities in several communities where migrants were received (i.e., local commissioner for refugees and migration, mayor, assistant to the mayor), relevant UN agencies present in Serbia, as well as frontline workers employed in migration management (i.e., staff working in the reception centers). Four local communities were selected as the focus —

---

[5] Even though the Ministry of Interior and security services were formally contacted with requests for permission to interview some of their employees, such permission was not received within the timeframe of task realization.

Belgrade (the capital, 8 interviews),[6] Subotica (northern Serbia, 2 interviews), Preševo (southern Serbia, 4 interviews), and Šid (western Serbia, 3 interviews), although the reception center in Banja Koviljača (western Serbia, 1 interview) was also visited due to its importance as the first established asylum center in Serbia. These four cities and municipalities were chosen according to two main criteria: the extent to which they were affected by the migrant crisis (the selected four cities and municipalities were the main entry (Preševo), transit (Belgrade) and exit (Subotica, Šid) points on the so-called Western Balkans refugee route), and the number of migrants staying in the reception centers on their territory upon the closure of the Western Balkans route (the selected four cities and municipalities accommodate the largest number of stranded migrants). Moreover, the very different structures of the local population in these four cities and municipalities made them particularly interesting and relevant for the research matter. The second major group of respondents consisted of members of several of the most prominent right-wing organisations and political parties in Serbia (five interviews), selected based on their activities in relation to the migrant situation in Serbia. In addition, three consultative interviews were conducted with representatives of academia.

VERLT and the migrant population in Serbia

The gathered insights on the risk of radicalization among the migrant population in Serbia can best be divided in three groups: behavior of migrants potentially relevant for the subject matter; the respondents' general impressions on the VERLT risks among the migrant population in Serbia; and the need for preventive measures against VERLT among migrants staying in Serbia.

---

6   Three interviews in Belgrade were conducted with respondents in charge of the situation in the reception centers in Belgrade only, while five interviewees were state officials in charge of the migrant situation in Serbia in general.

Migrants' behavior

While it would be wrong to treat any of the findings on the behavior of migrants as a kind of litmus test for radicalization among migrants in Serbia, it can serve to illustrate the conditions in which migrants in Serbia live and point towards the most important sources of their current frustrations. One of the most important findings in relation to the behavior of migrants in Serbia is that the location of the centers—not in relation to the city/municipality center, but to the state borders—seems to have a strong impact on the migrants' behavior. While respondents from Šid and Subotica reported a significant number of incidents and problems caused by the misbehavior of migrants, the situation in Preševo was much calmer, indicating that the situation near the "exit borders" can be far more troublesome than in the southern and central Serbia. Several respondents had similar explanations for this, arguing that "the closer to the EU they [migrants] are, the more impatient they become."

> "Preševo is the main entry point, where they behave perfidiously and are calm, knowing that they could be easily returned to Macedonia. In Belgrade, they behave like tourists since there are many organizations operating there, telling migrants what their rights are, etc. But this is all preparation for Subotica and Šid, where the problems start. They are one step from their goal, or at least they think so, and the tensions rise..."
> (An employee of the Ministry of Labour, Employment, Veteran and Social Issues 2017, pers. comm., December 31)

Aware of this situation, authorities allegedly sometimes (mis)use this psychological effect which the proximity to the border has as a form of a disciplinary measure, warning that they may transport those migrants who cause troubles in other centers to the center in Preševo, thereby sending the message to both them and the rest of the migrant population in Serbia that "some rules must be obeyed."

As for the type of incidents caused by migrants, by far the most frequently reported ones in all municipalities seem to be those of a criminal nature—looting, car and livestock theft, fights in public places, etc. Nevertheless, even though they have not supported their claims by any official police records, the respondents in all municipalities seemed to be rather convinced that these incidents should be blamed on those migrants who do not live in the camps, but remain "outside of the system." Even though all camps in Serbia are the open-type, meaning that migrants can leave camps whenever they want, some of them do not want to enter camps in any way, afraid that any type of registration could diminish their chances to move onwards. The situation in this regard seems to be by far worse in Šid, where it is estimated that approximately 300 migrants, who entered and stayed in Serbia completely illegally, live in abandoned buildings and sleep rough, hoping to cross to Croatia. In this way depriving themselves of food and other services which are available in camps, those groups are, according to respondents, "forced" to steal from the locals, thus arousing anger, and also exposed to far greater security risks than the migrant population living in the centers.

> "They are a huge problem, but they are also in a huge problem since they have no place to sleep, no food or any kind of protection"
> (A representative of the local self-government in Šid 2018, pers. comm., January 12).

The second group of incidents of great importance for considering the threat of radicalization among migrants currently in Serbia is related to incidents occurring among themselves. Almost all respondents agreed that the largest percentage of fights which have occurred since the beginning of the crisis were those between groups of migrants of different nationality, ethnicity, or religion, particularly between Afghans and Pakistanis and between Iranians and Pakistanis.

> "It [fight in the camp] happened because of their Sunni vs. Shia conflict, for sure, they confirmed"
> (An NGO employee working in the reception/transit center in Obrenovac 2018, pers. comm., December 28).

> "We once organized a celebration for the Afghani national holiday, but that caused a lot of troubles in the center because other groups were offended even though we promised to organize something for them too"
> (An NGO employee working in the reception/transit center in Preševo, 2018, pers. comm., January 22).

Nevertheless, while some findings do seem to indicate that different ethnic, religious and other sectarian grievances and tensions do not vanish even after several borders and continents are crossed, respondents from all the centers visited were also very keen to emphasize some more "material" causes of conflicts between migrants in the centers. Such reasons varied from those about the priority in receiving aid, to borrowing money and personal revenge, to the fight for informal rule inside or outside the center, often related to some kind of criminal activity, such as drug trafficking.

> "They don't fight because of religious differences, they fight for criminal reasons! They fight over the "rule" in the centre which is important to them for many reasons, but none of them is religion"
> (An employee of the Commissariat for Refugees and Migration, 2018, pers. comm., January 14).

In addition, easy access to alcohol (as previously noted, all camps in Serbia are open-type) was mentioned by several respondents as a "catalyst" of violent behavior not only between different groups of migrants, but also in, unfortunately, not so rare cases of family violence in the camps.

> "They are not used to alcohol consumption because of their religion, so they cannot control themselves when they get drunk. They come here and start fighting, so the police need to sometimes intervene"
> (An employee in the asylum center in Banja Koviljača 2018, pers. comm., January 31).

The third group of incidents include outbursts reflecting migrants' resentment towards local, but also global governments and populations. While migrants' protests in Serbia were more frequent in the height of the Western Balkan route, due to the frequent and unpredictable closures of the Hungarian and Croatian borders, as well as in the immediate aftermath of the route closure, not many migrants' protests have been seen since late 2016. The last protest occurred on the Croatian border in late December 2017, but was prevented from escalating by the local authorities and police forces (BIRN 2017). The absence of migrants' open protest should not, however, be confused with an absence of frustration and anger towards international migration policies which have captured them in their current situation, particularly since their stay in Serbia seems to add at least two local-specific grievances to an already inexhaustible list of migrants' grievances.

The most common added source of dissatisfaction among migrants currently staying in Serbia seems to be the duration of their stay in the country, which almost all of them see only as a temporary transit point (Danish Refugee Council 2017). Being stranded in a country in which they do to want to stay, living in crowded centers with almost no privacy, and not knowing whether and when the situation is going to change, migrants in Serbia often feel desperate and angry at the same time.

> "Oh, they are very frustrated with being held here, but they are also determined to endure till they find a way to move onwards to Europe"
> (A representative of the local self-government in Subotica, 2018, pers. comm., January 31).

Deprived of any legal way to move onwards and impatient to wait any longer, migrants more and more frequently turn to desperate measures, trying to illegally cross the Hungarian, Croatian, or Bosnian border by any means, though mainly with the help of smugglers. Since most such attempts end unsuccessfully and with migrants being either deceived by smugglers or brutally beaten by them or by the police (Oxfam 2017), their frustration and despair only exacerbate. Every new cruelty they suffer during their stay in, or while trying to leave Serbia, can reinforce their existing fears, perceptions of injustice and sense of discrimination, increasing their vulnerability to adopt radical ideas and reach for violent means.

General impressions

The majority of respondents were of the opinion that the threat of radicalization among the migrant population in Serbia was rather low. The most common reason for which the respondents were convinced that radicalization among migrants currently staying in Serbia was highly unlikely was related to the duration of their stay in Serbia, perceived as only temporary.

> "I am not sure how long the radicalization [process] lasts, but I guess it doesn't happen overnight... All of them leave Serbia sooner or later and I don't think they have time to radicalize while here"
> (An employee of a Belgrade-based NGO, 2017, pers. comm., December 22).

While some respondents consider the relatively short stay of migrants in Serbia (even though some of them have been stranded in Serbia for almost two years) as a main preventive factor to migrants' radicalization, other have referred to the structure of the migrant population currently in Serbia:

> "These are all economic migrants... They are interested in a better life, not in revenge, because they are not victims of violence. They will accomplish nothing if they radicalize... It is simply not rational to them"
> (An employee of the Commissariat for Refugees and Migration, 2018, pers. comm., January 23).

Finally, the remarkably strong belief among respondents' that Serbia and its people would not become a target of any kind of violent attack by migrants was underpinned by one more explanation. According to the respondents' experience and conversations with migrants, the "deep gratitude" and "sympathies" which migrants feel towards Serbia and its people for their "warm welcome" and help provided are, at least for now, directing any potential resentments away from Serbia. Only one respondent, however, had a completely different view based on the belief that "ISIS has no borders" (A representative of the local self-government in Belgrade 2018, pers. comm., January 12).

Nevertheless, while assessing the general risk of radicalization among migrant population in Serbia as fairly low, many respondents emphasized that the group most vulnerable to all kinds of abuses—from physical and sexual violence, to trafficking and all other potential vulnerabilities, including VERLT threats, are unaccompanied and separated minors. While most of them are reported to have already suffered some kind of abuse during the journey, their status and protection in Serbia is far from satisfactory (Boček 2017; Milić 2017; MSF 2017). Since there is no adequate mechanism in place for age determination, many unaccompanied minors lie about their age in order to avoid being assigned a guardian and other trustee who could deter them from leaving Serbia. They are then accommodated with other adult migrants and left exposed to those who might try to misuse their vulnerability for different criminal activities, radical ideas, or even violent abuse. Overcrowded centers and the lack of legal guardians, already warned about in several reports on the migrant situation in Serbia, only contribute to such risks. Emphasizing that all migrant children are in great danger of the above-mentioned risks, one of the interviewed frontline workers made an important note:

> "Boys are actually much more vulnerable than girls! There are fewer unaccompanied girls, so everybody notices them, and they get more attention" (An employee of a Belgrade-based NGO, 2018, pers. comm., January 12).

Preventive measures

Finally, when asked which actors were in charge of or involved in preventing radicalization among the migrant population living in the centers, all respondents pointed to the Ministry of Interior or other "security services doing their job." In addition to them, there is a security officer (sometimes several of them) responsible for maintaining order in each center. Nonetheless, according to respondents from both the government and non-governmental sectors, none of the frontline workers has any kind of specialized knowledge on identifying early signs of radicalization among migrants in the centers, nor have any kind of referral mechanisms been established in this regard. Moreover, the issue of potential VERLT among migrants as such seems to be absent from the agenda of all the institutions and organizations working directly with migrants in Serbia. The only respondent who said that he personally possessed some "informal knowledge" on recognizing potential radicalized individuals and extremists among migrants, emphasized that one of the signals that he followed was "the way they behave in critical situations," such as their behavior during incidents in the centers.

> "If they stay calm during incidents in the center, they must have undergone some kind of military training. They don't want to draw attention to themselves"

(An NGO employee working in the transit center in Belgrade, 2018, pers. comm., January 16).

One must caution against quick conclusions regarding the absence of any measures related to VERLT prevention among migrants in Serbia, as various activities are ongoing in the centers which, although indirectly and unsystematically, most certainly contribute to prevention. Those activities include regular individual and group psychological sessions, regular education and numerous extra-curricular activities for children, various recreational activities and vocational trainings for adults, as well as specialized preventive educational workshops on human trafficking, smuggling, family violence and other important issues related to personal security and well-being of both adult and children migrants, all provided by a network of governmental, non-governmental, and international organizations and funded by various national and international donors (Jelačić 2016). Although not explicitly named as activities aimed at preventing radicalization, these measures to a certain extent do coincide with the best practices for countering radicalization and violent extremism among migrants, so their impact on migrants' resilience to VERLT threats should not be overlooked.

VERLT and the host communities in Serbia

The findings on radicalization among the local populations in the affected municipalities can be best divided in three groups: those on radicalization among the general population, among right-wing organizations and parties, and the existing measures for the prevention of such radicalization.

General population

According to several public opinion surveys conducted in the municipalities affected most by the recent migrant crisis, the general attitude of local communities is divided[7] and varies from municipality to municipality due to numerous local-specific factors

---

7 According to an opinion poll conducted in August 2017, 44% of citizens had a negative opinion, while 43% had neutral attitudes towards migrants. The percentage of

(Ninamedia Research 2015a, 2015b; Group 484 2017; TNS Medium Gallup 2017). While such differences appeared during this research as well, the main findings on the drivers of both positive and negative attitudes in each of the target municipalities were strikingly similar.

In each municipality, the high tolerance and empathy which "characterize the Serbian people in general" were unanimously reported as the main source of positive local population's reactions to the migrants staying in their communities. In addition, respondents from each of the visited municipalities were eager to emphasize the reasons for which their exact community was particularly open and ready to accept migrants. For instance, "the experience of the 90s" was mentioned in all four municipalities, by which the respondents in Belgrade, Subotica, and Šid considered the experience of the Serb refugees who fled during the wars in Bosnia and Croatia (1990–1995), while the respondents in Preševo talked about Albanians who were forced to leave Kosovo and Metohija in the late 1990s.

> "A third of the population here are former refugees. We know how these people feel"
> (A representative of the local self-government in Šid, 2018, pers. comm., January 12).
>
> "Migration was once a solution for the Albanians, too. Many people in Preševo went through the same sufferings as migrants"
> (A representative of the local self-government in Preševo, 2018. pers. comm., January 22).

Besides empathy arising from common experience, religious solidarity was particularly emphasized by respondents in Preševo. The fact that the majority of migrants share the same religion with the dominantly Muslim population in Preševo seems to have a strong positive influence on the attitudes of the host community towards migrants.

> "Locals were distanced in the beginning, but everything changed when a local entrepreneur brought 300 burgers to migrants during Ramadan"

---

citizens holding a positive opinion was lower, with only 10% of the respondents reporting a positive opinion at that point (compared to 14% in the autumn of 2016) (Group 484 2017).

> (An employee of the Commissariat for Refugees and Migration working in the reception/transit centre in Preševo, 2018, pers.comm., January 22).

However, while emphasizing the importance of the religious factor in Preševo, one of the respondents emphasized that there were three different Islamic communities there, not all sharing the same level of compassion towards migrants transiting or staying there.

> "The Salafist community here did not help as everybody else did. Migrants were traitors, to them"
> (An activist of a Preševo-based NGO, 2018, pers. comm., January 22).

In addition to reasons which seem to be arising from solidarity, another important factor which constantly reappeared in comments on the positive attitudes of the local populations in all four cities and municipalities was the economic benefit which the host population — or at least some of its segments — has gained from the ongoing migrant crisis. The migrant crisis has significantly impacted the economies of the affected local communities since a significant number of new jobs was opened in the government-run reception centres, but also in a number of newly-opened small businesses, such as exchange offices, barbershops or fast food restaurants. In addition, local grey and black markets also flourished, according to respondents, since illegal taxi drivers and rental services, but also smugglers and drug traffickers, seem to have found ways to take advantage of the situation.

Finally, what seems to particularly contribute to the prevailing positive or at least neutral attitude towards migrants is a perception widely shared in all four local communities that the migrants are only "people in trouble passing by," and therefore represent a temporary problem. Once again, recent opinion polls indeed confirm that the majority of people in Serbia perceive migrants as someone whose stay in their country is certainly temporary and will end in the near future (Group 484 2017, 33).

> "People are not particularly happy that they are here, but everybody knows that they don't want to stay"
> (A representative of the local self-government in Obrenovac, Belgrade, 2018, pers. comm., January 17).

Nevertheless, in addition to these drivers of positive local attitudes, there are several drivers of seemingly rising and occasionally escalating resentment of the local populations towards migrants (Fondacija Ana i Vlade Divac, 2017). Far ahead of all other concerns of the local population in all four communities seem to be those of a security nature. While the spectrum of locals' security-related complaints is rather wide, according to respondents, the majority of those complaints are directed against allegedly frequent robberies, thefts and damage done to personal property by migrants. Since most of these criminal charges remain unresolved and the damage unreimbursed, citizens' dissatisfaction grows, occasionally escalating into direct physical clashes with migrants. What further contributes to such a situation is the fact that the immediate media reports on these incidents are often written in a sensationalistic manner, while the results of investigations are almost never later covered in the media, thus allowing the rumors to become the "truth" that only reinforces the existing prejudice and fears among the locals.

> "People started blaming migrants for everything. Whatever bad happens, regardless where, they attribute it to migrants. They interpret the news however they want. For example, when a woman was killed on the train at the train station in Belgrade, everybody was convinced that migrants did it even though no migrants were arrested for this"
> (A representative of the local self-government in Belgrade, 2018, pers. comm., January 21).

Local discontent with positive discrimination of migrants in their local communities underpins some other frustrations of the locals, as well, including those of an economic nature. According to respondents from all four cities and municipalities, complaints about migrants receiving abundant aid instead of the poor in Serbia can often be heard.

> "People often complain that migrants are being tolerated for things for which a local would go to prison. This is somewhat true"
> (A representative of the local self-government in Subotica, 2018, pers. comm., January 12).

> "Migrants go and sell the aid which they received on the local green market and do not pay the fees. Locals then come to me and ask me why they have to pay the toll and migrants don't"
> (A representative of the local self-government in Šid, 2018., pers. comm., January 12).

Those and similar economic concerns come immediately behind the security ones on the list of host communities' grievances. The attitude particularly noticed among the representatives of the local governments in Preševo, and, to a lesser extent in Šid, was that the municipality itself had not sufficiently benefited from the crisis, in a way that the "payback" for the hospitality offered was not adequately rewarded by both national and international donors. This perception of unfairness seems to be strong enough to cause a potential shift in the positive attitudes of local populations in the future.

> "Preševo was not sufficiently praised for its hospitality, we were not honored by the central government. [...] So much money was invested into the camp, and so little money was invested in the municipality. We now have huge problems with water restrictions and waste disposal. If a new wave of migrants come, no welcome policy in Preševo. Forget it!"
> (A representative of the local self-government in Preševo, 2018, pers. comm., January 22)

Regardless of whether it is grounded in a factual situation or not, this perception of unequal and unfair redistribution of "gains" seems to fall on the ground of already existing cleavages in the ethnically divided society of Preševo, threatening to contribute to local frictions.

> "The Serbs got all the jobs in the reception center and Albanians very few. That's not fair"
> (A representative of the local self-government in Preševo, 2018, pers. comm., January 22).

Perhaps unexpectedly, societal security concerns related to the different ethnicity and religion of migrants do not seem to rank high on the list of concerns and complaints of concerned and angry citizens. However, the fact that this issue was most vocally raised by local populations in autumn 2017 when it was decided that migrant children would go to regular schools, indicates that the so far relative absence of openly expressed fears of mostly Muslim migrants can be to a great extent attributed to the aforementioned prevailing opinion that the migrants' stay in Serbia is only short-term. The most massive protest of this kind was held in Šid in September 2017 (ANSA 2017; N1 2017).

> "Parents heard rumors that migrant children would pray during the lectures, that migrant children should not be touched with a left hand, and similar misinformation, and started protesting".
> (A representative of the local self-government in Šid, 2018, pers. comm., January 12)

Most of the parents' concerns which motivated the protest in Šid in autumn 2017 seem to have disappeared as soon as the school year started, since none of their fears regarding the "diseases which migrant children could spread" and the possibility of "migrant children praying during lectures" came true. One of three reception centers in Šid was, however, already closed as a result of the protest.

Right-wing extremists and political parties

While every new election cycle in countries across Europe confirms that the recent mass migration wave has greatly contributed to the expansion of right-wing extremism in Europe, it seems that the situation in Serbia is somewhat different since the migrant crisis has hit the top of the agenda of the main Serbian right-wing extremist organizations and right-wing parties only rather sporadically. While all the main right-wing organisations in Serbia, including *Srpski narodni pokret 1389, Srpski Obraz, Srpski narodni pokret Naši, Zavetnici, Nacionalni srpski front, Srpska liga*, etc., expressed some anti-immigrant and anti-Islamic attitudes, none of them had any strong and constant campaign against migrants in Serbia.[8] Moreover, the anti-immigrant activities of many of them, according to the

---

8   For more insights on the activities of the Serbian right-wing organizations, including those related to the current migrant situation in Serbia, see Ivanović, Marko, and Wentholt in this volume.

content published on their websites and social media, as well as according to their public appearances, weakened very soon upon the outbreak of the crisis — almost immediately after the government officially adopted the "no border closure" migrant policy.

The most vocal anti-immigrant appeal came from *SNP Naši* and *Srpski Obraz,* which announced a protest called, "Against the EU plan to settle 400,000 migrants in Serbia" in late August 2015, calling on people in Serbia to stand up against the EU's (unfounded) plan to turn Serbia into a "a collection center for hundreds of thousands of people with completely different cultural heritage, lifestyle habits and worldviews, whom our country can neither feed nor dress, let alone control" (Naši 2015). Even though this protest was banned by the authorities, another protest named "NO to dictatorship" was held a couple of days later by the same organizations, addressing the migrant crisis as well (NoviMagazin 2016). Nevertheless, while anti-immigrant stances were very loud and clear, no call for violence against migrants was heard from the speakers, and instead migrants were referred to as "unfortunates" who were the victims of the EU policy.

> "We, the Serbs sympathize with the sufferings and torment of every nation, but this issue will have to be solved by the EU and NATO member states, since they caused this humanitarian catastrophe" (Naši, 2015).

A similar anti-immigrant protest was announced by *Srpski Nacionalni Front* in October 2016 but was again banned by the authorities. Reacting to the ban, one of the organizers strongly refused to accept the label "fascist," justifying such attitude by referencing the similar anti-immigrant policy of numerous political parties in Europe:

> "Today, it is extremely stupid to call some people fascists if they have an anti-immigrant stance. Is Viktor Orban a fascist? I would not say so. Being against migrants does not make anyone a fascist. The ideology of blood and soil is not a controversial point at all, it is used by political parties in Europe for centuries" (Slobodna Evropa 2016).

Similar references to the correctness and efficiency of anti-immigrant policies in some European countries reappeared during all interviews with representatives of right-wing organizations, pointing to the strong echo which the rise of populism, nationalism, and xenophobia throughout Europe seems to have on the political scene in Serbia.

Different to the prevailing attitudes of the general population among whom societal security was not ranked as the greatest concern, all respondents from right-wing organizations emphasized either the "threat of the rise of Islam" in general or in relation to the "shrinking Serbian population."

> "A small number of us, the Serbs, is born, and a lot of us die. If they come and stay, what is our future in our own country?"
> (A leader of one of the Belgrade-based right-wing organization, 2018, pers. comm., January 19)

The inability of their successful integration into Serbian society due to different religious and cultural habits was also stressed by almost all in this respondent target group. Even though this concern was most often expressed in relation to the whole migrant population, some respondents were eager to emphasize that there were differences among migrants and that some are more acceptable than others.[9]

> "We do not have much against the Syrians. They are well educated and clean. We don't want the Afghans, they are uncivilized"
> (A member of a Belgrade-based right-wing organization, 2018, pers. comm., January 17).
>
> "It is fine for families to stay, but how do you explain the fact that 99% of people are young, male, military capable?"

---

[9] Similar attitudes seem to exist among the general population as well, since according to one of the recent opinion polls, there is "a strikingly positive attitude towards refugees from Syria, based primarily on a significantly higher degree of compassion, a human attitude towards people who have gone through the suffering and misery of a civil war, but also because of their behavior, which is mostly perceived as highly civilized" (Group 484 2017, 17). The survey adds that "Syrians are perceived as cultural and emancipated, and Afghans are uncivilized, prone to theft, unhygienic and violent behavior. The first group is usually associated with the idea of "real refugees" – people who have been forced to leave their country due to war and violence, which is strongly opposed to the idea of migrants who are perceived as only in search of a better life" (Group 484 2017, 33).

(A leader of one of major Belgrade-based right-wing organizations, 2018, pers. comm., January 19).

The urgent need for tighter controls was, nevertheless, emphasized by all of the respondents. They all said that a more rigorous security vetting system was needed in order to prevent terrorists from transiting or staying in Serbia, so Serbia "could avoid the destiny of Paris." Talking about the threat of terrorism, one of the respondents directly pointed to the possibility of radicalization of migrants living in Serbia, explaining such a possibility in mainly religious terms:

> "They are violating the rules of their religion and that must cause some frustrations among them. Islam is a violent philosophy and who knows how they can react. In Islam, there are no "international relations," only war"
> (A member of a one of the leading right-wing political parties, 2018, pers. comm., January 25).

The possibility of such development was supported by the reference to the "history of the Roman Empire", but also to "the experience of Serbia with Muslims in our region, in Bosnia and Kosovo."

> "Serbia was the first country to fight ISIS in the 1990s, here, in our own neighborhood [note: referring to Bosnia]"
> (A member of a Belgrade-based right-wing organisation, 2018, pers. comm., January 17).

In addition, the urgent need for separating "economic migrants" from "genuine refugees" was also raised, pointing to the growing potential for further radicalisation of right-wing activists towards migrants in Serbia, due to their firm belief that those migrants currently staying in Serbia were not forced to flee, but were only in search of a better life.

Finally, when asked what could potentially lead to their stronger reaction in relation to the migrant crisis in Serbia, most respondents gave one of these two reasons: the decision of the Serbian government to permanently resettle migrants in Serbia (while some said that they would not accept a single migrant, others said that a small number would be acceptable, but only "if they agreed to integrate into our culture"), and the decision of the EU to cut the funds for the migration crisis in Serbia, which would transfer all the burden to the people in Serbia who "did not cause the Syrian war."

Nevertheless, explaining what kind of action they would organize in those situations and invite people in Serbia to follow, respondents explicitly refused violence as an option. While expressing his disappointment with the absence of a "stronger reaction" from the citizens, one respondent stressed that he would not want to see a stronger reaction against migrants themselves, but against the Serbian government. An extraordinary remark was made by a respondent who said that "no wall should be built on the border with Macedonia since a part of Macedonia is Serbian, and a serious state policy should not abandon our people there," thus showing how a seemingly tolerant attitude could actually hide some harbored nationalistic beliefs.

The impact of the migrant crisis on Serbian right-wing political parties has been similarly moderate since no new right-wing political party has emerged out of the migrant crisis, while the majority of the existing ones have not put the migrant policy at the forefront of their appeals even during election campaigns. The most active right-wing parties in relation to the migrant issue have been *Dveri* and the Serbian National Party, followed by the Serbian Radical Party, all expressing some kind of anti-immigrant attitudes. The most radical attitudes could have been heard from the representatives of the Serbian National Party, which has actively advocated for the construction of a wall on the Serbian borders with Hungary and Macedonia from the very beginning of the crisis and continues urging the closure of the reception centers in northern Serbia and Obrenovac, Belgrade, often not hesitating to equate their arrival with the "invasion of jihadists" (Srpska Narodna Partija, 2016). *Dveri* has also been active during the entire course of the crisis, drawing attention to the potential risks which the migrants' stay in Serbia evokes—from personal and property security ones to those related to the potential change of the ethnic structure of the Serbian population. They have on several occasions strongly advocated against the opening of new centers, as well as against the recent adoption of the local action plans for the improvement of the position of migrants in the affected local communities (Dveri 2018). Finally, the Serbian Radical Party has on several occasions urged a stricter migrant policy, primarily advocating against the positive discrimination of migrants in comparison to the poor people in Serbia, but also pointing to the alleged rise in the criminal rate in those municipalities where migrants live. Nonetheless, except for the petition for the closure of the reception center in Obrenovac, Belgrade, launched by the Serbian National Party (Srpska Narodna Partija 2017), which ended without success, the mentioned parties have not made any serious attempts to mobilize stronger public support for the expulsion of migrants from Serbia so far.

Preventive measures

Maintaining direct contact with citizens seems to be the main way through which the representatives of local governments strive to prevent the rise of anti-immigrant attitudes among the local population. By directly responding to citizens' concerns, local representatives have a chance to provide citizens with accurate information, thus preventing all sorts of rumors to fit into already existing prejudice and fears among the local population. Direct talks with citizens are, according to the majority of respondents, a significantly better way of informing citizens on the migrant situation than the media, since media often give "either too sensationalistic or too general statements."

> "When I talk to them directly I can explain them how wrong they are… Sometimes I even twist their generalizations against them, perhaps by telling them that a number of migrants are Christians. And, it works"
> (A representative of the local self-government in Obrenovac, Belgrade, 2018, pers. comm., January 17).

Moreover, while considering an active media campaign as a potential way of preventing the rise of negative attitudes among the local population, one of the respondents from Belgrade expressed his deep doubts about the potential impact of such an attempt, convinced that "any stronger positive campaign would make the locals angrier" (a representative of the local self-government in Šid 2018, pers. comm., January 12). Nonetheless, most of the respondents agreed that more effective inclusion of media would contribute to the prevention of radicalization among local populations, but only if handled carefully. Recognizing the importance of professional media reporting on the migrant situation in Serbia, the Commissariat for Refugees and Migration, as well as several non-governmental organizations engaged in migration response in Serbia, organize different workshops for journalists in which journalists are educated on important terminology, informed on the most important developments in regard to the migrant situation in Serbia, or even taken to visit the asylum and transit centers.

In addition, various national and international stakeholders fund and implement numerous joint sport, cultural, art, and social activities aimed at decreasing the social distance between the local population and migrants, which—although not labelled as counter-radicalization measures—undoubtedly strengthen the host communities' resilience to all kinds of radicalism or violent extremism directed towards migrants (Đorđević 2017). Nevertheless, while some of these initiatives and programs predate the most recent migrant crisis and some are more recent, the room for maneuver for activities aimed at social inclusion of migrants into local communities seems to remain rather limited, since Serbia still identifies itself exclusively as a transit country. What could, however, happen while the discussions on successful inclusion of new migrants into local communities are put "on hold" is that the unaddressed resentment among both local and migrant population rises, making the risk of their mutual radicalization even more likely.

Discussion and conclusion

A better understanding of the extremely complex linkage between mass migration and VERLT can hardly be gained without a constant and vigilant search for country-specific and context-specific empirical evidence on the factors which contribute to the susceptibility of the affected population to turn to radical ideas or means. Only empirically-based knowledge can draw avenues for adequate policy adaptations aimed at preventing and countering further polarization and radicalization in each specific society. The case of Serbia is extremely valuable for discussions on mass migration-related VERLT since it sheds light on a rather different sort of protracted situation in comparison to the majority of the previous and ongoing refugee and migrant crises. The fact that migrants do not want to stay in Serbia, do not want to or are not able to return to their countries of origin, but continue to hope and try to find a way to move on towards Western Europe, creates an ambiguous status quo in which the maneuver for taking clear action with both the migrant population and the host government is narrowed. While this study's evidence on the initial consequences of this situation needs to be supplemented by continued and more focused research before any ultimate claims on mass migration-related VERLT in Serbia are made, it does provide a solid basis for some preliminary conclusions.

The first is that the grievances which the existing literature views as the main factors contributing to the migrants' vulnerability to VERLT are indeed present among migrants staying in Serbia. After enduring different hardships before and during their journeys, the migrants currently staying in Serbia feel additionally frustrated for not being able to move onwards, instead being forced to live in a limbo with no prospects for any change in the near future. Those frustrations are further exacerbated by different abuses they continue suffering when trying to leave Serbia illegally — all potentially contributing to their susceptibility to turn to violent ideas and means. Nevertheless, while incidents do occur, it seems that the majority of migrants' misbehaviour have not been motivated by some ethnic, religious, or other sectarian resentments against either the local population or other migrants, but have instead been driven by some more "banal" reasons of material, economic, and criminal nature, perhaps further stirred by the use of psychoactive substances. Therefore, even though the resentment of the migrants in Serbia seems to be high and growing, the nature of the incidents involving them seems to provide grounds for an optimistic belief that the radicalization among migrant population currently staying in Serbia is not a high-level threat at this moment.

The general impressions of those working directly with migrants also seem to support the conclusion that the potential for radicalization among migrants in Serbia is not alarmingly high, often attributing such belief to the migrants' short stay in Serbia and to their gratitude to the Serbian state and people for hospitality offered. While this evidence should not be taken for granted, it does resonate well with the existing literature, since many authors emphasize that "people who have just escaped civil war, oppression or poverty are unlikely to be interested in attacking the very society that has given them safety and the opportunity for a fresh start" (Schmid 2016, 50). Nevertheless, even such theoretical positions need to be taken with caution in the case of Serbia, since they are usually based on the assumption that first-generation migrants are "busy building a new existence for themselves and their children and have little time for politics or religious extremism" (Schmid 2016, 50), which is not the case in Serbia where migrants still live in a limbo between not wanting to stay and not being able to move onwards. Therefore, while the still prevailing belief that their stay in Serbia is only a temporary standstill on the way towards a better future has so far represented the main generator of migrants' hope and determination to endure, it cannot last forever.

The second claim which could be made based on the presented evidence is that the potential for radicalization among the local population in the most affected communities is also real, but not alarmingly high. The evidence seems to indicate that the majority of the general population in the affected communities have prevailingly positive or neutral attitudes towards migrants, but that a significant proportion of them also has various fears and concerns which need to be addressed if further polarization and radicalization is to be prevented. Different from what the majority of the literature predicts and the current situation in many affected European countries confirms, the fact that the majority of migrants are Muslims does not seem to be the major driver of fears and negative attitudes among host populations even in the Serbian municipalities with a very small Muslim population. However, the fact that the greatest concerns and dissatisfactions of the local population and local authorities are expressed in security and economic terms by no means indicates that the potential for radicalization of host communities does not exist, especially since the socioeconomic situation in the majority of affected local communities is quite bad. Nevertheless, what seems to largely, if not decisively, prevent the rise of negative attitudes among concerned citizens is the still prevailing belief that migrants are not going to stay in Serbia, but are being only temporarily held on their way towards Western Europe. On the other hand, the evident recent and continuing changes in such perceptions are exactly what warns against the underestimation of the existing potential for further polarization of the affected host communities in Serbia.

While the absence of stronger resistance among the general population could perhaps be explained by an apparently significant level of solidarity among the population in Serbia (based on their own refugee history, religious history in predominantly Muslim municipalities, or based on the long history of multiculturalism in some areas), or by some economic benefits which the local population has gained as a consequence of the migrant crisis, the absence of more radical attitudes and activities of the existing far-right and extremist organizations and political parties in Serbia is somewhat surprising, particularly when compared to the alarming situation in some of the long-standing democracies in Europe. What can be noticed from the presented findings is that the anti-immigrant activities of some far-right organizations were constantly banned by the authorities, while the activities of the others vanished very soon after the government adopted its own version of the "open door" policy towards migrants—all indicating that the government currently does have both formal or informal control over the right-wing extremists' activities in relation to the migrant situation in Serbia. However, since barely any evidence indicates that the Serbian government has adopted a responsible and systematic approach towards countering both registered and unregistered groups of extremists, not much space is left for grounded optimism that their current anti-immigrant policy is simply "not-now-violent" (Schmid 2014, 15).

Even though the majority of migrants have been living in Serbia for months and often over a year, Serbia is still sticking to the exclusively humanitarian approach, aimed at meeting migrants' basic needs, which was adopted at the very beginning of the crisis when migrants were indeed only transiting the country in the short term. While some initial updates of this approach have been made, the security issues, including those of VERLT, do not seem to be climbing up the humanitarian agenda. While the National Strategy and Action Plan for Combating Terrorism for the Period 2017–2021 acknowledges that "mass migration of the population, along with the porosity of the borders, can be used for the smooth movement of terrorists and can favor the rise of extremism both in transit and in the countries of the final destination" (Republika Srbija, 2017), no changes in this regard seem to have occurred on the agenda of the relevant stakeholders. None of the actors included in migration management, except the police and security services who are not constantly present in the reception centers, have any specialized knowledge on identifying early signs of radicalization among migrants, nor are any kind of early warning mechanisms in place. Accordingly, none of the stakeholders implements any kind of activities aimed at systematically preventing VERLT among migrants living in the centers, thus missing the chance to make all migrants more resilient to all kinds of radicalization and extremism. The prevention of radicalization among host communities is not satisfactory either since the current government's approach does not allow a more active policy of social inclusion, thus limiting direct contact between migrants and local populations. Since direct contact is considered the most effective measure for preventing and overcoming prejudice, stereotypes and fears that feed off radical ideas and projects, the lack of such contact, accompanied by often sensationalistic media reporting, can only contribute to further polarization of the affected local communities.

Therefore, while the current potential for radicalization among and between migrant and local populations seems to be promisingly low in Serbia, it can easily and rapidly elevate if these risks are left without adequate mechanisms for their monitoring and timely prevention, which now seems to be the case. The prevailing perception of only a temporary character of the current situation is still constraining the ongoing micro-radicalizations from escalating, but occasional (and more and more frequent) outbursts of resentment signal that patience is waning on all sides, urging the attention of all stakeholders included in the management of the migrant situation in Serbia. If all of them, led by the government of Serbia, do not step up from the initial humanitarian approach in order to address the potential security and development challenges which the changing dynamics of the migrant crisis may cause, the threat of reciprocal radicalization will go from minor to inevitable in a very short period of time, particularly if a number of migrants decide to stay in Serbia indefinitely. Stepping up from a humanitarian approach must not, however, mean the abandonment of humane treatment of migrants in Serbia or any kind of violation of their human rights; on the contrary, the adoption of policies should strengthen the protection of those very rights by addressing not only immediate needs and risks, but the long-term ones as well.

References

AlJazeera. 2017. "U Srbiji ostalo zaglavljeno 2000 izbjeglica." *AlJazeera*, 15. March 2016. http://balkans.aljazeera.net/vijesti/u-srbiji-ostalo-zaglavljeno-2000-izbjeglica.

ANSA. 2017. After initial "no", refugee kids admitted to Serbian schools. Accessed 7 May 2018. http://www.infomigrants.net/en/post/5191/after-initial-no-refugee-kids-admitted-to-serbian-schools.

Bailey, Gavin and Edwards, Phil. 2017. "Rethinking 'Radicalisation': Microradicalisations and Reciprocal Radicalisation as an Intertwined Process." *Journal of Deradicalisation*, 10, 255–281.

Beta. 2016. "Commissariat: Over 900,000 Migrants Pass Through Serbia." *Beta*, 18 December 2016. https://beta.rs/en/49084-commissariat-over-900-000-migrants-pass-through-serbia.

BIRN. 2017. "Serbia Police Remove Protesting Refugees From Croatia Border." *Birn*, 27 December 2017. http://www.balkaninsight.com/en/article/serbian-police-removes-protesting-refugees-from-border-12-27-2017.

Boček, Tomáš. 2017. "Report of the fact-finding mission by Ambassador Tomáš Boček, Special Representative of the Secretary General on migration and refugees to Serbia and two transit zones in Hungary". Council of Europe. Accessed 7 May 2018. https://rm.coe.int/report-of-the-fact-finding-mission-by-ambassador-tomas-bocek-special-r/16807be041

Cinoglu, Huseyin and Altun, Nurullah. 2013. "Terrorism, Interntional Migration and Border Control." *European Scientific Journal*, 9 (20), 100–114.

Danish Refugee Council. 2017. "Life in Limbo." Accessed 11 May 2018. https://drc.ngo/news/life-in-limbo-new-report-covers-the-situation-for-refugees-in-serbia.

Davey, Jacob and Ebner, Julia. 2017. *The Fringe Insurgency: Connectivity, Convergence, Mainstreaming of the Extreme Right*. London, Washington DC, Beirut, Toronto: ISD.

Đorđević, Biljana. 2017. *Community-based approaches to inclusion of migrants and refugees in Serbia*. N/a.

Dveri. 2018. "Pretraga: Migrant." Accessed 15 February 2018. https://dveri.rs/pretraga?keyWord=migrant.

Eatwell, Roger. 2006. "Community Cohesion and Cumulative Extremism in Contemporary Britain." *The Policital Quarterly*, 77 (2), 2014–2016.

Fekete, Liz. 2009. *A Suitable Enemy: Racism, Migration and Islamophobia in Europe*. London, New York: Pluto Press.

Fondacija Ana i Vlade Divac. 2017. "Stavovi gradjana Srbije prema izbeglicama i izbegličkoj krizi." Accessed 11 May 2018. https://www.divac.com/upload/document/kljucni_nalazi_istrazivanja_.pdf.

Group 484. 2017. "Citizens" attitudes towards refguees and migrants in the migration affected municipalities and recommendations for building social cohesion, European Union Support to Migration Management in the Republic of Serbia, European Union, Republic of Serbia." Accessed 15 September 2018. http://www.rs.undp.org/content/dam/serbia/undp_rs_QualitativeResearchCitizensAttitudesMigrants_Aug 2017.pdf.

Haider, Huma. 2014. "Refugee, IDP and host community radicalisation." Accessed 11 May 2018. http://gsdrc.org/publications/refugee-idp-and-host-community-radicalisation/.

Hakimi, Hameed. 2016. "Understanding the Drivers of Migration to Europe: Lessons from Afghanistan for the Current Refugee Crisis." Accessed 11 May 2018. https://www.bertelsmann-stiftung.de/en/publications/publication/did/understanding-the-drivers-of-migration-to-europe/.

Institute for Economics & Peace. 2018. "Global Terrorism Index 2017.| Accessed 11 May 2018. http://visionofhumanity.org/app/uploads/2017/11/Global-Terrorism-Index-2017.pdf.

Jelačić, Miroslava. 2016. *Izazovi migrantsko-izbegličke krize iz ugla OCD*. Belgrade: Grupa 484

Koser, Khalid. 2015a. "How Migration can help fight violent extremism." Accessed 11 May 2018. https://www.weforum.org/agenda/2015/02/how-migration-can-help-fight-violent-extremism/.

Koser, Khalid. 2015b. *IDPs, refugees, and violent extremism: From victims to vectors of change*. Washington D.C.: Brookings.

Koser, Khalid. 2016. "Migration and Violent Extremism in Contemporary Europe, The World Bank." Accessed 15 February 2018. http://blogs.worldbank.org/peoplemove/migration-and-violent-extremism-contemporary-europe.

Koser, Khalid and Cunningham, Amy. 2016. "Migration, violent extremism and terrorism: Myths and realities." *Global Terrorism Index 2015*. Institute for Economics and Peace, 83–85.

Koser, Khalid and Cunningham, Amy. 2018. "World migration report 2018." In *World migration report 2018*, 1–364. Geneva: IOM.

Lenos, Steven. 2016. "The refugee and migrant crisis: new pressing challenges for CVE policies." Accessed 11 May 2018. https://ec.europa.eu/home-affairs/sites/homeaffairs/files/what-we-do/networks/radicalisation_awareness_network/ran-papers/docs/ran_ex_post_paper_the_refugee_and_migrant_crisis_en.pdf.

Lukić, Vesna. 2016. "Understanding Transit Asylum Migration: Evidence from Serbia." *International Migration*, 54 (4), 31–43.

Martin-Rayo, Francisco. 2011. "Countering Radicalization on in Refugee Camps: How Education an Help Defeat AQAP." Accessed 15 February 2018. https://www.belfercenter.org/sites/default/files/legacy/files/Countering_radicalization-Martin-Rayo.pdf

Maunganidze, Otilia Anna. 2017. "Migration and violent extremism: a chain of false links?" Accessed 15 February 2018. https://issafrica.org/iss-today/migration-and-violent-extremism-a-chain-of-false-links.

Mc Sweeney, Damien Patrick John. 2012. "The Protection and Security of Vulnerable Populations in Complex Emergencies using the Dadaab Refugee Camps in the North Eastern Province of Kenya as a Case Study." PhD diss., University College Cork, Ireland.

McKeever, David and Chowdhury Fink, Naureen. 2017. "Complexity of Migration, Terrorism, and Violent Extremism Needs Comprehensive Response." Accessed 15 February 2018. https://theglobalobservatory.org/2017/11/migration-terrorism-violent-extremism-needs-comprehensive-response/.

Milić, Nikolina (ed.). 2017. *Unaccompanied and Separated Children in Serbia*. Belgrade: Belgrade Centre for Human Rights.

MSF. 2017. "Games of Vioelnce: Unnacompanied Children and Young People Repeatedly Abused by EU Member State Border Authorities." Accessed 11 May 2018. https://www.msf.org/sites/msf.org/files/serbia-games-of-violence-3.10.17.pdf.

Mullins, Sam. 2016. "Terrorism and Mass Migration: Terrorists rarely exploit refugee networks to conduct attacks", *Per Concordiam*, 7 (1), 22–30.

Sovilj, Miodrag. 2017. "Roditelji u Šidu protiv dece migranata u školama." *N1*, 11 September 2017. http://rs.n1info.com/a317284/Vesti/Vesti/Roditelji-u-Sidu-protiv-dece-migranata-u-skolama.html.

Naši. 2015. "Svi na protest protiv naseljavanja 400.000 migranata u Srbiji!" Accessed 15 February 2018. https://nasisrbija.org/svi-na-protest-protiv-naseljavanja-400-000-migranata-u-srbiji/.

Ninamedia Reserach. 2015a. "Stav građana Bogovađe, Tutina, Sjenice, Banje Koviljače i Krnjače (Beograd) prema tražiocima azila." Accessed 15 September 2018). http://www.kirs.gov.rs/docs/izvestaji/Stav gradana Bogovađe Tutina Sjenice Banje Koviljače i Krnjače Beograd prema traziocima azila jun 2015.pdf.

Ninamedia Reserach. 2015b. "Stav građana Republike Srbije prema tražiocima azila." Accessed 15 September 2018. http://www.kirs.gov.rs/docs/aktuelno/Stav gradjana Republike Srbije prema traziocima azila CATI maj 2016.pdf.

MŽ. 2016. "Obraz i Naši protestovali protiv vlade Aleksandra Vučića (FOTO)." *NoviMagazin*, 6 September 2015. http://www.novimagazin.rs/vesti/obraz-i-nasi-protestovali-protiv-vlade-aleksandra-vucica-foto. Accessed 5 August 2018).

Oxfam. 2017. "A DANGEROUS "GAME": The pushback of migrants, including refugees, at Europe"s borders." Accessed 11 May 2018. https://www.oxfam.org/sites/www.oxfam.org/files/file_attachments/bp-dangerous-game-pushback-migrants-refugees-060417-en_0.pdf.

RAN. 2016. "Tackling the challenges to prevention policies in an increasingly polarised society". Accessed 15 September 2018. https://ec.europa.eu/home-affairs/sites/homeaffairs/files/what-we-do/networks/radicalisation_awareness_network/ran-papers/docs/tackling_challenges_prevention_policies_in_increasingly_polarised_society_112016_en.pdf.

Ratković, Milijana. 2017. "Migrant crisis and strengthening of the right wing in the European Union", *Megatrend revija*, 14 (3), 47–60. doi: 10.5937/MegRev1703047R.

Reitano, Tuesday and Tinti, Peter. 2017. "Reviewing the Evidence Base on Migration and Preventing and Countering Violent Extremism (P/CVE)". Accessed 15 September 2018. http://ct-morse.eu/wp-content/uploads/2017/04/EU-CVE-Migration-.pdf.

Republika Srbija. 2017. *Nacionalna strategija za sprečavanje i borbu protiv terorizma za period 2017-2021. godina*.

Schmid, Alex P. 2014. "Violent and Non-Violent Extremism: Two Sides of the Same Coin?" The Hague: International Centre for Counter-Terrorism. Accessed 15 September 2018. https://www.icct.nl/download/file/ICCT-Schmid-Violent-Non-Violent-Extremism-May-2014.pdf.

Schmid, Alex P. 2016. *Links between terrorism and Migration*. The Hague: International Centre for Counter-Terrorism. Accessed 15 September 2018. https://www.icct.nl/wp-content/uploads/2016/05/Alex-P.-Schmid-Links-between-Terrorism-and-Migration-1.pdf.

Komarčević, Dušan. 2016. "Marš ultradesničara Beogradom: Za 'Veliku Srbiju', protiv migranata." *Slobodna Evropa*, 16 September 2016. Accessed 15 February 2018. https://www.slobodnaevropa.org/a/beograd-mars-ultradesnicari-migranti/27990127.html.

Srpska Narodna Partija. 2016. "Popović: Srbija u opasnosti da postane poligan za divljanja dzihadista!" Accessed 15 February 2018. http://srpskanarodnapartija.rs/popovic-srbija-u-opasnosti-da-postane-poligon-za-divljanje-dzihadista/.

Srpska Narodna Partija. 2017. "SNP pokrenula peticiju za izmeštanje centra za migrante iz Obrenovca." Accessed 15 February 2018. http://srpskanarodnapartija.rs/snp-pokrenula-peticiju-za-izmestanje-centra-za-migrante-iz-obrenovca-video/.

Sude, Barbara, Stebbins, David and Weillant, Sarah. 2015. "Lessening the Risk of Refugee Radicalization: Lessons for the Middle East from Past Crises." Accessed 15 February 2018. https://www.rand.org/pubs/perspectives/PE166.html.

TNS Medium Gallup. 2017. "TNS Medium Gallup Attitudes towards the Impact of the Refugee and Migrant Crisis in Serbia's Municipalities." Accessed 17 April 2018. http://www.rs.undp.org/content/dam/serbia/Publications%20and%20reports/undp_rs_QuantitativePublicOpinionSurveyAttitudesMigrant_Aug2017.pdf.

UNHCR. 2018. "Serbia January 2018 Snapshot." Accessed 15 February 2018. https://data2.unhcr.org/en/documents/download/61805.

United Nations. 2015. *Combating violence against migrants: Criminal justice measures to prevent, investigate, prosecute and punish violence against migrants, migrant workers and their families and to protect victims*. Vienna: Unitted Nations Office on Drugs and Crime.

Inclusive Intangible Cultural Heritage Protection as an Instrument for the Prevention of Identity-Based Conflicts: The Case of Serbia

Miloš Milenković

Introduction[1]

Intangible cultural heritage (ICH) consists of a core set of symbols, beliefs, and practices that are self-perceived key representations of the cultural (ethnic, religious, etc.) identity of a given social group. The global framework for ICH research and protection is the UNESCO Convention for the Safeguarding of the ICH. According to its structure and policy, UNESCO holds its member states/Convention parties accountable for ICH safeguarding. However, minority ICH is underrepresented in the national registers of states worldwide and profound dissatisfaction regarding this phenomenon has been reported, including in Southeastern Europe. Comparative anthropological and allied research indicate that minorities perceive the underrepresentation of their ICH elements as yet another way that nation-states purposively marginalize and suppress their identities for the purpose of their assimilation.

The goal of the research whose findings are being reported in this chapter was to set the stage for development of recommendations for a novel approach to the prevention of violent extremism and radicalization leading to terrorism (VERLT), based on inter-sectoral cooperation in the domains of ICH research, safeguarding, and promotion. The proposed shift engages academic knowledge on identity construction and application in conceptualizing and implementing policies oriented toward using ICH safeguarding as a

---

[1] The author is grateful to both known (V. Perry, S. Petkovska, N. Wentholt and D. Marko) and blind peer reviewers for their critique and recommendations. This study is partly supported by Serbian MoESTD project no. 177017.

peace-building, not conflict-provoking, tool. This chapter also reflects on the existing model of outreach as probed, and suggests reasons and ways it could be applied throughout the Western Balkans.

UNESCO's model, originally aimed at the worldwide preservation of cultural diversity, could de facto become its antithesis if there is not significant change on how elements of ICH are selected, researched, nominated, and safeguarded. This type of identity politics by nation-states should be preventively addressed as a potential trigger of VERLT, especially in the region of the Western Balkans. In that regard, an inclusive approach to ICH safeguarding as a VERLT-prevention tool is proposed. There is no evidence in the existing academic literature that the inclusive approach to ICH proposed hereafter has been used for that goal.

As the safeguarding of ICH in Serbia is delegated to a network of state-governed institutions in which ethnologists and anthropologists play pivotal roles, this chapter also includes a proposal for a paradigm shift. It is argued that the standard anthropological practice of deconstructing the reality of cultural identities is counter-indicative to the prevention of identity-based conflicts. As communities regularly perceive their identities as objective and real, and see a critical social theory approach to their customs and traditions as confusing, non-academic, illegitimate, or even offensive, a shift is proposed from constructionist criticism, typical in anthropology, to realist instrumentalism, typical of ethnology. Both UNESCO's and general anthropological aims could be better achieved by using concepts and methods typical of the humanities instead of the apparatus of critically oriented social science.

This chapter reflects existing work commenced in Serbia, proposing a shift in the politics and ethics of research on and safeguarding of minority ICH. As concluded, minority representatives should be preventively included in ICH protection in order to counterbalance the cultural fundamentalism, identity-based social segregation, irredentism, and separatism that solidly contribute to the emergence of VERLT. The development of sound guidelines for opening up ICH classification in a more inclusive manner is advocated, especially to those elements of ICH forming the core of cultural identities of national minorities and ethnic groups.[2]

Since 1989, UNESCO has protected intangible cultural heritage (ICH), a set of distinctive markers of a community's identity consisting of language and oral traditions, beliefs and rituals, performing arts and festivities, traditional social practices and knowledge systems (formerly known as folklore, customs or traditional culture, among other terms). Following the "Recommendation on the Safeguarding of Traditional Culture and Folklore," (1989)[3] UNESCO considers ICH an essential source and key manifestation of cultural identity, especially of indigenous peoples and minority communities. These recommendations were followed by the program "Safeguarding and Promotion of Intangible Heritage" (1993) that led to the "Convention for the Safeguarding of the Intangible Cultural Heritage" (2003), calling for the full participation of communities and individuals who create, maintain, or manage ICH (Art. 15).

The UNESCO "Convention on the Protection and Promotion of the Diversity of Cultural Expressions" (2005) suggested that states should envision culture and identity as inextricably linked to quality of life, and also encouraged the entwinement of cultural and developmental policies. The 2005 Convention is especially relevant to organizations such as the OSCE and the Council of Europe, as it emphasizes the recognition of, and dignity and respect for all cultures as well as individuals belonging to them, reiterating the principle of equality and emphasizing the fair treatment of minority and indigenous cultures by states. However, ICH protection throughout the Western Balkans has followed the 2003 (and not the 2005) Convention (which should be analyzed in a separate study).[4]

---

2   As culture and identify formation reflect a number of personal and broader community factors, see also Wentholt's and Dević's chapters in this volume. Given that young people are often at specific risk to the threats of online radicalization, consult also an additional analysis of this phenomenon in the chapter by Marko.

3   http://unesdoc.unesco.org/images/0008/000846/084696e.pdf#page=242.   [Date accessed January 14, 2018]

4   For now, it remains unknown to what extent minority ICH elements are underrepresented in neighbouring countries; comparative research in that regard would be an

The Republic of Serbia ratified the UNESCO Convention for the Safeguarding of ICH in 2010,[5] vowing to protect, preserve, document, develop, and treasure its ICH, consisting of elements selected solely at the national level. ICH is defined by the UNESCO Convention for the Safeguarding of the ICH (2003) as "the practices, representations, expressions, knowledge, skills—as well as the instruments, objects, artefacts and cultural spaces associated therewith—that communities, groups and, in some cases, individuals recognize as part of their cultural heritage."[6] In accordance with the Convention, the state launched and governs the Network on the Safeguarding of ICH, which encompasses various institutions and professionals, most of whom are ethnologists/cultural anthropologists. The National Registry of the ICH of Serbia was established as a key Convention implementation mechanism. Since 2012, 37 ICH elements have been recorded and inscribed in the Register as protected.[7] A summary list is included below:

Table 1:   37 elements in the ICH Registry in Serbia

1.	Patron saint's day ("Slava")	20.	Kaval playing
2.	Prayer – St. George's Ritual	21.	Slovak naïve art painting
		22.	Lazarica procession
3.	Belmuž – traditional shepherd dish made of unripened cheese	23.	Wooden flask making
		24.	Vuk's convocation
		25.	Ojkača singing
		26.	Urban songs from Vranje

---

    asset in prospective efforts to develop an effective VERLT prevention tool that connects cultural identity and collective security.

5   https://ich.unesco.org/en/state/serbia-RS. [Date accessed January 14, 2018]

6   http://unesdoc.unesco.org/images/0013/001325/132540e.pdf (Article 2). [Date accessed January 14, 2018]

7   See http://www.nkns.rs/ for information on institutions and other actors included in the Network, and also on the number and type of elements inscribed, with detailed descriptions. At the end of 2014, the "Slava" (the traditional Serbian celebration honouring each family's patron saint, and a key marker of ethnic identity for the majority of the Serbian (Orthodox) population) was inscribed on the Representative List of the ICH of Humanity by UNESCO, being the first ICH element nominated by Serbia at the international level. Since then, another ICH element, the "Kolo" (a traditional collective circle dance, an important element in festivities, religious and social events, such as weddings, throughout the Balkans and typical of many ethnic communities between the Caucasus and the Adriatic) has also been inscribed.

4.	Ritual of making and lighting farmer candles	27.	Easter ritual of Guarding Jesus Christ's Tomb
5.	Making of Pirot hard cheese	28.	Pirot-style storytelling
6.	Rug-making in Pirot	29.	St. George
7.	Filigree craft	30.	Plum brandy
8.	Craft of stonemasonry	31.	Coppersmith's trade
9.	Pazar meat pie	32.	Rug-making in Stapar
10.	Zlakusa pottery	33.	Skill and craft of making kajmak
11.	Kosovo-style embroidery	34.	Cipovka – skill and craft of making traditional bread in Vojvodina
12.	Singing accompanied by gusle		
13.	Groktalica-style singing	35.	Cooking of Žmar
14.	Clamor-style singing	36.	White fairy
15.	"Era" style humor	37.	St. Peter's candles
16.	Kolo dance		
17.	Rumenka-style kolo-dance		
18.	Bagpipe playing		
19.	Pipe-playing practice		

However, many ICH elements symbolic of the traditions of national minorities and minority ethnic groups in Serbia await inscription in relevant registries—out of 37, only 10% count explicitly as minority heritage, with some 10% more counting as the shared heritage of multicultural regions. Although implementation of the Convention has been more than satisfactory according to UNESCO's formal evaluation standards,[8] special attention is now needed in relation to the highly sensitive issue of minority cultural heritage protection—as ongoing ICH safeguarding practices, until now, have been directed primarily toward majority (Serbian Orthodox) cultural heritage markers.

As ICH is transmitted over generations and is a dynamic system, it is constantly being re-created by communities and groups in interaction with the natural world and their history, and also with other communities, the state, civil society, and international institutions or companies. ICH has the potential to provide communities with strong "objective" markers of identity and continuity, self-perceived as "authentic" and unquestionably "real." In that regard, it

---

8   https://ich.unesco.org/en/state/serbia-RS. [Date accessed January 15, 2018]

represents the core set of symbols and practices of a community's identity, recently deemed "worth dying for" in the Western Balkans' context, as a vulnerable region still recovering from the identity-related wars of the 1990s. As such, ICH is extremely prone to political manipulation, particularly in sensitive contexts of majority/minority relations.

Although "[s]trongly condemning the destruction of cultural heritage and religious sites, including the targeted destruction of UNESCO World Heritage sites, by terrorists, foreign terrorist fighters associated with ISIL and other terrorist groups," (p. 2) the OSCE Ministerial Declaration on Preventing and Countering Violent Extremism and Radicalization that Lead to Terrorism (Belgrade 2015) doesn't mention intangible aspects of heritage at all and there are no indications that ICH as a core of identity is considered a relevant sensitive issue.[9]

Keeping in mind that each community perceives their intangible cultural heritage as the core of their collective identity, its inclusive protection calls for urgent preventive intervention. Ongoing research among various "identity stakeholders" indicated that initial efforts by Serbian ethnologists and anthropologists to facilitate dialogue, strengthen institutional infrastructure, devise policy recommendations, and raise awareness among both stakeholders and decision-makers have proved successful yet insufficient, so relevant outreach and implementation activities are recommended in the final section.

Conceptual framework

The 2003 Convention opened a series of heated debates over the role of states and the position of minority cultures within the safeguarding system, especially in regard to pursuing cultural rights. Recent critical heritage studies and anthropology of cultural heritage scholarship has been largely reserved toward the safeguarding of ICH as promoted by the international policy framework. Diverse

---

9   http://www.osce.org/cio/208216?download=true. [Date accessed January 14, 2018]

literature points to heritage as a political means and an economic resource. While this chapter will not review critical heritage studies as a distinct field, the anthropological stance on cultural heritage protection could be summarized as follows:

- ICH protection is flawed; it contains inherent, structural errors in its treatment of cultural identity as a real phenomenon (and not as a social, historical, media or even market construct); in reality, cultural identity is a construal, a hybrid that is subject to constant (re)interpretation and transformation — it should not be constrained in "cultural islands" (Eriksen 2001; Nielsen 2011);
- The very *processes* of selection and safeguarding are cultural artefacts, too; they are neither objective nor natural; they are in fact processes of imposition and seclusion. Those who map, research, collect, digitize, promote and manage elements of ICH do not just make heritage accessible, but in reality, actively shape, re-create or even create it (Bortolotto 2010);
- Although often successfully rationalized by secondary functions (economic, political, educational, etc.) "heriditisation" involves latent homogenization of both majority and minority populations. Projects of exclusion of unwanted heritage are always implied in its background, although media, educators, and administrators regularly invoke the process's conceptual inclusivity. They disguise ICH as a tool of legalized omission, i.e., seclusion (Bendix et al. 2013; Kurin 2007). Kurin summarized the key issue a decade ago in a manner that deserves the following detail (Ibid., 13):

> "The biggest problem with government control over ICH safeguarding efforts is one of freedom and human rights. In many countries around the world, minority cultural communities do not see government as representing their interests — particularly when it comes to their living cultural traditions and their vitality as living, dynamic communities. Historically, government efforts have often been aimed at eliminating cultural practices — a native religion, a minority language, particular rites, certain instruments, and so on. Important parts of the ICH… may be seen as opposing government positions and practices… Government inventories of cultural practice may seem too much like cultural registries — officializing and de-officializing cultural practice, and allowing of all sorts of misuse of the

information. Having the government in charge of ICH activities could create uneven relationships of power between cultural regulators and cultural practitioners, where the latter may feel there was undue intrusion into the life of their community."

- Minorities of various types (ethnic, religious, racial, sexual, political, etc.) are left out of the standardization practices that create societal culture; these practices support a particular historical/heritage representation based on the mythologized past and culture of a dominant community or social/political elite, who seek to oppress counter-memories and to exclude interpretations of history or culture they find inappropriate (de Cesari 2010; Jackson 2010);
- Comparative global research points to the widespread instrumentalization of UNESCO's global authority to achieve, locally, goals that are opposite to its intentions (on Bolivia, see Sarrazín Martínez 2015; Japan, see Love 2013; South Africa, see Beresford 2012; and in Sweden, see Klein 2014; comparative, see Kearney 2009);
- It is unfortunate that the UN and other international organizations unwittingly have legitimized both legal and developmental ethnocide-like practices through heritage exclusion. This has enabled elites to oppress minorities via a mechanism through which they at the same time gain international authority and recognition. It verges on an internationally legalized violation of minority cultural rights (Logan 2007; Silverman and Ruggles 2007);
- Apart from general problems with intercultural relations, equally pressing is the issue of addressing minorities as homogeneous entities rather than recognizing their own internal diversity and complexity in the field (Oldham and Frank 2008; Brumman 2015; Brumman and Berliner 2016).

Generally, long forgotten in museums, galleries, and libraries, or confined to humanities classrooms, cultural heritage since the millennium has been among the crucial instruments used by the international community, especially in post-conflict regions, for reconciliation and peace building, for developing a common sense of belonging, and for promoting mutually respectful dialogue in culturally complex societies. It is, thus, dominantly interpreted through non-conflict and post-conflict lenses. This millennial conceptual integration of heritage in politics, is declared through three distinct but interconnected conventions—the Convention for the Safeguarding of the Intangible Cultural Heritage (UNESCO, 2003), the Framework Convention on the Value of Cultural Heritage for Society (also known as the Faro Convention; Council of Europe 2005), and the Convention on the Protection and Promotion of the Diversity of Cultural Expressions (UNESCO 2005). By promoting the intangibility of heritage and relating it to present identity struggles, emphasizing community engagement, and even opening the possibility of individuals' notions of having an identity to be respected, these documents provide a basis for yet *another* wave of politicization of heritage by diverse actors—communities, ethnic political parties, nation-states, and civil society and international organizations. The insistence on diversity, plurality, and inclusivity throughout the texts of these conventions has been envisioned as meeting the Western Balkans' pressing need for a post-war framework by which culture could be used as an integrative instead of a disintegrative tool.

Yet, insisting on intangibility has de facto resulted in movement away from contested monumental heritage, and has also challenged minority communities' efforts to stabilize their position within the societal cultures of the post-Yugoslav states. By defining heritage as practices, representations, expressions, and skills (knowledge, objects, artefacts, cultural spaces, instruments, etc.) prone to re-creation in space and over time by communities (and even individuals) as social actors, these conventions introduced insecurity and indecisiveness into the realm of ethno-politics at the moment in which minority communities in particular needed a firm basis for recognition (in what was later recognized as a segregative multicultural mode). Although many heritage scholars had waited for decades for conservative, static, or "authentic" notions of heritage to be replaced by a notion that recognizes its processual and construal character, it is precisely non-realist epistemology, embedded in the conventions, that made them potential sources of identity-related problems (instead of solutions).

It turned out that an instrumentalist approach to heritage as a means for (and source of) identity construction and management led to adverse effects. Communities are now competing with each other and being torn by the very instrument that was supposed to address their needs in the realm of the politics of culture and identity. It is precisely this conflicting nature of heritage safeguarding that should be kept in mind while reflecting on the relationship of identity to security. It was premature to suppose that the implementation of UN conventions or Council of Europe declarations that stress shared culture and customs would somehow automatically contribute to peace building between separated communities. In reality, both inter- and intra-cultural rifts emerged precisely because the opportunity arose to wage war by another (heritage) means (especially when the "politics of numbers" is at play, see Keil and Perry 2015).

There is another aspect of heritage protection that should be of concern for a socio-cultural approach to security issues. For the last two decades, heritage has been considered not only as an instrument of peace building and reconciliation but also as an instrument of economic development. In that regard, it is also perceived as a resource. This economically oriented perception of heritage should concern VERLT-prevention discourse since the economy is among the most typical drivers of political manipulation of ethnic and religious differences. Those in power within communities who manage to define what heritage is and claim that they are its "bearers" (i.e., owners, from the native's point of view) can, without corrective and preventive measures, profit more than those who are actually members of a given community (Brown 2004; Comaroff and Comaroff 2007). And that profit would not only be confined to direct monetary remuneration (say, to trade in ethnic or traditional goods, or control lucrative tourist sites), but to all other "fiscal" aspects of a given community's folk life (such as regular membership fees to ethnic political parties or to religious communities, interests gained through regional, local or even state government coalitions, etc.). Consequently, the power to define what is symbolic for a given community's identity is at the same time political and economic—an interplay of appropriation and commodification (Greene 2004; Feltault 2006; Smith 2006; Bendix 2009). It is through processes of monetization, and not only weaponization, that the notion of heritage got its appeal at the turn of the millennium.

It is important to underline that the notion of development, and particularly of its sustainability, was the key streamlining goal to which UNESCO directed its aims at the time of the passing the Convention. This is explicitly relevant for the overall aim and specific goals of the OSCE and allied international organizations seeking to promote human and cultural rights, as it was not only the preamble-like discourse (with "sustainability" a kind of buzzword at the time), but the concept of sustainable development that was underlined throughout the Convention, but which somehow faded in the following years (especially with the rise of the competitive and commercial aspects of heritage promotion, with "lists" and spectacular media coverage) (Hafstein 2009; Askew 2010; Frey and Steiner 2011). Nevertheless, it is precisely that notion of heritage as a tool for facilitating communities' involvement in shaping their own destinies that the OSCE and others could and should follow. In that regard, let us remember that Article 2.1 of the Convention (which defines ICH) requires parties to consider only ICH that is attuned to international human rights instruments and remain vigilant that ICH foster mutual respect among communities, groups or individuals. Nevertheless, the implementation of this vision wasn't without complications, as it was not clear at the time (nor is it now) how exactly to facilitate ICH's contribution to sustainable development in practice except through tourism (for the level of indecisiveness, see Bertacchini, Saccone, and Santagata 2011).

As a follow-up to the Convention, the operational directives were broadened (and adopted by the Intergovernmental Committee for the Safeguarding of ICH in 2015) and linked to the UN General Assembly's 2030 Agenda for Sustainable Development (an action plan, strictly speaking, that integrates culture with three major dimensions of sustainable development—economy, society, and the environment). The new chapter 6 of the operational directives stresses that ICH is a cornerstone of community well-being, and a resource for communities' socially and culturally rooted responses to developmental challenges. It directs states toward the utility of ICH in pursuing sustainable development and motivates them to integrate this renewed, detailed notion of ICH safeguarding into their other agendas (policies, strategies, action plans, etc.). This is especially important, as the change to the operational directives recognizes what scholars have stressed as the most vulnerable aspect of the 2003 Convention — the conflict-related dimensions of heritage safeguarding and its potential for discrimination (especially in fostering exclusion and inequality).

As Kisić (2016) demonstrated for the Western Balkans in general (focusing on monumental heritage, but raising the issue's relevance for ICH as well), mainstream heritage policy is unable to manage the existing heritage dissonance. It is especially inept at addressing conflicting claims over heritage in order to foster political goals, such as promoting dialogue or reconciling the (recent) past. Her research confirmed that the proclaimed heritage-for-reconciliation paradigm, which solely focuses on the unproblematic and uniting aspects of heritage protection, fails to grasp dissonant or completely opposing interpretations of culture, identity and the past, thus neglecting the power of safeguarding discourse to reproduce conflicting memories and related cultural practices.

The same goes for prominent EU institutional constructions of "European heritage," which have been shown to regularly exclude the "uncommon" heritage of European citizens of non-European origin (Nic Craith 2012) or populations, such as European Muslims, that are historically connected to "non-European" civilizations (Milenković and Pišev 2013). Among the many challenges that countries of the region face in the post-war period, the most destructive one may be the political re-invocation of ethnic and religious identities, which could potentially be (mis)used in a number of ways including what has been termed culturalized EU conditionality (Milenković and Milenković 2013). In that regard, scholars (e.g., Lixinski 2011) caution that safeguarding, as instituted, suspends the inherently discordant nature of heritage by its superficial bureaucratic uniformity, relying on political agendas to exclude specific ("problematic") ethnic, religious, and national identifications and to reduce heritage to its apolitical aspects. As a result, heritage-based conflicts between communities have been reduced and substituted by rifts over the control of heritization *within them*, which is also of importance for VERLT prevention and allied activities.

Analysis of Bosnia and Herzegovina (Perry 2015) showed the persistence of ethnic instead of civic notions of nationality and a kind of race to put as many ethnic-specific elements of monumental heritage into relevant national registers, calling for objective heritage evaluation criteria based on expert (scientific and technical) evaluation rather than ethno-political motivations (198). This is consistent with the *intentions* of international development instruments' perspective of heritage as common ground and a means for reconciliation. My position is different, yet complementary — I see ethno-politics as a rooted mode that is unlikely to change in the foreseeable future. Therefore, I recommend form (or process) rather than content as the focus in encouraging the introduction of inclusive ICH safeguarding. The post-war reconciliation potential of heritage safeguarding should be modified in order not to challenge persistent primordial constructions and collective loyalties while *simultaneously* introducing the goals of the international development instruments. Instead, bearers of ethnic identity politics should be motivated and trained to transform into bearers of ICH who safeguard and promote their heritages through common and unified practices, under the administration of UNESCO, and not as rivals in yet another identity war.

Perry (2015, 204) concludes:

> "Whether culture will ultimately be valued as an integrative tool, or used solely as a disintegrative tool, remains to be seen."

Yet, anthropological research worldwide demonstrates that national culture as represented by ethno-cultural identity is (outside of academic discourse) mostly a *disintegrative* tool. Therefore, we should not try to transform culture into something that it is unlikely to become. Instead, we should apply integrative tools to mend our already disintegrated society (and UNESCO's methodology is a promising one). This leads to the key research question: if it seems more conducive to achieve liberal ends by conservative means, what, then, would constitute true inclusion when it comes to ICH safeguarding?

My research shows that the vast majority of the population considers identities to be as real as the objects and processes of the physical world and are confused, annoyed, or insulted by a constructivist approach to what they consider the essence of their social being (Milenković 2014b). Outside of academia, and more precisely in the policy realm, there are not many who think like Benedict Anderson or Marija Todorova. Therefore, a socio-cultural approach to VERLT prevention should consider that standard anthropological and allied analyses of the social construction of cultural identities (and their instrumentalization in identity politics) are for the most part offensive for those who believe their identity is a natural kind. In that regard, standard scientific approaches to issues of identity construction are not only ineffective, they are counter-indicative in terms of international peacekeeping and stability-building efforts.

With that in mind, I undertook research on cultural heritage as the core of cultural (national, ethnic, religious) identities, realizing that this is exactly UNESCO's approach to community engagement in cultural heritage protection (though not explicated). This is why I have formulated notions such as "non-fundamentalist essentialism" (Milenković 2014) and "non-antirealist relativism" (Milenković 2013) in order to adapt ethnological-anthropological analyses to engage with extra-academic stakeholders on the "identity market" in social reality (i.e., not confined to the academic ivory tower). The present analysis of VERLT-prevention potential of inclusive ICH confirms my previous research results—an older, ethnologically realist, strategically essentialist ethnological paradigm, instead of anthropology's strong commitment to social theory, proved to be more conducive for understanding how it might contribute to policies and programs aimed at the use of UNESCO-based ICH safeguarding as a legitimate tool that would not be an intrusive and or provocative mechanism while preventing identity-based conflicts.

Explanation of data collection processes and findings

This particular research was designed to tackle the relevance of the previously unaddressed issue of the underrepresentation of minority heritage in the Serbian national ICH register to contribute interdisciplinary research on cultural identity and security in the OSCE's VERLT framework. Documents, literature, and institutions related to ICH research, protection, and instrumentalization were analyzed in order to address the data from a novel angle by reflecting on the findings (or lack thereof) from previous research on identity politics in the domain of ICH protection, including academic and policy analyses of relevant literature, legislation, governance practices, and existing policies either explicitly or tacitly related to the political instrumentalization of key symbols of identity by ethnic groups and identity-based communities in Serbia. Other data, such as individual and focus group interviews, participation in symbolically important minority festivities, and dialoguing with officials on national and regional levels was also used, as this analysis is linked to ongoing multi-year research by the author. This longitudinal qualitative research approach connects three types of inquiry that were not previously related:

1. research on the transformation of cultural identities in Serbia in the context of the EU accession process;
2. the search for a sustainable, inclusive model of minority intangible heritage safeguarding; and
3. the possibility of regulatory reform in the evaluation of social sciences and humanities research that would direct scholars toward knowledge-to-policy agendas.

This particular research was not based on filling the gaps in the literature model but on addressing the immediate issue model, as the issue to be tackled was already identified during previous research (Milenković 2016) and contextualized in the existing comparative literature on the anthropology of cultural heritage/critical heritage studies. Moreover, it is found that most of the professionals in ethnology, anthropology and related disciplines are familiar with the way that identity-related issues are typically addressed within institutions (dominated by ethnic and religious majorities). The data collection process was greatly affected by the strong will to challenge the deeply rooted and institutionally widespread distinctiveness of engagement that is a) purely academic, b) professional, and c) political/civil society organization (CSO) led.

The previous fieldwork, whose findings are here interpreted in the light of VERLT prevention, was conducted within projects of the Serbian Ethnological and Anthropological Society, the Department of Ethnology and Anthropology (Faculty of Philosophy, University of Belgrade), and my own research as a consultant with the Fund for an Open Society, PERFORM Helvetas or projects funded by the EU.[10] Over the period 2011–2017, the author visited minority communities throughout Serbia to discuss the issue of ICH with national minority representatives, with a special focus on the Bosniak, Jewish, and Roma minorities. This longitudinal research, together with ongoing desk research, in general and in light of this VERLT-relevant study, contribute to the basis for these findings and recommendations. Selected findings (2011 onwards) from this

---

[10] These include: "Towards evidence-based development of the guidelines for research evaluation policy reform in Serbia and the Western Balkans (PERFORM Helvetas 2017), "Protection of human rights by preservation of cultural heritage of Bosniaks in Sandzak region, Serbia (2017, Consortium of civil sector organizations, funded by Open Society Fund), DRIM – Danube Region Information Platform for Economic Integration of Migrants (2017, Slovenian Academy of Arts and Science and Partners, funded by Interreg/European Union), "Preservation, affirmation and development of Bosniak culture and tradition: Civic and cultural sector perspectives (2016, Consortium of civil sector organizations, funded by Open Society Fund), "Identity policies of European Union: Modification and Implementation in Republic of Serbia," (2011-, University of Belgrade, Faculty of Philosophy, funded by the Ministry of education, science and technological development of Serbia) "Toward Efficient Policies and Improvement of Life conditions for Roma People in Serbia – Social and Cultural Issues," (2015, SUPRAM, funded by Fund for an Open Society, Serbia) "Social and cultural potential of Roma people in Serbia," (2014, University of Novi Sad, Faculty of Philosophy, funded by Fund for an Open Society, Serbia) "Cultural Heritage within the Serbia EU Accession Framework," (2013–2015, Ethnological and Anthropological Association of Serbia and Lawyers Committee for Human Rights – YUCOM, funded by the Ministry of Culture and Media of Serbia) "Cultural Identities as Intangible Cultural Heritage," (2011–2012, University of Belgrade, Faculty of Philosophy, MCM) "Social Sciences and Humanities as Intangible Cultural Heritage." (2010–2011, Ethnological and Anthropological Association of Serbia, MCM)

ongoing multi-sited fieldwork were analyzed from the perspective of VERLT prevention. However, the findings could also be used in other collective and interdisciplinary efforts if the opportunity arises.

The first and most immediate effect of these projects was that representatives of official institutions caring for cultural heritage protection and minority representatives agreed to work jointly on the register of various intangible cultural heritage elements, which symbolizes the cultural identities of both the Serbian majority and the country's minorities (these studies focused on the Bosniak, Roma, and Jewish minorities, all perceiving themselves as autochthonous, and the first two without a nation-state). This effect of the research is a research finding in itself and points to a "means-as-ends" methodology typical of engaged anthropology.[11] Before this knowledge-to-policy intervention, these elements were normally gathered, analyzed, and safeguarded in a segregative multiculturalism framework, mainly by national councils of national minorities, and without the common framework UNESCO's ICH represents. However, the process is still in its early stages and there is no conclusive evidence that the jigsaw effect will be maintained — systematic action, education, and incentives are needed instead of simply enthusiasm and goodwill. The process is also occurring within a narrow circle of academic specialists, museum professionals and eminent stakeholders instead of reaching the wider population, which would impact its ability to contribute to peace and stability, as elaborated in the final section.

Interpretation of major findings

The UNESCO 2003 Convention was ratified in Serbia in 2010. However, ICH has been left on the margins of Serbia's legal and policy landscape and is still not addressed by its laws, strategies and policies on culture and media or human and minority rights. The national registry of ICH elements has been instituted and the National

---

11 For detailed elaboration of means-as-ends reflexive logic, and processual and engaged research methodology see: Bennet (1996); Simonović and Milenković (2008) and Hyland and Bennet (2013).

Network for ICH safeguarding is fully functional as per the Convention, yet the operational directives raise a number of possibilities and suggestions regarding the need for increased sensitivity to minority heritage by state parties that remain unaddressed.

Among professionals engaged within the Network it is found that the existing ICH safeguarding model "removes" ethnic and religious attributions from the safeguarding framework, probably in order to not provoke community tensions and to invoke the notion of co-constructing a common heritage in a proclaimed intercultural society instead. The fieldwork among community stakeholders showed that the prevailing approach is dissonant with the ways they have been fighting for recognition of their particular identities and pursuing collective rights in the cultural island/segregated multiculturalism mode. Not surprisingly, stakeholders interviewed are interpreting this dissonance not as a peace-making intercultural effort by ethnologists/anthropologists striving to relax the highly sensitive realm of ethnic relations, but as possible/probable *assimilationist* work aimed at creating a common societal culture in Serbia that would be tacitly dominated by heritage closely related to Serbian ethnicity and orthodox Christianity. This is the most relevant finding of the research, and one that needs further reflection and intensive policy work with both "sides" in the process of ICH safeguarding.

There are, however, more technical findings—not explicitly political but nevertheless sensitive. Most important among them is the fact that, although in terms of bureaucratic functioning the Network is very well set professionally, its work is not so publicly visible and almost unknown outside of specialist circles. Minority interviewees were mostly unacquainted with the Network at the beginning of earlier field research in 2011, and although the research itself contributed in a way to making the minority ICH safeguarding more visible, even now a large portion of politically influential minority representatives still needs to be informed, motivated, and creatively engaged. This presents a problem similar to that of the paradoxical underrepresentation of minority ICH elements in the registry—those who are unacquainted feel excluded. Exclusion may lead to dissatisfaction, and dissatisfaction could likely lead to the perception of intentional marginalization (which can be interpreted as oppression).

Although regional museums and cultural institutions (such as town libraries and cultural centers) have ICH protection competencies delegated to them, during fieldwork it was found that interviewed professionals working there are not formally included in safeguarding activities. The most striking finding, however, is that most of the stakeholders are still not aware that UNESCO provides them with the opportunity for their culture and identity to be formally researched, safeguarded, and promoted through publicly funded activities, and that the state is formally obliged to do so. A variety of stakeholders—from local administration, ethnic political parties, CSOs, libraries and cultural centers, museums, media, and research/higher education institutions—were interested in seminars, lectures, open discussions and individual and focus group interviews, with prominent community members showing a clear interest and willingness to pursue UNESCO-instituted activities. However, the pool of attendees didn't include elementary and high school teachers. An important finding, then, is that precisely this category of identity bearers and worldview makers should be included in the education/incentives model, given their influence on youth and the relevance that the VERLT paradigm puts on preventing extremism among younger members of any given population.

It is also found that UNESCO, as a highly respected and external/international actor, could serve as an "intercultural trustee," which is a perception on which relevant domestic bodies, the OSCE and the general international community could base further actions.

It is confirmed that communities are internally divided regarding the question of whether to prioritize ethnically attributed or regional/multicultural ICH elements (this is especially relevant for the Bosniak community). This was found to be interwoven with the architecture of the Network for ICH safeguarding, which was established according to ethnically insensitive administrative regions (with Sandžak being divided into the two districts, with administrative centers in Kraljevo and Užice). As these regions do not overlap with perceived cultural/ethno-political regions, many informants from Sandžak feel the architecture of the Network should change to reflect cultural realities as they perceive them, while Vojvodina *is* already established as a cultural region (which is also reflected in the Network, as there is an ICH coordinator solely for Vojvodina).

Further, the Network is perceived as expert-based yet ethnically biased, as *none* among eight posted coordinators or senior officials is of minority origin or expert in minority cultural heritage. Informants shared the belief that the Network should change in order to reflect ethno-cultural diversity personally, and possibly territorially.

The findings also point to diverse primary interests among interviewees and discussants: those cultural in the strict sense (the Jewish community), more social and oriented to well-being (the Roma community), and ethno-political (the Bosniak community). The most recent research directly connected to VERLT prevention through the research design, was conducted among Bosniak intellectuals, who reflected on 1) the current impediments of the minority ICH elements safeguarding system, especially in terms of underrepresentation; and 2) their needs and expectations regarding the linkage of their cultural heritage and their ethno-political identity. Most interviewees feel their ICH is underrepresented in the national register and that the current system does not reflect their perception of social fairness and political equality. However, a considerable amount of dissatisfaction was a consequence of participants' lack of familiarity with the standards and procedures required, and in some cases, the system was almost completely unknown to what would be apparent stakeholders.

Bosniak intellectuals interviewed perceive their ICH as the core of their collective identity. These findings coincide with those for the general population (cf. Žikić 2011) — cultural heritage and identity are perceived as an integrated set of beliefs, rituals, language, values, and various cultural practices that symbolize the uniqueness of a community in a wider social landscape. However, that does not mean that all of the interviewees were keen to opt for ethnically sensitive ICH protection, as almost half of them agreed that regional heritage should be safeguarded instead, reflecting the multicultural nature of the ethno-politically perceived region of Sandžak. Political activism proved decisive to that regard—those who are active as members of political parties or the national council clearly opted for ethnic attribution and ethnic-based selection of ICH elements for research and safeguarding. It is an indicator, as corroborated by this research, of the highly culturalized nature of politics in the region and that is precisely what this research results are pointing at—politically influential actors tend to position themselves as guardians of their communities' identity (regardless of particular ethnicity). More professionally oriented discussants opt for the simultaneous protection of ethnically and regionally attributed ICH elements.

In both cases, the fear of Islamist radicalization being supported by public figures in the region is exaggerated. The limited cases to date have been considered a fringe phenomenon that would not gain the support of prominent persons in the political and intellectual life of Sandžak, whose interests and hopes lie firmly within ethno-politics as conceived within the Serbian democratic multicultural landscape. None of the persons interviewed over time throughout these noted research efforts considers Islam a repressed religion per se, and their concerns are oriented toward the loss of traditionally based Bosniak cultural identity and folklore, which is a shared concern among ethnically oriented intellectuals generally. Among interviewed Bosniaks in Serbia, there is no "shift from political and economic reforms toward fierce nationalist divisions," as in, for example, Bosnia and Herzegovina (Office of the High Representative 2017, 1). I agree that "in a region where the rule of law remains weak and tensions between communities can be high, any form of anti-democratic extremism is destabilizing and must be combatted…] The threat to the region from radical Islamist ideology should not be overestimated. Too often, it has been portrayed as more prevalent than our evidence suggests. This is counter-productive, particularly when used to heighten ethnic tensions for political gain" (House of Lords 2017, 52). However, my findings point in a different direction. In this case, as opposed to the cultural particularity of the Jewish community or social problems of the Roma people, ethno-politics should be prioritized in the near future. Attention should be focused on preserving cultural heritage and establishing the full cultural autonomy of Bosniaks and their particular ethnicity in Serbia instead of reducing the whole community to the religious aspect of their heritage.

Conclusions and recommendations

Cultural identities based on ethnicity and religion have become distressingly "weaponized" throughout the former Yugoslavia since the 1980s. After the recent turmoil, which included the repeated political destabilization of the Western Balkans, the migration crisis, and the prevailing "end of multiculturalism" public discourse throughout Europe, we face a renewed need for cultural identities' urgent de-weaponization. Previous research clearly shows that de-weaponization is not feasible through mainstream academic deconstructionist notions that deny the reality of collective identification based on ethnicity, religion or "race" and form the dominant approach in the critical social sciences and humanities, particularly in anthropology. Communities throughout the region, and especially minority communities, feel that their underrepresentation in national ICH registers is just another wave of identity suppression. This undoubtedly alarms scholars interested in the relations between identity and security, because sentiments of exclusion and suppression can lead to exclusion, segregation, and fundamentalism that may lead to conditions conducive to radicalism and violent extremism.

These findings support the enhancement of existing levels of inter-sectoral cooperation by various institutions and organizations (professional, academic, political, administrative, and CSO) through a combined incentives-learning model, especially when it comes to integrating minority representatives into the Network for safeguarding ICH in Serbia (or, preferably, the Western Balkans) in order to facilitate intercultural dialogue and reinforce its legitimacy. Promoting and facilitating this dialogical modification of the existing ICH safeguarding network could be based on its programmatic opening to minority representatives, either through formal engagement (for example, by instituting "Standing Minority Representative/s") as civil servant/s or by introducing regional coordinators of minority origin/experienced researchers knowledgeable in particular minority heritages (and, preferably, respected by the relevant community representatives).

Prospective engagement of these "missing stakeholders" should not be confined to periodic, project-based, small-goal activities. It should be, instead, organized within state-governed, regionally or municipally co-funded, stable and respected cultural institutions, such as existing regional museums, libraries, and cultural centers, with close ties to the academic sector. In other words, the problem should be purposively "moved" from civil society and closed professional arenas, to which it has been confined so far, to more established institutions that have recognized cultural functions and with strong social authority.

The establishment of distinct ICH departments, with ethnologists and allied experts of minority origin (or professionally interested in minority ICH) posted, in all regional museums throughout the country, is recommended. That would most likely support sustainable infrastructure for an inclusive network for ICH safeguarding. As this is not common practice worldwide, this model could later be recommended for inclusion in the Register of Good Safeguarding Practices.[12]

An important step toward raising respect for the cultural rights of minorities on the national agenda would be to establish an institution specifically designed for research and the safeguarding of minority heritage. Its form — whether an agency, office or a policy institute, with decentralized structure (in order for its departments to cover all territorially dispersed minorities), or a combined academic/professional institution, also with territorial departments (and able to conduct research and teaching, alongside the administration of minority heritage) — is a technical issue that could be later deliberated. Either way, it should be responsible to the Na-

---

12   https://ich.unesco.org/en/register. [Date accessed January 27, 2018]

tional Assembly and relatively independent of the central government, in order to prevent heritage debates becoming an issue in daily politics.

An independent pressure group should be established to lobby for a law on cultural heritage and bylaws specific to ICH safeguarding; the group would consist of reputable individuals and representatives of the national councils of minorities, academic and cultural institutions, professional associations and prominent politically active NGOs. This law should establish the National Council for Cultural Heritage and corresponding Agency for Cultural Heritage Safeguarding, with executive powers conferred. This should be accompanied with an initiative to broaden the spectrum and definition of heritage in the drafted Strategy of Cultural Development of Serbia 2017–2027, that should emphasize the horizontal harmonization of rules and regulations, as the existing framework is untidy.[13]

Further coordination of existing national minorities' councils, emphasizing the activities OSCE has already commenced in that regard is also highly recommendable. This strategy is crucial given that bilateral EU conditionality has been intertwined with the perceived lack of minority cultural heritage protection and educational needs deprivation (as exemplified in the recent actions of the Republic of Romania and the Republic of Croatia, which could be also expected from other EU member states with national minorities present in Serbia).[14] Cooperation with national councils of minorities is especially important when it comes to (already exercised) identity-based bilateral EU conditionality. OSCE and other international support to prevention in that regard is strongly recommended.

Minority ICH safeguarding, including research, educational, and promotion activities, should be normalized—i.e., not limited

---

13 http://www.kultura.gov.rs/docs/dokumenti/predlog-strategije-razvoja-kulture-republike-srbije-od-2017--do-2027-/-predlog-strategije-razvoja-kulture-republike-srbije-od-2017--do-2027-.pdf. [Date accessed January 27, 2018]

14 http://www.dw.com/en/romania-blocks-serbias-eu-candidacy-for-now/a-15774734; https://www.eurotopics.net/en/171225/croatia-blocks-serbia-s-accession-negotiations. [Date accessed January 27, 2018]

only to specific, dispersed or occasional activities by national councils or NGOs, but incorporated into the regular state-funded programs of cultural institutions and municipal budgets.[15] Safeguarding of minority ICH should not be left solely to devoted individuals or expert groups, or enacted through occasional projects aimed at the research of specific elements or education of selected groups; it should be complemented by stable budgetary placement. As this is quite complicated, due to the fact that national councils of minorities are already allocated resources for exercising cultural autonomy, minority heritage safeguarding should be linked with safeguarding of the cultural heritage at the national level in order for it not to be treated as project-based or occasional, but as a regular, legitimate, and bureaucratized activity.

Since ICH safeguarding opens up new economic possibilities, especially to individuals and families who accept the responsibility of becoming "heritage bearers," the inclusion of a certain number of minority communities' members (preferably by quota, in order not to compromise the system at the very start of its implementation) is recommended in chambers of commerce on the state, regional, and local levels. This economic aspect of heritage need not to be seen as shameful commercialization, but as an important opportunity, especially in economically deprived regions. However, implementers should be mindful of intra-cultural rifts that economic opportunities may cause, and seek informed advice as they proceed.

Segregative multicultural policies that result in an "insularity effect" should be abandoned in favor of intercultural registers, preferably at the regional level. Inclusive intercultural ICH registers would more likely reflect the multicultural nature of both statistical and self-perceived regions, complementary with the central national register that would likely stay dominated by majority/com-

---

15 For examples on national councils activities see: Croatian (http://www.zkvh.org.rs), Bosniak (http://www.bnv.org.rs/wp-content/uploads/2013/01/Strategija-razvoja-kulture-sandzackih-Bosnjaka-u-Srbiji.pdf), Hungarian (http://www.mnt.org.rs), Roma (https://www.romskinacionalnisavet.org.rs/) and Jewish (http://savezjos.org/). [Date accessed January 28, 2018]

mon heritage elements in the future. However, existing multicultural minority-oriented cultural programs should not be abandoned, as swift and unprepared change to an intercultural approach would likely cause unrest and be counterproductive.

As ICH safeguarding is inextricably tied to notions and perceptions of human and minority rights, a community's dignity, and self-/mutual recognition, its inclusive transformation would directly achieve goals suggested by the international community for the Western Balkans. Yet, the fact that the existing legal framework is not harmonized should not be seen solely as an obstacle. On the contrary, the scarcity of legal instruments at the national level opens possibilities for the direct institutional implementation of declarations, conventions, decisions and recommendations by UNESCO, the CoE, OSCE, and other relevant international organizations. Although perfectly harmonized legislation would be an asset and would be an ideal, an approach focused on means-as-ends may be more conducive to the fulfilment of short-mid-term goals.

A combined incentives-learning approach should also be applied in reforming the academic sector, as the value of ICH for security and identity studies should not be left to individual initiatives. Thorough reform of the research evaluation system and pay grade scale in the research sector should include policy-oriented research, especially in the humanities (where it is quite rare), as currently, knowledge-to-policy academic work is devalued. Scholars in public universities and research institutions are reviewed for promotions, salaries, and overall academic standing according to certain "points" defined by rules and regulations that do not recognize knowledge-to-policy publications. This reflects a contradiction between the research assessment indicators and proclaimed strategic goals. While the "value" of research results is measured by their internationalization, the regulatory framework stresses their social utility at national/regional/local levels. In that way, the current evaluation system for the social sciences and humanities community prevents it from having societal impact. Instead, an approach advocated by UNESCO and the CoE, which considers social sciences and humanities (SSH) not only as a research of, but as an integral part of the cultural heritage of a nation/society/community, is something that should be considered by prospective regulatory reform and not confined to a traditional view of academic work.[16]

The issue of legitimacy of social and political reforms is reported as perhaps the most relevant to informants coming from outside of the capital city (or from underrepresented disciplines). They underline that regulation in sectors of culture and media, and research and higher education, had been constantly imposed in a totalitarian manner by bodies (the National Council, field-specific councils, various working groups and committees) that are not balanced in terms of disciplines, regions, gender, and ethnicity. On ethnicity, research conducted in the Sandžak region clearly shows double exclusion or a "minority within minority" position of Bosniak intellectuals, who feel doubly excluded from the regulatory process (both in terms of their professional affiliation as social scientists/humanities scholars, and their ethno-cultural identity). Diversification of participation in education, science and culture related policymaking is recommended, either by introducing a model based on predefined quotas for minorities and geographical regions, or by introducing regional bodies with delegated duties to culturally and socially contextualize what is considered SSH-quality output. Informants belonging to underrepresented disciplines, regions, genders, and ethnicities all concur that excellence in SSH research should be searched for in its relevance. Therefore, introducing regional research assessment panels to valorize the impact of directed SSH research outputs is recommended.

Due to lack of financial resources and a prolonged economic crisis, talented young pupils throughout Serbia are being systematically oriented away from studying the arts and SSH. This is not a purely academic issue but a security-related issue, too, as in just one and a half generations, most minority populations will likely be left without the human resources capable of channeling debates in core

---

16 This is not just some local social issue or fringe problem in evaluation studies; it is directly relevant for centering identity research and safeguarding in peace and stability efforts by international community in the region. Inquiry on the relationship between research evaluation and the societal impact of SSH throughout the Western Balkans would assist OSCE missions, as well, and is highly recommended.

collective identity-related issues such as history, culture or language. Consequently, it is likely that the political instrumentalization of identity-related issues and identity-based conflicts would again be hijacked by ethno-entrepreneurs, religious fundamentalists and the like (as in the 1990s) — thus, the prospect of minority identity politics would be either linked to radicalization or to assimilation (neither of which is an outcome expected by the international development instruments). Further, this means that minority communities would lack the capacity to negotiate sensitive identity-related issues and be more prone to politically adventurous interpretations of heritage (and its lack of safeguarding) that form the basis of prospective VERLT-like behavior. In that regard, preventive work is needed to foresee the cultural and educational needs of smaller/dispersed minority communities in particular, and reorient both school/academic curricula and allocation of resources toward such a goal.

Applied humanities types of research and teaching should be introduced and facilitated, as many of these disciplines hold a wealth of knowledge on historical and cultural heritage of communities at risk for VERLT. The existing policy pressure for sociocultural research to have social impact should be scrutinized, and disciplines like ethnology/anthropology, history, archaeology, the history of art, and language and literature studies should be directed by identity and security policies with more focus and enthusiasm. Both project-based incentives for younger researchers (especially those of minority origin or those focused on minority issues), and institution-based funding of research groups, departments or institutes should be strategically introduced into policy frameworks.

These conclusions and resulting recommendations could be (and in the authors' opinion, should be) developed into the Guidelines for Minority ICH Protection in Serbia, should the opportunity arise. This prospective development seems prudent, in addition to developing a Western Balkans perspective on these issues through joint research activities with individuals, research groups, and institutions from neighboring countries. The European Year of Cultural Heritage (2018) should be considered a "booster" for all of the actions proposed.

If the identity-driven conflicts that have splintered our society and the wider region for decades are to be overcome, identity stakeholders need to be reassured that UNESCO-based cultural heritage protection in Serbia will not become yet another instrument for their marginalization; instead, they should be motivated to participate in acknowledging their own significant cultural practices. If carefully balanced by adding upstanding minority representatives, the ICH safeguarding system could prove to be a powerful instrument for promoting intercultural dialogue and sustaining existing peace efforts. When proven useful, an inclusive registry of ICH might be applied to comparatively relevant contexts, both regionally and around the globe, and be nominated for UNESCO's Register of Best Safeguarding Practices, making this policy intervention a channel through which cultural heritage could be acknowledged for its peacekeeping potential worldwide.

References

Askew, Marc 2010. "The magic list of global status: UNESCO, World Heritage and the agendas of states." In *Heritage and Globalisation*, Labadi, Sophia and Long, Colin (eds.), 19–44. London: Routledge.

Bendix, Regina F. 2009. "Heritage Between Economy and Politics: An Assessment from the Perspective of Cultural Anthropology." in *Intangible Heritage*, Smith, Laurajane and Akagawa, Natsuko (eds.), 253–269. London: Routledge

Bendix, Regina F. et al. (eds.) 2013. *Heritage Regimes and the State (Göttingen Studies in Cultural Property*, Göttingen: Universitätsverlag.

Bennett, John W. 1996. "Applied and Action Anthropology: Ideological and Conceptual Aspects." *Current Anthropology* (Supplement: Special Issue, Anthropology in Public), 37 (1): S23-S53.

Beresford, Alexander. 2012. "The politics of regenerative nationalism in South Africa." *Journal of Southern African Studies*, 38 (4): 863–884.

Bertacchini, Enrico, Saccone, Donatella and Santagata, Walter. 2011. "Embracing diversity, correcting inequalities: Towards a new global governance for the UNESCO World Heritage." *International Journal of Cultural Policy*, 17 (3): 278–288.

Bortolotto, Chiara. 2010. "Globalising intangible cultural heritage? Between international arenas and local appropriations." In *Heritage and Globalisation* Labadi, S. Long, C. (eds.) 97–114. London: Routledge.

Brown, Michael Fobes. 2003. *Who Owns Native Culture?* Cambridge: Harvard University Press.

Brumman, Christoph. 2015. "Community as Myth and Reality in the UNESCO World Heritage Convention." In *Between Imagined Communities and Communities of Practice: Participation, Territory and the Making of Heritage (Göttingen Studies in Cultural Property, 8.)* Adell, Nicolas et al. (eds.), 273–289. Göttingen: Göttingen University Press.

Brumman, Christoph and Berliner, David. 2016. "UNESCO World Heritage—Grounded." In *World Heritage on the Ground: Ethnographic Perspectives (EASA Series, 28)*, Brumman, Christoph and Berliner, David. (eds.), 1–34. Oxford: Berghahn Books.

Comaroff, John L. and Comaroff, Jean. 2009. *Ethnicity, Inc.* Chicago: University of Chicago Press.

Council of Europe 2005. *Framework Convention on the Value of Cultural Heritage for Society.* https://rm.coe.int/1680083746.

De Cesari, Chiara. 2010. "Creative Heritage: Palestinian Heritage NGOs and Defiant Arts of Government." *American Anthropologist*, 112 (4): 625–637.

Eriksen, Thomas Hylland. 2001. "Between Universalism and Relativism: A Critique of the UNESCO Concept of Culture." In *Culture and Rights: Anthropological Perspectives.* Cowan, Jane. K., Dembour, Marie-Bénédicte, and Wilson, Richard A. (eds.), 127–148. Cambridge: Cambridge University Press.

Feltault, Kelly. 2006. "Development Folklife: Human Security and Cultural Conservation." *Journal of American Folklore*, 119 (471): 90–110.

Frey, Bruno S. and Steiner, Lasse. 2011. "World Heritage List: Does it make sense?" *International Journal of Cultural Policy*, 17 (5): 555–573.

Greene, Shane. 2004. "Indigenous People Incorporated? Culture as Politics, Culture as Property in Pharmaceutical Bioprospecting." *Current Anthropology*, 45 (2): 211–237.

Hafstein, Valdimar. Tr. 2009. "Intangible heritage as a list: from masterpieces to representation." In *Intangible Heritage* Smith, L. Akagawa, N. (eds.) 93–111. London: Routledge.

House of Lords Select Committee on International Relations. 2017. "The UK and the future of the Western Balkans. 1st Report of Session 2017–19 (HL Paper 53)." https://publications.parliament.uk/pa/ld201719/ldselect/ldintrel/53/53.pdf.

Hyland, Stanley E. and Bennet, Linda A. 2013. "Responding to community needs through linking academic and practicing anthropology: An engaged scholarly framework." *Annals of Anthropological Practice*, 37 (1): 34–56.

Jackson, Antoinette. 2010. "Changing Ideas about Heritage and Heritage Management in Historically Segregated Communities." *Transforming Anthropology*, 18 (1): 80–92.

Kearney, Amanda. 2009. "Intangible Cultural Heritage: Global Awareness and Local Interest." In *Intangible Heritage* Smith, L. Akagawa, N. (eds.) 93–111. London: Routledge.

Keil, Soeren and Perry, Valery. 2015. "The Politics of Numbers in the Post-Yugoslav States." *Contemporary Southeastern Europe*, 2 (2): 43–49.

Kisić, Višnja. 2016. *Governing Heritage Dissonance: Promises and Realities of Selected Cultural Policies*, Amsterdam: European Cultural Foundation.

Klein, Barbro. 2014. "Cultural Heritage, Human Rights, and Reform Ideologies: The Case of Swedish Folklife Research." In *Cultural Heritage in Transit: Intangible Rights as Human Rights*. Kapchan, Deborah A. (ed.), 113–124. Philadelphia: University of Pennsylvania Press.

Kurin, Richard. 2007. "Safeguarding Intangible Cultural Heritage: Key Factors in Implementing the 2003 Convention." International Journal of Intangible Heritage, 2: 10–20.

Lixinski, Lucas. 2011. "Selecting Heritage: The Interplay of Art, Politics and Identity." *The European Journal of International Law*, 22 (1): 81–100.

Logan, William S. 2007. "Closing Pandora's Box: Human Rights Conundrums in Cultural Heritage Protection." in *Cultural Heritage and Human Rights*. Silverman, Helaine and Ruggles, D. Fairchild (eds.), 33–52. New York: Springer.

Love, Bridget. 2013. "Treasure hunts in rural Japan: Place making at the limits of sustainability." *American Anthropologist*, 115 (1): 112–124.

Milenković, Miloš. 2013. "O izvorima antirealističkog pogleda na relativizam u sociokulturnoj antropologiji" ("On the sources of an anti-realist view of relativism in sociocultural anthropology"). *Antropologija* 13 (3): 27–47.

Milenković, Miloš. 2014. *Antropologija multikulturalizma: Od politike identiteta ka očuvanju kulturnog nasleđa (Anthropology of Multiculturalism: From identity politics to cultural heritage safeguarding) (Etnološka biblioteka, knj. 80)*, Beograd: Odeljenje za etnologiju i antropologiju Filozofskog fakulteta Univerziteta u Beogradu i Srpski genealoški centar.

Milenković, Miloš, 2014b. "A Return to 'Courtly Science'? Towards a Consequential Consideration of the Future of Ethnology/Socio-cultural Anthropology in Serbia and Croatia." *Studia ethnologica Croatica*, 26 (1): 5–23.

Milenković, Miloš. 2016. *Povratak nasleđu: Ogled iz primenjene humanistike (Return to Heritage: An Essay in Applied Humanities) (Etnoantropološki problemi – monografije, knj. 3)*. Beograd: Filozofski fakultet i Dosije studio.

Milenković, Miloš and Milenković, Marko. 2013a. "Serbia and the European Union. Is the "Culturalisation" of Accession Criteria on the Way?" in *EU Enlargement: Current Challenges and Strategic Choices (Europe plurielle/Multiple Europes, Vol. 50)*. Laursen, Finn (ed.), Peter Lang, 153–174. Bruxelles: Verlagsgruppe.

Milenković, Miloš and Pišev, Marko. 2013. "'Islam' u anti-multikulturnojretoricipolitičara i antropologa Zapadne Evrope: Kongruencija ili koincidencija?" ("'Islam' In the Anti-Multicultural Rhetoric of Western European Politicians and Anthropologists: Congruence or Coincidence?"), *Issues in Ethnology and Anthropology*, 8 (4): 965–985.

Nic Craith, Mairead. 2012. "Europe's Uncommon Heritages." *Traditiones*, 41 (2): 11–28.

Nielsen, Bjarke. 2011. "UNESCO and the 'right' kind of culture: Bureaucratic production and articulation." *Critique of Anthropology*, 31 (4): 273–92.

Office of the High Representative. 2017. "52nd Report of the High Representative for Implementation of the Peace Agreement on BiH to the Secretary-General of the UN." http://www.ohr.int/?p=98165&print=pdf.

Oldham, Paul and Frank, Miriam Anne. 2008. "'We the peoples…': The United Nations Declaration on the Rights of Indigenous Peoples." *Anthropology Today*, 24 (2): 5–9.

Perry, Valery. 2015. "Cultural Heritage Protection in post-Conflict Bosnia-Herzegovina: Annex 8 of the Dayton Peace Agreement." In *Bosnia and the Destruction of Cultural Heritage* Walasek, H. et. al., 185–204. Surrey: Ashgate.

Sarrazín Martínez, Jean Paul. 2015. "The protection of cultural diversity: reflexions on its origins and implications." *Justicia*, 20 (27): 99–117.

Silverman, Helaine and Ruggles, D. Fairchild. 2007. "Cultural Heritage and Human Rights." In *Cultural Heritage and Human Rights* Silverman, H. and Fairchild Ruggles, D. (eds.), 3- 22. New York: Springer.

Simonović, Dubravka and Milenković, Miloš. 2008. "Ponovno promišljanje šeme sredstava kao ciljeva: Metodološki potencijali društveno angažovanog istraživanja" ("Rethinking means-as-ends: Methodological potentials of socially engaged research"), *Issues in Ethnology and Anthropology* 3 (1): 205–228.

Smith, Laurajane. 2006. *The Uses of Heritage* London: Routledge.

UNESCO 2003. "Convention for the Safeguarding of the Intangible Cultural Heritage." http://www.unesco.org/culture/ich/en/convention.

UNESCO 2005. "Convention on the Protection and Promotion of Diversity of Cultural Expressions." http://unesdoc.unesco.org/images/0014/001429/142919e.pdf.

Žikić, Bojan (ed.) 2011. *Kulturni identiteti kao nematerijalno kulturno nasleđe (Cultural Identities as Intangible Cultural Heritage.* Beograd: Srpski genealoški centar i Odeljenje za etnologiju i antropologiju Filozofskog fakulteta Univerziteta u Beogradu,

Concluding Remarks

Valery Perry

In the preceding pages, the contributors to this volume have offered a wealth of insights and perspectives, and in addition to their primary data collection have added their own analytical value to a wide range of relevant literature. Some overarching concluding remarks will aim to briefly identify a few key cross-cutting observations and trends, and related programmatic and policy recommendations.

Observations and trends

The nature of extremist threats

First, the nature of extremist threats in Serbia corresponds with the literature, revealing more concerns about rising threats from the far-right than from ISIS-inspired militants. While research on foreign fighters returning from Syria has attracted significant attention in the security sphere among officials, researchers, and donors, there is little sense that this is a primary concern among people in Serbia. An exception is the far-right 4chan ecosystem explored by Milanović, which has integrated virulent opposition to migrants and Muslims into their broader world view, mirroring similar sentiments globally. Schmid's concept of "not now violent" extremism (2014) is useful in illustrating threats perceived as more present, reflecting the impact of simmering social vulnerabilities caused by a mix of contemporary dynamics and historical memories. Rečević's work explores these themes as relevant to migrants—a population often viewed as the biggest risk factor in Serbia, but in Europe as well— finding an impressive level of resilience to date, while cautioning against complacency. Ivanović's focus groups illustrate the manner in which young people assess and react to messages sent by extremists online, finding some regional variance but a certain impressive sophistication among a digital generation accustomed to online noise.

Reciprocal radicalization

Second, the research clearly demonstrates the applicability of reciprocal radicalization as a framework for understanding extremisms in the country, as well as the region. In-group/out-group framings and narratives do little to reduce perceptions of marginalization, or to build a stronger sense of commonality. These narratives draw inspiration from equally divisive historical constructs; they create very different understandings of the present. Wentholt and Marko's chapters each illustrate the "two sides of the same coin" characteristic proposed by Ebner, who points out that while seemingly diametrically opposed, these poles share a number of features. "[B]oth accuse the other side of lacking respect for their women. At the same time, misogyny and outdated gender perceptions are central to both Islamist and far-right ideologies" (Ebner 2017 10). She further points out far-right members positioning themselves as a bulwark of Christianity against Islam, while Islamist groups see themselves as in the front lines of efforts to prevent the "westernization of Islam" (ibid). Wentholt in addition points out the similarities in anti-west and anti-liberal sentiments.

This mutually reinforcing dynamic cannot be separated from unresolved issues and narratives related to the wars in the former Yugoslavia. Milanović's study of online memes and trends illustrates the central role of the war in these narratives, ranging from Srebrenica references to paramilitaries framed as heroes, while Ivanović also shares a range of youth perspectives on the impact of the wars on contemporary outlooks. As the status of Kosovo remains ever-present in the press and political discourse, there is an ongoing and real-time connection to the lingering legacy of Yugoslavia's dissolution. Dević's chapter explores such phenomena, adding in the regional dimension of neighboring Bosnia and Herzegovina and its internal politics that have as well been operationalized into broader Serbian-Russian symbolism and narrative construction. At the prominent Belgrade Book Fair, held in in autumn 2018, books by convicted war criminals were promoted (Gec 2018), viewed as simple free speech by some, and as dangerous revisionism by others.

Hate speech and dangerous rhetoric

Third, the topic of hate speech and dangerous rhetoric is present among the chapters in this volume, particularly in the online sphere. Marko's analysis demonstrates the sophisticated nature of speech of two key influencers, and their ability to avoid potential criticism of promoting hate, while still sending strong signals to their followers. Milanović's study of discourse in an anonymous environment provides a look at an online ecosystem freed from such constraints; whether this serves as a useful online safety valve for frustration and aggression, or contributes to an atmosphere in which spillover into real-world violence is inevitable, remains open to debate. However, it does seem unrealistic to imagine that there is no connection between hate speech and dangerous rhetoric and developments and events in the real world, and during the preparation of this volume there were reminders of the impact of normalized extremism. In summer 2018, a mocking Twitter comment about Srebrenica from a member of the Serbian Parliament shed light on hate speech among political actors, and the apparent lack of consequences of such public behavior (Rudić 2018). In October, high-level officials in both Serbia and Kosovo condemned an attack by stone-throwing individuals on two buses carrying Serbian pilgrims visiting a monastery (Morina and Rudić 2018).

However, while this condemnation is critically necessary and welcomed, the more general and difficult nature of public and political discourse related to the status of Kosovo is consistently heated. Recent attacks on two men speaking Albanian in the city of Novi Sad again raised a debate on the distinction between random or general crimes and hate crimes, and the difficulty of assigning motivation to such acts (Beta 2018). While investigations can demonstrate more complicated motivations, incidents and reporting can have a real impact on short- and long-term public perceptions, regardless of the eventually-established facts. The ever delicate balancing act between unfettered free speech and constructive civil discourse has been rocked by the impact of social media tools which allow for the rapid dissemination of news, but also stereotypes, rumors, and lies. The three authors studying the online sphere in Serbia describe this evolving debate, but acknowledge that this is still all new terrain. And this new frontier is emerging at the same time as Serbia, and the region as a whole, continues to grapple with the broader legacy of wartime and post-war manipulation, politicization, polarization, and public skepticism that has characterized the media environment for a generation.

The position of women in society

The impact of extremist worldviews and agendas on the position of women in society is also present. Marko reviewed the highly conservative language used in the sermons of Sead Islamović, and Ivanović observed more conservative understandings of gender roles among young respondents in different parts of the country (and from different religious/ethnic groups). In his 4chan study, Milanović touched on the reality that this online forum is largely populated by men, and can foster retrograde views of women's role in society, and at worst open misogyny. From another perspective, Dević's analysis shows the strong influence of a female thinker on Russian-Serbian affinities, calling to mind a documentary on influential women on the right in Serbia (Helsinki Committee in Serbia 2017). One can observe that while any worldviews that harken back to a real/imagined past will have inevitable consequences on gender roles that have changed in recent modernity, one cannot discount the participation of women in the active promotion of extremist thinking and actions.

Identity construction

Finally, the notion of identity and identity construction emerges through the research. Milenković's exploration of the links between cultural heritage and identity facilitates consideration of policies that can promote or deter the embrace of complex and multi-layered identities. Rečević and Ivanović describe how the position of migrants was at times viewed differently depending on the religious affiliation of respondents; Rečević's exploration of the views of some on the far-right places this issue in a broader "us vs. them" civilizational framing. Marko's study of key influencers sheds some light on how such a leader interacts with followers on the basis of a perceived shared sense of identity and belief. And both Dević and Wentholt explore historical markers that can reinforce or reify feelings of brotherhood or belonging. Not surprisingly, the bulk of examples frame identity in an essentialist, immutable way, black or white, with an individual either falling within or outside of some construct. Complexity, fluidity, and layering are absent, which is to be expected as extremist thinking has little space for nuance.

Recommendations

The authors in this volume offer a number of recommendations, many of which reflect some of the broad themes noted above. In addition, some additional overarching recommendations deserve to be repeated, or can be inferred from the collection. Few could be addressed solely through technical programmatic support, as they all require structural, political, and systemic commitment and effort (Carothers 2009). Notably, in these polarizing times many are similar to reforms needed in *other* countries (e.g., in the EU, the U.S., etc.); it remains to be seen whether the will to counter these trends exists there as well.

Research needs

It is a cliché for academics promoting their ideas to first note the need for more research. Perhaps a more finely-tuned recommendation could emphasize the need for better identification of research topics. As illustrated in the Introduction and the individual author literature reviews, while the number of policy studies on this topic in the region and in Serbia is increasing, there is a dearth of interdisciplinary and theoretically grounded research on the topic. While not explicitly noted by the contributors, their approach to the research, and the data they surveyed, remind of the need to rely on research professionals present on the ground to drive the research agenda, and to support a range of disciplines and specialties. This can have the added benefit of expanding the number of individuals thinking about these issues, to avoid a situation where certain countries—or even communities—are dominated by a sole and dominant research voice. Commissioning research on narrowly- and pre-defined topics will result in "products to order," and will have an impact not only on the body of literature but on resultant policy and practice in the field.

Education

The need for education, whether formal or informal, curricular or extracurricular, with young people or adults, was consistently noted. Media and digital literacy to better equip people—especially young people—to manage a torrent of information and opinion online and through social media is both explicitly noted and generally apparent. Civic education aimed at inculcating a sense of shared and responsible citizenship, and undergirded by a more civic understanding of what it means it be a Serbian citizen, would be essential to effectively address noted exclusionary identity politics. (However, in a system where students presently select *either* religious instruction or civic education, the challenges are substantial.) Milenković offers the positive option of cultural heritage as a bridging theme that could both reinforce minority groups' sense of inclusion, while also redefining and expanding the broader understanding of culture, and heritage, in Serbia past and present.

Wentholt's study illustrates the need for better history education, and a move away from the false premise that any one history text could be the sole "truth," and instead towards a more nuanced and multi-perspective approach grounded in documentary evidence. Dević similarly frames the need for more robust critical thinking about distant and recent history, a need made more urgent by ongoing revisionist endeavors.

In the world of P/CVE programming, intercultural education, civic education, and education about the risks of VERLT are increasingly common, including in Serbia. However the extent to which such ad hoc project-based activity can complement or even counteract what is learned in formal schooling, not to mention what is absorbed through mass media, requires consideration (Perry 2015). As noted throughout this volume, the unresolved legacy of the wars, combined with present political rhetoric that prizes sensationalism and division over measured thought (a trend that, while certainly not limited to Serbia, has plagued the region for over a generation), put limits on the impact of even the highest quality textbooks and classrooms.

Articulating narratives, or promoting values?

A discussion about identity, education, and history inevitably returns to the issue of contemporary and historical narratives. Several of the authors in this volume reference the role and power of narratives, most notably Wentholt, Dević, Marko, and Ivanović. Developing and promoting "counter-narratives" is an increasingly popular P/CVE activity as well, the goal presumably being to offer an alternative to (young) people other than the tempting narratives promoted by extremist groups (Hedayah and ICCT 2014; Hemmingsen and Møller 2017). Some such projects have been launched in the region, including in Serbia; for example, the "Life Stories" project being implemented by the Hague Center for Security Studies (Rrustemi 2018). Yet while these may be appropriate for some countries, particularly when focused on alternative religious interpretations as narrative cores, again in Serbia and the region the reciprocal nature of secular and faith-based narratives must be considered. There are few easy answers to what an effective alternative narrative might look like absent a broader shared articulation of a shared social, civic vision.

Again, some lessons from scholars of conflict analysis could be informative. The following could be easily found in a current study related to P/CVE, and is reminiscent of some of the themes explored by Wentholt: "Clashing narratives or worldviews produce dialogues of the mutually deaf, resulting often in mutual incomprehension and sometimes in tragedies" (Mitchell 2011, 93). Mitchell goes on to discuss strategic and tactical reframing possibilities, all of which integrate critical thinking, understanding of non-linear and multiple causality, and empathy. Such skills link back to education, and ensuring teachers, youth leaders, and others have the tools to engage in complex dialogue exercises. Some pilot efforts have been introduced in Serbia and the region, either under the new P/CVE rubric or through more than two decades of peacebuilding. However, structurally the conditions for broader adoption and integration remain absent, as does any shared and common social-political organizing principle and ideology.

The bigger picture question is by no means limited to Serbia. If individuals attracted to extremist groups are seeking meaning, purpose, and belonging, and rightly or wrongly are finding it in these spaces after finding it absent in their broader social realm, then what alternatives can genuinely be offered? The dissatisfaction with the operationalization of post-Cold War frameworks of liberal democracy, human rights, and market economics seem to have in fact contributed to the sense of a values vacuum, instead preparing the ground for reinvented tribalisms (Barber 2001). Any efforts to foster alternative narratives must contend with this much larger social challenge.

(Re)Framing the issue:
securitizing democratization or democratizing security?

Finally, as argued in the introduction, much of the P/CVE focus in Serbia and the region was born out of external concern of the potential for foreign fighters who gained experience on the battlefield in Syria to return to their Western Balkan communities, or perhaps go elsewhere in Europe. However, the numbers are in fact quite limited (and in Serbia must be compared to the numbers who went to Eastern Ukraine). Considering recent history, the impact of the war, lingering grievances, difficult living conditions and the difficulty many face in identifying a positive future outlook, vision or perspective, perhaps the question some might ask is why didn't *more* people go?[1]

---

1   For example, in Bosnia and Herzegovina some have noted that no individuals from the Bosniak/Muslim majority community of Goražde went to Syria and Iraq – the only such Bosniak/Muslim community. (Turčalo and Veljan 2018). Anecdotally,

The continued policy and funding focus on returning fighters, and on their deradicalization, rehabilitation, and reintegration, is leading to a large number of programs aimed at this incarceration and post-incarceration challenge; not to mention the social welfare challenges of addressing the needs of the families and children of the incarcerated. While these questions may be driven by concerns about radicalization, these bigger picture social welfare and psychosocial support issues have been long present. In the context of the Western Balkans there is increasingly a consensus that all elements of P/CVE require a "whole of society" strategy. The broad recommendations offered by the authors in this volume mirror this sensibility.

Research by Schirch (2018), Abu-Nimer (2018) and Perry (2017) have considered different elements of the overlap between P/CVE and general transformative development and peacebuilding. On the one hand, one could argue that this new attention offers opportunities to both bring a human rights perspective to traditional counter-terrorism approaches, and a renewed effort to shed light on liberal or democratic peace theory (Brown et al 1996). However there are also risks of securitizing the very rights being promoted, and at the same time of further marginalizing the marginalized through exclusive social profiling. Abu-Nimer identifies several problems in the P/CVE approach: securitization; the external imposition of programs and designs; and the questionable added value of P/CVE initiatives. "The question to ask is what the added value is of these programs, considering factors such as collapsing educational institutions, corruption, discriminatory governance and lack of a national vision, lack of policies to ensure the basic collective and individual freedoms, control and censorship of media and territorial occupation systems." (Abu-Nimer 2018, 7). Chayes (2015) makes similar arguments.

---

some attribute this to a relatively positive economic climate; others to the streamlined governmental administration (the cantonal and municipal levels of governance are the same, effectively reducing bureaucracy and administration); and the location of the community tucked into the Republika Srpska and connected to the rest of the country by a fairly narrow land corridor, thereby making the community fairly hostile to potential recruiters.

In light of the fact that the various countries in the Western Balkans have been the object of various peacebuilding and democratization initiatives for 15, 20 or more years (BCSDN 2012, Grødeland 2006), it is reasonable to question the limits of effectiveness of a project-based approach, and the presence of any broader structural drivers that are creating conditions in which, a full generation after the wars, extremist views are normalizing and even flourishing. In fact, one might fairly wonder whether P/CVE efforts are inserting new risks into still unconsolidated democratic systems. For example, the use of big data companies to scrape and crawl the Internet searching for keywords and linking IP geolocation research to identify individuals or clusters of people searching on certain terms could in fact end up providing support for more intrusive government surveillance, in the absence of robust human rights frameworks and privacy protections. It also leads to questions about the keywords being searched. (Why "jihad" and "ISIS," but not "14 words" or "race war"?) Intentional or unintentional framing of P/CVE as primarily a "Muslim issue," and leaving normalized far-right discourse untouched, could further inculcate a sense of otherness and grievance. A "first do no harm" approach to projects is therefore critical in the region, as is a strategy that does not seek to simply wish away the lingering impact of the recent wars.

Looking ahead

The contributions in this volume illustrate historical and contemporary manifestations of the actions, policies, perceptions, and narratives that can create fertile ground for extremist politics and potential violent consequences. While Serbia is the focus, the observations and findings are regionally relevant. Violence is never inevitable. However the social conditions that can amplify distrust, fear, and grievance can increase the likelihood of latent tensions spilling into real-world action.

While the war in Syria and ISIS's declaration of a Caliphate were key factors in raising the ubiquity and prominence of P/CVE policies, donor funding, and programming, the structural drivers underlying individual radicalization pathways are not new. As of this writing, the regional project/policy/publication pipeline has not yet adapted to the post- "territorial Caliphate" reality and accompanying geopolitical shifts. And yet manifestations of social and political polarization are flourishing—everywhere. The post-World War II experiment in and of the "liberal West" seems to have become unmoored, allowing for a normalization of far-right political ideas that in turn create their own escalatory dynamics of ideological and real-world confrontation.

On the one hand, it can seem natural to worry more about the impact of such trends on countries emerging from the multiple traumatic transitions of post-war political, economic, and social transitions—countries like Serbia. It is reasonable to question the resilience of these communities and the strength of independent checks and balances necessary in any open, democratic system. However, one could also consider the region as providing a playbook for how the politics of division and extremism works, based on over a generation of lived experience. In this sense, the reflections in this volume could be not only useful for readers in Serbia and the region, but may be even more instructive for countries unfamiliar with the potential consequences of these dynamics, and comparatively unprepared to grapple with and respond to contemporary and reciprocal radicalized social and political dynamics.

References

Abu-Nimer, Mohammed. 2018. "Alternative Approaches to Transform-ing Violent Extremism: The case of Islamic Peace and Interreli-gious Peacebuilding." Transformative Approaches to Violent Extrem-ism. Austin, Beatrix and Hans J. Giessmann (eds.) Berlin: Berghof Foundation.

Balkan Civil Society Development Network (BCSDN). 2012. "Donors' Strategies and Practices in Civil Society Development in the Balkans. Civil Society: Lost in Translation?" Accessed October 30, 2018. http://www.balkancsd.net/novo/wp-content/uploads/2012/02/81587797-BCP-8-Donor-Strategies-and-Practices-in-CSDev-in-the-Balkans.pdf

Barber, Benjamin R. 2001. *Jihad vs. McWorld: Terrorism's Challenge to Democracy*. New York: Ballantine Books.

Brown, Michael E., Sean M. Lynn-Jones and Steven E. Miller. 1996. *Debating the Democratic Peace*. Boston: MIT Press.

Beta. 2018. "Two Albanians heavily beaten in Serbia's north." N1. October 8, 2018. http://rs.n1info.com/a426240/English/NEWS/Unknown-attackers-heavily-beat-two-young-Albanains-in-Serbia-s-north.html

Carothers, Thomas. 2009. "Democracy Assistance: Political vs. Developmental." *Journal of Democracy* 20 (1): 5–19.

Chayes, Sarah. 2015. *Thieves of State; Why Corruption Threatens Global Security*. New York: W.W. Norton & Company.

Gec, Jovana. 2018. "Serbian govt criticized for publishing war criminals' books." The Associated Press. October 27, 2018. https://www.apnews.com/fca1a6232d3348748958f9efb2c574c6.

Grødeland Åse B. 2006. "Public Perceptions of non-Governmental Organizations in Serbia, Bosnia & Herzegovina, and Macedonia." *Communist and Post-Communist Studies* 39(2), 2006. pp 221–246.

Hedayah and International Center for Counter-Terrorism (ICCT). 2014. "Developing Effective Counter-Narrative Frameworks for Countering Violent Extremism: Meeting Note." Accessed October 29, 2018. https://www.icct.nl/download/file/Developing%20Effective%20CN%20Frameworks_Hedayah_ICCT_Report_FINAL.pdf.

Helsinki Committee in Serbia. 2017. "Šta hoće žene na desnici?" Helsinki Committee in Serbia documentary. Accessed November 6, 2018. https://www.youtube.com/watch?v=MGwskIpnSPg

Hemmingsen, Ann-Sophie and Karin Ingrid Castro Møller. 2017. The Trouble With Counter-Narratives" Accessed October 29, 2018. http://pure.diis.dk/ws/files/784884/DIIS_RP_2017_1.pdf.

Mitchell, Christopher R. 2011. "Conflict, Change and Conflict Resolution." Advancing Conflict Transformation. The Berghof Handbook II. Beatrix Austin, Martina Fischer and Hans J. Giessmann (eds.). Opladen/Framington Hills: Barbara Budrich Publishers, pages 75–100.

Morina, Die and Filip Rudić. 2018. "Kosovo, Serbia Condemn Attack on Serb Pilgrims." *Balkan Insight*. October 22, 2018. http://www.balkaninsight.com/en/article/kosovo-and-serb-politicians-condemn-the-attack-on-serb-pilgrims-10-22-2018.

Perry, Valery. 2015. "Countering the Cultivation of Extremism in Bosnia and Herzegovina: The Case for Comprehensive Education reform." Accessed September 10 2018. http://www.democratizationpolicy.org/pdf/DPCPolicyNote_10_ExtremismandEducationinBiH.pdf.

Perry, Valery. 2017. "Reflections on Efforts to Prevent and Counter Violence Extremism and Radicalization in the Balkans." Democratization Policy Council Policy Note #15. Accessed July 23, 2018. http://www.democratizationpolicy.org/summary/valery-perry-reflections-on-p-cve-efforts-in-the-balkans/.

Rrustemi, Arlinda. 2018. "HCSS 10 Years: Terrorism, Radicalization and Counter Measures in the Age of Digitalization." *Hague Center for Security Studies News*. March 5, 2018. https://hcss.nl/news/hcss-10-years-terrorism-radicalisation-and-counter-measures-age-digitalisation.

Rudić, Filip. 2018. "Serbia's Rightist MPs Pay No Price for hate Speech." *Balkan Insight*. July 27, 2018. http://www.balkaninsight.com/en/article/serbia-s-rightist-mps-pay-no-price-for-hate-speech-07-27-2018.

Schirch, Lisa (ed.). 2018. *The Ecology of Violent Extremism: Perspectives on Peacebuilding and Human Security*. London: Rowman and Littlefield.

Schmid, Alex P. 2014. "Violent and Non-Violent Extremism: Two Sides of the Same Coin?" Accessed September 15, 2018. https://www.icct.nl/download/file/ICCT-Schmid-Violent-Non-Violent-Extremism-May-2014.pdf.

Turčalo, Sead and Nejra Veljan. 2018. "Community Perspectives on the Prevention of Violent Extremism in Bosnia and Herzegovina. Country Case Study 2." Accessed November 10, 2018. https://www.berghof-foundation.org/fileadmin/redaktion/Publications/Other_Resources/WB_PVE/CTR_CaseStudy2BiH_e.pdf.

About the contributors

Ana Dević is a political and cultural sociologist who obtained her PhD from the University of California at San Diego, an MA from the Institute of Social Studies in The Hague, and a BA in Economics from the University of Novi Sad. Ana has specialized in nationalism, social movements, and the politics of arts, focused on the post-Yugoslav space. She worked at the University of Glasgow, Aarhus University, Brown University, and Fatih in Istanbul. Presently, Ana is a Marie Skłodowska-Curie senior fellow at the KU University of Leuven. Her current project is dealing with Turkish aid for the reconstruction of cultural monuments and educational development in Bosnia and Herzegovina and Serbia. Ana Dević's recent publications include: "Theatre of Diversity and Avant-Garde in Late Socialist Yugoslavia and What Came After" (2018), "Ottomanism and Neo-Ottomanism in the Travails of the 'Serbian National Corpus'" (2016) and "What Nationalism Has Buried: Powerlessness, Culture, and Discontent" (2015).

Kristina Ivanović is a researcher interested in politics, extremism and radicalization, policy analysis, and international relations. She is a consulting professional with an MA in Russian and East European Studies from the University of Glasgow and the University of Tartu. Currently, Kristina works in Belgrade as a Digital Transformation Consultant focused on business development.

Davor Marko holds a PhD in communication and culture from the Faculty of Political Sciences at the University of Belgrade. He has expertise in the analysis of communication trends in the offline and online spheres among young people, and in communication, policy making and advocacy capacity building. He is the author of many local and regional research papers, publications, and assessments, and has worked with leading academic, research and international institutions in the Western Balkans and abroad. He collaborated with USAID, the OSCE, the European Broadcasting Union,

UNESCO, the Zeit Stifftung in Hamburg, and the Thomson Foundation, and was an Open Society Fund research fellow in Bosnia and Herzegovina. His professional interests include strategic communication, the future of public service media, media and diversity, and the language of the media.

Boris Milanović received his BA from the Faculty of Political Science, University of Belgrade, and an MA from the Central European University in Budapest, both in international relations. As a researcher for the OSCE Mission to Serbia project on countering violent extremism project, he has had the opportunity to cement and help elaborate to others an understanding of extremism as it affects contemporary Serbian society. He has extensive experience in NGO work for various organizations, primarily related to CVE, humanitarian aid, and European integration. His primary research interests and competences lie in studying the Internet behavior of Serbian people today.

Miloš Milenković, PhD, is full professor of anthropological research methods and anthropology of science at the Department of Ethnology and Anthropology, Faculty of Philosophy, University of Belgrade. He has conducted various research projects funded by the Serbian Ministry of Science and Ministry of Culture, the Open Society Fund, the European Union and others. He also works as consultant in the area of Social Science Research and Development. Miloš serves in various regulatory bodies including the Council for Humanities at the Serbian Ministry of Education, Science and Technological Development, the Academic Council of Social Sciences and Humanities of the University of Belgrade, the Management Committee of COST CA 15137 ENRESSH - European Network for Research Evaluation in the Social Sciences and Humanities (Horizon 2020) and as the international representative of the Serbian Ethnological and Anthropological Association in the World Council of Anthropological Associations. He serves as academic coordinator of the Jean Monnet Module, "Anthropology of the European Union" at the University of Belgrade. Miloš regularly supervises MA and PhD theses in the Department, is editor of the monograph series *Issues in Ethnology and Anthropology*, and served as editor of the journal *Anthropology*. He authored and edited nine books and several dozen journal articles and book chapters.

Valery Perry has worked in the Western Balkans since the late 1990s, conducting research and working for organizations including the Democratization Policy Council (DPC), the European Center for Minority Issues (ECMI), the Public International Law and Policy Group (PILPG), the NATO Stabilization Force (SFOR), and several NGOs. She joined the OSCE Mission to Serbia as Project Coordinator on a project to prevent and counter violent extremism, serving in this capacity from autumn 2017 through early 2019. She previously worked at the OSCE Mission to Bosnia and Herzegovina in Sarajevo as Deputy Director of the Education Department, and Deputy Director of the Human Dimension Department. She has consulted for the UN Office on Drugs and Crime, the UN Development Program, the Regional Cooperation Council, USAID, IMPAQ International, and other organizations. Valery has also taught graduate level courses in a conflict analysis and reconciliation program at the Sarajevo School of Science and Technology. She received a BA from the University of Rochester, an MA from Indiana University's Russian and East European Institute, and a PhD from George Mason University's Institute for Conflict Analysis and Resolution. Valery has published numerous articles and book chapters, has spoken at conferences and policy events in the United States and throughout Europe, and has testified at the U.S. Congress. In 2015, Ashgate published a book she co-edited with Soeren Keil, entitled, *Statebuilding and Democratization in Bosnia and Herzegovina*.

Tijana Rečević is a Junior Researcher and PhD candidate in International and European Studies at the University of Belgrade, Faculty of Political Sciences. After obtaining her MA degree in International Security from the Faculty of Political Science in Belgrade, Tijana was granted a Chevening Scholarship by the UK Government to study Conflict Studies at the London School of Economics and Political Science (LSE). Her dissertation was awarded with the MSc

Conflict Studies Prize for Best Dissertation for the 2016/7 academic year. Her main academic interests are institutional design and intergroup relations in divided and post-conflict societies, security issues related to international migration, as well as the EU's conflict management capacity. In addition to her academic background, Tijana has practical work experience with the EU Delegation to Serbia and UNHCR in Serbia.

Niké Wentholt is a PhD candidate at the University of Groningen in the Netherlands. Her doctoral project, studying political parties' strategies towards dealing with the violent past in Bulgaria and Serbia in the context of EU accession, started in October 2014 and is funded by the Netherlands Organization for Scientific Research (NWO). For this currently ongoing project she conducted research in Bulgaria and Serbia. She obtained an MSc degree in Russian and East European Studies from the University of Oxford. She completed her undergraduate studies in History at the University of Groningen (*cum laude*).

ibidem.eu